Bruce Springsteen FAQ

Series Editor: Robert Rodriguez

Bruce Springsteen FAQ

All That's Left to Know About the Boss

John D. Luerssen

Backbeat
Books

An Imprint of Hal Leonard Corporation

Published in 2012 by Backbeat Books
An Imprint of Hal Leonard Corporation
7777 West Bluemound Road
Milwaukee, WI 53213

Trade Book Division Editorial Offices
33 Plymouth St., Montclair, NJ 07042

The FAQ series was conceived by Robert Rodriguez and developed with Stuart Shea.

Printed in the United States of America

Book design by Snow Creative Services

Library of Congress Cataloging-in-Publication Data

Luerssen, John D.
   Bruce Springsteen FAQ : all that's left to know about The Boss / John D. Luerssen.
      p. cm.
   Includes bibliographical references and index.
   ISBN 978-1-61713-093-9
1. Springsteen, Bruce. 2. Rock musicians–United States–Biography. I. Title.
   ML420.S77L87 2012
   782.42166092—dc23
   [B]
                                                              2012026374

www.backbeatbooks.com

For Heidi, Meredith, Hayley, and Jack

Contents

Foreword

Yorn in the U.S.A.

I first discovered Bruce Springsteen when I was ten or eleven years old, around the time that *Born in the U.S.A.* was big. I appreciated what he was doing from a distance, but I kind of rejected it. I was into the Smiths and the Cure, bands that my older brothers introduced me to when they came home from college. For me, side two of *Born in the U.S.A.* was the better half. I loved the energy and emotion of songs like "Bobby Jean" and the crumbling drums of "No Surrender," which was, for a long time, my favorite Bruce song ever.

When I was in college, I had this awakening about Springsteen after someone told me to smoke a joint and listen to *The Wild, the Innocent, and the E Street Shuffle*. Songs like "New York City Serenade" and "Wild Billy's Circus Story" and "Sandy" were just brilliant lyrically and so natural in their presentation. It opened a door and I walked through it, and I've been a proud fan ever since.

It's hard to pick a favorite album, but *Darkness on the Edge of Town* is up there for me. When people talk about *Darkness* as the real deal, they're on the money. Springsteen plays and sings like his life depended on it. And it probably did on some level. "Racing in the Street" and "Candy's Room" may be fiction in part, but they feel so genuine and sound so desperate and so heartfelt, there's no denying the brilliance of that record.

In April 2007, I had the opportunity to play my version of "Dancing in the Dark" and play drums behind Bruce on "Rosalita" when he appeared at a tribute show in Carnegie Hall. But as much fun as that was, it was a little hectic because bands like The Hold Steady, Steve Earle, and Patti Smith also played, so there wasn't much of an opportunity to interact. Thankfully, that wasn't my first encounter with him.

I first met Bruce Springsteen right before my debut album, *musicforthemorningafter*, was released. I went with my brother and Ed Burns to see him at the Staples Center in Los Angeles. And Ed had known Bruce and Patti because they both had songs in his movie, *No Looking Back*, as did I. Anyway, the whole time before the show we were partying, drinking beers, and Ed was like, "Bruce is gonna play 'Candy's Room,' I just know it. He told me he would." And we were kind of like, "Yeah, whatever."

Moving along, we really enjoyed ourselves at the show, which was probably the first time I saw Springsteen and really appreciated what he could do in a live setting. He was so powerful. Anyway, afterward the three of us are backstage in this small room and in walks Bruce. And he just looks at Eddie and smiles. We're looking at him and he goes, "I owe you a 'Candy's Room.'" It was a thrill to meet him and shake his hand. I couldn't help but feel nervous—I was awestruck to be in the presence of one of my heroes.

If I had to describe Bruce Springsteen—whom I admire although he probably has not had a direct influence on my songwriting—I'd say he's a beacon of musical hope. His dedication to his craft, his perseverance, his willingness to take chances, and his ability to not only still be relevant during his forty-year career, but sell out stadiums around the world at the same time, are fucking amazing. At the same time, I can't think of a time where he was ever corny. Well, maybe a track or two on *The River* or the production on "Born in the U.S.A." But even that he corrected in my opinion with the box set *Tracks*, when he revealed a raw, stripped-down version of that song.

For the bonus disc of *musicforthemorningafter* I did a Smiths cover of the song "Panic" and two Bruce tunes. I remember Don Ienner at Columbia telling me that Springsteen's daughter liked my version of "Dancing in the Dark" better than her dad's. That seemed cool. But Don also told me that Bruce favored my rendition of "New York City Serenade." Who knows, though? That might have been fuckin' bullshit.

When Bruce's website asked me to do another song for its "Hangin' on E Street" series, a lot of people were surprised I picked a more recent song, "Your Own Worst Enemy." But I love that song. Bruce only played that song live maybe once or something, but it's one that deserves to be revisited. When *Magic*, the album that it appeared on, came out, it really was magical to me. I loved that song. It really spoke to me.

When I signed to Columbia Records, the career-long home of the Boss, I couldn't help but be stoked. Growing up, that red Columbia label spinning on the turntable signified something special. It meant something, which is why I kind of insisted on my first few albums that the CD pay tribute to those red paper labels that could be found on *Born to Run* and *Darkness on the Edge of Town*.

When people ask if I would ever record with Bruce, all I can say is I wouldn't say no. But it's not something I'm actively seeking out. And honestly, I'm happy just to have heard and enjoyed his music. Sharing the stage with him at Carnegie Hall or shaking his hand—those things are just icing on the cake.

Pete Yorn
as told to the author
September 21, 2010

Pete Yorn is an acclaimed singer/songwriter who released his debut album, *musicforthemorningafter*, in 2001. The Montville, New Jersey–bred, Los Angeles–based rocker has covered "New York City Serenade," "Dancing in the Dark," "Atlantic City," and "Your Own Worst Enemy."

Acknowledgments

Thank you to my wonderful, beautiful wife Heidi for being my Jersey Girl and our three awesome children, Meredith, Hayley, and Jack, for always delivering awesome backseat chant-along choruses on "Mary's Place" and "The Rising."

Special thanks to Pete Yorn for a kickass foreword, Bruce Springsteen for the music and inspiration, John Cerullo, Robert Rodriguez, Bernadette Malavarca, Jaime Nelson, Wes Seeley, Dave and Pinky Luerssen, Paul Cavalconte and 101.9 WRXP (R.I.P.), Bill Crandall, Jessica Robertson, Kim Davis, Dan Reilly, Melissa Olund, Doug Waterman, *Brucebase*, Tom Jardim and Karen Fountain, Sheldon Ferris and Michelle Weintraub, Jenny Weintraub, Angelo Deodato, Liz Luerssen, Ann and John Crowther, Marie Garner, Marianne Mercer, Dick, Harriet and Jay Mercer, George Mercer, Dan Yemin, John Kieltyka, Nick Catania, Nick Helander, Dennis McLaughlin and Yvette Scola, Kenneth and Elizabeth Hoerle, Tasneem Baten Carey, Jose and Donna Rios, Marc McCabe, Rob and Anastasia Harrison, Scott and Noreen Singer, Jim and Monica Gildea, Doug and Dawn Heintz, William Cort, Mark and Chrissy Bradley, everyone in Westfield, New Jersey, that I may have forgotten, Jim Walsh, Mike Stefanelli and all my friends at PSE&G, the Yinglings, Ben Forgash, Kevin Houlihan, Kim and Pete Murin, Libby Coffey, Tim Dodd, Mary Glynn Fisher, and Mary Jane and Ray Aklonis.

Introduction

Baby, I'm a Rocker

In December 1980, Bruce Springsteen was already a household name. The dueling Boss covers of *Time* and *Newsweek* in October 1975 made damn sure of it. The success of 1978's *Darkness on the Edge of Town* and his new album, *The River*, cemented that notion. As a twelve-year-old suburban New Jersey kid who was breaking away from 77 WABC and the Top 40 format as a whole, that Christmas I received my very own "wish."

From my parents, David and Pinky Luerssen, I received my very first stereo. A Realistic console courtesy of the enterprising minds at Radio Shack, it was a bare-bones model with two small speakers, an FM receiver, and a turntable. It may have lacked frills, but it gave me hours and hours of rock-'n'-roll thrills.

A newspaper route delivering the *Suburban News* in my Westfield neighborhood the previous summer was my first opportunity to build up a record collection. Save for Supertramp's *Breakfast in America* and Billy Joel's *The Stranger*, which I already owned, I had little to listen to outside of New York's FM rock stations, WPLJ, and WNEW. After I spent my first paychecks on Joel's catalog, including his latest, *Glass Houses*, I looked for something else to check out.

My friend and Grant School classmate Nick Helander had turned me on to some cool sounds via his older brother, Alex. After we'd play touch football at their house on Tremont Avenue, some of us would hang out and listen to music. It was here that I heard records like *Candy-O* by the Cars, the Clash's *London Calling*, *Duke* by Genesis, and *Outlandos D'Amour* by the Police in their entirety for the first time. In early autumn of '80, I was also introduced to a couple of albums by a guy from our home state named Bruce Springsteen.

I can remember the first time I heard "The Promised Land" sitting on Nick's bedroom floor as local radio anticipated release of *The River*. Then, as Christmas approached, my grandmother asked what I wanted as a gift.

When I told her I wanted a pair of Bruce Springsteen albums, she gave me a funny look. I gave her specific instructions, telling her that Springsteen's new record—a double album—retailed for $12.99 at our hometown record store, the Music Staff. *Born to Run* was merely $6.99, I explained.

At sixty-nine, she seemed worried she might buy the wrong albums and insisted that I join her on a journey to the store on Elm Street. After paying the clerk, we left with the products in a lime green paper bag, and she went back to her apartment on The Boulevard where she'd wrap the records.

Fast-forward to Christmas Day. On my new stereo, I spent hours in my attic bedroom enjoying the chiming hooks of "Two Hearts" and "The Ties That Bind." But when I put on the song cycle that started with "Thunder Road" and ended in "Jungleland," I was floored as I carefully studied the lyrics.

Into 1981 and the years that followed, my mother would always yell up to me to "turn it down," flicking the light switch in the hallway to the third floor on and off in an effort to get my attention. Eventually, my parents sprung for a pair of General Electric headphones.

Anyway, it was the combination of these great gifts that first got me rockin' to Bruce. Three decades on, I owe a debt of gratitude to the late Emily Luerssen for the vinyl, which I still have and treasure. Of course, I no longer have the Realistic stereo, but I have to thank my mom and dad for the equipment, not to mention the electric typewriter from Christmas 1984 that I wrote my first record review on, and a million other things.

Thanks for listening.

John D. Luerssen
June 2012

Bruce Springsteen
FAQ

I Was Born Blue and Weathered

Springsteen's Childhood

Bruce Springsteen Is Born

B ruce Frederick Springsteen was born at Monmouth Memorial Hospital in Long Branch, New Jersey, at 10:50 p.m. on September 23, 1949. He was delivered by Dr. Frank Niemtzow, according to his birth certificate. The first child and only son of Douglas and Adele Springsteen, Bruce was raised in Freehold, New Jersey. At first, young Bruce and his parents lived with his fraternal grandparents, Fred and Alice Springsteen, at their home at 87 Randolph Street, while Doug saved up a down payment for a home of his own.

Bruce's Ancestry

Although his father's surname was distinctly Dutch—which earned Doug the nickname "Dutch"—Bruce's ancestry was predominantly Irish and Italian. Fred Springsteen was 50 percent Dutch and 50 percent Irish (O'Hagen lineage), while Alice, whose maiden name was McNicholl, was 100 percent Irish. Meanwhile, Bruce's maternal grandparents, the Zirillis, were born in Italy and were 100 percent Italian.

Doug Meets Adele

Douglas Springsteen was a World War II veteran who returned home to Freehold, where he met Adele Zirilli. They were quickly married and moved into an apartment briefly before settling in with his mom and dad. Doug—or "Dutch" as he was also known—was a nimble pool player and a proud man of service. Dutch went on to have a number of jobs, including factory worker, prison guard, and ultimately, bus driver. The latter was ideal for Bruce's dad, who loved driving and passed his appreciation for being behind the wheel on to his son. Motoring and traveling America's highways and local avenues would, of course, become prominent lyrical touches in Bruce's songs in later years.

In addition to being a homemaker and mother, Adele had a strong work ethic. She long held a job for Lawyer's Title, a land title company in Freehold. But most importantly, she was the Springsteen family's rock when times were tough. Because of her commitment to the family, Springsteen compared her to Superwoman in a 1975 interview.

Ginny

On December 8, 1950, Virginia Springsteen was born. Fourteen months younger than Bruce, she was two years behind him in school because she missed the State of New Jersey's October 1 cutoff requirement.

Ginny would go on to play an important role in her brother's pursuit of rock 'n' roll when a boy named George Theiss—who had a crush on her—came calling in 1965. Theiss was a member of a local band called the Castiles, and he hit it off with Bruce. They started talking music, and soon after, he joined Theiss's group.

Through the years Ginny would elect to keep her personal life quiet, but her famous brother took creative inspiration from the struggles in his sister's life. The character Mary, on the title track to 1980's *The River* album, is based largely on Virginia.

Ginny, like Mary, became pregnant as a teen and married before she was a legal adult. As with the song's character, she later fell on hard times when her union carpenter husband lost his well-paying job.

Bruce would reference his sister again in the unreleased autobiographical song "In Freehold," where he revealed Ginny "had her first little baby at seventeen." In his performance of the tune he explained that although folks in the town in the late 1960s looked down on her teenage pregnancy, he had nothing but love for his younger sister.

At the end of the song, Springsteen sings with a sense of relief at how they both "survived" Freehold.

Fred's Chair

Life on Randolph Street—where Springsteen lived for his first five years—was comforting as he remembered it. "My grandfather had this big stuffed chair next to a kerosene stove," he recalled. "And I'd come running home from school and sit [there] and I remember how safe I felt."

Springsteen would later admit that one of his earliest childhood memories was of his grandfather filling the spout in the rear of the stove. In the kitchen, a coal stove was used for food preparation, which he would shoot with his water gun when it was in use and watch the steam come off of it.

The stark, underdecorated room was centered around a picture taken in the 1920s of Doug's sister. Fred and Alice's daughter died tragically at the age of five in a bicycle accident near the gas station around the corner.

39½ Institute Street

In October 1954, shortly after Bruce's fifth birthday, the Springsteens bought a two-family duplex on Institute Street in Freehold, where they would live until 1962. On the lyric sheet for his 1984 classic *Born in the U.S.A.*, a photograph shows him leaning against a tree in the front yard.

But 39½ Institute Street was hardly a prestigious address. It was a half a mile east of his grandparents' house in a poverty-stricken area of Freehold called "Texas." Junked cars and appliances littered nearby yards in the rundown neighborhood where Doug and Adele reluctantly settled.

In "Texas" it wasn't uncommon for immigrants and Appalachian-reared laborers to live together in illegal boarding houses alongside the families of Nestle plant employees like Doug. Freight trains rumbling nearby were a soundtrack of the Springsteens' lives.

In 1974, he described living with a bathroom that had a big gaping hole in the wall that looked out at a neighboring convent. To avoid embarrassment, he told the area kids that an airplane had crashed into his house during the war.

In a 1978 feature in the *Aquarian*, Springsteen drove writer Mike Greenblatt down Institute Street. "I lived here all through grammar school," he said, pointing out the house, which had long since been painted. "There's a Nestle's factory near here. Man, when it rained we smelled that stuff all day long."

Always Broke

Money was mostly scarce, and smiles were often absent from Doug's face as he struggled to find work. Dutch bounced from jobs in the Karagheushian rug factory, where his dad also worked, to the nearby Nestle plant. He also worked at a local mental hospital and as a gardener. At some point, while working in a plastics factory, Doug lost part of his hearing.

Despite this financial strife, Adele was the inspirational, hopeful parent Bruce, Ginny, and Pam—who was born in 1962—needed. Speaking of his love and appreciation of Adele to *Time* in 2002, Bruce said, "When I was growing up, we didn't have very much, but I saw by my mom's example that a step into the next day was very important. Hey, some good things might happen!"

It was the outlook a youngster needed to break away from the tensions his father brought into the Springsteens' home. Bitter about his bosses, unhappy about his inability to find his calling, and disappointed with how his life had turned out, Doug would sit in their dark kitchen and find comfort in a six-pack of beer and cigarettes.

As Bruce listened to his father complain routinely about his overseers at work, he vowed to avoid landing in the kind of position where he could be looked down upon. Or as he once told concert promoter John Scher, "I'd say to myself, 'When I grow up, I'm gonna be the fuckin' boss!'"

Daddy's Buick

In spite of struggles to make ends meet, Doug and Adele had wheels. But the family car, an old Buick, was downright unreliable. In a 1995 interview with CBS Television's *60 Minutes*, Bruce and his mom joked about having to push it backwards out of parking spots because the transmission's reverse function was shot.

Affluence eluded the Springsteen family in the 1950s. Or as Bruce would say in the interview, "We weren't used to luck."

St. Rose of Lima Struggles

Bruce Springsteen began his education in September 1955 at Freehold's St. Rose of Lima School. Like his father before him (Doug had graduated from the Catholic grammar school in 1939), Bruce attended the secular school at 51 Lincoln Place from first to eighth grades.

During his years at St. Rose of Lima, he was stubborn and at first somewhat naïve. He was an outsider who struggled academically and found himself cast off by his peers and the nuns. In the third grade, Springsteen claims he was stuffed in a garbage can and pushed under a desk by a nun after misbehaving. She told him that was where he belonged; mouthing off meant corporal punishment.

"I was probably one of the smartest kids in my class at the time," he told *60 Minutes* reporter Scott Pelley in 2007, "except you would've never known it. Because where my intelligence lay was not, wasn't able to be tapped within that particular system."

Later, Springsteen was serving as an altar boy at St. Rose of Lima Parish when he was knocked down by a priest during Mass. The priest became enraged because Bruce—whose mother had pressured him to serve Mass—wasn't sure what he should do.

Part of his problem was his standoffish and self-reliant nature, which was mistakenly perceived by others as conceit. One nun, in fifth or sixth grade, disapproved of Springsteen's supposed haughtiness and sent him back down to first grade for discipline. As punishment, and at the nun's insistence, a first-grader named Jimmy came over and slapped Springsteen in the face.

Based on these rotten physical chastisements, it's little surprise Springsteen grew to loathe school and became completely disgruntled over time about the hypocrisy of life at St. Rose of Lima. Its mission—shaped in conjunction with the Sisters of St. Francis of Philadelphia—of shaping the intellectual, spiritual, emotional, and physical growth of every child was, as Springsteen would later describe, "utter crap."

White Trash

According to author Christopher Sandford in his unauthorized 1999 bio *Point Blank*, Springsteen's upbringing rendered him "white trash" by a classmate. Dirt-poor and dorky, he was ragged on for being "a very weird kid."

If his britches didn't help his image, his appreciation of rock music—what other schoolmates still called "nigger music" in the late 1950s—alienated him. Todd Grice, who knew him from Freehold, described young Springsteen—who got much of his culture from 1950s and 1960s television—to Sandford as "aloof and geeky," adding, "He always carried such a weight."

Although people thought he was peculiar because he walked around with a pained look on his face, Springsteen would eventually defend his outlook. "I was thinking of things," he told *Born to Run* author Dave Marsh of his years at St. Rose of Lima. "I was always on the outside looking in."

Elvis Presley

On January 6, 1957, Bruce Springsteen—merely seven years old—was allowed to stay up late enough to watch the last of three landmark Elvis Presley performances on *The Ed Sullivan Show*. The broadcast presented Presley from the waist up only, a result of the public's outrage over the future King's swiveling hips and legs.

If the show was the young Springsteen's first introduction to rock 'n' roll, it was also a signature moment in his life. From then on, he became an enormous fan of and identified with the Tupelo, Mississippi–bred superstar. Like the man the media had begun to call "Elvis the Pelvis," Springsteen was also from meager means.

There he sat in front of the television with his mouth agape. He looked over to his mom as Presley sang a medley of "Hound Dog," "Love Me Tender," and "Heartbreak Hotel," and told her, "I wanna be just . . . like . . . that." In fact, from that moment on, he couldn't imagine anyone *not* wanting to be like Presley.

First Guitar

Springsteen's newfound hero inspired him and instantly fed his interest in music. After repeatedly telling his parents that he wanted a guitar like Elvis's, they acquiesced and rented him an acoustic guitar.

Springsteen liked pretending to be Elvis by posing with the guitar in front of his mirror. But at such a young age he lacked the attention required to actually play the instrument.

Although Adele made him take lessons, her son's hands were too small, and he soon lost interest. "Guitar lessons at the time were like a coma, buzzing on the 3-string," he told Dave Marsh in the 1970s. "I knew that wasn't the way Elvis did it."

"I took a lesson or two, but they were horrible," he said in 2011 of his experiences as a nine-year-old working with his tutor at Deal's music in Freehold. "I needed instant gratification—I wanted to rock now," Springsteen told Steve Van Zandt in an interview for his syndicated *Underground Garage* radio show. "Not later, not after I learned the scales, these notes. I need to make a horrific noise right now!"

So his parents brought the guitar back. Although he grew to be enthralled with music, listening intently and thinking about how he might put his dream into action, it would be several more years before he would rediscover and master the guitar.

Chubby and Anita

In June 1962, Adele Springsteen took Bruce, then twelve, and Ginny, eleven, to their very first concerts in Atlantic City. The matinee show at the Steel Pier starred rock-'n'-roll pioneer Chubby Checker, who was known for songs like "The Twist"—which topped the *Billboard* Hot 100 in September 1960 and again in January 1962—and "Let's Twist Again" (1961).

Later in the day, the Springsteen family—sans Doug—attended a more subdued show by Anita Bryant, probably against Bruce's will. Bryant—a former beauty queen and future gay rights opponent—had four tepid Top 40 hits in the U.S. in the late 1950s and early 1960s, including the 1960 Top 5 smash "Paper Roses."

Pamela

On September 7, 1962, Pamela Springsteen was born to Doug and Adele. But because of the thirteen-year age difference, Bruce and his baby sister lived a life apart past her sixth birthday. As a budding local musical hero, he stayed in New Jersey when his parents moved to San Mateo, California, in early 1969.

Just after her thirteenth birthday, her brother became an international star. As a teenager, Pam was outgoing and attractive—far different from her adolescent brother. It was something he spoke about to the *NME* in 1975.

"My youngest sister, she's sixteen and she's very pretty and very popular," he said. "There's no way that she's gonna sit in her room for every waking hour. I didn't have that problem."

Pamela Springsteen went on to become an actress in the 1980s, appearing in the landmark teen movie *Fast Times at Ridgemont High* and the NBC sitcom *Family Ties* before starring as the killer in cult classic horror movies like *Sleepaway Camp 2: Unhappy Campers* and *Sleepaway Camp 3: Teenage Wasteland*. At one time she had been engaged to actor Sean Penn.

Pam ultimately married David Ricketts, one half of the duo David and David, who were known for the 1986 hit "Welcome to the Boomtown." By the 1990s, Pamela had divorced Ricketts and became a revered photographer. She shot album covers and publicity stills for the likes of Alan Jackson, Tears for Fears, and Ice Cube. In 1995, she contributed black-and-white photographs to a television commercial and subsequent music video for Springsteen's song "The Ghost of Tom Joad."

In recent years, Pamela has shot everyone from Keith Richards to Trent Reznor and her older brother. In 2002, a forty-one-piece photo exhibit of her work debuted at the Weisnan Art Museum at the University of Minnesota in Minneapolis, before it traveled to other museums in the U.S.

Radio-Loving Misfit

Despite attempts to fit in with his baseball- and football-loving peers, Bruce Springsteen marched to a different drum, and by the seventh and eighth grade, he sought refuge in his radio.

Springsteen was an ardent student of rock and soul music. He followed his love of Elvis with an appreciation of Eddie Cochran, whose 1958 singles "Summertime Blues" and "C'mon Everybody" had captured his attention at the age of nine. But by the time of Cochran's unexpected death in April 1960, Springsteen had schooled himself in all the current rock and soul hits, including Lloyd Price's "Stagger Lee," Roy Orbison's "Only the Lonely" or Elvis smashes like "Are You Lonesome Tonight?" and "It's Now or Never."

Tuned into New York's AM dial on his transistor radio when not checking out Dick Clark's national broadcast of *American Bandstand,* Springsteen devoured upbeat, soulful early 1960s Top 40 hits like Little Eva's "The Loco-Motion," Dion's "The Wanderer," and the Isley Brothers' "Twist and Shout."

He would continue to find exhilaration on the radio into the mid-1960s, with the likes of the Crystals and the Ronettes, while he maintained his hatred of formal education. This was especially true by his final year at St. Rose of Lima.

He was embracing the philosophy he would later sing about most famously on 1984's "No Surrender"—"We learned more from a three-minute record, baby, than we ever learned in school."

"It was like TNT coming out of those speakers," Springsteen explained to Kit Rachlis in the *Boston Phoenix* in December 1980. "It came and grabbed you by the heart and lifted you up. "Under the Boardwalk," "Saturday Night at the Movies"— those things made me feel real. Those songs said that life was worth living . . . . The radio—rock 'n' roll—went where no other things were allowed to go."

As an early record buyer, he was drawn to novelty songs like Sheb Wooley's "Purple People Eater" and Lonnie Donegan's "Does Your Chewing Gum Lose Its Flavor on the Bedpost Overnight?" He was also huge fan of the Four Seasons, splurging on every single of theirs that came out in 1962 and '63. He was also drawn to a 1963 single by the Orlons called "South Street"—it wasn't coincidental that he lived on a road with the same name. "It gave some magical cachet to my address," he laughed to Van Zandt, remembering that underrated Cameo/ Parkway act.

While music had become a diversion for some, it was much more than that to an adolescent Springsteen. It gave him a sense of purpose. "It was never just a hobby—it was a reason to live," he told the *Los Angeles Times.*

$18 Guitar

By the time he was thirteen, Springsteen had again set his sights on a real guitar, and sometime in eighth grade he managed to buy one secondhand at Freehold's Western Auto Appliance Store on Main for $18. After several years of listening to records, he was ready to try to play and turned to his cousin Frankie (Frank Bruno Jr.) for some guidance.

Frankie, who had become adept on both accordion and guitar, taught Springsteen his very first song, "Greensleeves."

"He taught me my first chords," Springsteen would remember four decades later. "He was super cool. I was 13 and I went to my aunt Edie's house where Frank played accordion in the living room. It was like Ted Mack Amateur Hour."

Well before Beatlemania had even hit the U.S., Springsteen was already on his way musically. The guitar, which Frankie had to tune for him, offered him a way to get his feelings out. The secondhand acoustic also gave Springsteen—who admittedly had low self-esteem at the time—an identity.

"It was real and it stood for something," he told Dave Marsh. Instead of dreaming of an escape from his reality, he now had the means.

"The first day I can remember looking in a mirror and being able to stand what I was seeing was the day I had a guitar in my hand," Springsteen added. He already knew rock 'n' roll was more than an obsession; it was the only thing that motivated him. Rock music would be his salvation.

68 South Street

In November 1962, ten months after Bruce welcomed his second sister, the Springsteen family sold their home at 39½ Institute Street and moved to a larger two-family duplex at 68 South Street in Freehold, which it rented from John W. Duckett. But it wasn't much of a step up, with its insufficient heat and poor lighting. Instead of living adjacent to railroad tracks, as they had on Institute, the South Street property was next to a highly active Sinclair gas station owned by a man named Ducky Slattery.

In the humid New Jersey summers of his early teenage years, Springsteen would drag his mattress out of his window and sleep on the roof, where he would observe the activity at the gas station, which was open until one in the morning. It was here that he would first formulate his dreams and visions of chrome machines as he observed motorists pulling in and out of Ducky's place all summer long.

Meanwhile, a small Raytheon television was the living room's focal point. Stucco walls, a photo of Doug Springsteen's deceased sister, and the omnipresent cigarette smoke were mainstays of home, where arguing between father and son soon became a regular ritual.

I Hear the Lead Singer Shoutin' Out, Girl

1965–1968

I've Got This Guitar

Anything that felt too much like school—including studying music—was something that Bruce Springsteen recoiled from. When his cousin Frankie turned him on to those first few chords, it was informal. As his skills developed, a teenage Bruce absorbed all the records he could, but he quickly favored working on his own material. It was easier and considerably more rewarding.

"The main reason I started doing my own arrangements and writing my own songs was because I hated to pick them up off the records," Springsteen said in 1974. "I didn't have the patience to sit down and listen to them, figure out the notes and stuff."

Through a process he called "assimilation," he was digesting Elvis and other Sun Records artists, Chuck Berry, the British Invasion acts, Dylan, the Byrds, Motown, R&B, and, later, psychedelia. He began crafting what eventually became his own legendary variation on rock 'n' roll.

The Rogues

Soon after he got his Kent guitar, the greenhorn rocker joined forces with a group known as the Rogues. Inspired by the Beatles and the British Invasion, the band—of which little is known—played a few area teen dances at the Elks Club and a mobile home park before Springsteen exited in early 1965.

"I got thrown out because they told me my guitar was too cheap," he would laugh during a 2009 interview with the Rock and Roll Hall of Fame's Jim Henke. "It kind of pissed me off. I remember I went home that night and I put on 'It's All Over Now' by the Rolling Stones and I forced myself to learn the lead."

Yellow Fender

By the spring of '65, Springsteen had stepped up to a yellow Fender guitar and had radically honed his chops by practicing incessantly. He was playing the guitar six hours a day, obsessing over Stones tunes like "It's All Over Now" and later the Who's "My Generation."

He also devoured classic soul sides as they poured out of his AM radio speaker. He would deconstruct the songs he loved in his bedroom until he could play them masterfully.

"The Coolest Voice"

Springsteen's appreciation of Bob Dylan didn't sit well with Adele. If she had been her son's biggest champion to date, the two had a huge disconnect when it came to the Columbia Records folkie-gone-electric.

Springsteen thought Dylan had "the coolest voice," but Adele balked that the Minnesota native couldn't sing. Not long after he got his hands on a copy of "Like a Rolling Stone," he was teaching the tune to all interested parties.

Thinking back in 1985 on his initial exposure to what may be Dylan's most famous song, Bruce remembered being stunned. "The first time I heard it, on came that snare shot that sounded like somebody'd kicked open the door," adding, "The way that Elvis freed your body, Bob freed your mind."

Boiling Over

By 1965, the rift between Bruce and his father ran deep. Around this time, Doug worked as a jail guard and would often come home angry and depressed and proceed to get drunk. Clutching his cigarettes and his six-pack of beer, Mr. Springsteen would sit in a dark kitchen. If either Bruce or Ginny tried to turn on the lights, he would freak out.

Some nights, when Bruce would come in the door after being out with his friends, he'd attempt sneaking into the house to escape Doug's wrath. Sometimes it worked, sometimes it didn't. He'd slick his growing hair back to keep his father from seeing how long it had become. And although their conversations started off pleasant enough, small talk often turned explosive. One time, things got so heated that Doug threw a full can of beer toward his son's head. The Freehold police showed up after they were presumably called by fearful neighbors on South Street.

Bruce began to escape when he could, and with a friend who was old enough to drive, they'd take off for the beach, where they might sleep all night on the roofs of oceanfront cottages. Or they'd head up to New York City, where they would wander Greenwich Village.

When the underage Springsteen was detained by Port Authority cops in the middle of the night, his dad wanted nothing to do with him. Adele would come

Early Gigs

The Castiles kept busy throughout the summer of 1965 by playing shows at a pizzeria in the Freewood Acres section of Howell and a Catholic Youth Organization dance held at Springsteen's old school, St. Rose of Lima. A repeat performance at the Catholic School followed in September, with shows at the Freehold Elks Lodge and the Farmingdale Mobile Home Park.

In a 1975 interview, Springsteen spoke about the Farmingdale gig, which found the Castiles performing alongside a female-fronted country band. "I remember starting at noon and we played until like 8 or 9 pm, when we had to stop," he said during his first tour of Europe. "That was one of the first gigs I ever did."

Into October, the Castiles played Howell's I.B. Club on Bergerville Road opening for a New York band called the Florescents on the 8th.

"Sidewalk"

Also in October 1965, the Castiles performed at a teen dance for the children of American soldiers stationed at Fort Monmouth. After the gig at the Fort Monmouth Recreation Hall, two kids at the show approached Springsteen with some unfinished verses and suggested he try to use them in an original song.

He obliged and left the U.S. Army installation with the piece of paper and returned home to write what would become his very first original composition. Tweaking the donated lyrics, he made them work as part of a musical number he had been working on. Called "Sidewalk," it was soon incorporated into the Castiles' live set.

"It's My Life"

By the time he was sixteen, Bruce Springsteen was 5' 10" and 150 pounds. With long hair and a thin build, he wore a leather jacket and Levi's when he wasn't in his rock-'n'-roll uniform. When he did actually put his guitar down, he was off freewheelin'.

With friends who could drive, he would escape. But his rocker look and defiant attitude couldn't help the gap-toothed kid escape the wrath of Doug.

"We'd start talking about nothin' much," Springsteen would famously tell audiences about his teen struggles with his father as he introduced the E Street Band's cover of the Animals' "It's My Life." "Pretty soon he'd ask me what I thought I was doin' with myself, and we'd always end up screamin' at each other."

Adele, watching television in the living room, would nearly always run in. Crying and trying to defuse Doug, she would typically help Bruce get away from her bitter husband. Exiting out the back door and heading down the driveway toward the street, Bruce explained how he would scream back at his father, "tellin' him how it was my life and I was gonna do what I wanted to do."

Underneath the Leather

If a motorcycle wreck eventually left the budding rocker with a slight limp, Springsteen's hood guise didn't run too deep at first. He never drank as a teen, perhaps in response to the alcohol abuse he witnessed at home.

And for all his future classics about cars and girls, he was among the last in his group of friends to actually drive; not to mention he was still a little shy around women.

He loved the Beach Boys, and went so far as to buy a madras shirt. He dug sports but preferred independent athletics like swimming and running over team activities. His obsession with singles like Sam the Sham's "Wooly Bully," the Who's "I Can't Explain," and the Animals' "We Gotta Get out of This Place" still took precedence over his studies.

He accepted that he wasn't like the others at Freehold Regional. With his acne, longer hair, and scorned look, some classmates had him pegged as a "nut," and he took pride in being different. While there were some who tried to test him, Springsteen could hold his own in a fight.

While his peers prepared for their college entrance exams, Springsteen earned C's and D's when he would bother to show up at school. Even when he was there, he was elsewhere. As he sat in class in his junior year, he daydreamed about rock 'n' roll.

Wedding Band

October 1965 found the Castiles following up their first-ever nightclub gig with a wedding performance at an unnamed reception hall in Monmouth County. The band's twenty-nine-song setlist—according to a document kept by a member of the Castiles—included an array of British Invasion classics by the Rolling Stones ("Satisfaction," "Play with Fire," "The Last Time"), the Kinks ("Tired of Waiting for You"), and the Yardbirds ("For Your Love").

The band also broke out its aforementioned, newly crafted tune "Sidewalk" and Sonny and Cher's July 1965 chart-topper "I Got You Babe" plus 1950s ballads like the G-Clefs' "I Understand" and Don and Juan's "What's Your Name." The softer material was delivered by the band at the insistence of Tex Vinyard, who knew he would need to cater to some of the wedding's older attendees.

Rockin' the Insane Asylum

If a wedding gig was perhaps too refined a venue for the Castiles, the group's rollicking performances at Marlboro State Hospital were completely chaotic.

Springsteen, Theiss, and the boys played some of their most memorable early gigs at this nearby psychiatric facility, and it was one that Springsteen wouldn't forget.

"We were always terrified at the asylum," he told *Newsweek* in 1975. "One time this guy in a suit got up and introduced us for twenty minutes sayin' we were greater than the Beatles. Then the doctors came up and took him away."

It was a far cry from the Rollerdome or the Elks Club, as Theiss explained to the fan site *Brucebase*. "There was a woman who was trying to seduce everyone," Theiss remembered. "And some guy was running around screaming 'Banzai!,' 'Banzai!'"

Shop Rite Rock

The Castiles kept active through the end of 1965, with November shows at the Hazlet Firehouse and a dance at St. Rose of Lima School, sponsored by the local Catholic Youth Organization. By this time, Springsteen was gaining confidence and began singing lead vocals on a couple of covers, including the Who's "My Generation."

Initially, Vinyard forbid Springsteen from singing lead vocals because he didn't think his voice was good enough. But songs like the aforementioned Who smash and Van Morrison's guttural Them classic "Mystic Eye" were exceptions where Springsteen's unrefined delivery was fitting.

Vinyard also booked the band to play at the Freehold Shop Rite supermarket grand opening that month. Held in the daytime in the parking lot of this grocery store—which still exists at the intersection of South Street and Route 9 in Springsteen's hometown—the Saturday afternoon performance exposed the band to area residents of all ages.

Bart Haynes Departs

As Christmas 1965 approached, the Castiles also played at the Freehold V.F.W. Hall. This December show marked the last performance of drummer Bart Haynes, who unexpectedly quit the band the same month.

Haynes, who was a year ahead of Bruce in school, graduated in June 1966 and joined the Marines four months later. In April 1967, he was shipped off to Vietnam where he was killed in combat in Quang Tri, South Vietnam on October 22, 1967, at the age of nineteen.

Goddamn Guitar

Despite his auspicious rock-'n'-roll path, Bruce and his dad still had a major disconnect in 1966. Doug wasn't thrilled with the course his son's life was taking, and when he came in the back door at night from band practice with his yellow

Fender—which the sixteen-year-old took with him everywhere he went—Doug often let him know it.

To Bruce, the Fender was his "key to the highway," but to his father it was "the Goddamn guitar." According to a 1978 story Springsteen would tell during the E Street Band's performance of "Growin' Up," "there were two things that were unpopular in my house. One was me and the other was my guitar."

Doug would knock on his door and tell Bruce to turn down that "Goddamn guitar." As Springsteen explained during the '78 tour, "he must've thought everything in my room was the same brand: Goddamn guitar, Goddamn stereo. Goddamn radio."

At the center of the rift was his father's belief that the guitar was okay as a hobby, but with adulthood looming, both Doug and Adele felt Bruce needed something bankable to fall back on. His dad wanted him to be a lawyer; his mother wanted him to be an author.

His parents felt it was a real crisis. They goaded him to seek help, and he reluctantly agreed. "So they say, 'This is a big thing. You should go see the priest," Springsteen told audiences. "Tell him we want you to be lawyer or an author—but don't say nothin' about that Goddamn guitar.'"

While there's no evidence Springsteen—who had an underlying distrust of religion after his unfavorable childhood experiences at St. Rose of Lima—ever actually sought the priest's advice, it didn't really matter. Deep down, he knew he was going to stick with the guitar.

Losing Battles

The Castiles got off to a slower than expected start in 1966, performing just four shows in the first third of the year. With a new drummer, Vinny Maniello, in place, the group played a "Battle of the Bands" show in January at St. Joseph's School in Keyport.

Competing with fifteen other teenage groups for a $200 grand prize, the band didn't even place, losing out to groups like the Clique, who were from nearby Red Bank, and the Rising Suns. The latter included keyboard player Bob Alfano—a future member of the Castiles.

Undaunted, the band next played a Freehold show on behalf of the Western Monmouth County Chamber of Commerce that February. It led up to a pair of shows at the Matawan-Keyport Roller Drome in late April.

On the 22nd, the group performed alongside two dozen local bands, placing third behind Sonny and the Starfires—which included future Springsteen drummer Vini Lopez—and first-place winners the Rogues, his former outfit. The following week, these top-placed groups were invited back by promoter Norman Seldin to open for national acts like the Crystals, the Dovells, and the Ad-Libs.

Lineup Shift

In early May 1966, during a gig at Le Teendezvous, a teenage club in New Shrewsbury, New Jersey, bassist Frank Marziotti—who was roughly ten years older than his bandmates—decided it might be time to step down from the group. After the show, Marziotti told his bandmates that he was leaving because he needed to increase his time commitment to the gas station he owned.

Frank later revealed that when a kid at the gig asked him if he was Springsteen's dad, he decided it was time to resign. With Marziotti out, the Castiles auditioned a bass player named Curt Fluhr who was in the same age range as the rest of the band. Like his new bandmates, Fluhr attended Freehold Regional.

"Baby I"

On May 18, 1966, the Castiles cut their first single at Mr. Music Inc. in Bricktown. Boasting two originals, "Baby I" and "That's What You Get," which were cowritten by Bruce Springsteen and George Theiss en route to this facility at the Brick Mall Shopping Center, the single remains one of the most sought-after collectibles among Springsteen fans.

The minuscule studio wasn't equipped to handle the loud volume the Castiles were used to delivering. The guitars had to be recorded on their lowest settings.

"We had to turn all of our amps to the wall and literally put covers over them," Springsteen told Jim Henke in 2009. "We couldn't get any distortion or speaker sound out of it. The recording studio was not set up in those days for any kind of overdrive."

If the Bricktown, New Jersey, recording facility wasn't exactly equipped for rock groups at the time, it still felt like an important moment for the Castiles. Although his memory of the exact amount is fuzzy, Springsteen revealed that the band plunked down somewhere between $100 and $300—a large amount of money in May 1966.

The session lasted a half hour and came about at the urging of Vinyard. "Tex just said, 'Let's make a record,' so we did," Theiss told *Backstreets*. Cut directly to disc, which resulted in inferior sound quality, the A-side was also affected when Springsteen's E-string snapped. On such a tight timeline, there was no time to scramble for a replacement.

If the Castiles didn't have any collective aspirations for getting signed to a label, its leaders were nonetheless dreaming of how it might take them out of Freehold.

"Bruce was probably thinking along those lines, and I know I did at times," George added. Unfortunately, the single was never officially released. However, it was pressed on acetate and four known copies of the original seven or eight made are still in existence.

And while the tangible copies of the disc are incredibly rare, the two-track recordings—which mark Springsteen's very first tracked vocals and guitar playing—can be heard if you look hard enough. Both tunes made it to the public via the 1993 bootleg *The Bruce Springsteen Story Vol. 2*. In 2009, Springsteen admitted that he had recently uncovered the two-track recording of his first single.

Where the Gigs Are

Three days after the Castiles' recording session, the group—consisting of five FRHS juniors—performed at their own 1966 Junior Class Prom. Late the following month, the band played the Woodhaven Swim Club, where they made their live debut a year earlier.

Springsteen, Theiss, Popkin, Fluhr, and Manniello booked three gigs in July and one in August 1966 opening for headliners the Rogues at the Surf 'N' See Club in Sea Bright. The Rogues—singer Thom White, drummer Mike Waters, and guitarist John Waasdorp—had tapped the band to be their support as the club's house band for four gigs during those two months.

On July 10, WMCA-AM radio host Gary Stevens emceed the event, which also featured national acts like Johnny Tillotson, the Jive Five, Dean Parrish, the Tymes, and the Shangri-Las. The Castiles performed a handful of songs, as did another local act called the Vik-turs.

A month later, on August 14th, Stevens returned to host a show headlined by established soul act Little Anthony and the Imperials. The Castiles were given a more prominent slot on this night, which also included a performance by the Shadows, a group that featured Springsteen's acquaintance Steve Van Zandt. Their hard work at the Surf 'N' See paid off when they were asked to coheadline their own gig with the Berries on September 17th.

Elsewhere that summer, the Castiles headlined the tenth birthday party of Loew's 35 Drive-In in Hazlet in late July. The group's hour-and-a-half set preceded darkness and the screening of the film, *The Russians Are Coming, the Russians Are Coming*. A week later, the Castiles rocked the Harris Gardens Firehouse in Union Beach.

The Castiles Take Asbury Park

Days before Springsteen began his senior year at Freehold Regional, the Castiles competed against Van Zandt's band the Shadows and another ten or so acts at the Arthur Pryor Bandshell in Asbury Park. While the gig marked Springsteen's first-ever in the city he would eventually help make famous, the show—held at the Fifth Avenue Pavilion complex adjacent to the beach—saw him lose out on prize money to his future bandmate Van Zandt.

When they went back to school, Springsteen and his bandmates were hardly hitting the books. Instead, they prepped for paying gigs at the Freewood Acres Fire Department Hall teen dance in Howell and another show in Red Bank.

Enter Bob Alfano

In late September 1966, the Castiles morphed into a sextet with the addition of organist and former Rising Suns member Bob Alfano. This incarnation of the group made its grand unveiling at a school dance at Red Bank Catholic High School.

Alfano, who was a year behind the rest of the Castiles at FRHS, gave the band more musical depth and allowed it to thrive into the fall of 1966 during an array of gigs, including several headlining events at the Middletown Hullabaloo and the Middletown V.F.W. halls. By November, the six-piece band played the aforementioned Matawan Roller Drome with the Shadows and another local outfit called the Clique.

Café Wha?

After a year on the Jersey Shore teen club scene, the Castiles asked Tex to see if he could get them some Big Apple bookings. Vinyard made some calls that fall and found out about Café Wha?, which was located on the same street as the Night Owl—where bands like the Mothers of Invention, the Lovin' Spoonful, and the Fugs were making a name for themselves.

At first, they were denied the chance to audition, but Vinyard convinced the powers that be at the Greenwich Village coffee house/nightclub to give the boys a shot. So in November 1966, the Castiles auditioned for an opportunity to perform at Café Wha? This successful tryout led to a long-running relationship with the New York venue, resulting in nearly thirty gigs during the next fifteen months.

For these shows, which began in December '66, the Castiles would typically play a weekend matinee gig alongside other bands. It was here that Bruce first met John Hall, who went on to form the '70s band Orleans and have Top 10 hits with 1975's "Dance with Me" and 1976's "Still the One."

Hall—a future Democratic U.S. representative from New York's 19th Congressional District in the Hudson Valley—spoke in 2009 to *AARP the Magazine* about their days performing alongside one another in the club, when Hall was in the band Kangaroo.

"We used to do six shows a day, starting about two in the afternoon," Hall remembered. "Kids from Long Island and New Jersey would come in and hear up-and-coming rock bands." The groups would play six sets each, alternating into the evening. For their efforts, each musician was rewarded with six dollars and all the potato chips they could eat.

Closer to home, the group's popularity also grew, thanks to a busy schedule that included gigs at the Middletown Hullabaloo and the Matawan-Keyport Roller Drome. Two days before Christmas, the Castiles also played a private Sweet Sixteen gig at the now-defunct American Hotel on E. Main Street in Freehold.

The New Uniform

By 1967, the Castiles had traded a refined look for one that reflected the rising psychedelic movement. The band was embracing the Sgt. Pepper–influenced fashions that the Beatles pioneered. Long military jackets and mod boots were matched by longer hair and songs that were more in tune with the time.

By now, Springsteen was out in front of the Castiles for a decent part of the set, singing "My Generation," the Beatles' classic "Eleanor Rigby," and two Jimi Hendrix tunes, "Purple Haze" and "Fire."

The group continued to play several weekends a month at Café Wha, with the occasional local show for the first half of 1967. In March, they returned to the Middletown Hullaballoo and headlined the Cage, also in Middletown.

April '67 saw the Castiles back at St. Rose of Lima for a CYO teen dance, with another school dance the following month at Howell High School. Then, on June 9th, the group—save for Alfano—performed their final gig as high school students at their own Freehold Regional, rocking the Class of '67's farewell dance.

Just Say No

Despite his appreciation of psychedelic rock, which grew increasingly popular in 1967, Springsteen continued to have little interest in drugs at a time when illicit substances—from pot to pills and acid—were becoming widely available on the Jersey Shore. Ironically, his hyped-up stage antics gave the impression he might have been taking something, but the allure of drugs completely escaped him.

Springsteen once suggested that he was able to avoid drugs because they were something people tended to take with friends, and as a teenager he never had many. As a result of this loner status, he avoided a lot of the social pressures that others experienced in high school. By the time he was established as a musician on the Jersey Shore, he was so focused on performing music that there wasn't any room in his life for mind-altering substances, save for maybe the occasional ice-cold beer.

Bruce the Bartender?

In his senior year, Springsteen's grades had plummeted. He was pulling C's and D's, and there was speculation that he might not graduate from Freehold Regional.

He was, for a spell, even considering a trade career in mechanics and engine repair. Springsteen, who was not a drinker, ironically mulled going to bartending school as a means to balance his musical pursuits. For a time, his dad was pushing him toward the military. Based on the nightly news reports about the Vietnam War, a fearful Bruce hit the books and managed to squeak by with his diploma.

Skipping Graduation

When Springsteen's 1963–1967 run at Freehold Regional High School was done, the budding rock 'n' roller skipped his graduation. He considered hitchhiking to California to catch the Who and Jimi Hendrix at the Monterey Pop Festival, but those plans fell through, and he instead escaped to New York for the night, much to the disappointment of Adele and Doug.

It had already been made clear to him that he wasn't wanted at the ceremony. His long hair made him an easy target among his peers. Long hair may have been accepted in June 1967 if you were one of the Beatles or the Rolling Stones, but if you were roaming the halls of FRHS, you were a lowlife.

According to rock-'n'-roll lore, Springsteen's rebellious appearance was deemed so disrespectful by one member of the faculty that the twelfth-grade instructor pressured him to either cut his hair—which was never an option—or ditch the formal ceremony. When the unnamed teacher asked if anyone objected to her suggestion, none of his classmates stood up for him.

If he wasn't well liked, he did have an ally in one English teacher named Robert Hussey. Hussey had such a significant impact on the future star that Springsteen personally thanked the teacher in his 1967 yearbook.

"This page is too small for me to write a fraction of the complimentary things I would like to say to you," he wrote in his inscription. "You have taught me things I could not get from any book. You have helped me understand people so much more than I had previously."

"This is not a mere thank you," Springsteen added in the yearbook—which Hussey sold in 1999 for $10,000 to a fan. "But it is a thank you that is felt deep within my heart."

That positive experience aside, Springsteen's time at FRHS was addled by an overall lack of acceptance by his classmates and faculty. Ironically, those lasting impressions never kept him from remaining interested in his alma mater as a rock star. When his schedule allowed for it, he could occasionally be seen in the bleachers at Freehold High School football games. At the height of his popularity, for instance, during the commercial heyday of *Born in the U.S.A*, he surprised droves of locals in the fall of '84 by popping in at a game.

Springsteen's 1967 Freehold Regional High School yearbook picture—taken in the fall of '66—depicts the budding rocker beginning to grow his hair out. His rebellious look—an apparent homage to groups like the Rolling Stones—was still quite uncommon at the time.   *Courtesy of E-Yearbook.com*

Surf 'N' See Again

Aside from the Castiles' ongoing Café Wha? commitment, the sextet rocked the Jersey Shore sporadically in the summer of 1967, playing at Sea Bright's Surf 'N' See Club on July 2. Springsteen and his bandmates were again asked to be on the bill for the third WMCA-AM "Good Guys" Spectacular.

Later in the month, the Castiles performed at the YMCA summer teen swim party and dance at Camp Arrowhead in Marlboro. In August, they returned to play an afternoon show on the 12th at the Surf 'N See. The band also rocked a massive private outdoor keg party in Howell around this time that was attended by approximately 500 people.

The Who Were Smashing

As much as he loved rock 'n' roll, Springsteen didn't get to see his first bona-fide rock-'n'-roll concert until August 12, 1967 when he caught a triple bill of the Blues Magoos, the Who, and headliners Herman's Hermits at the Asbury Park Convention Hall with some of his fellow Castiles. He went specifically to see the Who, a band he had loved since he first caught an earful of songs like "I Can't Explain" and "My Generation" some two years earlier.

Despite being the opening act for the Peter Noone–fronted Hermits, the Who delivered one of their notoriously chaotic rock-'n'-roll shows. Springsteen stood in awe as he watched Pete Townshend, one of his heroes, smash his Fiesta Red Fender Telecaster in half.

Bruce the Ladies Man

Springsteen was never into rock 'n' roll for the drugs or the booze, but he was into it for the women. An anonymous early colleague told Christopher Sandford that he remembered him "screwing most of our own chicks [like a] top dog marking his turf."

"We wanted to play because we wanted to meet girls, we wanted to make a ton of dough, and we wanted to change the world a little bit, you know?" he reflected to *Rolling Stone* in 1984. And if the money wasn't yet in heavy supply, Springsteen the local hero had no trouble making time with the ladies.

Castiles member Curt Fluhr confirmed that notion, describing Bruce as "the most heterosexual person I ever met."

Café Wha? Performance Footage

During one of the Café Wha? gigs sometime in 1967, the Castiles were professionally filmed and recorded performing, according to an interview George Theiss gave with the fan site *Brucebase*. Theiss revealed that a South African film crew had been in New York at the time producing a documentary on the Greenwich Village music scene. Sadly, the name of the documentary and film company are not known, and, as a result, this lost footage may never be recovered.

The Left Foot

In September 1967, the Castiles were offered the opportunity to play a pair of gigs at the Left Foot, which advertised itself as an "over 13/under 18 club" located in the recreation facility of St. Peter's Episcopal Church in Freehold. Hosted by the club's manager, Fred Coleman—who doubled as St. Peter's priest—these headlining gigs at 37 Throckmorton Street were captured on reel-to-reel tape for posterity.

Coleman's recordings of the first show, on September 16, trumped those from the second gig on the 30th. Although these tapes sat in storage for thirty-seven years, upon their rediscovery, the Episcopal priest was given the opportunity to broadcast portions of the thirteen-song set on National Public Radio in September 2004.

In conjunction with the broadcast—which included snippets of Springsteen-sung covers like Leonard Cohen's "Suzanne," Moby Grape's "Omaha," Donovan's "Catch the Wind," and an original called "Mr. Jones"—Theiss and Alfano gave new interviews about their time playing with Bruce.

By this point in the band's history, Springsteen had clearly begun to overtake Theiss on lead vocals, fronting the band on seven of the Castiles' thirteen songs at the first Left Foot gig. He was no longer the kid who was once content to play rhythm guitar.

Springsteen began to imagine himself as a full-time frontman, and he knew that within the confines of the Castiles, he couldn't completely overtake Theiss. He had already outgrown the band and began to think of new ways to deliver his music, but it would be several months before he would act on these ideas.

For those seeking out recordings of these and other songs from the sets at St. Peter's, they have surfaced on the bootlegs *The Bruce Springsteen Story, Vol. 1* and *The Bruce Springsteen Story, Vol. 2.*

The Thirteenth Grade

The Castiles may have been out of high school, but save for its yearlong run of Café Wha? shows, the band hadn't come very far as young adults. Early that autumn, Springsteen was still playing events like the Freehold Board of Education–sponsored West Freehold School Dance and the Christian Brothers Academy dance.

Into the fall, gigs at the Middletown Community Center and Freehold Regional High School—where the Castiles had headlined a Thanksgiving Homecoming event—were balanced by their marathon Saturday sets in Manhattan.

Nearing the End

Weekend afternoon gigs at Café Wha? in December 1967, coupled with local shows at the Ocean Side Surf Club in Sea Bright and Le Teendezvous in New Shrewsbury around Christmas, put an end to an active albeit somewhat disappointing year for the Castiles.

Despite its presence in Manhattan, the band couldn't get a record deal, and the sound of rock 'n' roll had gotten much heavier in the two and a half years since they first came together in Tex Vinyard's dining room.

Just the same, the Castiles trudged forth into 1968. The Springsteen-steered band continued to make its Saturday afternoon pilgrimage to New York until March. From there, they played a semiregular residency at Le Teendezvous, playing eight shows at the nearby venue between March and August.

By April, a new venue known as the Freehold Hullabaloo—opened by the owners of the similarly named Middletown and Asbury Park clubs—became one of the Castiles' monthly performance spots. Other places like the West End Casino in Long Branch and the Off Broad Street Coffee House in Red Bank, which opened that May, had also welcomed the Castiles in the spring and summer of 1968.

First Solo Gigs

The Castiles may have been fading, but they were still intact in May 1968 when the aforementioned Off Broad Street Coffee House opened for business. The Red Bank venue was an ideal forum for the singer/songwriter approaches Springsteen started developing in late 1967.

While it wasn't just an acoustic forum—Off Broad Street offered locals a variety of musical options, including the electrifying rock of the Castiles—it was, most importantly the home of Springsteen's earliest unplugged performances. According to *Brucebase*, Springsteen's folk songwriting style during this time was inspired by Donovan, Tim Buckley, and Leonard Cohen.

During the middle months of 1968, Springsteen mostly played originals during his gigs at the Red Bank coffee house. Song titles unveiled during this time included "Sunline," "Slum Sentiments," "New York Morning Love," "Alone," "Death of a Good Man," "Until the Rain Comes," "Inside the Castle Walls," "Upon This Day," "For Never Asking," "The Virgin Flower," "A Winter's Revelation in 9 Illusions," "The Window," "Crystal," "The War Song," and "Clouds."

Breaking Up

Around the time the Castiles opened for Screaming Lord Sutch on June 6, 1968, at the Freehold Hullabaloo, the band had already been in talks to dissolve at summer's end. Speaking of Sutch, the bizarre psychedelic rock eccentric from the U.K., who traveled to his gigs in a custom Rolls Royce hearse, delivered an eclectic and electric set. It left a significant impact on Springsteen as he thought about ways to stretch the boundaries of what could be done onstage.

In the weeks that followed, Springsteen wasted little time putting together his next group. But before he could completely get the new project off the ground, the Castiles decided to go out with a bang. They would wrap up their three-plus years together under the guidance of Tex Vinyard with a few commemorative area gigs.

First, they played two shows on August 9 at the Off Broad Street. The following night they played their final official headlining show at Le Teendezvous. Although the group came together for a one-time reunion performance at a wedding in 1969, the Castiles' breakup sent the members of the group in different directions.

Fluhr and Popkin abandoned their musical pursuits, Alfano and Manniello formed a new band they called Sunny Jim, while Theiss joined the prominent local band Rusty Chain. Springsteen—under the influence of Cream and the Jimi Hendrix Experience—executed his plan by launching a powerful quartet he had decided to call the Earth Band.

The events leading to the dissolution of the Castiles are unclear. At one point, Vinyard claimed to have fired the band. But according to Theiss, there was some infighting among some members, while others had decided to pursue college degrees. Springsteen took over any existing bookings, playing them with his new group.

Looking back on his run playing in the Castiles, Springsteen still felt a sense of pride as recently as 2009, as he explained to Henke: "For one of your first bands, we got around pretty good."

Earth

Merely a week after the Castiles played their final live show, Bruce Springsteen unveiled his new band—now known simply as Earth—with a pair of gigs at the Off Broad Street Coffee House. Aside from Bruce guitar and vocal duties, the band was rounded out by John Graham on bass, Michael Burke on drums, and a character named "Flash Craig" on organ.

Soon after Earth's August 16th debut, former Castiles organist Bob Alfano was tapped to replace Craig in the lineup that would remain intact until the band's split in early 1969.

Ooze and Oz

When Earth took shape in the summer of 1968, Springsteen didn't have a manager like Tex Vinyard looking after his affairs. But by September, a local promotion outfit called "Ooze and Oz Productions" began looking after the group's affairs.

Helmed by Francis "Fran" Duffy and Rick "Spanky" Spachner, their management company also looked after local acts like Brother Duck, Black River Circus, Sidewalk Theory, and the Clique.

Ocean County College

After a year away from academics, Springsteen decided to resume his education by enrolling at Ocean County College in Toms River in September 1968, although conflicting reports suggest it was September '67. Regardless of the year, the news came as quite a surprise to those who knew how much he loathed school. His decision—in part—was to appease his parents, with whom he was still living.

Springsteen was joined in his freshman year by his new bandmates, Graham and Burke. During his time at OCC, Springsteen contributed two poems—"My Lady" and "Untitled"—to *Seascapes*, the school's literary yearbook, published in January 1969.

Unfortunately, as with his high school experience, Springsteen's leather jacket, jeans, and sneakers resulted in complaints in his first semester, which were addressed with him by his academic advisor. His rocker attire caused the counselor to assume he was unhappy and had troubles at home. Neither of which—by now—was the case.

In his first Springsteen biography, Dave Marsh suggested that OCC students actually petitioned that Springsteen be dismissed for "unacceptable weirdness." But he ultimately left on his own accord, dropping out at some point in 1969, presumably at the end of the fall semester.

Familiar Haunts

Out in front of Earth, Springsteen kept a busy performance schedule in the final third of 1968. His band took the stage at a private wedding at a Brooklyn Veterans of Foreign Wars building in late August. Into the autumn, Earth rocked the same familiar spots—including Le Teendezvous and the Freehold Hullabaloo—that Springsteen had become accustomed to playing with the Castiles.

Earth also played a number of gigs at the Student Union on Ocean County College's Toms River campus beginning in September. Confirmed shows occurred at the school in October 1968 and January 1969.

Its sets were representative of the blues-influenced rock music that was popular and included Hendrix ("Purple Haze"), Cream ("Sunshine of Your Love," "Toad"), Traffic ("Dear Mr. Fantasy"), Doors ("Back Door Man"), and Steppenwolf ("Born to Be Wild") covers.

The group's proto-metal approach—steered by Springsteen's desire to play his recently acquired Gibson Les Paul as quickly as possible—left a lasting impression on his then-acquaintance and fellow Jersey Shore music pioneer

on Cookman in October 1975. "If there was a chance of any of us making a living through music, we figured it would have to happen through him."

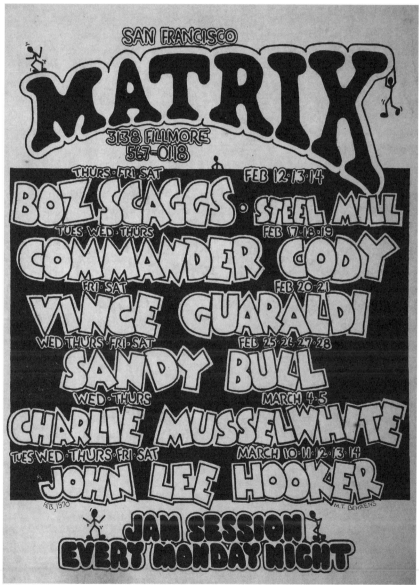

A flyer advertising Steel Mill's run of February 1970 dates with Boz Scaggs at the Matrix in Berkeley, California. The venue was owned by the Jefferson Airplane's Marty Balin.

Courtesy of Brucebase

Child Is Born

Springsteen ended Earth to join Child, an equally heavy blues-rock band that offered him the opportunity to play with new and advanced players. Child—which would also boast ex-Motif member Roslin—first came together officially for rehearsals in late February 1969.

The idea of forming a group that played original material dated back to 1967 when Lopez befriended Carl "Tinker" West. West was a local music enthusiast and aspiring manager who also owned a local Surfboard Factory called Challenger East that was based in the Wanamassa section of Ocean Township.

With more than enough room in his factory for a group to rehearse, West told Lopez to contact him should he ever form a band to play original music. By late 1968, Lopez was actively looking to make something happen, but his band didn't fully materialize until he heard Springsteen in early '69 and asked him to join them.

With a unique sound to set them apart from the other bands on the Shore, Child went to visit West in Wanamassa to find out if his year-and-a-half-old offer to Lopez still stood. Not only did West like what he heard from the foursome in a rehearsal/audition that included the Springsteen original "Jennifer," but he eventually offered the band a place to live.

Prior to this, Springsteen had been crashing with his close friend Steve Van Zandt at 610 Seventh Avenue in Asbury Park. He and Lopez occupied the uninsulated third-floor attic. They jumped at the opportunity to relocate. The accommodations were hardly plush—Lopez slept in one bathroom, Federici in the other. Meanwhile, Springsteen happily crashed in West's office on a mattress.

"I ended up living with [Tinker] in a surfboard factory for about a year and a half," Springsteen told the *NME*'s Andrew Tyler in November 1975. "It was dynamite up there."

"They used to make the surfboards downstairs," Springsteen told *The Aquarian* in 1978. "Tinker and I, we had a ball. Just one room! Two beds, a fridge and a TV—the rest of the room was filled with surfboards."

West and Springsteen became close friends, with Tinker acting like something of a surrogate dad and teaching the nineteen-year-old how to drive. Challenger East would remain the band's rehearsal facility, home base, and place of residence up until the summer of 1971.

Tinker West

Carl "Tinker" West was an iconic surfboard shaper and designer who first established Challenger at its original West Coast facility in San Diego's Mission Beach. But with tough competition in Southern California, and with the popularity of surfing on the rise on the East Coast, West set up shop on the Jersey Shore in 1967 to meet the demand of the sport's growing clientele.

Challenger was a legitimate operation with its own Pro Surfing Team, as evidenced by the ads and pictures of the Challenger Eastern crew in *Eastern Surfer* magazine. It's interesting to note that West was a rocket scientist at the Jet Propulsion Laboratory in the 1950s who had a knack for calculations and accuracy, which may explain why his boards were well received. He left the science world in his late twenties after he apparently became dismayed with the U.S. Government.

West was an avid guitarist and harmonica player who was in the process of establishing his own concert promotion enterprise, Blah Productions, but he wasn't interested in the cover bands that ruled the area clubs in the summertime. When he aligned with the members of Child, he found what he had been looking for.

Inside the factory, West kept things relatively relaxed. In the back room of Challenger's building, he kept a twenty-year-old woody station wagon that he was restoring alongside the surfboards that he was sanding. Dust was everywhere, as one might expect.

West was an unorthodox businessman, but a businessman just the same, whose dedication would help propel Bruce Springsteen's career beyond Asbury Park. He insisted—as Child's manager—on a certain level of professionalism. Contracts needed to be in order. Money was due when services were rendered.

In addition to band management, Tinker enjoyed jamming with anyone who would play with him, but was especially fond of playing with people like Steven Van Zandt, Garry Tallent, "Southside" Johnny Lyon, and an organist named Johnny Waasdorp.

West also had an interest in launching a recording studio (which he eventually did when he moved the surfboard factory to the Atlantic Highlands in 1970) and taped many of the band's gigs on a reel-to-reel machine that he would hook up to the soundboard. Unfortunately, due to the cost of tape, he had a tendency to record over them, which left few if any archival recordings as evidence from this era.

Bruce the Surfer

Aside from music, Springsteen developed a fondness for Challenger's wares. He didn't have much of a choice, after taking up residence in West's surfboard shop. Here, he was exposed to a crowd of locals who befriended the rocker and started goading him into giving it a try. At first he resisted, but eventually he gave in to the pressure. And along with the guys around him, Springsteen grabbed a board and began regularly visiting nearby spots like Manasquan Inlet, known to this day as one of the best surfing locations on the East Coast.

Because he was from Freehold, he was "considered inland," he told the *Aquarian* in '78. "I must have been some sight surfing for the first time," Springsteen explained, "but I'll tell you something—I got the hang of it pretty quick." For a time, hitting the waves was—along with cars and girls—one of his main interests outside of writing and playing rock 'n' roll.

Pandemonium Begins

Not long after the February 14, 1969, Grand Opening of Pandemonium in Wanamassa, the new music club began to hold what it advertised as "talent quests" each Thursday. These events were essentially jam sessions similar to those held after hours at the Upstage, but they also served as an opportunity for new bands like Child to ply their wares to the club's booker. During the group's first informal appearance at Pandemonium on March 13, the Bruce Springsteen–fronted band secured a run of headline gigs.

In advance of Child's official live unveiling, the band shot its earliest publicity photo inside Pandemonium. This picture was used to promote a run of dates that ran throughout April. Consisting of four or five sets, the band would play one lengthy show between 9:30 p.m. and 2 a.m.

According to *Brucebase*, Child's set consisted of original material like "Jennifer" and "Crown Liquor." The latter was actually written by Billy Chinnock, a former bandmate of Lopez's in Moment of Truth, and appropriated by Springsteen's group.

For these shows, the band's set also included a notable rendition of Buffalo Springfield's classic hippie anthem "For What It's Worth," which was a crowd favorite.

Attendance was strong after the club publicized the shows in local newspaper ads that read "Pandemonium gives birth to Child" and "It's a Birthquake with Child."

In addition to these gigs, Child rocked the Asbury Park Hullabaloo—which would eventually be rechristened the Sunshine In—and New Shrewsbury's Le Teendezvous, which Springsteen had played several times in earlier years.

Elsewhere, the group played an all-day event on May 5 in West End Park in Long Branch that was followed a week later by a music festival at Monmouth College. That event also included acts known as Tracks, Brother Duck, and Southern Conspiracy, but Child's performance was best received, a reviewer calling it "a wild, mind-bending show" in the school's newspaper.

"Brandy" Connection

Throughout the early summer of 1969, Child headlined regular gigs at Pandemonium, with additional performances at the short-lived Auction Coffee House in Long Branch. The band also took a gig at Blessed Sacrament Regional School in Margate in early June. The private school performance found Child sharing the stage with Tracks, a band that featured Peter Sweval and Jeff Grob, who were also the rhythm section for the '70s hitmakers Looking Glass. That band—which formed at Rutgers University in 1969—had an enduring

As for Mercy Flight's first show opening for Steel Mill, it went over well enough that it earned them additional opportunities. Springsteen suggested that the Richmond band open future shows for them if and when they returned to the area.

West Coast Plans

Back home on the Jersey Shore in early December, Tinker West and Steel Mill had conspired to travel to the San Francisco area, where Springsteen's parents had settled. The plan was to take a crack at making it on the same music scene that had given birth to bands like the Grateful Dead and the Jefferson Airplane.

In advance of the trip, the group played a pair of area shows. The first, which found them described on a poster that read "Steel Mill is Child under an assumed name," was held for Monmouth College students ahead of their Christmas Break.

This poster, printed in November 1969, was designed to promote Steel Mill's Richmond, Virginia, show that month, while informing Springsteen's growing group of followers in the region that his band had changed its name.   *Courtesy of Brucebase*

The following week, the band held an unusual fund-raising show at their practice facility in Wanamassa to finance the trip.

Goin' to California

Less than a year after his parents moved to the Bay Area, Bruce Springsteen made his first trek west with Tinker West and the other members of Steel Mill. They set off in the last week of 1969, caravanning in a station wagon following

West's Chevy truck. They were hoping their California trip might earn them the same kind of attention they had reaped from memorable gigs on the Jersey Shore and in the Richmond area.

As a warm-up after the drive across country, Steel Mill planned a pair of gigs at the Esalen Institute, a retreat center in Big Sur, some 120 miles south of San Francisco. The first show was held outdoors on New Year's Eve with other bands against the area's stunning backdrop. Two nights later, Steel Mill headlined an inside gig at the facility. In exchange for their services, West had arranged for a week's worth of accommodations in a log cabin on site.

"I've never been outta Jersey in my life and suddenly I get to Esalen and see all these people walkin' around in sheets," Springsteen told *Newsweek* in 1975. "I see someone playing bongos in the woods and it turns out to be this guy who grew up around the corner from me."

Attention!

Steel Mill's initial days in San Francisco weren't too promising. On January 8, 1970, the group failed an afternoon audition to perform a series of shows at the Avalon Ballroom. Two nights later, Steel Mill played the College of Marin in Kentfield in preparation for a show supporting Boz Scaggs at the Matrix, a Berkeley club founded by Marty Balin of the Jefferson Airplane.

Unfortunately, Scaggs wound up canceling because of illness, but *San Francisco Examiner* critic Philip Elwood didn't get word. Already at the venue, Elwood elected to review the sparsely attended show anyway and praised the Springsteen-fronted foursome in his article the following day. Elwood called the band's ninety-minute set "one of the most memorable evenings of rock in a long time," heralded Springsteen as "a most impressive composer" and surmised, "I have never been so overwhelmed by an unknown band."

The band's set—according to soundboard audio that has long been in circulation among Springsteen fans—included six-to-seventeen minute songs like "The War Is Over," "Lady Walking down the River," the politically charged "America Under Fire," "Guilty," "The Train Song," and "Goin' Down Slow."

In Elwood's closing remarks about Steel Mill, he wrote "they deserve and demand attention." The acclaim earned the group an invitation to audition night at Bill Graham's Fillmore West.

Burying the Hatchet

During his seven-week stay in Northern California, Springsteen spent a good deal of time at his parents' new home in San Mateo. He did his best to try and keep the peace with his mom and dad, and at one point, according to *Point Blank*, he and Doug worked hard to bury the hatchet.

But things became contentious during a weekend road trip where the two shared driving responsibilities. "We got in the car and drove," Springsteen explained. "[We were] arguing all the way. First I drove and my dad yelled at me, and then he drove and I yelled at him."

Still, things were hardly as tumultuous as they had been in Bruce's teen years. Much to Adele's happiness as time moved forward, the father and son—who always loved each other deep down—were actually coming to like and respect one another.

The Matrix

Steel Mill was invited back to the Matrix to support the Elvin Bishop Group on January 22nd, but in spite of the *Examiner* praise, the payoff was meager. The band was paid just $5 to open for the Chicago-based headliners.

Still, gigs were gigs, and Springsteen, Federici, Lopez, and Roslin returned to Balin's club the following month for a three-night stand opening for Boz Scaggs on February 12–14. Scaggs, a veteran of the Steve Miller Band, had returned to health since his cancelation for illness and was supporting his self-titled Atlantic Records debut.

Grin

After the newspaper praise, Steel Mill had earned from its first show at the Matrix, Bill Graham, the Bay Area's premier concert promoter and owner of Fillmore West, came down to check out Springsteen's group at one of the subsequent Matrix gigs. Graham liked what he had heard and hired them as a last-minute fill-in at his venue on February 9th, when another group canceled.

Again on the 18th, Steel Mill was tapped to play at the Fillmore, supporting the Maryland-bred band Grin. Fronted by singer/guitarist Nils Lofgren, this midweek gig marked the first-ever introductions between Springsteen and his future E Street Band guitarist.

$1,500 Offer

In addition to his venue and promotions businesses, Bill Graham had also recently established his own music label, Fillmore Records. Upon witnessing Steel Mill at Fillmore West, Graham became interested in signing the group and offered the band studio time to make a demo.

By now, the foursome was firing on all cylinders. They had an unbridled energy, a charismatic leader, and an arsenal of original material as evidenced by the two dozen songs Springsteen had since written for the group.

On February 22, 1970, Steel Mill entered Pacific Recording Studio at 1737 S. El Camino Real in San Mateo—not far from Springsteen's parents' home—to track a three-song demo. His trip to Pacific, which spawned classic albums like Santana's eponymous debut and the Grateful Dead's *Aoxomoxoa*, was only his second time ever inside a recording studio if you count the Castiles' thirty-minute 1966 session.

Graham—who had acts like Cold Blood and the aforementioned Elvin Bishop signed to his upstart record label—liked what he heard from the resulting recordings of "Going Back to Georgia," "He's Guilty (Send That Boy to Jail)," and "The Train Song" and made Steel Mill an offer. But after Tinker West and the band reviewed the contract, which offered unfavorable terms and a paltry $1,500 advance, they surprised the San Francisco music fixture by declining his offer.

Back East

Steel Mill closed out its eight-week West Coast visit with a second show at the College of Marin on February 24th. Following that gig, the band hit the road and traveled the 2,900 miles back east to make an already-booked, two-night return engagement at Richmond's Free University on February 27th and 28th.

"We had to get back to Richmond in 3 days to do a gig," Lopez said in an interview with the Bruce fanzine *Thunder Road* in 1979. "We made it. But that was a delirious show. I drove most of the way back, me and Tinker."

If the California journey wasn't the massive success Steel Mill had hoped, it was encouraging just the same. The foursome had gotten good press and label interest. They had nothing to be embarrassed about. If anything, their star was on the rise.

The group's weekend gigs in Richmond were chronicled on tape by West, and based on the recording—which has long circulated among fans—the band played as confidently as ever. Together, they tore through originals like "You Say You Love Me" and "On the Road" plus tunes like "Jeannie I Want to Thank You" and "Sweet Melinda."

These shows were also significant because they marked the final performances with bassist Vinnie Roslin. Speculation exists that Roslin wanted Steel Mill to take advantage of Bill Graham's record contract and was disappointed when they walked away from the offer. Although this has never officially been confirmed by the bassist, the idea that he was out of alignment with the rest of the group on the subject serves as an understandable excuse to quit the band.

The Upstage Scene Thrives

Alongside Steel Mill's increasing success, things continued to thrive late night at the Upstage into 1970. The commercial location of the club kept neighbors from complaining about the loud jams—which ran until daybreak. Tom Potter had a highly capable sound system courtesy of the hundreds of 15-inch speakers that lined his venue's back wall. Area musicians—some just off their local bar gigs—would plug into the house amps and roar for hours.

But despite the appearance that things were going smoothly, university officials had already relayed to Steel Mill that they were receiving complaints regarding their volume levels. Springsteen—based on the recording—seemed irritated about the warning.

"There's a weird thing going on between your officials and us" he told the crowd, proclaiming, "there should be no restrictions on me."

When the curfew hour of 11 p.m. rolled around, the audience clamored for more, and Steel Mill intended to keep playing. However, VCU authorities cut the power. Vini Lopez kept on drumming disobediently while the crowd kept on dancing until things escalated. Security jumped onstage and arrested Lopez. He was carted off to jail on a disorderly conduct charge.

Asbury Park Riots

Aside from a high-profile slot opening for Grand Funk Railroad at Bricktown's Ocean Ice Palace on June 13—which came about on short notice after the tour's support act, the MC5, got hung up in Connecticut—the early summer of 1970 was highlighted by June gigs at Freak Beach, the String Factory down in Richmond and the Clearwater Swim Club in Atlantic Highlands. The latter, which opened the club's summer season on June 21, was such a success that another event featuring Steel Mill was promptly booked for September.

But things weren't as upbeat when Independence Day rolled around in downtown Asbury Park, where the Upstage called home. Five nights of rioting caused by friction between the community's black poor and white shop owners broke out. Rocks shattered windows downtown, Molotov cocktails were thrown, and gunshots rang out. The end result was destruction from which the city would never recover.

Parking Deck Rock

Steel Mill kept plugging away, performing a gig at Asbury Park's Sunshine In just two weeks after the riots subsided, but area music fans were understandably timid about coming out at night so soon after the mayhem. Summer gigs became scarce, leaving the band with a monthlong pause before its next show, at a parking deck at 7th and Marshall Street in Richmond.

That August 14 headlining performance—which included a new tune called "We'll All Man the Guns"—came at just the right time for the band, which was running out of momentum. Steel Mill needed a change, and a lineup augmentation seemed like a good solution.

Funky Dusty and the Soul Broom

The Upstage was home to a performance by Van Zandt's side project, Funky Dusty and the Soul Broom, on July 27. The lineup also included Southside Johnny (formerly of Maelstrom), plus Tallent and "Big" Bobby Williams, from the area band Glory Road, which also featured future E Street Band member David Sancious and scene fixture Billy Chinnock.

This group laid the groundwork for future scene outfits like the Big Bad Bobby Williams Band and Sundance Blues Band, which would take shape in late 1970 and spring 1971, respectively.

Robbin Thompson Joins

After the parking deck gig, Springsteen pulled Mercy Flight frontman Robbin Thompson to the side for a private conversation, during which time Springsteen asked him to join Steel Mill as a second vocalist and songwriter. Of course, Robbin would be expected to move north to the Jersey Shore, which he contemplated.

Thompson gave notice to his existing bandmates the following week and moved to Wanamassa to begin rehearsing with Steel Mill. The practices ran long during the next few days as the band prepared to play at the Nashville Music Festival in Tennessee on August 29.

Like Springsteen, Thompson—a Florida native—had gotten his start fronting Sunshine State garage bands like the Hanging Five, the Five Gents, the Tasmanians, and Transcontinental Mercy Flight between 1963 and 1968. In 1969, he went north to Richmond for college and formed the band that regularly supported Steel Mill.

"[Bruce] asked me to join the band because he wanted another singer and writer," Thompson told Torsten Mörke of the *Castiles.net* fan site in June 2000. The thinking was that with Thompson in the band, Steel Mill would be more versatile. It also gave them an even stronger link to the Richmond music scene, where it was already thriving.

Music City

Steel Mill rolled into Nashville on August 29 for a performance at the 3rd Annual Nashville Music Festival, which was sponsored by local radio station WMAC and held in the city's Centennial Park Band Shell.

The fest was long on lesser-knowns like Ballin' Jack and Ten Wheel Drive, and headlined by country performer Ronnie Milsap and early rock legend Roy Orbison, one of Springsteen's childhood favorites who he later mentioned, of course, in "Thunder Road."

For Springsteen, the Nashville journey was also a rare opportunity to stay in a hotel. He and the rest of the band were mostly used to crashing with hospitable fans and, when all else failed, sleeping in the back of Tinker West's truck.

Springsteen would vividly remember this day in 1987 when he inducted Roy Orbison into the Rock and Roll Hall of Fame. Incidentally, this show apparently drew fifty thousand area music fans, making it the biggest crowd Springsteen had played to date.

Cut Loose Like a Deuce

1971–1972

Open Mike

In early 1971, Bruce Springsteen was still being managed by Tinker West, although he had no proper band to call his own. He finally had wheels—an old Ford he used to get around after tiring of being reliant on others to shuttle him places. He needed mobility as he plotted his next move.

That's not to say he ever had thoughts about giving up the stage. On January 29 and 30, he participated in jam sessions at the Upstage with its headliners, Steve Van Zandt and the Big Bad Bobby Williams Band. With a lineup that also included bassist Garry Tallent, organist David Sancious, and Johnny Lyon on harmonica and vocals, Springsteen was clearly among friends.

On February 12, he made the first of approximately ten "open mike" appearances at the Upstage, where he performed solo material and jammed with other shore-area performers over the next five weeks. This led up to Springsteen's first billed performance as a solo act on March 18 at the Deal Park Recreation Center in Deal. For the gig, which was sponsored by the Young Hebrew Association, he was backed by Van Zandt, Lopez, Tallent and Sancious.

Friendly Enemies

In February'71, Tinker West received a call from the manager of the Sunshine In asking if Steel Mill wanted to open for the Allman Brothers at their March 27 show. When West broke the news that the band had split, the venue's overseer evidently replied, "give me Springsteen, I don't care how."

Springsteen and Van Zandt were enormous Allman fans who were anxious to take the gig, plus they both needed the money. So the two gathered together their friends from the Upstage and formed a new ten piece band that West had temporarily named "Friendly Enemies." The group—which consisted of two drummers (Lopez and Williams), two guitarists (Bruce and Steve), two keyboardists (Sancious and ex-Rogues member John Waasdorp), and two saxophone players (Albee Tellone and Bobby Feigenbaum), plus one bassist (Tallent) and one harmonica player (Lyon)—was modeled after large but successful bands of the era like Joe Cocker's Mad Dogs and Englishmen and Leon Russell's Shelter People.

For the Sunshine In show, there were also a group of Upstage regulars who performed skits while a foursome sat at a table and played Monopoly during the gig. It was a way for Springsteen to include his nonmusical friends in the performance. In doing so, his pals could say—at least for the night—that they were in the band.

The Allman Brothers evidently found Springsteen's outfit—which had already settled on a new handle, Dr. Zoom and the Sonic Boom, for future shows—highly entertaining. According to reports, the late Duane Allman even told Springsteen, "That's one cookin' band, man."

Monopoly Wizard

The Monopoly players were an extension of an activity that Asbury Park area musicians regularly shared, especially during winter weeknights of early 1971. Springsteen was a competitive Monopoly enthusiast who was almost always on hand at Van Zandt's apartment—which was just up the street from Palace Amusements—on the evenings when the Upstage was closed and/or there were no gigs.

Steve would organize the games, which eventually morphed from Monopoly into poker. In addition to musicians, including his roommates Lyon and Tellone, scene regulars like Danny Gallagher were almost always present. Gigs were hard to find in Asbury Park in the winter after the riots, and the games were a way to occupy the musicians' time as they lived on a dollar or two each day.

Putting a local spin on the game, they gave the Atlantic City–themed pastime an Asbury Park twist. There was a Chief McCarthy card, named for the Middletown Police official who sent Federici into hiding. Anyone who pulled that card could send any opponent to jail. And then there was a Riot card, which made light of the recent local racial crises. Anyone who was lucky enough to get the latter could firebomb the real estate of any other gamer.

Springsteen would show up with snacks for the Monopoly sessions that he would trade with hungry players for property. This, of course, gave him a keen edge over the others.

"He had no scruples," Johnny Lyon told *Time* in 1975. He would show up and barter Pepsis and Drake's Cakes for hotels. If that wasn't enough, Springsteen was also a mean pinball player and could usually beat the pants off of his pals.

Bruce's Jams

On the second weekend of April 1971, Springsteen lined up a pair of acoustic gigs at the Green Mermaid under the billing "Bruce Springsteen Acoustic Jam." These gigs were an unplugged but slightly more formal take on what he had long been participating in at the Upstage.

The following weekend, he went electric, moving the shows upstairs to the Upstage, where he steered the "Bruce Springsteen Jam Concert" over two shows. In doing so, Springsteen was working toward the right combination of musicians that would comprise his yet to be finalized new band.

These concerts, which also provided a payday for Springsteen, continued for an additional weekend before wrapping up on April 24. While they weren't technically Dr. Zoom shows, they were celebratory in nature and did encompass many of the same musicians.

"Southside" Johnny

In advance of the Friendly Enemies gig supporting the Allmans, some of the members went to a thrift shop to pick up clothes for the show. When Johnny Lyon returned to Challenger East, where the giant group rehearsed, Springsteen was highly amused by his getup.

Lyon looked like an old Chicago blues dude in his secondhand suit and fedora hat. According to Tellone, Springsteen yelled, "Hey man, it's Chicago Johnny." To which Lyon snapped back, "From the Southside."

From that point on, all of the Asbury Park music scene insiders called him "Southside" Johnny.

"The Doctor"

Springsteen had accumulated his own nicknames during his time on the Shore music scene. While they didn't stick very long, he was at first known as "Baby" and, later, "Gut-rock" for his love of junk food. During the Sonic Boom era, he was referred to as "the Doctor" and, later, "God."

"Everybody had to have a nickname," Springsteen told *Mojo* in 1999. "There was no one in Asbury Park that did not have a nickname." Of course, his most infamous nickname had yet to become widely known.

Dr. Zoom and the Sonic Boom

On May 14, 1971, Dr. Zoom and the Sonic Boom were booked to play the Sunshine In with a subsequent show the following day at Newark State College in Union, the future site of Kean University. These were the band's only two official performances, and as Vini Lopez remembered to *Castiles.net*, "It was the sound of the Upstage Club brought out to a large concert venue. We did a mix of tunes like Bob Dylan, Chicago Blues, Carole King and Bruce's originals."

Among them was a song he wrote called the "Southside Shuffle" that prominently featured Johnny Lyon, plus a twelve-minute take on King's "Will You Love Me Tomorrow." A look at the band's May 14 setlist reveals the Steel Mill staple "Goin' Back to Georgia," the blues classic "Bo Diddley," and a timeless medley of Chuck Berry's "Roll Over Beethoven" and "Reelin' and Rockin'." For this show, the sprawling band was augmented by female backing singers known as the Zoomettes, plus a lady baton twirler.

"We had everybody that could play and some that couldn't," Springsteen told *Crawdaddy* in 1973. But Dr. Zoom was never meant to be a serious endeavor. It was just a gathering of assorted friends. After its second performance at Newark State's first annual "Ernie the Chicken Festival"—an all-day outdoor party—the Sonic Boom was over.

Sundance and the Hot Mammas

In April 1971 and in tandem with Dr. Zoom and the Sonic Boom, Van Zandt and Lyon played their first gigs fronting the Sundance Blues Band. The group— which was evidently named after the Paul Newman and Robert Redford movie of the time, *Butch Cassidy and the Sundance Kid*—also featured Lopez on drums, Tallent on bass, and a rhythm guitarist named Joe Hagstrom. Shows held at the Student Prince throughout the spring of 1971 usually featured a guest performance by Springsteen, who was asked to join the group in mid-May after Hagstrom quit.

Also in May, Springsteen fronted his own group for a series of gigs at the Upstage, which were billed as Bruce Springsteen and the Hot Mammas. Backed by some of the female singers who had accompanied the Dr. Zoom shows under the handle "the Zoomettes," Bruce was helped by most of the guys in the Sundance Blues Band for these late-night performances, which took place after their own Student Prince obligations had been met.

After roughly a dozen gigs with Sundance, Springsteen officially stepped away from the group after a July 4 show. Keyboardist David Sancious was added to the lineup to try and fill the void. Of course, Bruce's departure was amicable as he continued to guest with the group until it splintered in 1972.

The Bruce Springsteen Band

In the summer of 1971, Springsteen launched himself as a marquee performer fronting a diverse, eleven-member band that boasted his core group—Van Zandt, Lopez, Tallent, Federici, and Sancious—plus a small horn section and female backing singers. Sax player Bobby Feigenbaum was a Dr. Zoom survivor, and with the addition of trumpet player Harvey Cherlin from local band Lazarus plus singers Barbara Dinkins, Delores Holmes, and Francine Daniels, the band had crafted a unique and powerful sound.

Mixing covers like "C. C. Rider," "Not Fade Away," and "Route 66" with originals like "You Mean So Much to Me"—later recorded by Southside Johnny and the Asbury Jukes—and the Steel Mill holdover "Goin' Back to Georgia," the BSB played its first show at Brookdale Community College in Lincroft, New Jersey, on July 10.

Humble Pie

For its second gig on July 11, the Bruce Springsteen Band was asked to open for Humble Pie, the British band fronted by future rock sensation Peter Frampton, at the Sunshine In. Frampton, at the time signed to A&M Records, was so impressed with the group that he offered to get them an audition with the label. He also wanted to take the BSB on the road with him across North America as his opening act.

"He talked to me and most of the band members about getting a contract with A&M and going on tour with them," Harvey Cherlin explained to *Castiles. net.* Although it sounded like the break Bruce had been waiting for, his manager famously declined both generous offers on the spot.

"Tinker said no way was he going to sign with a major label—they were scavengers," Cherlin added.

Lincoln Center

The BSB kept an active performance schedule throughout the summer of '71, playing shows in Richmond's Monroe Park, South Amboy's D'Scene, Asbury Park's Sunshine In, Garfield Park in Long Branch, and, perhaps most impressively, at Damrosch Park in New York City's Lincoln Center.

The latter was part of the Guggenheim Memorial Concert Series and featured original Springsteen compositions like "Jambalaya," "You Mean So Much to Me," "I'm in Love Again," and "You Don't Leave Me No Choice." The last two titles were sung by Delores Holmes instead of Springsteen. The show was advertised in advance on the pioneering rock station WNEW-FM.

Recording Practice

Around this time, Springsteen began recording himself alone and with his band, setting up a makeshift studio in Tinker's surfboard factory, where he still lived. The idea was to become more comfortable with how he sounded on tape.

In addition to a slew of originals, the band laid down covers, including a slow, soulful rendition of Bob Dylan's "It's All Over Now, Baby Blue." It's unknown if these tapes still exist, but based on the observations of Ken Viola, a friend of the Springsteen camp at the time, Springsteen was unhappy with the results.

The Prince of the Student Prince Meets Clarence Clemons

From early September to late October 1971, the BSB dominated Asbury Park's the Student Prince, performing for two and a half hours in total each night with a forty-minute intermission. What the dingy club lacked in ambience, Springsteen more than made up for with enthusiasm as he led the band through

Chuck Berry's "Little Queenie" and the original tune "Don't You Want to Be an Outlaw."

It was during this residency that Springsteen would first encounter saxophonist Clarence Clemons, who had been playing as part of Norman Seldin and the Joyful Noyze at the nearby Wonder Bar. Clemons apparently dropped in on the Student Prince gig to see what all the fuss was about, and he and Springsteen were introduced. Although a jam session occurred, Clemons was still a good year away from officially joining up with Springsteen.

Tumbleweed Connection

The Bruce Springsteen Band was booked to play a headlining show at the University of Richmond on October 23 that also featured two additional bands Tinker West had been working with at the time. Named Black Forrest Rhodes and Tumbleweed, these bands also supported the BSB for a Halloween night gig at the National Guard Armory, which, incidentally, was the band's final performance with backing singers.

Aligned with West's Blah Productions, the acoustic-based Tumbleweed—formerly known as Montana Flintlock—had already been working in a Nashville under the direction of Mike Appel. Appel was a music industry veteran who Tinker would soon introduce to Springsteen.

The Upstage Shuts Down

On October 29, 1971, Springsteen led a group of area musicians—as he had done countless times before—through a jam session at the Upstage. Including the core members of the BSB, Bruce steered the 2 a.m. to 5 a.m. performance on what would be the second to final night that the Tom and Margaret Potter–owned venue would be open.

Due to a commitment to play at Virginia Commonwealth, the band was rocking down in Richmond on the club's final night. Regardless, it was a sad night for the Jersey Shore music community.

The unrest in the city the prior year had drastically hurt the local merchants, including the Potters. The members of the Bruce Springsteen Band had held on all along, hoping for an economic recovery, if not a social one.

"The place went down to the ground, and we rode right down with it," Steve Van Zandt told *Time* in 1975. But before it all crumbled, they had the time of their lives, and the Upstage was the main hub of their joy.

"Those were wonderful days," Lyon added in the same article. "We were all young and crazy."

Pocketful of Tunes

On November 4, 1971, Tinker West brought Springsteen to a meeting at Pocketful of Tunes, a music publishing company owned by Wes Farrell that employed Mike Appel. This was at the suggestion of Vini Lopez, who had heard from some other musicians that there was a pair of producers in New York looking for singer/songwriters.

"I mentioned this to Tinker and suggested there might be something in it for Bruce," Lopez told Marc Eliot in 1992's *Down Thunder Road*. "I knew Bruce was having a hard time and I thought this might get him some work."

West came by Springsteen's house in Highlands that afternoon while he was out on his front porch. Yelling through the car window, West told Springsteen that he had befriended a music publisher in New York City and suggested he go with him for an introduction. Springsteen grabbed his guitar and took the ride.

Here, Springsteen—sporting torn jeans and a T-shirt—performed a couple of tunes using his acoustic guitar and the office piano.

Appel—a Flushing, Queens, native who got his start in the psychedelic band the Balloon Farm and cowrote their 1967 hit "A Question of Temperature"—wasn't immediately blown away by Springsteen, but liked the creativity in the lyrics to the song "Baby Doll." The meeting wasn't incredibly promising, as Appel, who also helped pen Paul Anka's "Midnight Angel" and songs for the Partridge Family, let him have it.

"I told him they were the worst songs I ever heard," Appel told Eliot. "[They were] utterly devoid of any pop potential."

Just the same, Appel left Springsteen with a glimmer of hope about a publishing deal. He told him to keep writing and come back when he had some better songs and they would see where it might lead. There were no commitments from either side.

Firing West

November 1971 also marked Springsteen's amicable split from Tinker West. As much as he loved his manager for his guidance and generosity, Springsteen had outgrown the Jersey Shore scene and the routine Richmond runs.

West's discharge was triggered by an argument that occurred in a bar between Tinker and Lopez. "I came by and told him [I] didn't want him to manage us anymore," Springsteen explained in *Point Blank*. West had been working on the band's equipment truck at the time. "He said, 'Okay,' and that was it.'"

Under Springsteen's direction, with business guidance from a local music aficionado named George "the Attorney" Francis—who also helped the Sunshine Blues Band—the group carried on, playing as a five piece into mid-December 1971 and continuing its run as weekend headliners at the Student Prince.

During this era, the BSB performed Springsteen originals like "She's Leaving," "Sure Can Feel the Pain," and John Lee Hooker's "Sweet Miss Sally."

Springsteen closed out the year with a performance at the Rutgers University Student Union in New Brunswick on Thursday, December 17. Two days later, the BSB played its last-ever shows at the Student Prince, marking the end of a successful run at the now-historic Asbury Park venue.

Christmas Break

In the third week of December, Springsteen left New Jersey with Tinker West—with whom he still remained friends—and they drove to California. West had business and family matters in the Golden State, while Springsteen had plans to spend Christmas, as he had the previous two years, with his mom and dad in San Mateo.

Before his exit, Springsteen conveyed to his band members that there was no guarantee when he'd be back. He might be gone a few months or a few weeks. There was no formal split. While he was away, Van Zandt stepped up and kept the organization together.

After trying his hand at performing as a solo act in the Bay Area, Springsteen could tell things were going to be tough. The only rock-'n'-roll action he could find was playing with some fourteen-year-olds in a nearby garage.

"There were too many good musicians," he explained in *Songs*. "I'd left my rep as 'bar band king' in Jersey, so it was back home for me."

In his absence, Gary Tallent and David Sancious had accepted short-term jobs as session musicians at a Richmond recording studio called Alpha Sound.

Commitment to Song Craft

In the weeks and months after meeting Appel, Bruce Springsteen began to write like a madman and felt guilty when he didn't keep a busy songwriting schedule. Although he wasn't exactly rolling in money, the $100 he could earn performing locally each weekend was a far cry from poverty in early 1972.

He knew his future as a performer and recording artist depended on the quality of his craft. Springsteen wanted to live up to Mike Appel's challenge and completely overwhelm him when he had the chance to meet with him again.

The Captain's Garter and the Back Door

With their future uncertain while Springsteen was away in San Mateo, Lyon, Van Zandt, Tallent, Lopez, and Sancious booked shows as the Sundance Blues Band at the Captain's Garter in Neptune in early '72. Upon his return to New Jersey, Springsteen joined the band in its residency on January 21–23, playing guest rhythm guitar and leading them through high-energy renditions of Walter Brown's "Confessin' the Blues" during the group's respective sets.

With Springsteen back in town, the BSB was reactivated for two shows opening for an adaptation of the musical *Jesus Christ Superstar*—also at the Captain's Garter—on the final weekend of January. The Bruce Springsteen Band remained busy the next month with an eight-gig engagement at the Back Door in Richmond over the first, third and fourth weekends of February. Recordings

Afterward, Hammond informed Springsteen that he would arrange for the performer to return to CBS to cut a solo demo the following day, which was the next step toward a record deal. Springsteen was totally elated. After the showcase, according to Appel's account, Springsteen was so excited by the news that he was jumping into the air as he ran down the street.

Bruce Signs to Columbia

After his promising performance, Springsteen's joy turned to conviction. He intended to make the best of the golden opportunity John Hammond was presenting to him. He would put his all into the studio demo audition that Hammond would hopefully bring to his boss, Clive Davis.

Alternating between the acoustic guitar on songs like "Mary Queen of Arkansas" and "Growin' Up" and the piano on "Jazz Musician" and "If I Was the Priest," Springsteen's CBS demo may have exhibited power over prowess, but the inventiveness in his lyrics—evidenced by the Catholic imagery of the latter—stayed with Hammond for years.

Hammond took the demo tape (which also included "The Angel," "Arabian Nights," "It's Hard to Be a Saint in the City," "Southern Son," "Street Queen," and "Two Hearts in True Waltz Time") to Davis. Hammond was both excited and nervous—it had been a while since he discovered a major act.

Davis loved what he heard on his office stereo and even took the tape with him to play for Paul Simon at the latter's birthday party that evening. Springsteen was offered a preliminary deal with Columbia Records, which was finalized on June 9, 1972.

Not So, Epic

Because Springsteen was a young artist, Hammond had pushed for him to sign to Epic Records, a subsidiary of Columbia. The staff was comprised of younger people, and he believed Springsteen might be better served there.

But in Appel's mind, Springsteen—like Dylan before him—deserved the distinction that came with the red label the parent company was known for. Davis finally stepped in and kept Springsteen on Columbia.

Shop Around

Before Springsteen's contract with Columbia was actually finalized, Appel tried to see if he could drum up a better offer. But his hopes for a bidding war stalled after he got a flat-out rejection from the A&R director at Elektra Records—home of the Doors, the Stooges, the MC5, and Tim Buckley, a favorite of Springsteen's.

A&M Records also rejected Springsteen, making Appel realize how lucky he had been with Columbia.

Slavery Deal

While Columbia was readying the paperwork on Springsteen's contract, Hammond would later reveal that he had an attorney take a look at the production and management agreements Springsteen had recently signed with Mike Appel. The lawyer summed up the Springsteen-Appel agreements as "a slavery deal."

Springsteen wasn't actually signed to Columbia. Appel and Cretecos' production company, Laurel Canyon, held that distinction. The indirect contract he had inked with his handlers affirmed the twenty-three-year-old Springsteen was anything but wise about his finances.

He signed a one-year management deal with Appel and Cretecos that gave them four one-year options. A separate contract gave Laurel Canyon the exclusive right to his recordings for the same length of time. That agreement also stipulated Springsteen would need to make five albums for Laurel Canyon, for which he would get 3 percent of the retail selling price. Meanwhile, Appel and Cretecos would get three times that through Laurel Canyon's arrangement with the label.

Springsteen would later concede that he was far too trusting of Mike Appel. He never hired an attorney to review the recording, production, or publishing documents he signed. As Jim Mahlmann, a New York music booker who had dealt with Appel, would explain in *Point Blank*, "deal-wise, [Mike] was a thug."

On the flipside, Springsteen was the exact opposite, as Hammond told Time in 1975, "In all my years in music, he's the only person I've ever met who cares absolutely nothing about money."

That would come back to bite Springsteen in the ass.

Appel's Amendment

In *Down Thunder Road*, Appel contested the term "slavery deal." He claimed it was he who took his Springsteen contracts to Bill Krasilovsky, the lawyer Hammond recommended.

When Krasilovsky advised him that the management split was too high, even at a net figure, Appel went back to his own lawyer, Jules Kurz, and they elected to reduce Laurel Canyon's commission to 20 percent in June 1972.

According to Appel, Springsteen was well aware of the contract amendment, which was to the artist's advantage.

The Esquire

Springsteen acquired his trademark 1952 Fender Esquire Electric guitar in May 1972. The model, designed by Leo Fender and George Fullerton, debuted in 1950. Springsteen's beloved axe—which he can be seen clutching on the cover of his 1975 breakthrough album *Born to Run*—has seen some minor modifications through the years.

Purchased for $185, Springsteen later told RockHall.com, "it was my official 'you just signed a record deal, you get a guitar' guitar. Previous to that, you would not have $180 dollars at a single moment." In the company of Mike Appel, Springsteen went to Phil Patillo's Guitar Shop in Belmar New Jersey on Highway 34 and made the buy.

"I wanted a Telecaster, because I played a Telecaster previously when I was younger," Springsteen explained, citing the fact that two of his guitar heroes, Jeff Beck and Pete Townshend, had both played them. He believed Telecasters were versatile. They were good for playing soul music a la Steve Cropper or the kind of rock music James Burton was known for.

Springsteen bought it without asking any questions, only to find out later that it wasn't a stock instrument, which would explain its distinct sound. He would come to describe it as "a bastard" because its Telecaster body was fused to the neck of a different guitar.

Interestingly, Springsteen has embraced the practice of applying a special household sealant to the outside of it and all of his guitars in an effort to protect them. According to Gary Graff, author of *The Ties That Bind*, Springsteen first began to coat the Esquire in the 1980s after he began dumping a full bucket of water over his head to cool off during his marathon shows.

The sealant, of course, shielded the guitar's wiring and pickups from water damage, which Springsteen—or more likely his guitar technician—would test by pouring a two-liter bottle of water over the instrument before plugging it in.

With him for nearly every performance he'd play over the course of more than four decades, the instrument would come to represent everything that Springsteen accomplished as an artist and world-class performer. The Esquire symbolized the fulfillment of his rock-'n-roll dreams. Like Springsteen, it was versatile and durable.

Not So Big Advance

Aside from the Esquire, Bruce Springsteen bought himself one lone gift—a Harley-Davidson motorcycle—with his share of his Columbia Records advance. The total amount advanced for his first record deal was $65,000, including a $25,000 lump sum and a $40,000 recording budget.

Contrary to his infamous line on 1973's "Rosalita," Springsteen's deal may have been more money than he'd ever seen, but his share of the money wasn't big enough to change his lifestyle. His uniform—T-shirts, jeans, sneakers or boots, and his scraggily beard—remained unaltered.

He kept an apartment in Asbury Park above a drugstore where he could write music on his guitar and an old upright piano that had been bought by his aunt. But based on his propensity to couch-surf, he listed his permanent address as care of Cretecos—who maintained a residence in Bedford, Massachusetts—on his Columbia contract.

Johnny Superstar

Not long after his record deal was inked, Springsteen reportedly called his mom and dad in San Mateo to tell them that—after a decade of hard work and dedication to rock 'n' roll—he had finally landed a record deal. Dutch suggested he think about using a stage name and had a good suggestion.

"I got a doozy. *Johnny Superstar*," Mr. Springsteen proposed. Bruce kindly declined the recommendation and said he'd call home again when he had more news.

6

Just Like a Supernova

Greetings from Asbury Park, N.J.

Writing Greetings

Upon his return from San Mateo in early 1972, but before he had again made contact with Mike Appel, Bruce Springsteen began writing the songs that would eventually shape *Greetings from Asbury Park, N.J.*

The tunes were a far cry from his electrified efforts with Steel Mill and the BSB. His solo material was written in an acoustic style and was more in line with the coffeehouse songs he had sporadically experimented with starting in the late 1960s.

Largely crafted on his old hand-me-down upright piano in the back of a closed beauty salon beneath his apartment, the material was lyrically driven and emerged from a series of notebooks where Springsteen stored his thoughts and prose. Surrounded by old hairdryers and sinks, he penned the songs for *Greetings*. The lyrics came first. He set them to music after.

"Most of the songs were twisted biographies," he said in Songs, citing virtually every tune that made up his debut. "I wrote impressionistically and changed names to protect the guilty. I worked to find something that was identifiably me."

Calling Up the Band

Because he was signed as a solo artist after auditioning alone, Springsteen's label and handlers had envisioned marketing him as a singer/songwriter along the lines of Bob Dylan or James Taylor. But when it came time to create his debut album, Springsteen insisted on putting together his own band.

Appel resisted the band concept at first because he was caught up in his client's lyrics. After the initial acoustic presentation of Springsteen's material, Appel had difficulty imagining a song like "Spirit in the Night" translating with a full band. Springsteen, the young visionary, was surprised at Appel's close-mindedness.

Meanwhile, Hammond was also skeptical of how Springsteen might pull off songs like "Growin' Up" and "It's Hard to Be a Saint in the City" with such accompaniment. But the A&R executive trusted Springsteen and gave him the opportunity to form his own group.

Springsteen sought out friends and former bandmates from the Asbury Park scene like Vini Lopez, Steve Van Zandt, David Sancious, and Garry Tallent. He offered them all the chance to play on his first studio album.

Van Zandt Declines

Despite the invitation, Steve Van Zandt had to decline Springsteen's offer to participate in the making of *Greeting from Asbury Park, N.J.* because of financial pressures. Lack of cash prompted him to take a well-paying construction job.

Although he would return to music full time the following year—taking a steady gig touring with the oldies band the Dovells—he kept strong ties to the Jersey Shore music scene. While it would be a couple of years until Van Zandt would again join his friend in a formal capacity, he managed, as explained below, to leave his mark on Springsteen's debut album.

The *Greetings* Band

In the second week of June, Bruce and his band began to rehearse the songs that would make up *Greetings from Asbury Park, N.J.* in nearby Point Pleasant. The core members of the group that played on the album sessions were:

Vini Lopez

"Mad Dog" was as capable as he was volatile and definitely earned his nickname. As Springsteen's loyal kit man and resident screwball since the Steel Mill days, Lopez once slapped short-lived BSB trumpeter Harvey Cherlin in the mouth.

Garry Tallent

Everything Springsteen could have wanted in a bassist at the time; Tallent's last name said it all. In the studio or onstage he was stoic but dependable, drawing comparisons to legendary players like the Rolling Stones' Bill Wyman and the Who's John Entwistle.

David Sancious

A natural-born musician and multi-instrumentalist who served as Springsteen's keyboardist, Sancious was a blistering guitarist in his own right. Sancious—who was just eighteen during the sessions for *Greetings*—would go on to play with the likes of jazz favorite Stanley Clarke, Peter Gabriel, Eric Clapton, and Sting.

914 Studios

In July 1972, Bruce Springsteen and his hand-picked band began recording at 914 Studios in Blauvelt, New York. The recording studio—which was located thirty-five miles north of New York City—was hardly state of the art, but for Springsteen it was far more advanced than his other official recording sessions with the Castiles and Steel Mill.

The 914 Studios—named for the area code in Rockland County where it stood—was a no-frills setup on Highway 303 that backed up against a football field. It was located in the vicinity of a Carvel ice cream store and the Blauvelt Diner, which became a favorite of Springsteen's.

Housed in a converted garage that would ultimately revert back to an auto body shop, the studio had subpar acoustics and suffered from a leaky roof. Springsteen would later describe 914 as "a crapper," but by 1972 analog standards, 914—launched just a year earlier and owned by sound engineer Brooks Arthur—served its purpose well.

The initial two-and-a-half-week recording session only took $11,000 from the $40,000 Columbia had offered for the album's budget. Had Laurel Canyon reserved a top-notch Manhattan studio, it could have easily burned through that advance money. Instead, Appel and Cretecos chose a reasonably priced albeit out-of-the-way alternative.

"I thought it would be a great idea to have a workshop where artists and producers could hang out for a week at a time, relax and build a record at affordable rates," Arthur told *Mix* magazine in June 2005. As for its modest environs, Appel would suggest it was fine for the time, telling Eliot, "there was nothing we were doing that needed the excellence of an [upmarket] studio."

Solo Summer

Just before completion of the songs Springsteen believed would comprise his debut album for Columbia, he resumed performing. Save for a full-band show at a private Point Pleasant residence in advance of the *Greetings* sessions, his summer '72 itinerary was a completely solo endeavor.

On July 1, he performed impromptu alongside future saxophonist Clarence Clemons during a Norman Seldin and the Joyful Noyze gig (see below). Later that week, on July 5, Springsteen made a solo engagement at the Cinema III in Red Bank, playing a benefit show for 1972 presidential candidate George McGovern.

Elsewhere in July, he accompanied the Bank Street Blues Band—which featured Southside Johnny and would ultimately evolve into the Blackberry

Booze Band and finally the Asbury Jukes—for a pair of Asbury Park gigs at the Student Prince.

London Publishing Demos

Around the time he recorded *Greetings from Asbury Park, N.J.*, in July 1972, Springsteen went into Media Sound in New York City to track material that his publisher had hoped to use to sell his songs to other artists.

Tracks distributed to Intersong Music in 1972 included "Arabian Night," "Circus Song" (which would later be known as "Circus Town" and ultimately "Wild Billy's Circus Story"), "Cowboys of the Sea," "Henry Boy," "If I Was the Priest," "Marie," "No Need," "She's Leaving," "Song for the Orphans," "Southern Son," "Street Queen," "Tokyo," "Vibes Man" (which would later evolve into "New York City Serenade"), "Visitation at Fort Horn," and "The Word." These were among the demos of some sixty songs Springsteen apparently tracked during the year.

No Single

In July 1972, after Appel had delivered the first few songs to Columbia, Springsteen got word back about the shape his debut album was taking. Sure, there were some great songs, but John Hammond's boss, Clive Davis, didn't hear a single.

Determined to make the powers that be at CBS happy, Springsteen went back to work and returned with two memorable numbers, "Blinded by the Light" and "Spirit in the Night."

Davis would later tell *Backstreets* that he was pleased with how well Springsteen took his feedback when he told him it lacked a "breakthrough radio cut."

This poster advertised Springsteen's February 1973 concert with Dan Hicks and His Hot Licks at Virginia Commonwealth University.   *Courtesy of Brucebase*

"Most artists, if you discuss that, they get very defensive," Davis explained. "But he said, 'You know, you're right. Let me spend some time with this.'"

Calling Up Clarence

Bruce Springsteen first encountered Clarence Clemons in September 1971 at the Student Prince when Clemons—during an intermission for his own gig with Norman Seldin and the Joyful Noyze at the Wonder Bar—wandered across the street with his saxophone and joined him for a spontaneous jam. Ten months later, while he was perfecting his debut album, *Greetings from Asbury Park, N.J.*, Springsteen began to ponder ways to enhance the tracks Clive Davis asked him to append to the disc.

Springsteen thought again about Clemons's tenor sax work and sought him out in July 1972 at a Joyful Noyze gig at the Beacon Manor Hotel's Ship Bottom Lounge in Point Pleasant. After jamming with him once again, Springsteen liked how things clicked.

He invited the saxophonist up to Blauvelt for his next session at 914 Studios. Clemons agreed to play on "Blinded by the Light" and "Spirit in the Night," the two tracks Springsteen was adding to the final sequence of his debut.

Session Players

While Clemons was a featured player on *Greetings*, other performers on the record included Richard Davis, who would play double bass on "The Angel" and pianist Harold Wheeler, who can be heard on "Blinded by the Light."

Meanwhile, Steve Van Zandt came to visit the studio one weekend and punched a hole in the head of an amplifier. The feedback he generated during "Lost in the Flood," resulted in a sound effects credit on the track.

Max's Kansas City

In mid-August 1972, Springsteen played six dates at New York's revered club Max's Kansas City at the bottom of a bill that included Doris Abrahams and headliner Dave Van Ronk. These were his first official shows since signing to Columbia, and it is believed that John Hammond—a good friend of Van Ronk's—arranged to have Springsteen added to the bill for these gigs at the last minute to keep his artist active.

Two of these shows were videotaped for promotional use as evidenced by the use of snippets of Springsteen performing "Growin' Up" and the song "Henry Boy" in a 1990 documentary about John Hammond called *From Bessie Smith to Springsteen*. During these gigs, Springsteen mixed things up, playing other songs that were recorded at 914 Studios for album consideration, including "Arabian Nights," "Two Hearts in True Waltz Time," "Let the Words," "Balboa vs. the Earth Slayer," and "Calvin Jones and the Thirteenth Apostle."

Springsteen would return to the venue at the end of August, opening for American blues icon Odetta. He also played five early evening shows at the club in late August and early September on the same dates as a young David Johansen.

"I used to come down to Max's Kansas City and play by myself," Springsteen told *Musician* in November 1992. "And then late at night the New York Dolls would play at Max's—they'd play at 2 a.m."

Meeting Jackson Browne

Following one of Springsteen's early shows at Max's Kansas City, folk singer David Blue asked him to come along to his own gig at the Bitter End.

It was here that Blue introduced Springsteen to Jackson Browne—who had just had a surprise smash hit with "Doctor My Eyes" (U.S. #8, Spring 1972)—and both encouraged Springsteen to take the stage and open the show. It was the start of a forty-year friendship that may have reached its apex when Bruce inducted Browne into the Rock and Roll Hall of Fame in 2004.

The Return of Danny Federici

Danny Federici and Springsteen had parted company when Steel Mill splintered in 1971, with the Passaic-born, Flemington-based keyboardist left to fend for himself by taking money gigs. He was working with Billy Chinnock on Long Island when Springsteen managed to track him down in the late summer of '72.

He wanted Federici for his touring band. Although Federici had missed out on the sessions for *Greetings*, Springsteen wanted to make things right with him. "I went up to Bruce and said, 'Well, what's the story?'" Federici explained to Marsh in 1981's *Born to Run*. "He said, 'It's not an audition.' There was no audition; it was a rehearsal. And we went out on the road seven days after and we've been there ever since."

Full Band, Fall Tour

Bruce Springsteen's debut album was bumped from November to January to accommodate the additional work Clive Davis required for it to be released. This allowed Springsteen to consider how he wanted to present the album to audiences. With Federici back in the fold and Tallent and Lopez also on board, he also hired Clemons to play in his touring band.

Clemons gave his final performances with Norman Seldin's Joyful Noyze at the Club Plaza in Bayville on October 21. He joined Springsteen and the others when rehearsals started at the Beacon Manor Hotel two days later. Three lengthy practice sessions gave way to an unannounced, full-length gig for friends at the hotel's own Shipbottom Lounge on October 25.

Springsteen's new band made its official debut on October 28, playing a short six-song set at the West Chester University Field House opening for the a capella act the Persuasions and comedy headliners Cheech and Chong. The next night, the band was back on the Jersey Shore, playing a Halloween gig at the National Guard Armory in Long Branch that was promoted by Springsteen's former manager, Tinker West.

November '72 was highlighted by a York College of Pennsylvania gig opening for Crazy Horse and a show at Detroit's Cobo Exhibition Center. The latter, arranged by Mike Appel, was a free promotional appearance at the 1972 Detroit Auto Show.

Kenny's Castaways, Sing Sing, and Ohio

Between December 5th and 10th, Springsteen was booked into a six-night, twelve-show residency at the Greenwich Village venue Kenny's Castaways. Midway through the band's ninety-minute performance, which was comprised of songs from his forthcoming album, Springsteen played a solo mini-set of two or three newer numbers like "Bishop Dance," "Song of the Orphans," and "Circus Song."

Before his evening set at the club on December 12, Springsteen and the group traveled ninety minutes north to New York's West Chester County for a gig at Ossining Correctional Facility. Hoping to draw publicity for his client, Mike Appel successfully lured writers from *Crawdaddy* to report on the gig.

Held before inmates in the "Sing Sing" prison chapel, the two-hour show of cover songs was distinctive. According to sound manager Albee Tellone, Clemons offered a unique vocal take of Buddy Miles's "Them Changes." Elsewhere, an inmate joined in on saxophone during a blues tune, and the prisoners in attendance—who had just been treated to a double bill of Joan Baez and B. B. King two weeks earlier—were appreciative and respectful.

According to *Brucebase*, Springsteen spoke of the event in a press release following the show. "They're tough dudes," he said of the prison audience. "They got nobody to impress at all. It was good that they liked us."

Following the 1972 Christmas holiday, Springsteen, Federici, Tallent, Lopez, and Clemons closed out the year with a pair of Ohio gigs as the undercard to Brownsville Station and '50s nostalgic headliners Sha Na Na. The first gig was held at the Dayton Hara Arena on December 29, with a subsequent show the next night at the Ohio Theatre in Columbus.

Jersey Pride

As his debut album's cover would later assert, Bruce Springsteen wanted to be identified as a New Jersey artist. From the disc's title to its postcard-derived artwork, he made it known that his label might be based in New York, but he was a product of the Jersey Shore.

"[Columbia was] pushing for this big New York thing—this big town thing," Springsteen explained in his own defense to Marsh. "I said, 'Wait, you guys are nuts or something? I'm from Asbury Park, New Jersey. Can you dig it? New Jersey.'"

The Storyteller

In addition to their individual skills as musicians, Springsteen, Clemons, Federici, Lopez, and Tallent worked hard in advance of the release of *Greetings from Asbury Park, N. J.* to bolster their performances beyond the scope of a mere rock show. The band—especially Clemons and Federici—wore stage clothes and followed Springsteen's lead with aplomb.

Springsteen also began to tighten up his storytelling. According to future girlfriend Lynn Goldsmith, he would practice incessantly in front of the mirror. He also worked on his comic timing.

He'd later cite his Italian background—specifically his grandparents—for giving him the gift of gab. And as the years wore on, Springsteen's ability to deliver a tale became part of his fame.

At the dawn of 1973, Springsteen was well on his way to captivating his crowds not only with music, but with spectacle and story. He could elicit laughs from audiences and then play for them. He knew how to get a reaction.

Greetings Held Up by the Powers That Be

Although *Greetings from Asbury Park, N.J.* was finished by the second week of September 1972, it wasn't released until January 1973, because there was no real support for it from Columbia at the outset. The album's single, "Blinded by the Light," was delayed until February because no one at the label believed it had a shot at charting.

"They didn't think it would sell," an unnamed Columbia executive would tell Marc Eliot. The in-house joke at the label was that the album hadn't been released, it escaped!

Greetings from Asbury Park, N.J. Is Released

On January 5, 1973—after a decade spent mastering the electric guitar and playing in the bars and bandstands of New Jersey—Bruce Springsteen released his debut album to modest acclaim. As an unknown artist dropping his first batch of songs on the unsuspecting music world, rock fans in many cases first learned about him in the era's rock-'n'-roll periodicals.

One thriving publication, *Crawdaddy*, summed up *Greetings from Asbury Park, N.J.* with the kind of praise that couldn't help but send curiosity seekers into their nearest Record Town or Licorice Pizza. "Bruce Springsteen has been hiding in New Jersey writing these incredible songs," Peter Knobler wrote in his famous

The lyrics focus on their friendship as they hang out, drink wine, and, in the case of the narrator and Crazy Janey, fuck at a spot known as "Greasy Lake." That body of water still actually exists in Lakewood, New Jersey, although it is officially known as Lake Carasaljo and located "about a mile down on the dark side" of Route 88 (as Bruce describes it) and U.S. Route 9.

The song was Springsteen's second single. Although it bombed at the time of its release in 1973, Manfred Mann's Earth Band scored a Top 40 hit in the U.S. with a 1977 cover. It has been a career-long favorite of Springsteen's live show and another album rock classic.

"It's Hard to Be a Saint in the City"

Considered the song that started Springsteen's career, this was the tune that made Mike Appel believe he would be a star. It was also the first number he played for John Hammond during his Columbia audition.

Fast paced and long on bravado, it was understandable how the song jump-started Bruce's career. He exuded confidence as he sang, "I was the pimp's main prophet I kept everything cool/Just a backstreet gambler with the luck to lose."

"Saint in the City" remains one of the album's classic songs and a welcome part of the set when it popped up in Springsteen's shows during postmillennium tours.

Critical Reception

Crawdaddy was one of Springsteen's earliest supporters, pledging allegiance to Springsteen often throughout 1973. Elsewhere, accolades were mostly strong, with the music trade publication Cashbox getting behind the record and Stereo Review proclaiming it 1973's "Record of the Year."

Still, Dylan comparisons were plentiful, if not inevitable. In Rolling Stone, Ken Emerson said *Greetings from Asbury Park, N.J.* "was like "Subterranean Homesick Blues" played at 78 RPM" adding that "a typical five-minute track [was] busting with more words than this review."

SATURDAY RAMPAGE WEEKEND '72
Bruce Springsteen
The Persuasions
Cheech and Chong
October 28, 8 P.M.
Hollinger Fieldhouse
Sponsored by College Union Activities Board

Springsteen's performance at West Chester University on October 28, 1972, marked the public unveiling of his legendary backing band, which consisted of drummer Vini Lopez, keyboardist Danny Federici, bassist Gary Tallent, and saxophonist Clarence Clemons. This advertisement appeared in *The Quad*, the school's student-run newspaper. *Author's Collection*

7

The Aurora Is Risin' Behind Us

The Wild, the Innocent, and the E Street Shuffle

W ork on Bruce Springsteen's second album got underway in May 1973. After a week at 914 Studios, he returned to the road, while Appel took his client's new material to Columbia. And although Appel got the green light for the second album, the face of the company was changing fast.

Clive Davis Exits Columbia

Days later, label chief Clive Davis—one of Springsteen's few supporters at Columbia—was fired in a cloud of controversy over allegations of financial wrongdoing and drug abuse.

This didn't bode well for Springsteen, whose inferior album sales had hardly improved despite the release of a second single. That May, his classic 45 "Spirit in the Night," which was backed by the equally timeless "For You," was released to industry indifference.

Appel Does Radio Promo

If Springsteen's immediate future was safe for the moment at the label, Appel was nervous. Columbia wasn't putting any of its resources into promoting *Greetings* to radio.

Appel thought it still had some life in it. So he began working the phones himself, calling up program directors hoping to sway them.

When they were unresponsive, he'd send them a photo of Springsteen as a child sitting with Santa Claus coupled with a lump of coal. According to lore, Appel once sent ripped up ten-dollar bills to radio programmers who refused his calls.

Sancious Joins the Touring Band

On Memorial Day weekend 1973, Springsteen played a three-night stand at Washington's Childe Harold club. Many of his loyal fans from Richmond traveled to D.C. for these two-hour gigs, resulting in long lines for admission that caught the venue's owners completely off guard.

These shows were more significant because they marked the informal entrance of David Sancious, who would play with the band off and on over the next four weeks before formally joining on June 22.

Chicago

In an attempt to strengthen Springsteen's position, Appel arranged to have Springsteen signed to the concert booking department of the world-famous William Morris Agency, where they worked with Sam McKeith and his assistant, Barry Bell. One of the first outcomes of this alliance was a run of East Coast shows supporting the jazz-pop giants Chicago.

On paper it seemed like a good idea to pair Columbia's biggest-selling act with its latest discovery. It would also show that Springsteen was a team player. But in Springsteen's eyes, it all went horribly wrong.

He would describe the late May and early June shows to Marsh as "a soul destroying experience" as he played to disinterested fans waiting to hear "Beginnings," "Color My World," and "Saturday in the Park." Forty-minute arena gigs in Fayetteville, Hampton, Baltimore, New Haven, Philadelphia, Boston, Springfield, Binghamton, and New York City tested his resolve.

With the exception of Springfield—where ten thousand attendees erupted in support of him—Chicago's audiences were at best polite and at worst rude. Audiences threw rolls of toilet paper at him.

At the Spectrum in Philly, Springsteen was booed for the first and only time in his career. He responded defiantly, continuing to sing while giving the audience his middle finger.

By the time he'd rolled into Madison Square Garden, Springsteen had had enough of the support act bullshit. He ran offstage and unloaded on Appel. In tears, he threatened to quit, insisting he'd never play another arena and, according to Mike, "never as someone's butt-fuck." Columbia suits—even those who loved him—were visibly dismayed.

Appel conceded to book him into small clubs, theaters, and colleges. The college circuit wound up being where Springsteen would make his mark and his living during the next two years of his career.

Back to the Beach and Back to Blauvelt

Ahead of his formal 914 Studios sessions for the second album and after the pressure and frustration of his stint with Chicago, Springsteen gladly took a run of headlining club shows at Fat City in Seaside Heights. These gigs, on the weekend of June 22–24, also signified keyboardist David Sancious's placement in Springsteen's band.

Following these gigs, he and the band spent the next week and a half working through the songs he had earmarked for what would become *The Wild, the Innocent, and the E Street Shuffle*.

Nine more gigs over five nights were booked at the band's favorite new haunt, the Main Point, in Bryn Mawr, Pennsylvania near Villanova University. Following his final show there on July 9, the band traveled back up to Blauvelt, New York, to record the material that would comprise his sophomore album.

Orphaned by Columbia

Although Columbia Records had given Springsteen the option of making his second album, Mike Appel sensed that Charles Koppelman, an A&R representative who rose through the ranks under Davis, wasn't always Springsteen's corner.

Koppelman, who became more influential after his former boss's exit, focused most of his attention toward the career of singer/songwriter Billy Joel, who had a substantial hit with his 1973 album Piano Man. Meanwhile, Kip Cohen, who had assisted Hammond with A&R duties, had since exited to A&M, leaving the Springsteen camp short on allies during the making of *The Wild, the Innocent, and the E Street Shuffle*.

In an effort to maintain interest in Springsteen, Appel would take copies of positive reviews and regularly tape them to the office doors of CBS executives.

Working on the Cheap

On July 10th, Springsteen and the band started working at 914 Studios. In under two weeks, they tracked the nuts and bolts of the album.

They recorded during the graveyard shift, when studio time was less expensive. As musicians who were used to working into the night, the band was happy with the midnight to 8 a.m. recording schedule.

Springsteen continued to tweak the record, mixing and mastering it into September. The cost of recording the second album totaled $17,882.29 when all was said and done.

Bruce and Bob Marley

In an effort to keep the band afloat, Springsteen kept busy by playing an array of gigs in New York, which allowed him to retreat to 914 if necessary. Beginning on July 18th, he headlined twelve shows over six nights at Max's Kansas City.

These shows found Springsteen supported by future reggae legends the Wailers—which included Bob Marley and Peter Tosh—on their very first U.S.

motive for the tune, as he explained in Songs, was to "describe a neighborhood, a way of life, and I wanted to invent a dance with exact steps."

Hanging out at "Easy Joe's," the track's "teenage tramps in skintight pants" had scuffles with troopers, just as Springsteen and his bandmates once did. Unlike most dance songs, where novelty wins out, this upbeat and exhilarating album opener balanced captivating lyrics with an irresistible groove. Unfortunately, it wasn't the hit with fans Bruce had envisioned, and he altered it into a slow, soulful number before he completely abandoned it from his live set in late 1975.

"4th of July, Asbury Park (Sandy)"

Known to fans simply as "Sandy," this summertime ballad quickly became one of Springsteen's most loved early numbers. Conjuring up images of young lovers strolling arm in arm along the floundering boardwalk of Asbury, Springsteen calls out the greasers, "switchblade lovers," and "stoned-out faces" crashing on the beach and hanging around the arcades.

At the time he wrote the song, he'd been booted from his Asbury Park apartment and was shacking up with his then-girlfriend in a garage apartment in Bradley Beach, minutes from the shore town he was becoming synonymous with. Ironically, "4th of July, Asbury Park (Sandy)" signified the end of Springsteen's youthful days spent in the dilapidated shore town. As for the song's subject, "Sandy" was a composite of several girls he'd known during those years.

The tune grew out of earlier compositions like "Casper" and "Glory Road." Its depressing atmosphere—coupled with the male subject's tales of previous relationships where he's blown it—promised little hope for the couple. Although it was penned at a time when the Asbury boardwalk was crumbling around local fortune-teller Madame Marie, the shore culture would live on and thrive in Jersey locales like Seaside Heights, Wildwood, and Point Pleasant.

When Springsteen described the tune to an audience in March 1974, he said, "You travel

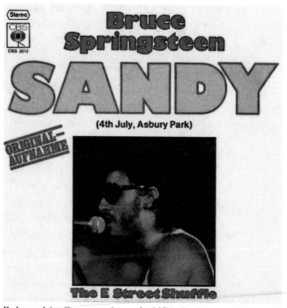

Released in Germany in early 1975, Springsteen's first 45 issued outside of the U.S. was incorrectly titled "Sandy (4th of July, Asbury Park)."   *Courtesy of Lost in the Flood*

around [to] Nashville, Atlanta, Tennessee and [people say] 'Hey! What's Asbury Park like?' and I play them this number. This is a song based in New Jersey or actually anywhere along the coast."

"Kitty's Back"

Focusing on a heartbroken character named "Catlong," "Kitty's Back" finds Springsteen telling the tale of an unlucky dude who has been abandoned by his lover for "some top cat." "Catlong" takes her back, but the fact that she's been with someone else causes him to ruminate over her infidelity. Still, he is unable to resist her charms.

In a live setting, the song's jazzy approach allowed for Springsteen and his band to get creative midway through the number, whether for jamming, story-telling, or both. A seventeen-minute take on the tune, featured on Springsteen's *Hammersmith Odeon London '75* live album, for example, was an opportunity for keyboardist David Sancious to display his chops.

Springsteen said he got the idea for the swing tune from the jazz/rock he had played in some of his earlier bands. The idea at the time was to have longer songs that could capture the attention of crowds that may not have been completely familiar with his work.

Inspired by the finales of soul revues he had witnessed, the tune—like his live staple "Thundercrack"—was crafted to leave the audience in suspense. Just as concertgoers thought the tune was about to end, he'd take the band in a different direction, bringing the music to a higher plane.

"Wild Billy's Circus Story"

Based on Springsteen's childhood memories of the Clyde Beatty/Cole Bros. Circus and traveling carnivals that would touch down across from the raceway in Freehold each summer, "Wild Billy's Circus Story" explores the life of carnies, living on the fringes of society. It was something Springsteen, at just twenty-four, found relatable to his own tours, as he crisscrossed the fruited plain, building up and taking down equipment from town to town.

He does an exceptional job observing and depicting the transient circus folks, from the freaks to the fire-eater and the fat woman. By the time Billy is introduced at the tail end of the tune, Springsteen—in the role of the ringmas-ter—seeks to lure him into the big-top life.

Describing the song during a show in March 1974, Springsteen said, "Around this time of night at the carnivals is when you start breaking it down to the real freaks. If you've ever been at one of those old circuses, between 12 and 1, just before they break down and move on—these are some of the people that are left."

That same month, he spoke about the tune to *Sounds*, saying, "To me a song is a vision, a flash, and what I see is characters and situations. I mean I've stood around carnivals at midnight when they're clearing up and I was scared, I met some dangerous people."

"Incident on 57th Street"

Despite his sharp threads, "Spanish Johnny" struggled to find love in "Incident on 57th Street," one of two Springsteen tributes to New York City on his sophomore waxing. Steering his beat-up Buick away from the pimps that have branded him a cheater, the song's central character takes up with "Puerto Rican Jane," and they make a new start in another part of the city.

But soon enough, Johnny is lured back into the "easy money" life by his thug friends. Based on a real person or people Springsteen once knew, the song's realistic and poignant lyrics are matched by Danny Federici's dazzling organ playing, Springsteen's distinct vocal, and a rare but welcome Garry Tallent bass solo.

"Rosalita (Come Out Tonight)"

Before it became an enduring rock song and one of the Rock and Roll Hall of Fame's "500 Songs That Shaped Rock and Roll," the seven-minute "Rosalita (Come Out Tonight)" was simply the strongest number on Bruce Springsteen's second album. In this semiautobiographical opus of love between Springsteen and the title subject, Rosie's parents disapproved his rock-'n'-roll lifestyle, but he urges her to stick with him anyway.

Written as a humorous kiss-off to all of the naysayers who underestimated him and put him down during his first two decades of life, the song's key line, "Someday we'll look back on this and it will all seem funny," suggested that Springsteen had an idea about the stardom that would follow with his next album. Although it was never actually released as a single—none of the tracks on his second album were given that distinction in the U.S.—"Rosalita" became the album's emphasis track. When "Born to Run" became a radio favorite a year and a half later, rock radio stations across the U.S. began to play the song continuously.

In his original *Rolling Stone* review of *The Wild, the Innocent, and the E Street Shuffle*, Ken Emerson called "Rosalita" a "raucous celebration of desire." The song was a fixture of Springsteen's live set from its introduction in 1973 up until late 1984, when he inexplicably dropped it after his Tacoma gig on October 19. It has since reappeared from time to time for special occasions such as the closing night of the Meadowlands run of gigs in 1999.

"New York City Serenade"

"New York City Serenade" stemmed from two earlier Springsteen tunes known as "Vibes Man" and "New York Song." A long and somewhat self-indulgent number, its lyrics were about two thieves named "Billy" and "Diamond Jackie,"

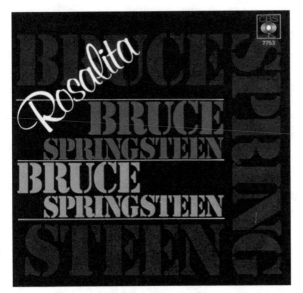

"Rosalita" wouldn't officially be released as an A-side single until 1979, when this pressing—backed with "Night"—was made available in Holland. A 12-inch single with a completely different picture sleeve was also released. Both "Rosie" singles are now highly sought after by Springsteen collectors.   *Courtesy of Lost in the Flood*

a money-hungry prostitute dubbed "fish lady" and the "jazz man"—who Springsteen advises to "save your notes/don't spend 'em on the blues boy."

The song was clearly a forum for the piano work of Sancious, and not long after his departure Springsteen abandoned the steady jazz-inflected number from his live set. The tune wasn't played live for twenty-four years after he dropped it on August 10, 1975. On August 11, 1999, he revisited it again with the band as part of his Reunion tour.

Ron Oberman

Although Springsteen lost a huge ally when Clive Davis exited CBS, he still had the enthusiasm of the company's publicity director, Ron Oberman. If the promotional budget for the second record was minimal because its predecessor was initially deemed unsuccessful, Oberman still kept his staff motivated, making the record a top priority at a time when the radio promotion department had moved on to push albums by Boz Scaggs and Billy Joel.

Oberman's loyalty stemmed from the fact that he had seen what Springsteen was capable of during his own headlining shows, and he knew that the "New Dylan" hype of his first record was inaccurate. So while others at the company couldn't get the failing image of him opening for Chicago at Madison Square Garden earlier in the year out of their minds, Oberman was sure that critics would see what he saw. He was right.

Saved by Critical Acclaim

The Wild, the Innocent, and the E Street Shuffle received lofty praise, which helped sustain momentum at the label and the Springsteen camp, even when record sales were modest. Instead of pointing to sales charts, his booking agent Barry Bell used the weighty acclaim to lure promoters to hire him.

"Great" was how Creem's Ed Ward described the new record, writing that he was "mystified and entertained" in a way that he hadn't been since Van

Morrison's 1968 landmark Astral Weeks. In his aforementioned *Rolling Stone* review, Ken Emerson called the album "one of the year's best."

Elsewhere, the *New York Times*' Bruce Pollock gave Springsteen additional love, calling the album, "a stone, howling, joyous monster of a record," and naming him "a word virtuoso." For Pollock, *The E Street Shuffle* was "a precise and exuberant picture of teenage romance in the '70s."

On the strength of the two albums that comprised his entire 1973 output, Cashbox named Springsteen—along with Elliott Murphy and Larry Norman—its Best New Male Artist of the year in its January 6, 1974, issue.

Slow Start at Radio

The E Street Shuffle got a slow start at rock radio, but disc jockeys on some of North America's more open minded, free-form FM stations took notice. Ed Sciaky from Philadelphia's WMMR was one who continued to gravitate toward Springsteen's music and became one of Bruce's most ardent and vocal advocates.

Elsewhere, radio stations like WHFS in Washington D.C., WBCN in Boston, KILT in Houston, and WMMS in Cleveland, all cities where Bruce had a strong following, were equally supportive of his second album. Oddly, Springsteen's local station, New York's WNEW-FM, was slow to the party, even though tunes like "Incident on 57th Street" and "Rosalita" seemed ripe for its listeners in the city, on Long Island, and over the Jersey state line.

Commercial Response

Sales of the second album achieved 175,000 copies during its first eighteen months of release. And when all was said and done, Springsteen had a record he could forever be proud of, even if it didn't equate commercially with the critical praise it received.

With its emergence, the Dylan and Van Morrison comparisons of its predecessor were pretty much gone. Springsteen hadn't only established his own identity—he proved he was a vibrant and powerful force in rock 'n' roll.

"The new album was a little more what I wanted to do," he told Jerry Gilbert humbly in 1974. "There was more of the band in there and the songs were written more in the way I wanted to write."

Money Worries

Although *The Wild, the Innocent, and the E Street Shuffle* had made its mark on the music world, Springsteen was still uneasy about where he was financially. He was hoping his best-known fan David Bowie might release a version of one of his songs, as was suggested. Meanwhile, he was banking on an influx of money from Columbia.

For all of his, and his band's, hard work, he had no security to show for it, yet. His only real comfort was that nearly every fan who bought his album became a convert—with many of those same record buyers coming to see him repeatedly as he built himself into a cult artist. But if being notorious for having one of the best live acts of the day was important to him, it was still a struggle to pay the bills. There were some fringe benefits yet little glamour. He was still living a modest life, and money—or lack of it—was always on his mind by 1974.

The Wild, the Innocent, and the Outtakes

Although Springsteen's second album had just seven songs, he walked into 914 Studios with an abundance of contenders for *The Wild, the Innocent, and the E Street Shuffle*. Songs left off the album included live favorites from the era like "The Fever" (which Springsteen demoed as part of his publishing deal and eventually offered to Southside Johnny and the Asbury Jukes), plus "Thundercrack," "Zero and Blind Terry," and "Bishop Dance."

Additional songs from this time such as "Santa Ana"—a mid-tempo love song also known as "Contessa" that included lyrics that eventually helped shape 1975's "She's the One"—and "Seaside Bar Song" were planned for the album, but were supposedly vetoed by Columbia. Recordings of each of these songs wound up being pressed as an acetate for Springsteen's U.K. song publisher, Intersong, with the hopes that other artists might record his tunes.

According to the 1989 book *Backstreets*, other unreleased Springsteen songs from the 1972–1973 time frame were plentiful and included titles like "Angel's Blues," "Architect Angel," "Balboa vs. the Earthslayer," "Ballad of the Self Loading Pistol," "Calvin Jones and the Thirteenth Apostle," "Casper" (which evolved into "Sandy"), "Cherokee Queen," "Full of Love" (which was a precursor to the 1984 B-side "Pink Cadillac"), "Funky Broadway," "How the West Was Won," "Lonesome Train," "Texas," "Secret to the Blues," and "Over the Hills of St. Croix."

Northeast Gigs Close Out '73

Following the release of *The Wild, the Innocent, and the E Street Shuffle*, Springsteen kept close to home for much of November, playing well-attended shows at Trenton State College in Ewing, New Jersey, a three-night run at My Father's Place on Long Island, and a pair of shows at the Roxy Theatre in the Manayunk section of Philadelphia.

A Thanksgiving week gig at the University of Massachusetts supporting British blues icon John Mayall rounded out the month. A week later, Springsteen and the band were again opening for Mayall, this time at Connecticut's Quinnipiac University. After a three-night stand at Washington's Childe Harold—part of which has long been in circulation with fans thanks to a live broadcast on Georgetown University's WGTB-FM—Springsteen was back in New England in mid-December for an underattended gig at Pinecrest Country Club in Shelton, Connecticut.

Appel the Antagonist

Despite the fact that *The Wild, the Innocent, and the E Street Shuffle* was a hit with critics, insufficient label support for radio promotion irked Mike Appel. Appel's determination to make his lone client a star reached abrasive levels in late 1973, when FM rock stations failed to pick up on the magic of "Sandy" and "Rosalita."

According to Dave Marsh, Appel sent a letter to unresponsive radio programmers in major U.S. markets, replete with torn up photocopies of $20 bills. In a couple of instances, he actually used real $10 bills to suggest that they were taking payola, a claim Appel later denied. In any case, he scolded many of them by telephone, suggesting that they were either deaf or had no taste.

If that didn't cause them to recoil, Appel put a nail in the album's coffin when he sent bags of coal to a few specific programmers that December. While he claimed it was a gag, it did severe damage with CBS executives, who needed allegiances at radio to promote releases by all of its artists, not just Springsteen. Efforts to push the album were over by early 1974 and because of Appel's actions, the powers that be at Columbia Records were secretly and seriously considering releasing Springsteen from his contract.

"Santa Claus" Beer Brawl

Back home, Springsteen and the boys returned for a three-night commitment at the Student Prince in Asbury Park between December 17 and 19. But unlike previous years, he did not visit his parents in San Mateo. Instead, he took on shows at the Bristol [Rhode Island] Motor Inn and Sandy's in the Boston suburb of Beverly, Massachusetts, on the 20th and 21st.

During these shows, and subsequent ones at Uncle Al's Erlton Theatre Lounge in Cherry Hill and the Rova Farms Function Center in Jackson on December 22 and 23, the band unveiled "Santa Claus Is Coming to Town." The latter gig, held at a local Russian Orthodox congregation center, also marked the reconnection of Springsteen and his Castiles' bandmate George Theiss, whose band, Doo Dah, was also on the bill.

According to *Brucebase*, the Rova Farms show had an open beer bar, which resulted in a rowdy audience turning violent. A brawl during "Santa Claus" caused the Jackson police to respond; however, the promoter managed to keep the show in progress.

Barry Rebo

Springsteen closed out an active 1973 with a four-night, eight-show post-Christmas run at the Main Point. While the band took New Year's Eve off, its first gigs of 1974 got underway with a three-night stand at Joe's Place in Cambridge, Massachusetts.

Some or all of these January 4–7 shows were filmed by Barry Rebo, who went on to film various Springsteen shows until 1976. Springsteen evidently owns all of the Rebo footage shot during this era.

Exuberance and Enormous Energy

Looking back on the era that spawned his first two records, Springsteen—with three decades of hindsight—still felt the discs held up well. In an interview with *Entertainment Weekly* in 2003, he acknowledged that those albums were "very freeing" because he had yet to establish a broad fan base.

Springsteen credited the purity of both *Greetings from Asbury Park, N.J.* and *The Wild, the Innocent, and the E Street Shuffle* largely to the fact that he had yet to react to his success. "I just had this explosion of youthful creativity and exuberance," he told the magazine.

"I had heroes I was emulating, but I also had my own little world that I was trying to give life to," he continued. "Those records always bring me back to the street life of my early 20s and the boardwalk."

8

I Wanna Be a Slave to the Beat

Artists Springsteen Opened For

A lthough Bruce Springsteen has been a headlining act for more than thirty-five years, in the days before he became an icon of rock 'n' roll, he shared the stage with a number of prominent musicians. Between 1969 and 1974—fronting Child, Steel Mill, the Bruce Springsteen Band, and finally, the E Street Band—he supported everyone from Black Sabbath to Bonnie Raitt.

It was tough going in the early days, as he acknowledged in 1981. "I've opened for Black Oak Arkansas, I've opened for Brownsville Station, and I've opened for Sha Na Na," he told *Creem*. "I'm 31—and I've been playing bars since I was 15. And I've faced a lot of audiences that don't give a shit that you're onstage."

Chicago Transit Authority

Billed as "Child—Steel Mill," Springsteen and his band—who were transitioning from one name to the next—were reportedly paid $650 to support Chicago Transit Authority at Randolph-Macon College in Ashland, Virginia, on November 21, 1969. CTA's eponymous 1969 debut was released on April 28 on Columbia Records and eventually produced the hits "Questions 67 and 68," "Does Anybody Really Know What Time It Is?," and "Beginnings" during the disc's two years in the charts.

Although Springsteen and his bandmates alternated two forty-five-minute sets with the headlining act, Chicago—as they would soon officially become—was supposedly paid $3,000. It wouldn't be Springsteen's last time supporting the hit-makers. As explored elsewhere, he went on to open for his future label mates during a disastrous run of arena gigs in 1973.

Iron Butterfly

The second of two support shows at Randolph-Macon's 3,500-seat Crenshaw Gymnasium, "Child—Steel Mill" opened for psychedelic hard rockers Iron

Butterfly in Ashland on November 22, 1969. Springsteen's group played an hour-long set before the San Diego-bred Butterfly took the stage to perform its epic 1968 anthem "In-A-Gadda-Da-Vida," which clocked in at seventeen minutes. The group apparently earned $7,500 for its headlining set—quite a staggering amount for a college gig in 1969—making Springsteen's $650 payday seem paltry by comparison.

The Elvin Bishop Group

According to Steel Mill's bassist, Vinnie Roslin, the group was paid a meager $5 to support the Elvin Bishop Band at the Matrix in San Francisco during Springsteen's first tour to California on January 22, 1970. Bishop, who had previously played with the Paul Butterfield Blues Band, went solo in 1968 and earned $90 for the headlining gig in support of his solo debut *The Elvin Bishop Band.*

In 1976, with the help of future Jefferson Starship vocalist Mickey Thomas, Bishop earned the distinction of one-hit wonder with the U.S. #3 song "Fooled Around and Fell In Love."

Boz Scaggs

Steel Mill performed three shows supporting Boz Scaggs at the Matrix in San Francisco on February 12–14, 1970. Scaggs—who was years away from hits like "Lido Shuffle" and "Lowdown" from his 1976 U.S. #2 album *Silk Degrees*—was supporting his 1969 self-titled Atlantic Records debut with these shows.

Grin

Fronted by future E Street Band guitarist Nils Lofgren, Grin's February 18, 1970, headlining gig at San Francisco's Fillmore West was supported by Steel Mill. Marking the first time the Maryland-based Lofgren and Springsteen would meet, the gig was the beginning of a friendship that would last forty-plus years.

Grand Funk Railroad

Supporting Flint, Michigan's favorite sons, Grand Funk Railroad—who had become one of the most successful bands in the U.S. by 1970 on the strength of the albums *On Time, Grand Funk,* and *Closer to Home*—in its own backyard was an opportunity Steel Mill couldn't pass up. Offered the slot at Bricktown, New Jersey's Ocean Ice Palace on June 13 after the last-minute cancellation by the MC5, Steel Mill acknowledged its local roots by closing its eight-song set with the Springsteen-penned "Garden State Parkway Blues."

The Ike and Tina Turner Revue

In the fall of 1970, Bruce got his first exposure to Ike and Tina Turner when Steel Mill supported the notorious and volatile soul performers at the Mosque in Richmond, Virginia, on October 11. A rare audio recording of part of the show in this 3,000-seat venue reveals a polite albeit somewhat disinterested crowd, but that doesn't stop the openers from serving up lengthy originals like "Sherlock Goes Holmes" and "I Can't Take It."

Black Sabbath

On the bottom of a three-act bill with Cactus and metal pioneers Black Sabbath—then fronted by Ozzy Osbourne, who allegedly received death threats before the gig—Steel Mill weren't exactly stoked about their undercard slot at Asbury Park's Sunshine In on November 27, 1970.

An existing audio recording chronicled a generator power failure at the eight-minute mark of a nearly fourteen-minute rendition of "Dancing in the Streets." Springsteen is upset enough to complain. According to, he balked, "We must be the Guinea Pigs here tonight."

Humble Pie

The Bruce Springsteen Band—consisting of Steven Van Zandt, Gary Tallent, Vini Lopez, and David Sancious—opened for the Peter Frampton–fronted Humble Pie at Sunshine In on July 11, 1971, in Asbury Park.

Oddly, Springsteen's then-manager and sometime conga player Tinker West inexplicably declined both of Frampton's potentially lucrative offers to take the band on the road as its North American opening act and arrange for an A&M Records audition. An explanation for Springsteen's refusals—guided by Tinker West—remain a mystery.

Crazy Horse

Twice in 1972, the Bruce Springsteen Band supported Neil Young's off and on backing band Crazy Horse. The first show took place on February 12 at the Sunshine In in Asbury Park. A second gig late in the year at York College in York, Pennsylvania, occurred on November 11 where the BSB delivered an eighty-minute opening performance.

Jackson Browne

On September 4, 1972, Bruce Springsteen performed an ad hoc guest set, opening for Jackson Browne at New York's Bitter End. At the suggestion of David

Blue, who was Browne's official support for the six-night, twelve-show run in Manhattan, Springsteen was given the impromptu slot.

"He went out there for about an hour and proceeded to do the greatest songs I'd ever heard, with just his guitar and [my] piano," Jackson said of Springsteen's performance in a 1979 radio interview. "When he got off stage I said 'Man, where the hell have you been hiding!'"

A year later, Springsteen and Browne would coheadline a concert at the Villanova University Field House on October 6, 1973. Springsteen—who was playing the final night of his *Greetings from Asbury Park* tour—performed first, serving up a ninety-minute set. Browne followed with a show that was equal in length. Tickets for this gig were a mere $4.

Cheech and Chong

Maybe it was the dope, but marijuana humorists Cheech and Chong didn't exactly take it kindly when Springsteen was added to a Pennsylvania concert bill at the last minute that also featured a capella group the Persuasions. According to lore, C and C's management objected to a third act on the bill at West Chester University on October 28, 1972, forcing Springsteen and his band to cut their set to just six songs.

But that's not what made this gig historic. It was the public debut of what would eventually become known as Bruce Springsteen and the E Street Band, with a lineup that included Clarence Clemons, Danny Federici, Vini Lopez, and Gary Tallent.

Sha Na Na

In December 1972, Springsteen—just days away from the January 5 release of his debut album *Greetings from Asbury Park, N.J.*—opened a pair of Ohio shows for 1950s nostalgia act Sha Na Na. Also on the bill ahead of him was Michigan's then-up-and-comers Brownsville Station, who would be known for their 1973 U.S. #3 "Smokin' in the Boys Room." These shows took place at the Dayton Hara Arena and the Ohio Theatre in Columbus during Christmas week.

At the Dayton gig, which was billed as "a holiday rock festival," Springsteen was incorrectly billed as "Rick Springsteen." The promoter presumably had him confused with Australian pop singer Rick Springfield, who had a U.S. #14 hit that year with "Speak to the Sky."

Nearly four months later, on March 18, 1973, Bruce again opened for Sha Na Na at the Keaney Gymnasium at the University of Rhode Island, performing future classics like "For You" and "Spirit in the Night." Springsteen and his band were delayed in starting the gig by an hour, having arrived late from an afternoon club gig at Oliver's in Boston.

Blood, Sweat, and Tears

On March 2 and 3, 1973, Springsteen opened a pair of California gigs for Blood, Sweat, and Tears at Berkeley's Community Theatre and the Santa Monica Civic Auditorium, respectively. The headliners—who had peaked three years earlier with hits like "You Made Me So Very Happy" (US #2, 1969) and "Spinning Wheel" (US #2, 1969)—may have been on the decline, but Springsteen was clearly on the rise.

As evidenced by a soundboard recording that has been in circulation among fans for some time, Springsteen was already peppering his live set with new material like "Circus Song" and "Thundercrack." The former would become known as "Wild Billy's Circus Story" when it was released six months later on his sophomore album, *The Wild, the Innocent, and the E Street Shuffle*. The latter was an outtake from the same era that eventually saw the light of day on the 1998 rarities box, *Tracks*.

Lou Reed

On March 23, 1973, Springsteen opened for one-time Velvet Underground frontman Lou Reed at the Palace Theatre in Providence, Rhode Island. Reed—backed by the Tots—was supporting his heralded sophomore solo album, *Transformer*, which was released the previous December. Produced by David Bowie and his guitarist Mick Ronson, Reed's album included such enduring classics as "Perfect Day," "Satellite of Love," and "Walk on the Wild Side."

Stevie Wonder

On March 29, 1973, Springsteen and the boys were tapped to open for soul giant Stevie Wonder at Kutztown University as part of the school's "Black Cultures Weekend." Springsteen's hour-long appearance gave way to Wonder's two-hour set, which saw him perform recent hits like 1971's "If You Really Love Me" (U.S. #8), 1972's "Superstition" (U.S. #1), and his then-current *Billboard* chart-topper "You Are the Sunshine of My Life."

The Beach Boys

Springsteen was offered a pair of gigs in April 1973 opening for the Beach Boys at the Scope Arena in Norfolk, Virginia, and the Omni Coliseum in Atlanta, Georgia, on the 7th and 11th respectively. Looking for opportunities to play in the Southeast, he took the gigs.

Sadly, the Beach Boys were still more than a year away from their 1970s resurgence, which came with the band's U.S. #1 1974 hits compilation *Endless Summer*. According to reports, less than 20 percent of the sixteen thousand potential tickets for the Atlanta gig were sold.

The Eagles, Blood, Sweat, and Tears, Joe Walsh, Billy Preston, and Others

On April 27, 1973, Springsteen played at the bottom of an all-star bill that included Billy Preston, former James Gang guitarist Joe Walsh, rising stars the Eagles, and, once again, Blood, Sweat, and Tears at the Ohio University Music Festival in Athens, Ohio.

Eagles drummer and singer Don Henley took a tip from his friend Jackson Browne, who raved about Springsteen, and made a point of checking out his performance. "I sort of wandered in alone and checked out his set. He was just a warm-up act at this show. After watching him I remember thinking to myself that this was a guy that wasn't gonna be warming up the crowd for us—or for anybody—for very long."

Chuck Berry and Jerry Lee Lewis

Not only did Bruce Springsteen open for iconic headliner Chuck Berry and the second-billed legend Jerry Lee Lewis at the University of Maryland on April 28, 1973, he and his band wound up backing the iconic Berry—who was back in favor after the success of his October 1972 U.S. #1 hit "My Ding-a-Ling."

Springsteen supposedly learned that the promoter was seeking a backing band for Berry a week ahead of the gig. He even offered to take the gig without an additional fee. Although Springsteen and his band—which included Southside Johnny for this legendary gig—never had time to rehearse with Berry, the show apparently went well. At the end of the gig, Berry praised Southside Johnny's harmonica efforts, telling the crowd, "That white boy can blow, can't he?"

In fact, demand for tickets in and around College Park was incredibly high for the sold-out 5,500-capacity Cole Field House performance. Twenty people were arrested, according to a report by the university's school newspaper at the time, for trying to crash the concert by entering through a ladies' room window left ajar. But not before a couple hundred people snuck their way into the show.

New Riders of the Purple Sage and Dr. Hook and the Medicine Show

Springsteen was the first performer on a triple bill held May 1, 1973, at L.A.'s Ahmanson Theatre. Part of a week of promotional shows arranged by Columbia Records to promote the many artists on its label, he and his group flew in from New Jersey. Film footage of this performance was shot and exhibited at the CBS Sales Convention, which was held in July 1973 to hype his second album. Audio of Springsteen performing "Circus Song" was also released on the label's promotional EP series *Playback* that same month.

John Mayall

Supporting *The Wild, the Innocent, and the E Street Shuffle*, Springsteen opened for British blues fixture John Mayall at the University of Massachusetts on November 25, 1973. Springsteen's seventy-minute set included "Walking the Dog," "Spirit in the Night," "New York City Serenade," "Does This Bus Stop at 82nd Street?," "Kitty's Back," "Thundercrack," and Wilson Pickett's "634-5789 (Soulsville, USA)."

Freddie King

If Springsteen's appearance at the 300-seat Muther's Music Emporium as the opening act for Texas bluesman Freddie King on January 29, 1974, seemed a little beneath him by this point in his career, manager Mike Appel had a method to his madness. Springsteen was booked as a special guest in the Nashville venue during a CBS sales and marketing convention with the hopes that the 200 company employees would turn out to see him and the band.

Appel's plan failed, despite the fact he had slipped handbills under the hotel room doors of all the CBS sales and marketing reps in Nashville that week. Based on the soundboard recording, only a few of the company men and women turned out to hear Springsteen perform powerful renditions of "Incident on 52nd Street" and "Rosalita."

Bonnie Raitt

On May 9, 1974, Springsteen performed two separate shows opening for Bonnie Raitt at the Harvard Square Theatre in Cambridge, Massachusetts. The E Street Band—as his group would be introduced as officially for the first time—rendered a rare take on the Patti Labelle and the Blue Belles blues classic "I Sold My Heart to the Junkman" in the first set. They closed the second set with a fiery rendition of "Twist and Shout."

This show would become infamous after music critic Jon Landau—who attended the second set—wrote in *Real Paper*, "I saw rock and roll's future and its name is Bruce Springsteen." During that show, Springsteen unveiled the song that would help define his career—"Born to Run."

Dr. John

On July 25, 1974, Springsteen and the E Street Band opened for New Orleans blues/pop/zydeco fusionist Dr. John—best known for the hit "Right Place, Wrong Time"—at the Santa Monica Civic Auditorium in California. Although the venue was only part full, *Phonograph Record* critic Michael Davis wrote "from the third song on each number was followed by a standing ovation." Perhaps much of the crowd was there to see Springsteen perform classics like "Spirit in the Night," the yet-to-be-recorded "Jungleland," and set-closer "Rosalita."

Anne Murray

In one of the more bizarre concert pairings of his career, Springsteen was billed as the support act for Canadian soft-rock singer Anne Murray at the Schaefer Beer Music Festival in New York's Central Park on August 3, 1974.

Held in the Wollman Ice Rink Outdoor Theatre, the show was initially slated to be headlined by Boz Scaggs with Murray as the undercard when it was first announced. When Scaggs withdrew his commitment, concert promoter Ron Delsener replaced him with Springsteen. But when Murray's managers complained that she was more deserving of the top slot, Delsener acquiesced with the permission of Springsteen's manager Mike Appel.

With four-fifths of the audience there for Springsteen, after the E Street Band's eighty-minute set, most of the fans left, leaving Murray to perform for about one thousand attendees, some of who were Bruce fans there to boo the Canuck.

John Sebastian

Although Sebastian was billed as the headliner, he caught wind of what happened in Central Park, and decided to let Bruce close this show at the Capitol Theatre in Passaic, New Jersey on October 18, 1974. This effectively ended Springsteen's run as an opening act for good.

Folk singer Dan Fogelberg opened the show before handing the reigns to John Sebastian—the former Lovin' Spoonful frontman promoting his album *Tarzana Kid*. From there, the E Street Band took the stage for a thirteen-song set that included future *Born to Run* tracks like "She's the One" and "Jungleland" plus fan favorites "Spirit in the Night" and "4th of July Asbury Park (Sandy)."

9

Out on a Midnight Run

After *The Wild, the Innocent, and the E Street Shuffle*

Cretecos Quits

After twenty months working with Springsteen, Appel's partner in Laurel Canyon stepped out of the picture. A lack of income since the pair had quit Pocket Full of Tunes to launch their own venture, coupled with pressure from his new wife to be closer to his Suffern, New York, home caused Jim Cretecos to step down.

Appel agreed to give his partner $1,500 for his half of their publishing, and Cretecos walked away from their organization in January 1974.

Firing Mad Dog

In February 1974, following a run of shows up and down the East Coast, Springsteen fired his longtime drummer, Vincent Lopez, after his temper got the best of him. Things first became heated between the kitman and Mike Appel when the latter failed to make Clarence Clemons's alimony payment.

This oversight on Appel's part led to Clemons being arrested before the group's January18 gig in Cleveland. Although Appel managed to have the money paid, the child support was taken from the salary of the others in the band. This didn't sit well with Vini, who let his frustrations be known.

Meanwhile, shows in Richmond, Norfolk, Nashville, Cleveland, Springfield, Massachusetts, and Atlanta were carried out, but before the group's gig in Lexington at the University of Kentucky, Lopez and Appel's brother, Steve—who was the band's road manager—got physical.

After the February 12 show, Springsteen spoke of the incident by phone with Mike Appel, and the two decided to ask "Mad Dog" to resign. In doing so, shows in Toledo, Columbus, and Cleveland were canceled as the band returned home to plot its next move.

"Sometimes I don't think I got treated really fairly in the whole deal, because I started the whole goddamn thing," Lopez told Marc Eliot. "I asked Bruce to join *my* band, I brought him to Tinker, and Tinker in turn found Mike Appel. And Tinker got his finder's fee and all that. I got nothing. No royalties, no credit for anything."

The drummer's discharge weighed heavy on Springsteen's mind. When asked about by *Sounds* that March about firing Vini, Springsteen spoke to Jerry Gilbert. "He'd been with me four years," he explained. "There were various pressures—it was a difficult decision to make."

Boom Carter Joins

Ernest "Boom" Carter joined Springsteen's band on extremely short notice after the discharge of Vini Lopez on February 12. Carter—who was an Asbury Park native—and Sancious became friends after playing together as session musicians in a Richmond recording studio a year and a half earlier.

Bassist Garry Tallent—who played on some sessions at the same facility with Carter in 1972—was also friendly with him. In fact, Carter's audition took place at Tallent's parents' house. He was recruited in time to play with Springsteen at a gig booked at the Satellite Lounge in Cookstown, New Jersey, on the 23rd.

Carlo Rossi, Gangster Promoter

Carter auditioned days later, and Springsteen liked what he heard, but trying to pull off a gig with a guy who had less than a week to learn his band's repertoire was a challenge. Springsteen initially tried to have Appel pull out of the gig, but the club's owner, Carlo Rossi, was something of a gangster.

When Appel called Rossi to cancel the show, as he explained to Eliot, he was told, "If you don't play the fucking date, I'm going to come up there and fuck you up! And fuck [Bruce] up!"

Appel tried to explain that Springsteen wanted to play the show near Fort Dix, but he didn't want to disappoint his fans because he was still working the drummer in. But Rossi didn't care and in a subsequent phone call went so far as to threaten to kill Appel and Springsteen if the show didn't go on.

Appel knew the guy meant business. A few weeks earlier at a Foghat show in his club, Rossi emptied his revolver into the band's amps while they were onstage in front of three thousand people because they refused to turn down the volume. A month earlier, when the James Gang played at the Satellite Lounge, he slit the tires in the band's equipment truck and dumped it in a South Jersey swamp.

Fearing for their lives, they played the show. According to Appel, the gig was fantastic, and no one in the audience could tell that Carter was a new drummer. After the show—which got underway after midnight and incorporated two seventy-five-minute sets that went well past 3 a.m.—Rossi circulated backstage congratulating the Springsteen camp for a job well done.

Rockin' with the Flu

The next two nights were spent at The Main Point in Bryn Mawr, one of Springsteen's most loyal venues. And while the two gigs on the 24th were without incident, the next night was a struggle for Bruce, because he was playing with a case of influenza.

The show on February 25 was almost canceled, but in keeping with Springsteen's work ethic, he carried on, even if it meant playing songs like "Rosalita" and "Wild Billy's Circus Story" from a chair, because he was too weak to stand.

Upon his return home, he spent the next week in bed, seeking the care of a doctor after coughing up blood. This caused the cancellation of his March 1 show opening for Richie Havens at the State Theater in New Brunswick. A gig at the Joint in the Woods in Parsippany the next night also had to be scratched.

As sick as he was, Springsteen loathed canceling these shows. They were in his own backyard where his fan base was strongest.

Drug Free

Save for sucking down a couple of beers under the Asbury Park boardwalk with Clemons, Springsteen remained drug free during his 1974–75 ascent, not to mention his entire career. When offered a hit on a joint or a bump of cocaine, which was common at the time, he always respectfully declined.

Like all rockers, he got high on the music. But unlike so many of his peers in the 1970s, that was all he needed. As with powders and weed, Springsteen never touched pills—aside from the occasional aspirin or vitamin.

Holiday Inns

After years sleeping on floors and crashing in equipment trucks, Springsteen was enjoying the small luxuries that came with being a touring band on the rise. Motel rooms with clean sheets and hot showers were something he was starting to appreciate.

"When our band goes into a Holiday Inn, I step up in the world," he told *Rolling Stone* in early 1974. "The beds are nice. They got color TV. I love them places."

Big in Houston

Following a pair of post-influenza shows at Georgetown University on March 3, the second of which was broadcast on the Washington D.C. school's own WGTB-FM, Springsteen and his band departed by train for the lengthy trip to Houston by way of New Orleans.

His representatives at William Morris had booked a four-day, seven-show residency at Liberty Hall. This commitment allowed Springsteen and his group the opportunity to play for more than two thousand fans while gaining some strong radio exposure in the largest city in Texas and building on an already strong regional following.

On March 7, he and the E Street Band's first Texas gig was broadcast via rock station KPFT-FM. The next afternoon, he was interviewed on competing KLOL-FM by host Ed Beauchamp.

The following day, Springsteen was invited back with the entire E Street Band for a lengthy afternoon radio performance that included highlights from both his albums, plus a rendition of "The Fever." The latter had become a favorite on KLOL after Appel had serviced the demo of the song to the station without the authority of CBS.

Austin's Armadillo

Springsteen did equally well in Austin, headlining the 1,500-capacity Armadillo World Headquarters in mid-March. For these gigs, he and the E Street Band were supported by a western swing band called Alvin Crow and the Pleasant Valley Boys.

When asked about the March 15 and 16 shows in 1980, he revealed to *Performance* that he and Mike Appel were both a little concerned about the unique billing, but the merger of rock and country was triumphant.

"It worried me a little bit," Springsteen remembered. "I knew for sure we weren't cowboys and I didn't know how they [the crowd] would act. But, you know, they were up and dancing by the second song . . . I didn't think there were people like that, able to shift from one extreme to another so quickly."

Dire in Dallas

Because of the success of Bruce's shows in Houston and Austin, the band was booked into a four-night, eight-show run at the Dallas nightclub Gertie's. However, with just fifty to one hundred people at each gig, the March 18–21 engagement wound up being quite a disappointment.

Springsteen had yet to become a national act. Strong pockets of fans in certain regions like Philadelphia, Boston, and Houston couldn't prevent him from an underwhelming response in a city like Dallas.

Scraping By

Despite his increasing notoriety, Springsteen was still only getting by. The money that he made after expenses was still funneled back into Laurel Canyon.

It didn't help that Appel would book shows based on agreements scrawled on napkins. When all was said and done, the Texas trip was good for exposure

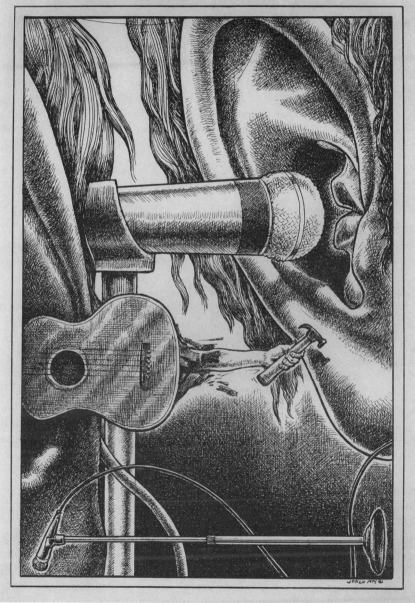

This unique poster advertised Springsteen's March 1974 gigs at Armadillo World Headquarters in Austin, Texas. It was rendered by Jim Franklin, who was the Armadillo's primary poster artist at the time.   *Courtesy of Robert Rodriguez*

and little else. After Appel and the band took their cut from the shows, all Springsteen had to show for it was a few nights of rest in modest motels and four twenty-dollar bills.

The Guest DJ

To promote his March 24 concert at the Celebrity Theatre in Phoenix, Springsteen took to the KDKB airwaves for a brief interview a day earlier. When the DJ asked him to spin some records, he happily obliged, taking over the station for an hour to play some of his favorites and provide anecdotes.

His charm carried over to the gig, which marked his first time playing on a revolving stage. After the show, he was interviewed by reporters from the Phoenix *New Times* and the Arizona State University newspaper in tandem, which has since been released as a bootleg called *The Inner View.*

Changing Hats

Back on the East Coast, Springsteen booked a weekend of shows close to home, including performances at Widener College in Chester, Pennsylvania;, Burlington County College in Pemberton, New Jersey; and Seton Hall University in South Orange.

Beginning with the Widener show, Springsteen began to sport what he referred to as a "gangster hat" instead of the beret he had become known for. He had acquired this 1920s-era hat during his Texas excursion.

Meeting Mighty Max

On April 7, 1974, future E Street drummer Max Weinberg introduced himself to Springsteen during his gig at the Bishop Dougherty Student Center at Seton Hall University. Weinberg, who was a student at the private South Orange-based Roman Catholic university, played in the show's opening act, the Jim Marino Band.

Weinberg briefly introduced himself and expressed his appreciation for Springsteen's live show. Neither of them knew at the time that in just five short months, Max would be a member of the E Street Band.

Spontaneous Combustion

Part of what made Springsteen shows circa spring '74 so popular among fans in the know was his unpredictability. Set changes were constant. Old material would be reworked, and new songs would evolve in front of audiences.

But more than that, the concerts were brimming with confidence and passion. Every night he put himself on the line, pouring all of his strength into his live act.

After ten years in bands, Springsteen had experience on his side. He didn't need to rely on routines. Every night was a revelation, replete with new songs, new covers, or new antics. It kept his increasingly loyal group of followers coming back to his shows again and again. His William Morris booking agent Barry Bell would succinctly explain his own fascination with Springsteen's gigs in *Born to Run*. "I wanted to be there the next night, to see what the new surprise was gonna be."

Giving Up Half

Sometime in 1974, Springsteen had approached Mike Appel about giving the band half of his income. As his manager, Appel tried to talk him out of it.

Springsteen was the star, Appel argued. Ultimately, Appel convinced him it was a bad idea. The only problem was that Springsteen had already shared his intentions with the band. Telling them that they would remain on salary would be unpleasant but necessary.

Marathon Live Shows

Springsteen believed in giving his fans their money's worth. A decade earlier, when the Beatles toured the United States for the first time, their live sets were around a half an hour. At this point in Springsteen's career, his shows were typically two hours.

His band shared the same commitment at lengthy sound checks, where they would uncover new places to go with the music. During the shows, his energy was unmatchable as he would conquer the stage and leave audiences astounded, exhilarated, and clamoring for more.

The only blowback came from promoters, who weren't used to bands playing for so long. Concerts in excess of an hour were still somewhat rare in 1974. But Springsteen had a self-administered obligation to his fans. Whenever he left the stage thinking that maybe he could have given the crowd a little more, he would toss and turn that night, unable to sleep.

At the time, cynics assumed that he must be hopped up on something to deliver such a high-energy gig. But the truth was quite different. If Springsteen seemed scrawny, even fragile, the truth was he was amazingly agile—an athlete going strong onstage for hours each night. As his stamina and his songbook built up over the next decade, the shows would top out at an inconceivable three and a half hours.

The Storyteller

While other rock groups churned out their hits onstage in 1974, Bruce Springsteen and his backing band broke the mold in terms of what a concert experience could be. He shared memorable reflections from his life with his fans. His stories were relatable, dramatic, and, many times, downright funny.

Tales of life as an outsider battling naysayers at school, accounts of struggles at home with a challenging father, and embellished stories of how he befriended Clarence "The Big Man" Clemons one dark, scary night were augmented by the band's sonic inflections as interludes or segues.

As he delivered these anecdotes and others, all eyes were fixed on him.

Springsteen's stories, like the rock 'n' roll that would bookend them, would almost always get a great audience reaction. He thrived on the crowd's response and the joy he and his band shared with his devoted fans. For Springsteen, the key was to never forget about that kid in you.

10

Will You Walk with Me out on the Wire?

Landau Discovers Bruce

One day in the summer of 1973, while tooling around Boston in his car listening to WBCN, the city's leading rock station, Jon Landau first *heard* Bruce Springsteen. The song playing out of his speakers reminded him a little of the Band, Robbie Robertson's group.

When the DJ announced the song as "Blinded by the Light," Landau committed it to memory and decided he would investigate *Greetings from Asbury Park, N.J.* Although he hadn't actually heard Springsteen's debut, he was familiar with its existence.

As *Rolling Stone*'s record editor he had assigned it to eccentric critic Lester Bangs earlier in the year. Bangs proceeded to give it a good mauling.

When *The Wild, the Innocent, and the E Street Shuffle* was released, he took a more diplomatic approach. An eager writer named Ken Emerson pitched a review of the album, which he ran. He also gave the album his own write-up.

The Real Paper

Just days before Bruce Springsteen's run of April 1974 appearances at Charlie's Place in Cambridge, Massachusetts, Landau reviewed *The Wild, the Innocent, and the E Street Shuffle* in the Boston-area arts weekly, the *Real Paper*, in anticipation of the New Jersey rocker's Boston-area arrival.

In the article, Landau dubbed Springsteen's sophomore effort, "the most under-rated album so far this year" calling it "an impassioned and inspired street fantasy that's as much fun as it is deep."

His words—which were timed to help the musician draw new fans—carried a lot of weight. And for all the acclaim, Landau—who was also an experienced record producer—used the piece to tactfully name the disc's two major flaws.

In a nutshell, Landau felt the album could stand some production tweaks. He also called out Springsteen's recently dismissed drummer Vini Lopez as "the album's consistent weak spot."

Hitting It Off

The second night of his Cambridge engagement, Springsteen—who had just given an acoustic radio appearance of favorites like "Growin' Up," "Sandy," and "Rosalita" on Boston's renowned rock station WBCN a day earlier—walked outside ahead of one of that night's late performances to get some air. Landau had never met Springsteen but the bartender pointed him out.

Landau spotted him as he was eyeballing his review of . . . the E Street Shuffle in the club's window. He approached him to see what he thought of it. Springsteen, who was standing outside in just a T-shirt despite the fact it was a cold night, told him that he liked the write-up.

Calling it one of the best he'd ever seen, Springsteen told the inquisitive fan that this Landau guy had his "shit together." With perfect timing, Landau then told the twenty-four-year-old rocker that it was he who had written the piece.

They exchanged a chuckle. And talked some more, hitting it off instantly. As they walked back into Charlie's together, talking, Springsteen introduced Landau to Mike Appel. Landau, in turn, introduced his friend and fellow music scribe Dave Marsh.

As the four took a table, Appel wanted to know what was wrong with the production on Wild. Landau told him that the low end and the top end of the record were unclear—that there was too much midrange. He also said that the instruments sounded too separate. Appel was kind of offended, but Springsteen was mostly attentive. He soaked up every word Landau said.

Jon Who?

While attending Brandeis University in Waltham, Massachusetts, in 1966, Jon Landau worked at a Harvard Square record store. It was here in Cambridge that he was first introduced to Paul Williams, the man behind Crawdaddy magazine.

Landau's assessment of the first few issues of Williams's magazine—which were sold in the store—wasn't favorable. When he relayed his opinion to the Crawdaddy chief, he also volunteered his services. Before long, he was shaping the vibe of the publication.

Rock magazines were few and far between at the time, which helped him earn the attention of Jann Wenner. Wenner was getting his own magazine, Rolling Stone, off the ground in San Francisco and recruited Landau to contribute in time for the first issue.

Landau went on salary at Rolling Stone as a critic and columnist, earning $70 a month until he stopped in 1969. He had been hired by the MC5—a notorious but commercially unsuccessful Detroit band—to produce their second album,

A collectible concert poster that announced Springsteen's November 1974 gigs at Armadillo World Headquarters in Austin, Texas—this art was the work of Michael Priest.

Courtesy of Robert Rodriguez

Back in the USA. He earned 3 percent of the retail price of the record, which sold roughly seventy thousand copies and netted him around $6,000.

Like Springsteen, music was in Landau's blood at an early age. He studied the guitar for eight years, played in rock bands in high school and college, and even landed a demo deal of his own with Columbia Records that resulted in a contract offer for his group, Jelly Roll. When he realized he might have to sacrifice his educational pursuits, he declined the offer and continued his studies.

Following his efforts with the MC5, Landau took on production roles with Livingston Taylor and the J. Geils Band that were ill fated. He returned to music journalism in 1971, when he was hired for $10,000 per year as a music writer and editor for the *Boston Phoenix*, which became the *Real Paper* in 1973.

Part of this decision was due to the fact that Landau—who contracted Crohn's disease in 1967—had seen an increase in symptoms related to the emotional and physical strain of production work. By 1972, he was also hired as the record editor at *Rolling Stone*, a post he held until June 1975.

Along the way, Landau left Boston for New York and became separated from his wife, future *New York Times* movie critic Janet Maslin. He also underwent surgery in the summer of 1974, which ultimately cured him of Crohn's disease.

He also seriously considered record company A&R work and hoped to talent scout. He took interviews with Ron Oberman at Columbia and Clive Davis at Arista. And then, of course, he met Springsteen.

Charlie's

The shows at Charlie's that resulted in Springsteen meeting his future manager Jon Landau were the result of a fire at another area venue, Joe's Place. Springsteen had to postpone his Boston gigs, which were scheduled for the weekend of April 2-4, by a week. Because the altered venue was smaller, Appel arranged for eight shows over four nights beginning April 9 instead of the originally proposed three-show, three-night run.

On the final night of the April 9–12 engagement, Springsteen and his opening act, blues singer Mighty Joe Young, each donated their performance fees to the Joe's Place Disaster Fund. The owners of Charlie's also donated their proceeds from the same night to the cause.

Harvard Square Theatre

Springsteen returned to Cambridge in May, following a productive run of shows close to home at Monmouth College in Long Branch, the State Theatre in New Brunswick, plus Pennsylvania shows at Ursinus, Swarthmore, and Bucks County Colleges. He and his band also played Southern New England gigs at Brown University, University of Connecticut, and the University of Hartford, leading up to their historic concerts at Harvard Square Theatre.

For the pair of gigs, he opened for headliner Bonnie Raitt. Yet the blues woman was generous enough to let Springsteen play his usual two-hour performance—twice!

Aside from being notable for his renditions of the Blue Belles' 1961 single "I Sold My Heart to the Junkman" and Fats Domino's "Let the Four Winds Blow," these concerts again found critic and new friend Jon Landau present and accounted for along with Maslin and *Rolling Stone* writer Emerson.

In his subsequent review of the gig in the *Real Paper*, the nationally known scribe would render what would become career-making praise of Springsteen and his band.

"I Saw Rock and Roll's Future"

Landau didn't make it to the Harvard Square Theatre until the late show, which marked the performance of two new songs, "She's the One" and "Born to Run." He referred to the latter in his *Real Paper* review as the song with the "Telstar" guitar opening.

After catching the show, Landau—who was about to turn twenty-seven—retreated home to his apartment to write his "Loose Ends" column. A few days later, he wrote, "Last Thursday at Harvard Square Theatre, I saw my rock and roll past flash before my eyes. And I saw something else: I saw rock and roll's future and its name is Bruce Springsteen."

Landau went on to write, "he made me feel like I was hearing music for the first time." Within a few weeks, Columbia and Mike Appel would use Landau's opinions of Springsteen to help make him a rock star.

Bruce Calls Jon

According to Landau, Springsteen called him soon after his Harvard Square gig, and they talked for several hours. It was the beginning of an allegiance that continues to this day.

Springsteen was initially struck by their conversation outside of Charlie's a month earlier and Landau's critical discussion with Appel about the production on his last record. But most importantly, they shared a love of music.

For Springsteen, Landau was an interesting guy. A proven producer and critic with the kind of insights he had never been exposed to before. Springsteen—who was still going through a tough time with Columbia—was dying to pick the brain of an industry vet like Landau. His phone call caught Landau a little off guard—he had never given Springsteen his number. Springsteen had to hunt it down.

Ironically, he had no idea about the article Landau had already penned about the Cambridge gig. He telephoned Landau after the scribe had written his article, but before it ran.

Reaffirmed

Springsteen was floored when he read what Landau had written about him. Landau's article left him feeling elated and vindicated.

At the time, he and the band were making just $50 a week. "It helped me go on," Springsteen told *Newsweek* the following year. "I realized I was getting through to somebody."

Hyping Landau's Quote

Columbia Records took Landau's line, "I saw rock and roll's future and its name is Bruce Springsteen," and used it to plug Springsteen's back catalog in national and regional ads. It was a quick change of heart from the label that had all but quit on his sophomore disc two months earlier.

The attention, coupled with his continued touring efforts throughout 1974 and the help of airplay in key radio markets like Cleveland, Austin, and Phoenix, helped Springsteen's *The Wild, the Innocent, and the E Street Shuffle* rack up sales of one hundred thousand copies. In the Philadelphia area—thanks to the dedication of WMMR's Ed Sciaky and David Dye—Springsteen sold more than half of those preliminary numbers.

Nashville?

Before Landau helped the powers that be at Columbia to change their tune about Springsteen, label executive Charles Koppelman was looking to send him to Nashville to record his next album. Because of his lack of commercial success, Koppelman wanted Springsteen to work without the E Street Band with an array of producers and studio players.

In one of his earliest confidential discussions with Landau, Springsteen conveyed his frustrations over the idea. Koppelman and his staff at CBS were clearly out of touch to even suggest implementing such a thing. Of course, Springsteen and Appel had no intentions of ever going through with the idea.

Springsteen Bonds with Landau

As 1974 elapsed into 1975, Springsteen—much to Mike Appel's chagrin—would continue to trust and rely on Landau, bringing him in to help produce what would become his breakthrough third album.

Landau had definite ideas about how songs should be arranged and how drums and guitars should sound. At first he served as a friend and a consultant, but ultimately as a producer. Landau offered a security and level of trust that just wasn't there with Appel.

Landau offered a fresh perspective and unique suggestions at a time when Springsteen needed them. Early sessions at 914 Studios were problematic, but Landau's inventiveness would be an important force in the realization of *Born to Run*.

In Landau's opinion, the commercial struggles of Springsteen's first two records were a good thing. Springsteen was allowed to evolve and study many of rock's existing varieties. His depth came from his Jersey Shore roots at a time when Asbury Park was still untainted by record company A&R men.

"He had the humility to make it look effortless," Landau told *AARP the Magazine* in September 2009. For Landau, it was as much about Springsteen's distinctive, extraordinarily truthful and genuine voice as it was his undeniably instinctive approach to rock-'n-'roll music.

Monday When the Foreman Calls Time

The Boss

Springsteen's nickname first emerged in the early 1970s, when—as the leader of bands like Steel Mill, Dr. Zoom and the Sonic Boom, and the Bruce Springsteen Band—he took responsibility for making sure his players got paid at the end of the week. Eventually, the chore of doling out the money went to somebody else, but his alias, "the Boss," stuck and has stayed with him for more than four decades.

In addition to being the money man, Springsteen's early leadership qualities and deep dedication to his craft supported the branding. He would crank out five or more songs a week and bring them to his musicians, who were in awe.

For several years, "the Boss" was a handle that was only used among Springsteen's band and handlers, at first behind his back. But around 1975, some radio deejays and reporters—including Jay Cocks from *Time*—helped make the nickname widely known.

Through the years, Springsteen has had mixed feelings about being called "the Boss." "It was never meant for public dissemination," he told *Mojo* in 1999. "I personally would have preferred that it had remained private." He also relayed to *Creem* in 1981 that he hated bosses and hated being called 'Boss'.

However, Springsteen seemed cool with it around the time word began to spread about the moniker. When concert promoter John Scher first asked him if it bothered him, he said no.

Scher told *Backstreets* that Springsteen once told him, "'When I was growing up, somebody else always was the boss. The boss had control of people's lives.' Then he gave me a big smile and said, 'Now I'm The Boss.'"

12

And the Band Played

The E Street Band

The Incredible Jersey Jukers

Although the members of the E Street Band first came together in 1972, the group did not assume its proper handle until mid-1974. In letters sent to Student Directors at East Coast Colleges earlier that year by Mike Appel soliciting gigs, Springsteen's band was referred to as "Bruce Springsteen and His Incredible Jersey Jukers." It was a name that his good friends Steve Van Zandt and John Lyon would appropriate somewhat for their own as Southside Johnny and the Asbury Jukes.

The "E Street" reference was bandied about in the spring of 1974, and it stemmed from a handful of practices that Springsteen and the boys held at the Belmar home of David Sancious. Although Sancious and drummer Boom Carter announced plans to exit the group that August to form a jazz outfit they'd call Tone, Springsteen and the others decided to hold onto the moniker anyway. It had a nice ring to it.

While debate exists as to when they actually became known as Bruce Springsteen and the E Street Band, the group was first professionally billed as such in posters advertising their August 14, 1974, gig at the Monmouth Arts Center in Red Bank, New Jersey. As early as Springsteen's Harvard Square Theatre show in May, however, the group was apparently being introduced to audiences by emcees as the E Street Band.

Bad Credit Okay

In the first stage of their career with Springsteen (1972–1988), the E Street Band helped shape a series of landmark studio albums, beginning with 1975's *Born to Run* and running up to 1984's *Born in the U.S.A.* Although their contributions were weighty on these discs—plus 1978's *Darkness on the Edge of Town* and 1980's *The River*—Springsteen took full credit on the respective album sleeves. His band's members were given individual credits by track.

By *The River*, the E Street Band graduated to liner note mentions. Its members were also depicted in memorable inner sleeve photographs. But it wasn't until the 1986 concert box set, *Live/1975–85,* that the group received part of an album credit. Bruce Springsteen and the E Street Band was spelled out in block letters. Since then, all subsequent concert releases involving the group have been fully credited as such.

Perhaps this speaks to the band's live impact. Performances were nearly always a spectacle since the dawn of the band. In addition to the great music, a highlight of any Springsteen show would be when the Boss took the time to spotlight each key player, including longtime members "Phantom" Dan Federici, Garry "W." Tallent, "Miami" Steve Van Zandt, "Mighty" Max Weinberg, "Professor" Roy Bittan, and, of course, the "Big Man," Clarence Clemons. Upon their joining the band in 1984, Nils Lofgren and Patti Scialfa both earned similar acknowledgments nightly.

Studio Hands

In addition to their work with the Boss, the past and current members of the E Street Band have recorded individually and collectively with a who's-who of rock legends, including Bob Dylan, David Bowie, Peter Gabriel, Sting, Stevie Nicks, Dire Straits, the Grateful Dead, Santana, Meat Loaf, Ian Hunter, Ringo Starr, Ronnie Spector, Darlene Love, Southside Johnny, Lucinda Williams, Steve Earle, Emmylou Harris, Aretha Franklin, and others.

Decade-Long Hiatus

In 1989, after the E Street Band's participation in the *Human Rights Now!* tour a year prior, Springsteen notified his group that he was putting them on hiatus. For his 1993 albums *Human Touch* and *Lucky Town*, he assembled all-new session players for recording and touring purposes. E Street members Bittan and Patti Scialfa were the only exceptions.

On his next studio album, 1995's *The Ghost of Tom Joad*, Springsteen again used the services of Roy and Patti. He also tapped Danny Federici to contribute. That year also marked the brief regrouping of the E Street Band for the recording of four new songs that were appended to his *Greatest Hits* package.

Reunited and It Feels So Good

Four years later, following the late 1998 release of his rarities box set *Tracks*, Springsteen put the E Street Band back into service for a successful 1999 reunion tour. That regrouping brought joy not just to all of the band's members but to its millions of fans, who rallied behind Springsteen.

The positive reaction of Bruce's global audience spawned his collective's rebirth for recording and touring purposes over the next decade. Based on how the Boss joyously introduced his band onstage as recent as November 2009, calling them "the heart-stopping, pants-dropping, house-rocking, earth-shaking, booty-quaking, Viagra-taking, love-making, legendary E Street Band," relationships were still strong.

In 2010, Springsteen and the E Street Band came together to perform songs from his lost 1978 album, *The Promise*, in a live setting for a future DVD release. This left the door open for further potential activity.

Roll Call

Before they became members of the world's most famous backing group, the players in Springsteen's E Street Band forged their own unique individual paths. Hailing from the swamps of Jersey and beyond, Springsteen's cast of ragamuffin rockers created a distinctive, magical, and often unforgettable sound that has thrived and flourished for more than forty years.

Danny Federici

Like many children of the 1960s, Danny Federici—the E Street Band's late organist and accordionist—took inspiration from *The Ed Sullivan Show*. On October 18, 1964, Federici was mesmerized as he caught The Animals' U.S. television debut performance of "House of the Rising Sun."

The song's blues-rock fusion, augmented by keyboardist Alan Price, was right up the Flemington, New Jersey-bred performer's alley. At just fourteen, Daniel Paul Federici (who was born on January 23, 1950) had already joined his first rock band, the Legends, on accordion.

Federici first picked up accordion when he was seven years old, taking early cues from *The Lawrence Welk Show*. He went on to become proficient in polka and classical styles, and his mother found him paying gigs at parties and clubs. After studying classical accordion for several years, he switched over to organ, because the Cordovox was a better fit for the rock 'n' roll he played in the Legends, who his mother managed, and The Storytellers, which he joined in 1967.

Federici left Hunterdon Central High School before his senior year to play organ with the Storytellers, a band based in Millburn, New Jersey, that was steered by Bill Chinnock. The quintet managed to release a single, "Cry with Me/Little Boy Sad," on Tristereo Records, an imprint of Artie Ripp's Kama Sutra Records that was distributed by MGM.

The single was a regional success that led to gigs at the Jersey Shore's Hullabaloo teen clubs in Freehold, Middletown, and Asbury Park, but the Storytellers splintered by 1968. Chinnock and Federici launched a new group that also consisted of Shore-area drummer Vini Lopez and bassist Wendell John. Known as the Downtown Tangiers Band, the quartet recorded an album, but it was never released.

By 1969, John was out and a bassist named Garry Tallent had taken over. But that lineup didn't last. When Chinnock split for Maine, Federici and Lopez decided to continue their musical pursuits.

As chronicled elsewhere in this book, Federici and Lopez met Bruce Springsteen at the Upstage in Asbury Park and asked him to join their new band Child, which soon became Steel Mill. In homage to Chinnock, they covered a Tangiers holdover he penned called "Crown Liquor."

As much as he loved playing in Steel Mill, Federici at times loathed rehearsals because Springsteen was so prolific, things were constantly changing. Every day he'd have a new song. "Bruce is the kind of guy who just says, 'Oh—that was yesterday,' and throws it all away," Danny would tell Robert Hilburn in his 1985 *Springsteen.*

The Boss introduced him to crowds as "Phantom" Dan because of his ability to escape arrest following an infamous Steel Mill show at the Middletown Pool, where dozens of others were captured. Also nicknamed "The Blond Bombshell" because of his hair and appreciation of fine leather, Federici's talents would help define Springsteen's best records.

Whether it's the accordion solo on "4th of July, Asbury Park (Sandy)" or his organ fills on Springsteen's 1980 smash "Hungry Heart," Federici's musicianship in the E Street Band was undeniably great. His mastery of another unique instrument, the glockenspiel, helped shape "Thunder Road" and "Candy's Room," two of the E Street Band's finest numbers.

In a 1997 interview with *Backstreets*, Federici explained what makes the E Street Band so successful. "The key to [it] is looking at the big picture, not letting the little things get in the way. Little junk that doesn't amount to anything, that's not important. That's why I'm so into that band, because we know each other so well. We've been playing with Bruce for so long, he just has to say '1, 2 . . . ' and we know what song he's going to do just by the way he's counting off."

In his personal life, Federici and his first wife, Flo, had a son, Jason, in 1969, but they were both very young and divorced before long. In 1987, he married a flight attendant named Kathlynn Helmeid, whom he had met two years earlier, during the *Born in the U.S.A.* tour. Together they adopted two daughters, Madison and Harley, but they wound up separating in 2000 and divorcing in 2002. Helmeid, who suffered from Crohn's disease, died in 2007.

The same year, on November 21, Federici—who had been living in Upper Black Eddy, Pennsylvania—announced he would need to take a leave of absence from Springsteen's *Magic* tour to pursue treatment for melanoma, which he had already been living with for two years. In a statement, Springsteen said, "Danny is one of the pillars of our sound and has played beside me as a great friend for more than 40 years. We all eagerly await his healthy and speedy return."

Although Federici did return to join the E Street Band for one final performance in Indianapolis on March 20, 2008, that show would be his last. Sadly, he succumbed to melanoma within a month, passing on April 17, 2008, at the Memorial Sloan-Kettering Cancer Center in New York.

Soon after his death, the Danny Federici Melanoma Fund was launched to help with the research and development of treatments for melanoma through funding for clinical trials at Memorial Sloan-Kettering. The fund, which also aims to help raise awareness for the disease, received a nice boost thanks to Springsteen.

That July, he and the E Street Band released an EP of audio and video tracks to digital outlets like iTunes for download. Known as *Magic Tour Highlights*, and all proceeds went to the fund. Among the tracks included was the performance of "4th of July, Asbury Park (Sandy)" from Federici's final appearance with the band. Springsteen also dedicated his 2009 studio album, *Working on a Dream*, to Federici.

In his downtime from the E Street Band, during its period of inactivity, Federici kept busy recording solo material. In 1997, an album of jazz instrumentals known as *Flemington*, which included guest stints from Tallent and E Street guitarist Nils Lofgren, was released on the Masters Jazz label. A subsequent jazz record, *Sweet*, was released in 2004 and reissued as *Out of a Dream* the following year.

Vini "Mad Dog" Lopez

Although he never actually played under the banner of the E Street Band, original Bruce Springsteen drummer Vini Lopez—a product of the Shore area—was a formative member of the group before it had its official name. Raised in Neptune, he attended Neptune High with an Asbury Park musical icon, Southside Johnny Lyon, and his future bandmate Garry Tallent.

A self-taught drummer who got his musical start playing the soprano valve bugle in an area Drum and Bugle Corps, Lopez first played with an Asbury Park drummer and DJ named Buzzy Lubinsky. Lubinsky—whose dad owned Savoy Records in Newark—encouraged Vini to join a band to hone his craft.

Lopez was still in high school when he unsuccessfully auditioned for Bill Chinnock's band, the Storytellers. Soon enough, he managed to land behind the kit with Sonny Kenn's band the Blazers. He stayed with Kenn as that group morphed into Sonny and the Sounds and Sonny and the Starfires.

By 1968, Lopez—who graduated high school a year earlier—joined Chinnock and Danny Federici in the Downtown Tangiers Band. He also played with future E Street Band bassist Garry Tallent in Moment of Truth before he and Federici asked Springsteen to join forces with them as Child in February 1969.

Before the year was out, the quartet—which also included bassist Vinnie Roslin—was reborn as Steel Mill. Around this time, Lopez made ends meet by working a day job at Carver's Boatyard in nearby Point Pleasant.

When Springsteen pulled the plug on Steel Mill, Lopez continued to play for him in all of his short-lived Asbury Park-based early 1970s ensembles, including the Friendly Enemies, the Sundance Blues Band, Dr. Zoom and the Sonic Boom Band, and the Bruce Springsteen Band. These outfits—which were precursors to what would become the E Street Band—also included Federici, Tallent,

Southside Johnny, Roslin's Steel Mill replacement Steve Van Zandt, and pianist David Sancious.

When Springsteen signed to Columbia Records in 1972, Lopez remained in the fold, playing on his first two albums and touring with him. During the making of this album, Columbia Records head Clive Davis gave Lopez his fitting nickname "Mad Dog."

In addition to being a vibrant player, Lopez at times had a volatile personality, which made "Mad Dog" all the more fitting. His outspoken nature prompted his discharge from Springsteen's band in February 1974.

When asked for his version of events by *Backstreets* in September 1985, Lopez explained, "Mike Appel's brother and I had a few words. I pushed him and he went down. After that I was told to leave the band . . . I resented it, but there was nothing I could do except ask for a second chance. Which I did. But I didn't get it.

"Those were great days for me," he remembered. "I wish they never had to end. I guess I would do things differently. But what happened, happened."

Lopez may have been out of Springsteen's band, but he remained a fixture on the Jersey Shore throughout the 1970s, playing in local outfits like Cold Blast and Steel and Maddog and the Shakes.

In 1977, Lopez moved to Maine to play drums on Chinnock's album, which he titled and released as *Badlands* before learning that Springsteen had a song with the same title in the works. Chinnock, who had long been compared with Springsteen, couldn't help but feel cursed.

In the late 1970s, Lopez joined the Lord Gunner Group. Ironically, he replaced Boom Carter in this band. When Lopez departed, he was supplanted by future Bon Jovi kitman Tico Torres.

Lopez eventually teamed with Paul Whistler, formerly of the Blackberry Booze Band, and they played in acts like the Wheels and the Asbury All-Stars, which also included Patti Scialfa's brother Mike. In the mid-1980s, he played in groups like Opus I and the Acme Boogie Company.

By 1987, he was reunited with Vinnie Roslin in J. P. Gotrock, and in 1989 joined Live Bait, a band led by singer/songwriter Laura Crisci. It was during this time that Lopez began tackling old Springsteen rarities like Steel Mill's "Goin' Back to Georgia" and the BSB's "Cowboys of the Sea." In the 1990s, Lopez started his own bar band, Maddog and the Disco Rejects.

More recently, in 2004, "Mad Dog" launched Steel Mill Retro, a band that played material, most of which was penned by Bruce, from Steel Mill's heyday. In 2007, they released *The Dead Sea Chronicles*, an album comprised of Steel Mill–era songs.

Through the years, Lopez—who has worked as a golf caddy—has reteamed with Springsteen on several occasions. They first jammed together with the Blackberry Booze Band—which was the precursor at the Stone Pony—six months after their falling-out on September 8, 1974.

Then, on January 18, 1989, Springsteen brought Lopez and his former Castiles frontman George Theiss with him and Scialfa, to the 4th Annual Rock and Roll Hall of Fame Dinner at New York's Waldorf Astoria Hotel. Springsteen invited Vini to play with him during the jam session, where he backed the Boss during a performance of Roy Orbison's "Crying" and shared the stage with rock luminaries like Little Richard, Mick Jagger, Keith Richards and Stevie Wonder.

On July 21, 2003, at Giants Stadium, Lopez joined the E Street Band for a rendition of "Spirit in the Night." He did so again at the Wachovia Spectrum in Philadelphia on October 20, 2009.

Lopez and Springsteen also shared the stage at the Wonder Bar in Asbury Park on April 2nd, 2011. Along with Southside Johnny and other members of the city's original rock community, the two celebrated the musical history of the town they first made famous on 1973's *Greetings from Asbury Park, N.J.*

David Sancious

There's been some discrepancy over whether David Sancious ever actually performed in Springsteen's group under the moniker of the E Street Band. But as Springsteen's original pianist, he did indeed officially play with that name. It happened just once, at the group's August 14, 1974, show in Red Bank, New Jersey, although proof exists that Springsteen's band was introduced under that name by emcees in the months prior.

The first advertised gig as the E Street Band was also Sancious's last with Springsteen. After several years playing and recording with him, Sancious was anxious to start his own jazz fusion group. So in August 1974, he left with Springsteen's blessing and took his good friend and the group's drummer Ernest "Boom" Carter with him to form Tone.

Before his departure, the Belmar-raised Sancious was an essential part of the early Bruce Springsteen sound. Born in Asbury Park on November 30, 1953, Sancious came up in the same Jersey Shore music scene as his future colleagues, first encountering them at the Upstage on Cookman Avenue when he was barely sixteen.

In 1960, when he was merely seven years old, Sancious began to learn classical piano. By the time he was eleven, he was self-taught at the guitar.

A few years on from that, when he was still a sophomore in high school, the prodigious young musician found a place in the late 1960s Upstage scene. Sancious became a hot commodity in the area into the early '70s, making the rounds at the underage club and eventually playing in Glory Road, Dr. Zoom and the Sonic Boom, the Bruce Springsteen Band, and the Sundance Blues Band.

In early 1972, the eighteen-year-old multi-instrumentalist landed a job as a studio musician at Alpha Studios in Richmond, Virginia, playing on radio jingles and artist sessions. It was here that he befriended Carter, the studio's drummer. Surprisingly, Boom also hailed from Asbury Park.

When Sancious's old friend Springsteen landed his record deal with Columbia a few months later, he called Sancious and asked him to play on the sessions for his debut, *Greetings from Asbury Park, N.J.* that same summer. By July 1972, however, with that commitment honored, Sancious returned to his paying gig in Richmond until the following June, when he permanently joined Bruce's touring and recording band before the sessions for Springsteen's second album, *The Wild, the Innocent, and the E Street Shuffle.*

Sancious made a significant impact on this record. His ability to inflect classical and jazz into Springsteen's songs gave them a tinge of sophistication, as evidenced by his piano efforts on "New York City Serenade." He also arranged strings for that track, injected a memorable organ solo into "Kitty's Back," and lent his vast abilities to other numbers like "The E Street Shuffle," for which he played soprano saxophone.

Sancious's friendship with Carter paid off in February '74, when Vini Lopez was asked to resign. On his recommendation, Carter joined Springsteen's band. While Sancious and Carter helped craft the title cut to Springsteen's third album, *Born to Run,* at 914 Studios, they both stepped down to form Tone.

Ironically, at one time, Tone—which explored progressive rock and jazz fusion sounds—would feature Patti Scialfa, the woman who wound up joining the E Street Band and eventually married Springsteen. By 1978, after a series of well-received records, Sancious had left Tone behind for a full solo career, which he has augmented with high profile session and touring work, playing with artists like Sting and Peter Gabriel.

It was during the latter's tour as part of 1988's Amnesty International *Human Rights Now!* trek that Sancious briefly reunited with the E Street Band. On certain dates, Sancious sat in with his former bandmates, and a few years later, when Springsteen was recording the solo album *Human Touch,* he asked David to play on it.

In the years since, Sancious has performed with everyone from Seal to Bryan Ferry to Natalie Merchant and Eric Clapton. In 2005, he appeared in the Springsteen documentary *Wings for Wheels,* which chronicled the sessions for that notorious 1975 album.

Garry W. Tallent

Born Garry Wayne Tallent on October 27, 1949, the E Street Band's Detroit-bred, Jersey Shore–reared bassist officially teamed with Springsteen in 1971. But before that forty-plus year alignment, he was already a well-known bassist on the Jersey Shore.

Tallent was one of seven children who moved around the Southern United States often as a boy until his parents settled in Neptune, New Jersey, in 1964. By the time he decided on electric bass, Tallent—yes, that's his real last name—had tried flute, clarinet, violin, guitar, tuba, and upright bass.

Inspired by the likes of Motown session player James Jamerson, the Beatles' Paul McCartney, Chas Chandler of the Animals, Booker T. and the MGs Donald "Duck" Dunn, and the Band's Rick Danko, Tallent first attempted the instrument he became known for when he borrowed an electric bass from his musically inclined neighbor, "Southside" Johnny Lyon.

With that Hagstrom loaner, Tallent made friends with other musicians at Neptune High School. Before long, he shifted to his very own Framus Star bass and began to play in various outfits along the Jersey Shore. Devoted to his musical craft, he kept his bass by the family television set when he was seventeen so he could learn the bass solo to "Secret Agent Man," the theme to the 1960s television series *Secret Agent.*

In 1969, around the time he also played a short stint in the Downtown Tangiers Band with Federici and Lopez, he fell in with the Upstage crowd where he and local drummer Big Bad Bobby Williams became the club's house rhythm section. This assignment served as a great development opportunity for Tallent, who played a Danelectro bass he built for himself while working at the guitar manufacturer's factory in Neptune City. It was here that he befriended Springsteen and the future members of the E Street Band.

Upon teaming with Springsteen, Tallent adhered to the same approaches that served Rolling Stones bassist Bill Wyman. Content to keep a low profile, he let his music do the talking on early tracks like "Incident on 57th Street," the mid-70s Springsteen stage staple "Fire," and the 1980 hit "Hungry Heart." The bass line on the latter was originally hatched as a staccato tuba part.

As he said in Gary Graff's 2005 book *The Ties That Bind,* "nobody notices I'm there, until I'm not."

When pressed in an interview for *Bass Player* in May 2008 for his favorite Springsteen tracks, he cited "Point Blank" from *The River.* "The bass and Bruce's voice are the predominant elements of the track," he said, "and with a band as big as ours, I don't get to play that role often."

In the 1970s, Tallent took some of his royalties and bought a 1948 Rock-Ola jukebox. At the time of Springsteen's 1976 *Playboy* article, Tallent had amassed three thousand 45 singles.

In addition to his efforts performing on Springsteen tours and albums, Tallent has played on recordings by Little Steven and the Disciples of Soul, Southside Johnny, Ian Hunter, Gary U.S. Bonds, Emmylou Harris, and Steve Earle. In 1987, Tallent turned to production, overseeing Marshall Crenshaw's *La Bamba* soundtrack inclusion, "Crying, Waiting, Hoping." He went on to produce albums by Jim Lauderdale and Steve Forbert.

In 1989, Tallent moved to Nashville, drawn to the country music scene. He played on countless sessions before opening his own MoonDog recording studio during the E Street Band's 1989–1999 hiatus. He also launched the D'Ville Record Group label.

In 2006, after returning to the E Street Band in the summer of 1999 during its Reunion trek, Tallent moved to Whitefish, Montana. Outside of his work touring and recording with Springsteen and playing on sessions via the Internet, Tallent has been learning piano and studying musical theory.

Clarence Clemons

Clarence Clemons—"the Big Man" as he was known to fans—was born on January 11, 1942, in Norfolk, Virginia. The son of Clarence Sr., a fish market owner, and Thelma, a homemaker, Clarence was the oldest of three children.

Gospel music was a fixture of the childhood of this grandson of a Southern Baptist preacher. On his ninth Christmas, his father presented him with an alto saxophone and bought him a series of lessons. He flourished on the instrument and by the time he was in high school, Clemons had switched to baritone sax, which he played in a local jazz band.

His uncle bolstered his interest in pop music by giving Clarence records by King Curtis, who was known for his horn work with the Coasters. Curtis played tenor sax, which prompted Clemons to take on that variety of saxophone.

Aside from music, his size—he was six foot four—and athletic ability helped him thrive as a football player in high school. He wound up attending Maryland Eastern Shore University on a dual scholarship that acknowledged his skills as a sportsman and a musician.

As a lineman, Clemons played with future Pittsburgh Steelers Running Back Emerson Boozer in college. He also seemed destined for the National Football League, landing a tryout with the Cleveland Browns. En route to the team's camp, however, Clemons was involved in a car accident that put an end to his pro sports ambitions.

Clemons fell back on his music, which had already earned him some fame. In 1960, he entered the recording studio for the first time, playing sax on sessions with Tyrone Ashley's Funky Music Machine. The Plainfield, New Jersey–based band was also made up of future Parliament-Funkadelic members Ray Davis, Billy Bass Nelson, and Eddie Hazel.

The always-revered Clarence Clemons, replete with saxophone, on the cover of his 1983 debut album *Rescue*. Recorded with the Red Bank Rockers, the disc—which featured the vocals of J. T. Bowen—included a Springsteen original, "Savin' Up," complete with rhythm guitar by the Boss.   *Author's Collection*

In 1961, while still in college, Clemons played classic soul and R&B music with his first band, the Vibratones. "We were all music majors," he told *Mojo* in *May* 1998. We'd play for beer and hot dogs. James Brown covers." The band lasted until 1965, when they splintered and Clemons moved to Newark, New Jersey. He spent the second half of the 1960s working as a counselor with emotionally disturbed kids at the Jamesburg Reform School.

Working with troubled kids that society had given up on, Clemons "loved helping them," he confessed in his 2009 book *Big Man*. "Seeing even a little progress gave me joy. Most of the kids were mentally handicapped and never had a chance to begin with. Combine that with ignorance and poverty, and it spelled jail or death."

He also played semipro football in the late 1960s, until a 1968 crash, caused when the accelerator in his Buick Riviera jammed, nearly killed him. Paramedics thought he was gone after he collided with a tree. He remembers feeling no pain as he floated above his body. "I was there in this light," he'd say. "All I felt was euphoria. I felt like I should let go, but then I thought, 'I'm not finished. I've got to go back.' So I did." Surgeons had to reattach his ear.

Around this point, Clemons and his first wife had two sons, Clarence III and Charles. Although he had a family, he was anxious to play saxophone in bands and hopefully make a living at it, which caused domestic strife. Determined, he went to New Jersey's musical haven, Asbury Park, with his horn and joined forces with a country duo called the Bobs. By 1969, he was playing on the Jersey Shore in bands like Lord Sims and the Untouchables, Little Melvin and the Invaders, and the Entertainers. Soon after, he was asked to join the popular shore act Norman Seldin and the Joyful Noyze. The band played the Crossing Inn up in Princeton, the White Elephant and the Wonder Bar in Asbury, and various other clubs in Seaside Heights.

Karen Cassidy, the female vocalist in the Joyful Noyze, was responsible for encouraging Bruce Springsteen to check out Clemons's playing and vice versa. And in September 1971, Clemons did just that, walking across the street from the Wonder Bar to the Student Prince.

On a break between sets on a rainy, windy night, Clemons opened the door. "The whole thing flew off its hinges and blew away down the street," he explained to *Mojo* in the aforementioned article. "[Bruce and the band] were onstage, but staring at me framed in the doorway. And maybe that did make Bruce a little nervous because I just said, 'I want to play with your band,' and he said, 'Sure, you do anything you want.'"

Clemons remembered that the first song they played was an early take on "Spirit in the Night," and from there they knew they were, as he puts it, "the missing links in each other's lives."

For Springsteen, that first evening was epic. "The night I met Clarence, and he got on stage, a sound came out of his horn that—it seemed to rattle the glasses behind the bar and threaten to blow out the back wall," he told the *Star-Ledger* in July 1999.

Clemons would describe the Boss as equal parts "scrawny little kid" and "visionary." When Springsteen finally recruited the saxophonist for his band the following summer, after additional jams with Seldin's group, Clemons went to tell Seldin that he was quitting. After three years with the Joyful Noyze, it was a tough conversation. Seldin told "the Big Man" he was crazy and that Springsteen had no future.

Clemons knew otherwise. Driven by a mutual love of music, he quit his day job. Fifteen bucks a week just wasn't worth it. He also left his classical music–loving first wife. She hated that he was playing rock 'n' roll. Besides, the musical differences were at the surface of a much deeper rift.

After playing on "Blinded by the Light" and "Spirit in the Night," the two tracks that finalized *Greetings from Asbury Park, N.J.,* Clemons played his final shows with Seldin at the Club Plaza in Bayville, New Jersey, on October 21, 1972. Four days later, he officially appeared with Springsteen, marking the start of a forty-year alliance.

Clemons's saxophone efforts have gone on to highlighted many of Springsteen's most memorable numbers, including "Rosalita," "Born to Run," "Thunder Road," "Jungleland," "Badlands," "The Ties That Bind," "Sherry Darling," "I'm Goin' Down," and "Bobby Jean." Always a significant presence in E Street Band shows, Clemons has been referred to on stage by Springsteen as "the Big Kahuna" and "the Biggest Man You've Ever Seen."

Arguably the most identifiable member of the E Street Band, Clemons kept active outside the band. In 1983, he released his first solo album, *Rescue,* as part of Clarence Clemons and the Red Bank Rockers. A year earlier, he launched his own nightclub, Big Man's West, in Red Bank, New Jersey.

In 1985, he had a hit duet with Jackson Browne, "You're a Friend of Mine." The same year, his sax performance helped define Aretha Franklin's "Freeway of Love."

In addition to his other solo records—*Hero* (1985), *A Night with Mr. C* (1989), and *Peacemaker* (1995)—the Big Man released three studio albums with his band Clarence Clemons and Temple of Soul—*Live in Asbury Park* (2002), *Live in Asbury Park, Vol. II* (2004), and *Brothers in Arms* (2008). Clemons also collaborated on records by an array of well-known artists, including Gary U.S. Bonds, Ringo Starr, Southside Johnny and the Asbury Jukes, Pezband, Ronnie Spector, Little Steven and the Disciples of Soul, Ian Hunter, Michael Stanley, Joan Armatrading, Twisted Sister, the Four Tops, Todd Rundgren, Lisa Stansfield, Joe Cocker, Nils Lofgren, and Roy Orbison. In 2011, Clemons was back on the pop charts, providing a saxophone solo on Lady Gaga's smash "Hair."

Clemons was also the first member of the E Street Band to get bit by the acting bug, appearing in various movies and television series beginning with 1977's *New York, New York.* For that Martin Scorsese musical, he played a trumpet player. After a guest role on *Diff'rent Strokes* in 1985 to promote his aforementioned album, *Hero,* he was cast as one of the Three Most Important People in the World for 1989's hit movie *Bill and Ted's Excellent Adventure.* Television roles on *Jake and the Fatman* and *Nash Bridges* followed into the 1990s. He also had a well-received role on *The Simpsons* in 1999 as a narrator in the episode "Grift of the Magi." Fittingly, Clemons starred on two episodes of HBO's *The Wire* in 2004 as the head of a Baltimore youth program.

Clemons also become a philanthropist, helping to raise money to put musical instruments and programs into underfunded U.S. public schools as part of "Little Kids Rock." That nonprofit organization presented him with the inaugural "Big Man of the Year Award" at the "Right to Rock" charity gala.

Sadly, Clemons—who was married five times and had two other sons named Christopher and Jarod—died on June 18, 2011, of complications he suffered from an unexpected stroke a week earlier. His passing rocked the music community, but it was the Boss who spoke with the most clarity of his lifelong friend.

"Clarence was big, and he made me feel, and think, and love, and dream big," Springsteen wrote on his website, adding "Clarence doesn't leave the E Street Band when he dies. He leaves when we die."

Roy Bittan

After answering Bruce Springsteen's ad in the *Village Voice* for a keyboardist who could play "classical to Jerry Lee Lewis" in August 1974, Queens, New York native Roy Bittan auditioned for the E Street Band. He was asked to join days later.

Bittan was a product of Rockaway Beach, where he was born on July 2, 1949. His piano and keyboard work quickly found his way into the heart of Springsteen's sound, as evidenced by his contributions to 1975's epic *Born to Run,* which also included his backing vocals on many of the songs.

Bittan studied accordion and piano as a child. As a young adult, he took premed classes at Brooklyn College and played in bands for extra cash. Soon enough, he switched majors to music education before quitting school.

With the E Street Band, Bittan quickly earned the nickname "the Professor" as something of a tribute to his hero, one-time Fats Domino pianist Professor Longhair. Roy would go on to play piano, organ, accordion, and synthesizers for Springsteen, who he first met during his April 1974 shows at Charlie's. According to one account, Bittan actually asked to sit in on piano, and Springsteen obliged.

"When I joined the band, Bruce's material brought something out in me," Bittan said in the 1993 book *Local Hero: Bruce, In the Words of His Band.* "I felt very strongly about what he was writing. He was writing about themes that touched me deeply."

Although Bittan's vocal contributions waned after *The River,* Springsteen continued to utilize the Professor for recordings and tours, even after the E Street Band went on hiatus in 1989. Since the E Street Band's Reunion tour in 1999, Bittan's Yamaha grand piano has been a focal point of Springsteen's stage.

His first studio work outside of Springsteen was significant. David Bowie asked him to play on his 1976 album *Station to Station* and used him again for 1980's *Scary Monsters (and Super Creeps).*

Meat Loaf producer Jim Steinman was such a fan of Bittan's playing on *Born to Run* that he tapped him to play on the former's enormously successful 1977 debut *Bat out of Hell.* Bittan was also recruited in 1978 for Peter Gabriel's second solo album. He can be heard on fan favorites like "On the Air" and "D.I.Y."

After his piano work on Patti Smith's '78 hit, "Because the Night"—which Springsteen cowrote with her—Roy was asked by Dire Straits' Mark Knopfler to play on that band's 1979 album *Making Movies.* When Fleetwood Mac singer Stevie Nicks recorded her solo album *Bella Donna* in 1981, Bittan was asked to help. He also toured with her in support of that multiplatinum record.

Max Weinberg

E Street Band drummer "Mighty" Max Weinberg joined forces with Bruce Springsteen after he responded to the Boss's *Village Voice* ad for a drummer in August 1974. "No Jr. Ginger Bakers, please" read the classified placement that resulted in Weinberg's successful audition at SIR studios in Manhattan late that month.

At the time, Weinberg was working in the pit band for *Godspell* on Broadway. He showed up with a basic drum kit and played "Sandy"—a song he had played during his time in the Jim Marino Band. In late August, Max accepted the job, which initially paid $450 a month. He made his public debut with Springsteen at the Main Point in Bryn Mawr, Pennsylvania, on September 19.

Weinberg was born in Newark, New Jersey, on April 13, 1951 and took to the drums at a young age. The son of an attorney named Bertram and a teacher named Ruth, Max grew up in the South Orange-Maplewood Schools, where he—like his sisters Nancy and Abby—attended Columbia High School.

Weinberg first dreamt of being a rock drummer after he saw Elvis Presley's kitman D.J. Fontana play on the *The Milton Berle Show* around the time of his fifth birthday and picked up the sticks when he was six. The Jewish-reared musician planned to become an attorney, but after studying Dixieland Jazz, polkas, cha-chas, and British Invasion rock, he wound up playing with Springsteen instead.

Inspired by Buddy Rich, he also admired Ed Shaughnessy—who was the drummer in Johnny Carson's *Tonight Show* band. To Weinberg, the idea of a steady television gig seemed like a dream job. As a student of Ringo Starr, he played in the Epsilons, a New Jersey–based outfit that rocked the 1964 New York World's Fair.

Around this time, Weinberg's father suffered financial devastation when the two Pocono Mountain summer camps he owned went under. This taught the thirteen-year-old the importance of hard work and keeping his options open as his family sought comfort in its congregation at Temple Sharey Tefilo-Israel in South Orange. Here he embraced the concept of Seder. It was this appreciation of order that helped Weinberg to serve the frontmen in his respective bands.

A year after his graduation in 1969, he landed a record deal with Epic as part of Blackstone, but that band's eponymous LP lacked staying power. Weinberg studied at Adelphi University in Long Island before moving home to attend Seton Hall University in South Orange.

He was just two classes short of his degree when he quit college for life in the E Street Band. Although he knew how to play "Sandy" pretty well, Weinberg later admitted that it was his drumming on the Fats Domino song "Let the Four Winds Blow"—a Springsteen live staple—that earned him the gig.

Like Bittan, Weinberg's contributions on *Born to Run* were significant. Although he didn't play on the landmark title track, his presence on the album's other classic rock staples, "Thunder Road" and "Jungleland," help to define them. During the 1977 and '78 sessions for Springsteen's much labored-over *Darkness on the Edge of Town,* Weinberg turned out essential performances on "Badlands," "Candy's Room," and "Prove It All Night."

Although he later suggested his drumming on 1980's *The River* felt inferior to him, fans of "Cadillac Ranch" and "Out in the Street" didn't notice. Meanwhile Weinberg's playing on the title cut to '84's classic *Born in the U.S.A.* and winners like "No Surrender" and "I'm Goin' Down" was top-notch.

The album—which was Springsteen's commercial triumph—was Weinberg's artistic height. "Max was the best thing on the record," Springsteen would say in Marsh's 1987 book *Glory Days: Bruce Springsteen in the 1980s.* As for the title track, the Boss would add, "to me, he was right up there with the best of them on that song."

Explaining Weinberg's ability to thrive under Springsteen's direction, guitarist Steve Van Zandt said, "What nobody understands is that not only is Max a great drummer, Max reads Bruce's mind. You can't learn that." He was also a true professional, whose modus operandi was, "Show up, do a good job, and give them more than their money's worth," as he explained to the *New York Times* in January 2001.

Even when he was suffering from tendinitis and repetitive stress injuries to his hands and wrists, as he was in the early 1980s, Weinberg learned how to deal with the pain, thanks to the help of revered jazz drummer Joe Morello and seven surgeries.

Weinberg was named Best Drummer in the 1986 *Rolling Stone* critic's poll. But his approach has always been simple, even as he shifted brands from Ludwig to Pearl to DW drums over the years. "I've got four drums. Anything more is redundant," he said to *Musician* in February 1981.

That same year, he married a Tinton Falls, New Jersey–reared high school teacher named Rebecca Schick. After the E Street Band played at their wedding, the couple settled on a Monmouth County farm. In between commitments, Weinberg wrote a book, *The Big Beat: Conversations with Rock's Greatest Drummers,* which was released in 1984. In 1987, he became a father to Ali, and in 1990, his son Jay was born.

Although Weinberg played on Springsteen's *Tunnel of Love* album and its supporting tour, when Springsteen put the band on indefinite hiatus in 1989, Weinberg found himself with a lot of time on his hands. He returned to Seton

Hall and finished his bachelor's degree in 1989. He also enrolled in Yeshiva University's Cardozo School of Law but withdrew after just six weeks.

After several years of anonymity, Weinberg went back to performing, even playing bar mitzvahs. He sat in with 10,000 Maniacs during its 1992 tour after that band's drummer got hurt, and joined them at the January 1993 inauguration of President Bill Clinton. That fall, after a chance meeting with budding talk show host Conan O'Brien, he was hired to oversee the jazz- and blues-influenced Max Weinberg 7 for NBC's *Late Night.*

When Springsteen reunited the E Street Band for live work in 1999, O'Brien allowed Weinberg to balance both gigs, juggling sessions and tours with television for the next ten years. In 2009, Weinberg relocated to Los Angeles when O'Brien briefly assumed *The Tonight Show.* But when O'Brien was unfairly ousted from his spot at NBC later that year, he abandoned Max Weinberg and the Tonight Show Band and television altogether.

Aside from his work with Springsteen, Weinberg can be heard on Meat Loaf's classic 1977 *Bat out of Hell* album and has recorded hits with Bonnie Tyler, Air Supply, Carole King, Southside Johnny and the Asbury Jukes, Gary U.S. Bonds, and bluesman Johnnie Johnson, among others. In 2000, he released a self-titled album with the Max Weinberg 7.

Suki Lahav

Violinist Suki Lahav was a short-term member of the E Street Band who played with the group from September 1974 until March 1975. Lahav first appeared with Springsteen for shows in New York's Lincoln Center, where the audience response was substantial.

"We carried on with it," Lahav told *Backstreets* in December 1985. "Bruce used the violin only for the romantic side of him. I played only on the slow songs."

Born Tzruya Lahav in Kibbutz Ayelet HaShahar in the Upper Galilee in Israel in 1951, she initially played kibbutz harvest music and classical. Completing her service in the Israeli military, she settled in the United States with her husband, recording engineer Louis Lahav.

After befriending Springsteen during sessions for his first album, Lahav wound up singing backing vocals on his second, *The Wild, the Innocent, and the E Street Shuffle,* on the track "4th of July, Asbury Park (Sandy)." She also played on the third album, lending her violin to the nine-minute and thirty-three-second album closer, "Jungleland."

Despite speculation that Lahav and Springsteen were romantically involved, neither party has ever confirmed this. The Lahavs had a daughter, Tal, during their time in the United States, who was killed in a road accident when she was just three years old.

In the spring of 1975, the couple moved to Israel and eventually divorced in 1977. Suki Lahav remarried and had two children with her second husband,

Moshe Albalek. In the 1980s, she returned to a career in music, playing violin and viola with the Israeli Kibbutz Orchestra.

In the 1990s, she rose to prominence in her homeland as a lyricist. Her songs were performed by Israeli artists like Rita, Yehudit Ravitz, Meir Banai, Yehuda Poliker, Gidi Gov, Rami Kleinstein, and Ricky Gal.

Lahav has also authored acclaimed screenplays, including the 1996 Israeli crime movie *Kesher Dam,* and two novels: *Andre's Wooden Clogs*—which is based on *The Swamp Queen Does the Tango,* a true-life story of a boy's survival of the Holocaust in Holland—and an adult fairy tale. She lives in Jerusalem.

Steve Van Zandt

Although Steve Van Zandt didn't officially join the E Street Band until July 1975, his friendship with Bruce Springsteen had already dated back a decade at the time he was invited into the fold. Van Zandt was, of course, a product of the same Jersey Shore scene as Springsteen. Together, they jammed into the night at the Upstage in Asbury Park in the late 1960s and early 1970s, and Van Zandt played in the final incarnation of Springsteen's early band, Steel Mill.

Springsteen's guitarist was born Steven Lento on November 22, 1950, in Winthrop, Massachusetts, where he lived until he was seven years old. When his mother Mary remarried as a child, Steve assumed his stepdad William's last name. When he was in the second grade, the family relocated to the Garden State, settling in Middletown Township in Monmouth County.

Van Zandt was enthusiastic about the Beatles on *The Ed Sullivan Show,* but his real rock-'n'-roll awakening came when the Rolling Stones made their U.S. television debut on *Hollywood Palace* in June 1964. In subsequent interviews, Van Zandt would describe this as his moment of clarity. After the show, he obtained a guitar and diligently learned how to play it.

By the end of the summer of 1964, he had formed his first band, which he named the Whirlwinds. Influenced by the surf-rock instrumentals that were popular at the time, the band—which also included drummer Neils Lybeck and accordionist Bruce Gumbert—played together in the garage until early 1965 when Van Zandt formed a new, Stones-inspired group, the Mates. The following year he and Gumbert played together again in the Shadows.

Van Zandt continued to play with the Shadows at the same venues as the Castiles, which is how he first befriended Springsteen. Together, they discovered they had an appreciation for the same kinds of records, like the Isley Brothers' "Twist and Shout," plus sides by the Stones, the Who, the Beatles, and an endless run of soul and R&B singles.

Although his parents encouraged him to go to college, Van Zandt's sole interest was rock 'n' roll. But after a lengthy tenure in and out of bands, including the Source and Steel Mill, Van Zandt decided to quit music for construction—the family trade—by early 1972. It was a short-lived career shift. Within two years, after breaking his finger playing football, Van Zandt started playing guitar in a band again. His drummer was a cousin of a member of the Dovells.

Through that connection, he took a paying gig supporting the '60s Philadelphia band that was best known for the song, "Bristol Stomp." On the oldies circuit, he played Madison Square Garden and Las Vegas, plus arenas throughout the country. He performed with his hero, Dion, and met others like Little Richard, Gary U.S. Bonds, and the Drifters. He was surprised they didn't consider themselves more important to the roots of rock 'n' roll. It was this firsthand exposure to classic oldies music that helped forge his next group, Southside Johnny and the Asbury Jukes.

With longtime Springsteen associate John Lyon out in front on vocals and harmonica, Van Zandt was content to focus on song craft and musical direction while Lyon took the spotlight. When Springsteen tapped his old friend Steve to join him in the E Street Band shortly before the release of *Born to Run*, "Miami"—as Springsteen called him in deference to his pal's love of the Florida sunshine and surf and soul music—was happy to oblige.

"It was a way of getting out of town," Van Zandt told the *Star-Ledger* in October 1999. "It wasn't anything bigger than that at the time. He was obviously someone who was a friend of mine, and I figured if anybody's going to make it, he had a shot."

It was during his creative struggles to make his third album in late '74 and early '75 that Springsteen first called on Van Zandt to help him arrange the horn part for "Tenth Avenue Freeze-Out." With his vast knowledge of '60s soul, Van Zandt helped to strengthen the song. Perhaps even more importantly, he helped Springsteen perfect his newly penned song "Born to Run" by adding its memorable guitar line. In the 2005 documentary *Wings for Wheels*, the Boss called his friend's input on the track "arguably Steve's greatest contribution to my music."

Van Zandt provided an effective rhythm guitar presence that heightened the E Street Band's harder-rocking sound. He was also skilled at arranging the Miami Horns, a five-piece band that played with the E Street Band for fifty gigs during 1976 and 1977.

Miami—who by this point almost always wore a hat or bandana to cover the permanent hair loss he incurred when his head hit a windshield in a car accident—still felt loyal to the Asbury Jukes. He continued to work with that group, helping to write and produce music for them, including Southside's 1976 debut single "I Don't Wanna Go Home." He remained involved in the production and songwriting processes for his former group's first three albums, including 1978's *Hearts of Stone*, which featured the Bruce-penned "Talk to Me." Van Zandt was also instrumental in helping produce Springsteen classics like *Darkness on the Edge of Town*, *The River*, and *Born in the U.S.A.* and worked with the E Street Band on singles and album projects with Ronnie Spector and Gary U.S. Bonds.

Van Zandt's songwriting and production efforts on Bonds's comeback albums *Dedication* and *On the Line* led to his own solo deal with EMI America. In

The sleeve for Little Steven's single "Out of the Darkness." This song was extracted from 1984's politically themed *Voice of America* and peaked at #8 on the Norwegian singles survey. The album was Van Zandt's second with the Disciples of Soul and first since leaving the E Street Band.

Author's Collection

1982 he recorded an album, *Men Without Women*, under the banner of Little Steven and the Disciples of Soul. He was backed by an assortment of E Street Band and Jukes members on the record, which spawned an MTV hit called "Forever."

A subsequent, politically charged single, "I Am a Patriot" was released in 1983 as he balanced his work with Springsteen and songwriting for his next solo record, *Voice of America*. In 1984, in advance of that album's release and the unveiling of Springsteen's own *Born in the U.S.A.*, Van Zandt announced his amicable departure from the E Street Band.

"I had mixed feelings about it but felt I needed to learn about myself," he told the *Star-Ledger*. "When you're doing that, you need to confront as many of your fears as you can. I thought maybe I had some fear of success, or fear of realizing my potential. I was writing stuff that was very personal and very political, and it felt appropriate to be a solo [artist]."

The political charge of Van Zandt's second solo record fed into his 1985 all-star project, Artists United Against Apartheid. This industry activist collective featured Springsteen, Bono of U2, the Who's Pete Townshend, Bob Dylan, Joey Ramone, Lou Reed, and dozens of other high-profile artists who used the single "Sun City" as a means to declare they weren't going to play at the South African resort of the same name.

"I'm happy with the way it reached people," Van Zandt told *Backstreets* in March 1987. "Our main goal was to reach the entertainment world. And as far as I know, no major star has played Sun City since the record came out. We wanted to increase awareness about the issue and we wanted to give the whole movement a little push."

During the sessions for the "Sun City" single and album—which featured a rendition of the Bono song "Silver and Gold" with accompaniment from Keith Richards and Ron Wood of the Rolling Stones—Van Zandt befriended the U2 singer. When he finished a third solo album, *Freedom—No Compromise*, in 1987, the Irish giants asked Steve to support them on their massive *Joshua Tree* stadium tour.

Subsequent albums like 1989's *Revolution* and 1999's *Born Again Savage* gave way to an unexpected opportunity, when Van Zandt was brilliantly cast as Silvio Dante in the HBO mob drama *The Sopranos*. The show's creator, David Chase, got the idea after he watched the humorous way he described brokering to bring together the disputing members of the Rascals during his induction speech for that group at the Rock and Roll Hall of Fame in 1997.

Also in '99, Springsteen reunited the E Street Band with his old friend Steve back in the group to stay for touring and recording purposes.

A longtime love of garage rock prompted Van Zandt to contribute the rollicking song "Affection" by his next band, the Lost Boys, to *The Sopranos: Pepper and Eggs* soundtrack. The mafia-based show, which was a massive hit and ran for a decade, featured Van Zandt forgoing his trademark bandana headdress for a pompadour toupee. His role as a strip club owner and Soprano family consigliere was one of the most memorable characters on the beloved program.

In 2010, Van Zandt revealed plans to appear in a Norwegian television series as a mafia boss who has been relocated to Lillehammer, Norway, as part of a witness protection program.

Van Zandt has also established a significant radio presence with the advent of *Little Steven's Underground Garage* radio program, which has been syndicated globally since 2002. He also programs SiriusXM Satellite Radio Channels *Underground Garage* and *Outlaw Country* and launched his own record label, Wicked Cool Records, in 2006 as a means to release the garage rock records he loves.

Steve married Maureen Santoro—a former ballet dancer who played his wife Gabriela Dante on *The Sopranos*—on December 31, 1982. Reverend Richard Penniman (aka Little Richard) officiated the New York City ceremony, Springsteen was his best man and singer Percy Sledge was hired to perform his legendary "When a Man Loves a Woman" at the reception.

Nils Lofgren

When guitarist Nils Hilmer Lofgren was officially hired by Bruce Springsteen to replace Van Zandt in May 1984, the performers had already known each other for more than a decade. Before joining the E Street Band, Lofgren had an active solo career that grew out of his 1970s tenure fronting Grin. When he was just seventeen, he accompanied Neil Young on the Canadian icon's 1970 classic *After the Gold Rush* and later played alongside him in Crazy Horse.

Lofgren was born in Chicago on June 21, 1951, to a Swedish father and an Italian mother. His family relocated to Bethesda, Maryland, when he was a youngster, and he first studied accordion there when he was five. He pursued that instrument for ten years, before shifting away from classical and jazz as a teen. He engulfed himself in rock music by the mid-1960s and set his sights on the piano and, ultimately, the guitar.

Lofgren was drawn to the sound of harmonics and studied under Roy Buchanan, who pioneered the Telecaster guitar sound. Buchanan taught him how to achieve unique tones on his guitar. "He was the first person I heard who made harmonics sound like bells," Lofgren told the *O.C. Register* in January 2009. By 1967, Lofgren—who had been a competitive gymnast in high school—launched Grin with bassist Bob Gordon and drummer Bob Berberich.

The next year, Neil Young asked Lofgren—by now a Los Angeles-based teenage guitar whiz who played by ear—to join his band. He wound up playing guitar on *After the Gold Rush,* and although Lofgren was fairly inexperienced, Young gave him the task of playing piano on the record, which was tracked in a small Topanga Canyon studio.

"It was strange," Lofgren told the *Washington Post* in 2008. I hit the road at 17, went out to L.A. with my band Grin. Neil Young and [rock producer] David Briggs kind of took us under their wings, and I moved in with David. I saw Neil regularly with David, which was great. When I was 18 years old, Neil called and said he was doing this project, *After the Gold Rush,* and wanted me to be in the band, which was an honor."

Lofgren was petrified because, although he knew accordion, he wasn't really a piano player. He told Young and Briggs this, but they had a confidence in him that he himself lacked. "Both Neil and David felt like because I had played classical accordion for 10 years—I'd studied it seriously—that I shouldn't have any problem working out a few simple piano parts," he told the newspaper. "They had more faith in me than I did. They told me they thought I could handle it. They were right and I was wrong, thank God."

As a way of thanking Lofgren, Young gave the multi-instrumentalist his Martin D-18 guitar, which would remain one of the most cherished in his collection. Lofgren also played on Young's *Tonight's the Night* album and toured with him through 1971. With Lofgren fronting them, Grin had a regional radio hit,

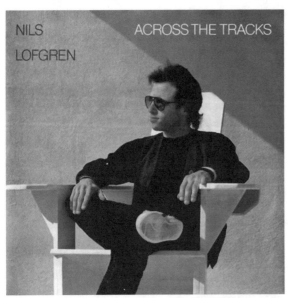

NILS LOFGREN
ACROSS THE TRACKS

"Across the Tracks" was a modest hit for Nils Lofgren in 1983 and the last single he released before joining the E Street Band the following year. Its parent album, *Wonderland,* was recorded in Bermuda and originally released on the MCA Records imprint Backstreet.   *Author's Collection*

"White Lies," around Washington and released four acclaimed but overlooked albums in four years.

By late 1974, Lofgren had gone solo, earning praise for his self-titled solo debut from the likes of *NME* and *Rolling Stone*. Future Springsteen manager Jon Landau touted it as one of the finest rock albums of 1975, and according to Lofgren, it was carefully studied during sessions for that year's breakthrough album *Born to Run*. The following year, his album *Cry Tough* was rated by *NME* as the fifth-best album of '76.

Lofgren's live shows highlighted his penchant for acrobatics, and he was often seen doing flips on a trampoline while holding his guitar. He continued to have a prolific and modestly successful solo career, and even landed on MTV in 1983 with the somersault-laden music video for "Across the Tracks." The same year, he signed on to play a European festival tour with Neil Young.

In the spring of 1984, before Van Zandt announced he was leaving, Lofgren got a call to come to New Jersey to check out Springsteen's next studio album.

"I'd been up to visit Bruce when he finished *Born in the U.S.A.* but before it was released, just to listen to the mixes and visit him for a couple of days," Lofgren told *Backstreets* in August 1985. "At the time nobody knew, including Bruce or Steve, what was gonna really happen. Just in passing, I mentioned that if he needed a guitar player I wanted an audition. A couple of months later, just before the album came out, he called me up and asked me to come up and jam, and I went up and jammed with the band for a couple of days. He asked me to join."

Lofgren won the job and has held onto it ever since, touring with the E Street Band until Springsteen dissolved it in 1989. Continuing to write and perform in the decade the group was apart, when the band reunited in 1999 with Van Zandt back in the lineup, Lofgren saw it as an opportunity instead of a threat. He challenged himself to augment the songs by learning new instruments including pedal steel, Dobro, lap-steel, and others. Or as he told the *Post*, "I think the E Street Band is the greatest toolbox in rock-and-roll, and Bruce is a master carpenter."

In his downtime, Lofgren has remained busy, working as a solo artist, accompanying Patti Scialfa, appearing in Ringo Starr's All Starr Band and even releasing an acoustic album of Young covers titled *The Loner—Nils Sings Neil* in 2008. In September of that year, he underwent successful hip replacement surgery after years of gymnastics, onstage flips off of drum risers, and decades of pickup basketball took their toll. The next year, however, he was back to work, touring with the E Street Band across the globe.

Speaking of his place in the group, Lofgren told *Guitar World* in October 1995, "I just love being part of a great band; I'll play tambourine or anything. I've been fortunate throughout my career to never have to do things I couldn't put my heart into. With Bruce it was easy; it was a lot of work, but it was being part of something I love . . . I've always been pulling for Bruce, whatever he needs to do."

Patti Scialfa

In May 1984, Bruce Springsteen's future wife, Patti Scialfa, was added to the lineup of the E Street Band. A Jersey Shore native, the vocalist and guitarist was born Vivienne Patricia Scialfa on July 29, 1953, in Oakhurst, New Jersey, to Joseph, a Sicilian American, and Patricia (Morris), a Scottish-Irish American.

Scialfa's maternal grandfather was her earliest musical inspiration. He would play his own songs to her on his piano and ask her which endings she preferred. By the time she was eight she was a fan of pop music and was instantly drawn to the Chiffons' smash "He's So Fine." It opened her mind. "Sicilian families are very male-based," Scialfa told the *Observer* in 2004. "To hear a woman singing on the radio, I started to realize that there are a lot of choices out there beyond the confines of my own hometown and people."

When she was twelve, the Scialfas moved from the Oakhurst house that her father—a television store owner turned real estate developer—had built to one in the more affluent town of Deal. She joined the glee club in junior high but was mostly a quiet, shy girl who wrote poetry and listened to the likes of Bob Dylan, Joni Mitchell, and Dusty Springfield. Around the age of fourteen, she began singing in her older brother Michael's rock band. From there she found her own group to front, learned the guitar, and honed her songwriting skills.

In 1971, she graduated from Asbury Park High School and set off for the University of Miami's Frost School of Music, where she studied jazz alongside classmates like Bruce Hornsby and Pat Metheny, but before long she transferred to New York University, where she earned a music degree. "I was very single-minded," Scialfa told the *Asbury Park Press* in 2004. "I was taking demos to labels by the time I was 18 or 19, and I got close three or four times."

Scialfa stayed in Manhattan and waitressed and performed in Greenwich Village, forming a street group called Trickster with Soozie Tyrell and Lisa Lowell, who would remain her close friends and future collaborators. In 1979, Asbury Jukes guitarist Billy Rush—who knew Scialfa from high school—called her and asked if the members of Trickster would back Southside in the studio and on tour.

She performed at clubs like Kenny's Castaways and Asbury Park's the Stone Pony, briefly joining the latter's early 1980s house band, Cats on a Smooth Surface. Through the Jersey Shore music scene, Scialfa was introduced to Bruce Springsteen in 1983, and they became casual friends.

"Once in a while I'd bump into him," she explained to the *Observer*. "We'd be in the same bar and we'd sit and talk and when the night was over he'd always give me a ride home or we'd go out for a hamburger. We just became friends."

The following year, Scialfa was asked by Springsteen to sing at rehearsals just days before the *Born in the U.S.A.* tour was slated to launch. Springsteen wasn't sure he had a place for her, but because Nils Lofgren had contracted mononucleosis and couldn't sing his backing vocals, she was asked to join the trek. Scialfa didn't know all of Bruce's back catalog and had to learn it in a panic.

When the tour wrapped in mid-1985, Scialfa wasn't yet an official member of the E Street Band, but the exposure landed her work with the Rolling Stones. She sang backing vocals on the legendary U.K. band's 1986 hit, "One Hit (To the Body)," and went on to work on Keith Richards's 1988 solo album *Talk Is Cheap*, which was produced by an old friend and future collaborator of hers, Steve Jordan.

In support of Springsteen's 1987 album, Scialfa was invited back for the *Tunnel of Love Express* tour the following year, earning a more prominent and provocative role in the live set on numbers like "You Can Look (But You Better Not Touch)" and "Tougher Than the Rest." Meanwhile, as Springsteen's marriage to actress Julianne Phillips was ending (they divorced in '89), his romance with Scialfa was heating up.

Scialfa became pregnant and gave birth to Evan James Springsteen in 1990. On June 8, 1991, she and Springsteen married at their Beverly Hills, California, home. A daughter, Jessica Rae, and a son, Samuel Ryan, followed in 1991 and 1994, respectively. As the Springsteens put the E Street Band on the back burner for domestic pursuits, they continued to pursue music together. Scialfa sang on Bruce's 1993 albums *Human Touch* and *Lucky Town*, while he coproduced her debut album, *Rumble Doll*, released the same year.

Eleven years later—and five years after Springsteen reunited the E Street Band—Scialfa released a second solo album, *23rd Street Lullaby*. The 2004 disc was comprised entirely of original Scialfa compositions. It was produced by Jordan and featured assistance from Lofgren and minimal input from Springsteen. In 2007, Scialfa dropped the critically praised *Play It as It Lays*, which—like its predecessor—was recorded in her Colts Neck farmhouse studio.

At times during postmillennium E Street Band tours, Scialfa has had to juggle motherhood with her obligations to the group. During their 2003 tour behind *The Rising*, Springsteen apologized for her absence, saying, "Patti sends her regards, she couldn't be here. The kids need her more right now than the band." Scialfa was also absent from stretches of the 2007–2008 *Magic* tour so that she could tend to the needs of her children.

As for her solo career, she has endured her share of criticism from naysayers who treated her first album as a pet project. "That's just the price that comes from being married to someone who's really famous," she told the *Observer*. "But that's okay because I am confident that the music can stand on its own."

Soozie Tyrell

Vocalist and violinist Soozie Tyrell befriended Patti Scialfa in the late 1970s, when they collaborated musically in the New York–based group Trickster. Through this affiliation, Tyrell worked with Patti on her 1993 *Rumble Doll* album and landed infrequent work with Springsteen. She became an auxiliary member of the E Street Band in 2002. Ironically, her earliest ties to the Jersey Shore sound date back to 1980, when she appeared on Southside Johnny and the Asbury Jukes' *Love Is a Sacrifice.*

Tyrell was initially credited as a special guest, but was sourced as "violinist with the E Street Band" by 2006. Born Soozie Kirschner in Pisa, Italy, she was the daughter of a military serviceman and relocated frequently as a child before her family settled in Florida. She studied music theory at the University of South Florida before moving to New York, where she met Scialfa.

In addition to work with the Jukes, she formed a country outfit, Soozie and High in the Saddle, before aligning with Buster Poindexter (aka David Johansen) and backing him on his smash 1987 single "Hot-Hot-Hot."

By 1992, she was backing Springsteen on *Lucky Town* and has since provided violin and vocal work on all of his studio records, including non-E Street efforts like *The Ghost of Tom Joad* and *Devils and Dust.* Her violin playing was a notable element of Springsteen's 2002 album *The Rising* and its resulting world tour. In addition to her efforts with Springsteen, Tyrell released a debut studio album, *White Lines*, in 2003.

Charles Giordano

Charles Giordano got his start playing keyboards with Pat Benatar in her 1980s heyday before he went on to perform with David Johansen's Buster Poindexter and the Banshees of Blue. Giordano, who was born in 1954, is a multi-instrumentalist known for his accordion abilities, which first earned him a role alongside Springsteen in his Sessions Band, for the 2006 album *We Shall Overcome: The Seeger Sessions.*

Giordano had earned the attention of Springsteen through his studio work on Madeleine Peyroux's 1996 album *Dreamland* and Bucky Pizzarelli's 2000 album *Italian Intermezzo.* In 2007, when Danny Federici announced he was undergoing treatment for melanoma, Giordano was asked to accompany the E Street Band on keyboards and organ for its touring efforts behind *Magic.* He became a permanent member during the campaign to promote *Working on a Dream.*

13

Pulling out of Here to Win

Born to Run

One Last Chance to Make It Real

After a couple of failed attempts at 914 Studios beginning in June, Bruce Springsteen committed himself to work on his third album in August'74. Making the new record their priority meant that the band would only book a few nearby gigs that summer. Although keeping themselves out of the lucrative summer concert season hurt Laurel Canyon's cash flow, Springsteen and Appel needed to ease the contractual suspension Columbia had forced on them after they failed to provide two albums yearly in accordance with Appel's arrangement with CBS.

From a business standpoint, Columbia could have gone either way with Springsteen, who had yet to earn the company a profit. After mulling their options, the label gave him the green light. Th e first track that was finalized was "Born to Run," which took a staggering half a year to perfect.

Appel knew the song was brilliant and pushed for it to be released as a single in advance of the album. But the powers that be at CBS declined. They didn't even like it.

In reality, there was no finished album to sell to fans. Deep in debt to the company, the label was also concerned about the lineup changes and the fact that the material wasn't coming along. Springsteen was laboring over a new song called "Jungleland," but the notion of an actual finished studio album was long off.

Predictions for His Third Album

Springsteen's initial plans for his next album included chick singers and horns, according to an August 1974 interview with *Zig Zag*'s Jerry Gilbert. He also spoke of "Born to Run," which was far from finalized.

"I'm still fooling with the words for the new single, but I think it'll be good," he said, adding, "I've written a lot of stuff for the new album but when I get into the studio I'll have a clear picture." Or so he thought.

"Born to Run"

At the time he wrote "Born to Run," which he debuted live in May 1974, Springsteen was living in a West Long Branch bungalow at 7½ West End Court. Here he rediscovered the depth of classic 1960s pop records by Roy Orbison, the Ronettes, and the Beach Boys. Noodling with the guitar, sitting on the edge of his bed, the title popped into his head.

Working the song's arrangement out with the band on the road, Springsteen struggled with the fact that his seven-piece band couldn't offer him the Phil Spector–minded Wall of Sound he was after. It took him six months to perfect, but served as the catalyst for the rest of the album.

Designed to fuse the excitement of a lengthy fan favorite like "Rosalita" with his own desire to write the ultimate rock song, Springsteen long agonized over the tune.

Springsteen spoke of how he obsessed over "Born to Run" during his time in Blauvelt when he spoke to *NME* in November of the next year. "I was there for months," he explained. "I had this girl with me and she'd just come in from Texas and she wanted to go home again and she was going nuts and we were in this room and it just went on and on. I would come home and she would say, 'Are you done? Is it over? Are you finished?' And I said, 'No, it ain't over, it ain't over.' I'd come home practically in tears."

Recorded on August 6, 1974, right before pianist David Sancious and drummer Ernest Carter left the band, the legendary drum roll that launches the song was Springsteen's idea. As Carter relayed to *Backstreets* in April 1986, "He told me what he wanted and I played it."

Appel Breaks "Born to Run"

In an act of desperation and defiance, Appel went against the wishes of CBS and serviced cassette tapes of the song to markets where they had allies. He sent out about three dozen copies of the song to Kid Leo at WMMS in Cleveland, Ed Sciaky at WMMR in Philadelphia, plus stations in Phoenix and Boston. The song took off like a rocket, becoming the most requested song in Cleveland overnight. WNEW in New York City quickly picked up on it.

The brazen move wasn't without a backlash. Fans were going into record stores in these markets looking for the new Springsteen hit. The problem was, there was no single to buy. Appel had bootlegged Springsteen's music so that his fans could hear it, but they couldn't buy it. There was no product to sell, and Columbia Records was pissed.

This iconic poster for Springsteen's career-making run of 1975 Roxy gigs symbolized him on the cusp of superstardom. In addition to a who's who of L.A. media types, the Boss played in front of Hollywood stars like Warren Beatty and Jack Nicholson, as well as music legends David Bowie and George Harrison. *Courtesy of Robert Rodriguez*

Appel knew he could still sell concert tickets and Springsteen's fan base was only growing on the popularity of the song. So while Springsteen continued to ponder the shape that his third album might take, he went back on the road. After all, the organization had bills to pay.

Segelstein's Son Saves Springsteen

In support of his show at Brown University, a reporter from the college newspaper asked Springsteen about his situation with Columbia Records. He admitted that he didn't feel like he was getting the treatment he deserved.

Unbeknownst to Springsteen, the son of Irwin Segelstein—the president of CBS Records—was an ardent fan who went to Brown. When Irwin's son's friends began to chastise him for his father's ignorance, he called his dad out on it. Soon after the article ran, Segelstein phoned Appel to grill him about the interview.

Appel wasn't even aware that Springsteen had made the remarks, but played them to his advantage on the phone. He reminded Irwin that Springsteen had an upcoming interview scheduled with *Rolling Stone*, and promised Springsteen would really let Columbia have it.

Segelstein pleaded with Appel against that idea. He suggested an imminent lunch meeting with Springsteen at Mercurio's in Manhattan. During the meal, while Springsteen remained mostly silent, Irwin assured them that CBS would back him. They even agreed to finance the rest of the album at a state-of-the-art Manhattan studio.

A Work in Progress

With the financial support of CBS to make the record, Springsteen pushed everyone involved with the project to exhaustion on a regular basis. The band would record a particular song live and then continue to tweak and rerecord it—at times for days—only to discard it altogether.

As evidenced by some of the original working titles attempted below, Springsteen had a tendency to recycle song ideas and lyrics. At one point during his yearlong efforts on *Born to Run*, he worked through songs like "Walking in the Street," "American Summer," "War and Roses," "Up from the Street," "Sometimes at Night," "From the Churches to the Jails," "The Legend of Zero and Blind Terry," "The Hungry and the Hunted," and "Between Flesh and Fantasy."

Springsteen's original plan was to make a concept record chronicling a full day in the character's life. At one point, he considered launching the album with an acoustic rendition of "Thunder Road" and closing it with an electric, full band version.

When he first planned the record a year earlier, he wrote out a list of tunes he wanted on it. They included "Angel Baby," "Architect Angel," "Thundercrack," "Vision at Fort Horn," "Two Hearts," "Here She Comes," "Glory Road," "Wild

Billy's Lullaby," "You Mean So Much to Me" (later recorded by the Asbury Jukes), "Janey Needs a Shooter" (later covered by Warren Zevon), "Still There," and "Jungleland."

The finished project only held on to one of those titles. Of course, "Jungleland" remained. Another song, "War and Roses," was earmarked early on by Springsteen for the title track.

The Record Plant

While 914 Studios had served Springsteen well, the facility had begun to have some technical inadequacies. After completing "Born to Run," Springsteen—who had started to lose confidence in himself—was looking for someone or something to blame for his creative struggles.

Under the guidance of Landau, he decided he no longer wanted to work at 914 Studios. Landau convinced him that as a first-rate performer he had no business recording in a second-rate facility.

As Appel feared, production costs soared, to $125,000—a lot of money in 1975. But at least things started to progress, assuaging Columbia's anxiety over getting the album done for a third-quarter release.

"We moved down to Manhattan, to the Record Plant, where we went over our budget in two seconds," Appel said in *Down Thunder Road*. "[That] money, of course, came out of our pockets."

Springsteen and Landau

In 1974, while Jon Landau was recuperating from surgery related to Crohn's disease in Boston, Springsteen sent his new friend a cassette of "Born to Run." Soon after, when Landau had completed a planned moved to New York, their alliance became stronger. They hung out, studied records, went to movies, and, when Springsteen felt like he was struggling to complete his album, he asked for Landau's help.

Settled into the Record Plant in February 1975, Springsteen would regularly crash at Landau's apartment instead of retreating back to the Jersey Shore late at night by bus. Before long, he asked his friend to visit the sessions. Springsteen solicited Landau's insights.

Landau told him candidly that Weinberg and Tallent were having trouble with a particular transition on "Jungleland." Springsteen agreed. He pointed out the thump of a piano foot pedal that was affecting the same track. Springsteen concurred and knew he had to get Landau officially involved as a producer.

With Landau in tow, Springsteen hoped the long, difficult sessions for the record might get some relief. At the very least, Landau showed him a way to improve on things and be the best that he could be.

Appel on Landau

As work progressed on what would become *Born to Run*, Landau's idea sharing took on a formal role. Springsteen called Mike Appel in late February and told him he wanted to hire Jon as a coproducer.

Landau had as much experience with production as Mike Appel, who was aware of Landau's power and influence as a music critic. He could already see how Landau helped bolster Springsteen's confidence and shared his insights about the music business, and that, in Appel's estimation, was a good thing.

At the same time, Appel very quickly felt as if Landau was desperate to be involved, and he found it peculiar. Once Landau branded Springsteen "rock and roll's future," Appel began to see how Landau was pushing his way into the fold.

By February 1975, Landau had managed to land a production credit that became official by April. Appel was threatened, and based on how things would play out, he probably had a right to be.

Debt Killing Idea Axed

Laurel Canyon was $50,000 in debt in February 1975. At the time, Springsteen's fan base in Philadelphia was large enough that a run of gigs could have paid it off. Springsteen, who had been juggling other tour dates with album efforts, needed to focus on the record and rejected the idea.

The following month, when the E Street Band was back on tour, Springsteen insisted that Appel arrange for a Ferris wheel to be brought onstage for the group's March 7 show at the Painter's Mill Music Fair in Owings Mills, Maryland. When Appel told him it was impossible to bring such a large item indoors and that it would eat away at their payday, Springsteen got downright surly.

Springsteen Pays the Crew

Before he went back on the road in March 1975, Springsteen was met with hesitation from his road crew before a run of East Coast shows. They were owed for their work the month prior, and Appel was giving them the "check is in the mail" routine.

According to Springsteen's account in a 1976 lawsuit deposition, "They were bitching to me they were never paid."

"Mike owed them this and Mike owed them that," Springsteen testified. "I had to borrow money here and there just so these guys would come on the road."

To Sign or Not to Sign

In March 1974, Appel wanted to sign the members of the E Street Band as a separate group. Clarence Clemons, David Sancious, and Boom Carter had all expressed an interest in having him manage their individual careers.

Because he was already operating as their manager, he wanted to make it official. He also didn't want other management outfits swooping in to lure them away because it might complicate matters for Springsteen and Laurel Canyon. Springsteen agreed.

A year later, Clemons and Danny Federici finally came into Laurel Canyon and signed contracts with Appel. But when Springsteen got word they had done this, he took exception and called Appel about it. At his request, Appel tore the contracts up.

Although he never came right out and said it, Springsteen knew that if he ever broke away from Appel, the E Street Band's contracts with Appel could prevent him from playing and recording with them.

Paying Landau

Some of the animosity between Landau and Appel stemmed from the fact that he was so cheap. Appel offered Landau just $150 a week to help produce the record, what the members of the E Street Band were earning at the time. This didn't sit well with Springsteen, who felt Landau he deserved a reasonable paycheck, like the two points (percent) of the retail price Landau had suggested.

Springsteen pushed for a royalty agreement, and Appel had a contract drawn up between Landau and Laurel Canyon Ltd. Landau was given a $3,500 advance and royalties, and, after much hemming and hawing, the deal was finalized on April 13, 1975. Half of Landau's cut came from Appel's company, and the other half came from Columbia Records.

Columbia Takes a Cue from Appel

Well in advance of the official release of the "Born to Run" single, CBS's regional promotion staffers mimicked Mike Appel. With cassette copies of the track, field men went out to visit radio programmers and record distributors in the spring 1975. The plan was to lay the groundwork for Springsteen's third album.

With Columbia's muscle finally behind Springsteen, the label was gearing up to make Bruce a star. CBS had already bought print ads in regional arts weeklies and magazines like *Rolling Stone* in February, plugging his back catalog and letting the world know that a new studio record was forthcoming.

Power Struggle

In Springsteen's eyes, Landau filled a production void that Mike Appel never could. Because Appel wore multiple hats and had other managerial considerations, Springsteen started to feel as if Appel wasn't the good fit he once was.

Appel was at times uncommunicative, at other times distracted, and sometimes absent altogether. As a result, he overlooked the sonic details Landau was picking up on. Landau made himself available to Springsteen around the clock, something Appel couldn't do and run Laurel Canyon.

Springsteen confided to Landau that he was frustrated with Appel. At one point, he revealed to Landau that after *Born to Run* was finished, Appel would be out of the picture, at least when it came to record making.

Landau saw an opportunity, and by the spring of 1975, a power struggle was on between him and Appel. Appel began to think that Landau had a plan all along to try and infiltrate the Springsteen camp and stage a coup.

According to Appel, Landau pushed to have his name above his in the production credits for the album. Appel raised an eyebrow, but relented. Still, Landau's persistence over such matters made Appel certain Jon was going to be trouble.

In Appel's opinion, Landau seemed obsessed. Each step—from friend to confidant to producer—was calculated. In Landau's eyes, Appel had a crooked business arrangement with his new best friend.

Landau Kick-Starts the Album

According to Springsteen, Landau's input on his third album was indispensable. He worked with Springsteen on his songs, came to band rehearsals and made astute suggestions, and essentially taught Max Weinberg how to thrive as a rock drummer.

Creative Concerts, Cellar Door, & WGOE Present

Tonight 8:30 P. M.!!

Bruce Springstein

and

The E St. Band

Mosque

Reserved Seats $6, $5 On Sale at Mosque

This Richmond newspaper advertisement, which misspells Springsteen's last name as "Springstein," helped draw attention to the E Street Band's August 1, 1975, gig at the Mosque Theatre.

Courtesy of Ray Bonis/Brucebase

"He taught this guy [Max], man, you know . . . how to attack them things," Springsteen said in a 1976 deposition related to his eventual lawsuit against Mike Appel and Laurel Canyon. "He changed the tide of the whole thing. He changed all of a sudden, hey, everybody had felt good and things were getting done and things were happening and we weren't laying in the quicksand anymore and we were coming out of it."

Even Appel would concede in depositions for his countersuit the same year, "I would say that the most important thing that he did was to kick start the album and get Bruce off his rump."

Appel Is Asked to Leave the *BTR* Sessions

At one point, Springsteen's work at the Record Plant had come to a standstill. There was tension in the room, no one was communicating, and it would get to the point where the project's engineer Jimmy Iovine—who had worked on Harry Nilsson's *Pussycats* album and John Lennon's Phil Spector–produced album *Rock and Roll*—couldn't help but nod off during the overnight proceedings.

At one point during the July 4, 1975, holiday—Springsteen suggested to Landau that if Appel left—in his words from the aforementioned deposition "Mike was not performing any useful function"—it might be better.

Landau called Appel and explained that because they were going nowhere, that the chemistry between the three of them had become a problem, it might be best if he stayed away for a while. Appel told Landau that he felt it was unfair for them to cut him out after almost a year of work on the record, but he acquiesced and left the city. He retreated to the beach for the weekend.

Springsteen Asks Appel to Come Back to the Studio

When Springsteen showed up at Laurel Canyon's offices the Monday after, Appel—who had already spoken to Iovine and knew things were unproductive in his absence—asked him how it went. He admitted there was no progress.

According to Appel's account, Springsteen was withdrawn and clearly embarrassed as he asked him to come back to the sessions. Soon after, Landau apologized to Appel, and for a short while, the fences were mended.

Landau had come to the realization that Appel was only a minor part of the problem. The real problem behind the completion of the album was Springsteen, who couldn't get past the pressure of delivering the album that would either make or break his career.

A Monster

In an era when most radio singles were around three minutes, "Born to Run" was nearly two minutes too long. Because of its nature, and its gigantic sound, Columbia's in-house engineer couldn't find a place to edit the song down. Ultimately, the company would select it as the lead single anyway.

The biggest problem with the album was Springsteen's own perfectionism, as he told *Creem* in 1975. "I had this horrible pressure in the studio," he explained of his perfectionist approach. "The album became a monster. It wanted everything. It just ate up everyone's life."

As Landau would tell Dave Marsh in his book *Born to Run*, "The biggest thing I learned from [Bruce] was the ability to concentrate on the big picture. 'Hey, wait a minute,' he'd say, 'the release date is just one day. The record is forever.'"

The Live Album Is Quashed

In early 1975, Appel, Springsteen, and Columbia Records executives had begun to discuss releasing a live album. Springsteen's live shows were already notorious, and Appel and Columbia thought that having a stopgap release out in between the second and third studio albums would be a way to keep his name alive, draw increased airplay, and bring in new revenue. Appel also knew it was a way to satisfy another album in Springsteen's contract, which called for seven more records.

At first, Springsteen was excited by the notion, and several live dates were recorded. But later, when he changed his mind, he neglected to tell Appel.

It was Landau who lowered the boom one night at the Record Plant, when they were wrapping up *Born to Run*. The exchange resulted in an argument between Landau and Appel on the roof of the Manhattan recording facility.

Appel went to confront Springsteen, who had begun to recoil from interacting with his increasingly harsh and insensitive manager. Appel told him that canceling the live album was a mistake. He let Appel know that it was his career, and he had no plans for a studio album anytime soon.

Crushing Appel

For the first time in his career, Springsteen—under Landau's guidance—was standing up to Appel. And Appel clearly didn't like the friction.

He made it known to Springsteen that, in his estimation, he was being brainwashed by Landau. Springsteen dismissed this notion, but Appel soon had a reason to believe what he was saying to his client was true.

In *Down Thunder Road*, Appel revealed that one of his secretaries, Chouteau Merrill, overheard Landau saying that if he wanted, he could "get rid of [Appel] as producer, manager, everything. He said all he had to do was tell Bruce."

Later, during a recording session with Southside Johnny and the Asbury Jukes and in the presence of Jimmy Iovine and Steve Van Zandt, Landau evidently proclaimed he had "a plan to crush Mike Appel."

Miami Steve Officially Joins

Although Steve Van Zandt had helped Bruce with certain parts of the record—most notably he envisioned the horn parts on "Tenth Avenue Freeze Out"—he didn't officially join the E Street Band until sessions were just about finished on *Born to Run*.

Springsteen put the offer out to Van Zandt, who decided to leave the Asbury Jukes. "[Bruce] was something special and I just wanted to help him become a success," Van Zandt told *Guitar World* in October 1995. "I felt he deserved it: I had an emotional stake in it because he was my friend, and the only representative of our area, in a way. He carried the flag for all of us. I felt we would be stronger together than apart."

Van Zandt also liked the idea of letting someone else control the reins. "One of the reasons I left the Jukes to join Bruce's band was I didn't want the responsibility and pressure of running a band and fighting with the club owners any more," he admitted to Robert Hilburn in 1985's *Springsteen*. "I also didn't want the focus on me. It was easier to just lay back and watch someone else take over on stage."

For Springsteen, one significant benefit was that his old friend "Miami" had a great ear for arrangements. But most importantly, Van Zandt had the uncanny ability to elicit the musical ideas from Springsteen's brain, something that would be a major asset to forthcoming projects.

The Album Is Done

After recording was completed in July 1975, Springsteen continued to obsess over the final product. He insisted on nearly a dozen mastering sessions for the album. At one point, he even threatened to scrap half the record and substitute the songs with live recordings.

Jon Landau—who had gone on vacation to San Francisco—called Springsteen and told him that the album was as good as it was ever going to be. Landau convinced him to let it go—it was time to be released. And on September 1, 1975, it was.

Nearly three decades later, Springsteen tried to explain his obsession with the project. "With that [album] I was shootin' for the moon," Springsteen told *Entertainment Weekly* in 2003. "I said, 'I don't wanna make a good record, I wanna make The Greatest Record Somebody's Ever Heard.' I was filled with arrogance and thought, I can do that, you know?"

Songs Left Off of *Born to Run*

During the sequencing of Springsteen's third album, Appel fought to keep its cinematic interlude, "Meeting Across the River" on the album. Meanwhile, Landau and Springsteen pushed for two songs, "Lonely Night in the Park" and "Linda, Let Me Be the One," to make the final cut.

After a heavy discussion, Appel—who felt the songs were inferior to the others on the record—won out. Of those leftovers, only "Linda" ever made it to official release. The lilting, Spector-esque number appeared on 1998's four-CD box set, *Tracks*.

The *Born to Run* Tour, Part One

Because Springsteen labored over *Born to Run* up until the final minutes of the mixing process, rehearsals for the E Street Band's tour to support the record suffered drastic delays. This meant rehearsing together in a room a floor above the Record Plant's studio in order to ready the group for its upcoming tour.

According to *Brucebase*, Springsteen conducted a marathon rehearsal that began on July 19 at 3 p.m. and wound down the following morning at 10 a.m. This allowed little time for rest, considering the group's trek—which started six weeks before the album would hit store shelves—got underway in Providence, Rhode Island, at 8 p.m. that night. This show at the Palace Theatre marked the official live debut of rhythm guitarist "Miami" Steve Van Zandt.

These Eastern dates in cities like Geneva, New York; Lenox, Massachusetts; Washington; Norfolk; Cleveland and Akron, Ohio; and Pittsburgh were where the band was perfecting its live show in advance of a much-publicized run of New York City dates to showcase Bruce to the music industry. The mood was loose and celebratory at these gigs, with Springsteen teasing Van Zandt for fucking up his parts, forgetting certain lyrics, and being out of step during certain dance numbers.

The Bottom Line

Springsteen's legendary five-night, ten-show run of dates at the Bottom Line in New York City came about after he refused Mike Appel's plan to book him into Madison Square Garden. Springsteen's lone experience playing MSG was tainted by the 1973 experience opening for Chicago, where he choked in front of Columbia execs and Peter Cetera fans alike.

The 400-seat Bottom Line venue in Greenwich Village was a much better fit, and with ten gigs, Springsteen would reach four thousand fans during the August 13–17, 1975, run. He would also shatter the venue's previous attendance records, grossing a cool $20,000 in the process. Columbia Records snatched up 980 of the tickets to distribute to members of the media and encouraged radio personnel and music journalists to come and see for themselves.

It worked. Local radio personalities like WNEW-FM's Dave Herman—previously a nonbeliever—jumped on Springsteen's records the morning after and his radio station hastily arranged to simulcast Bruce's fifth show. The *New York Times* raved, "The shows will rank among the great rock experiences of those lucky enough to get in. Mr. Springsteen has it all—he is a great lyricist, a wonderful singer, guitarist and piano player, has one of the best bands anybody has ever heard, and he's as charismatic a stage figure as pop has produced," proclaiming, "A star was born."

Finally, future Springsteen biographer Dave Marsh championed Bruce's appearance at the Bottom Line in *Rolling Stone*, writing, "Not since Elton John's initial Troubadour appearances has an artist leapt so visibly and rapidly from cult fanaticism to mass acceptance," and adding, "It was a time to hail from Jersey with pride."

Shutting Down the Cash Registers

In late August 1975, the E Street Band traveled to Atlanta to play a three-night stint at the Electric Ballroom, a large music club owned by Georgia concert promoter Alex Cooley. According to Cooley, via his official website, Springsteen approached him after the first night's performance with an unorthodox request.

"He asked if we could shut down the cash registers because they were making too much noise!," says Cooley, who obliged. "That's the only time I ever did that."

Track by Track

When *Born to Run* was released to the media in the last week of August 1975, it was the breakthrough everyone in the Springsteen camp hoped it would be. Critical acclaim and commercial success validated that the struggles to complete the album over the prior year were worth it.

Artistically, it was an achievement that signified Springsteen, nearly twenty-six, had begun to grow up. On *Born to Run*, he moved past his teenage interpretations of love and liberty.

"Thunder Road"

Before it became the lead-off track on one of rock 'n' roll's greatest studio albums of all time, "Thunder Road" was initially known as both "Wings for Wheels" and "Glory Road." Publicly unveiled at the Main Point in February 1975, Springsteen's future anthem endured a series of lyrical shifts as it morphed into its final version. Most notably, the song's character, Mary, was introduced as both Angelina (or "Angie") and Christina (or "Chrissy") in early versions.

The song's depictions are downright cinematic, as Mary's dress waves, Roy Orbison graces the airwaves, and Springsteen lures her off of the front porch and into his front seat to head out on the open road. Taking its title from the 1958 Robert Mitchum movie of the same name, Springsteen told *Rolling Stone* in December 2004, "I never saw the movie, I only saw the poster in the lobby of the theater."

Despite its categorization as a masterpiece by fans and critics alike, the Boss has publicly dismissed his lyric, "Well I got this guitar and I learned how to make it talk." In a 2005 *VH1 Storytellers* appearance, he called it, "Probably the hokiest line I ever wrote."

According to Springsteen, the song also signifies his shift away from the regional approach to music heard on his first records. "When the screen door slams on 'Thunder Road,' you're not necessarily on the Jersey Shore anymore," he wrote in *Songs*. "You could be anywhere in America."

As for its title, Springsteen told Australian rock critic Ian "Molly" Meldrum in 1995 that he "wanted the band to sound like thunder, I wanted to feel that sort of power."

"Tenth Avenue Freeze-Out"

Before it became the unofficial theme of the E Street Band, this song chronicled how Springsteen (who refers to himself as "Bad Scooter" in the opening line) and his legendary outfit first came together. Proudly namechecking 10th Avenue in Belmar, the road that intersects with E Street where the group once held occasional rehearsals, it's a musical history lesson of sorts.

Although Springsteen declared in the *Wings for Wheels* documentary that he had no idea what a "Tenth Avenue Freeze-out" actually was, accounts from early insiders claim that it stems from one wintry night when his band's van broke down within walking distance of the home of pianist David Sancious's mother. Together the members of the band hoofed it to the warmth of Mrs. Sancious's house.

In general, the song is an account of the group's teamwork early on. It makes special notice in the third verse about when Clarence "Big Man" Clemons joined the band, which is augmented by the saxophonist's vibrant horn part.

Randy Brecker, the jazz trumpeter hired to play on the song, told Christopher Sandford how he came in to remedy matters as the sessions for the tune started to break down. "We were the New York pros," the horn player explained, "and this wild-looking gypsy guy tears up the charts and sings the lick. From then on, things took off."

Despite its buoyant, musical "block party" outcome, the tune—which was the second single from *Born to Run*—didn't fare too well on the pop charts. It stalled at #83 after its release.

Over time, the song has become part of the public's consciousness, especially in Belmar, where there is an ice cream stand at the intersection of 10th and the Boardwalk appropriately named 10th Avenue Freeze Out. When the E Street Band performed a four-song set with Springsteen during half-time at Super Bowl XLIII in 2009, they opened their appearance with a version of this classic rock staple, but not before he told the millions watching at home to "put down the guacamole dip and chicken fingers."

"Night"

A precursor to a lot of the themes that would embody Springsteen's fourth studio album, *Darkness on the Edge of Town*, "Night" chronicles a blue-collar guy who gets home from a long day at his job and heads out on the town in his fast machine. Like the album's signature anthem, this tune finds Springsteen singing of "rat traps" and the "chromed invaders" that line up and down the Circuit of Asbury.

Arguably the least acknowledged song on *Born to Run*, its high-energy bass line and expressive vocal delivery made "Night" a song that the E Street Band would come to rely on to open many of its 1976 concerts and revisit during the 2007–2008 *Magic* trek.

But this is no mere hot-rodding ode—"Night" is a song about loneliness. As its greaser/loner subject searches to find love to fill the void in his life, he acknowledges he'll have to "run sad and free," at least for the time being.

"Backstreets"

As the song that concludes side one of *BTR*, "Backstreets" is an epic piece of Springsteen's catalog that launches with Roy Bittan's sweeping, declarative, and emotive minute-long piano and organ introduction. While some of the lyrics suggest that the song is the tale of a heartbroken guy reminiscing about the loss of his girl, Terry, other lyrics—coupled with the spelling of the name—suggest it might very well be about a man.

Much speculation exists among fans, but the song appears to be about either a good buddy he would up having a falling-out with or a woman who left him in the lurch. It could also be based on an amalgam of severed platonic or romantic relationships.

As the song explains, together they crashed in abandoned beach houses, got drunk, went to drag races, and lived as misfits hanging on the boardwalk away from the 9-to-5 world. These could be the activities of a couple in love—but more likely, they are indeed the experiences of two extremely close friends who drifted apart.

While it's unknown if the tune was written in homage to Terry Magovern— Springsteen's best friend from childhood—Springsteen often played it in tribute to Magovern after his 2007 death on the *Magic* tour. The song's title would eventually become the name of the Springsteen fan magazine and website, *Backstreets*.

A rare Spanish pressing of "Tenth Avenue Freeze-Out" from 1976, this 45—titled "Enfrentamiento en la Decima Avienda"—was backed by another *Born to Run* cut, "She's the One," which is listed as "Ella Es la Que Quiero."

Courtesy of 991.com

"Born to Run"

Released one week ahead of the album that shares its name, Springsteen would ultimately call his career-defining single "My shot at the title" in the liner notes to 1995's *Greatest Hits*. With a desire to break free of the limitations of the Jersey Shore and leave modest success behind for stardom, the song's main character coaxes Wendy to hop on his Harley and get out of the Garden State while they're young.

Together they roll past Palace Amusements, swarms of kids from the inland towns, and Mopar-made Hemi-powered rides as the E Street Band rises to a throbbing, sax-infused crescendo. Ultimately, Springsteen would call it "the song of my youth" in a 2005 interview with National Public Radio.

Fans shared this sentiment. On June 12, 1979, "Born to Run" was named New Jersey's "Unofficial Youth Rock Anthem" by the New Jersey State Legislature after a campaign was initiated by Carol Miller, a DJ at New York rock station WPLJ. In March 1980, fans again petitioned to make it the official state song of New Jersey. Springsteen always considered the idea ironic because, as he put it at the time, it was "about leaving Jersey."

"She's the One"

Springsteen once claimed that he penned this song so that he could hear Clarence Clemons play the sax solo he heard in his head. He wrote the melody for "She's the One" before he penned the lyrics. Topically, it deals with an extremely beautiful but hurtful woman who breaks the heart of the tune's obsessed subject. Some fans have speculated that Karen Darvin, his girlfriend at the time, inspired some of its lyrics.

Its song structure was influenced by Bo Diddley, which Springsteen has acknowledged in concert. In a live setting, Springsteen has incorporated parts of "Bo Diddley," "Who Do You Love?," and "Mona" into a medley with "She's the One." He first played the song live in October 1974.

The song was attempted several times during recording sessions for *Born to Run* in the spring of 1975. The final version was recorded in mono instead of stereo.

"Meeting Across the River"

This song's jazzy, dramatic music was the backdrop for this tale about two criminals who head into New York from New Jersey to meet up with a drug connection. The song's character—who is already in hot water with his old lady for pawning her radio—wants to catch a ride from his friend, Eddie, in search of a $2,000 payday.

Guest trumpeter Randy Brecker and upright bassist Richard Davis give the song a high-end jazz feel. Countered with Springsteen's tale of two desperate and seedy men, "Meeting Across the River"—which was originally listed as "The Heist" in early pressings of the album—has a definite film noir vibe. Eccentric singer/songwriter Tom Waits once said that he wished he had written the song.

"Jungleland"

At nine minutes and thirty-three seconds, the ambitious number that wraps up Springsteen's third album is easily the record's artistic peak. From Suki Lahav's violin introduction to the soaring yet eloquent collective achievements of the E Street Band, "Jungleland" is his very own operatic rock triumph and a brilliant close to *Born to Run.*

The song weaves the tale of "Magic Rat"—a heavy-footed hood from New York—as he courts his Jersey-based lover, the "Barefoot Girl." Before long, however, Rat has gone back to his thug life and finds himself being pursued by police on both sides of the state line. By the song's closing, she abandons Rat, and he ends up being gunned down by police. His death is met with indifference as the ambulance pulls away.

Devoted Springsteen fan Melissa Etheridge praised the song to RollingStone. com, saying, "When Bruce Springsteen does those wordless wails, like at the end of 'Jungleland,' that's the definition of rock and roll to me. He uses his whole body when he sings, and he puts out this enormous amount of force and emotion and passion."

The Praise

Upon its release, *Born to Run* was bestowed with the finest critical praise of Springsteen's career. *Creem* wrote, "Street-punk image and all, Bruce Springsteen is an American archetype," and promised it "will probably be the finest record released this year." Meanwhile, the *New York Times* asserted, "*Born to Run* seems to be one of the great records of recent years."

The *Los Angeles Times'* Robert Hilburn wrote, "He is the purest glimpse of the passion and power of rock and roll in nearly a decade," adding that the album "comes to grips with the emotional essence of rock and roll so well that I think it could give even Elvis chills."

Elsewhere, *New Times* cemented Springsteen as one of America's greatest "heroes," and *Crawdaddy* publisher Peter Knoebler penned a six-page piece he headlined, "Burning Up the Backstreets with BRUCE SPRINGSTEEN, A Star Is Born to Run."

And *Rolling Stone* heralded it as "a magnificent album that pays off in every bet ever placed on him—a '57 Chevy running on melted down Crystals records that shuts down every claim that has ever been made. And it should crack his future wide open."

The album continued to fare well with *RS* in future issues, listing it at #8 in its 1987 ranking "100 Best Albums of the Last Twenty Years." Sixteen years later, the magazine's "500 Greatest Albums of All Time" issue ranked *Born to Run* at # 18.

Breaking Through

Columbia Records propelled *Born to Run* into the upper regions of the U.S. album charts with the help of a $250,000 promotional campaign, including television commercials. The label took a two-pronged approach, working to alert the music industry and the record-buying public that Springsteen—thanks to Landau's quote—was "rock and roll's future." With massive publicity and Springsteen's first significant but critical AM radio play, the album debuted at #84 on the *Billboard* Top 200 on September 13, 1975, before jumping to #8 a week later.

On September 27 and October 4, respectively, the album held strong at #4, and by the middle of the month, Springsteen held steady at #3. During his first commercial triumph, *Born to Run* became his first gold record. As his breakthrough album, it remains one of the favorites of his catalog.

Born to Run charted again in late 1980 and in the summer of 1984 after the respective releases of *The River* and *Born in the U.S.A.* It remained on the chart for much of 1985 and went on to sell more than six million copies. The 1975 record is listed in the Library of Congress's National Recording Registry of historic recordings.

"I Hated It"

Despite all the accolades, Springsteen would be his own harshest critic when it came to *Born to Run*. With the goal of making a record where the vocals resembled Roy Orbison and the music recalled Phil Spector's finest efforts, Springsteen went back and forth with his feelings about the record.

Yes he was elated when he finally finished the album's title track. But after twelve tense months fixating over the rest of the record, he'd clearly had enough.

At one point, according to *Point Blank*, Springsteen trashed what nearly everyone else in the rock world had treasured. "I hated it," he said. "I thought it was the worst piece of garbage I'd ever heard."

The *Born to Run* Tour, Part Two

The *BTR* tour resumed on September 6, focusing on a four-week run of dates through the South and Midwest. Shows in New Orleans and the major Texas cities gave way to gigs in America's heartland.

Boz Scaggs joined Springsteen on a set-closing rendition of "Twist and Shout" at NOLA's Performing Arts Center on the trek's opening night. Midway through the tour, Bruce and the E Street Band got good news via Mike Appel—the new album was in the U.S. Top 10!

The mood was high on the road, as evidenced by the leg's final gig on October 4 at Detroit's Michigan Palace. Springsteen delivered a fiery rendition of Mitch Ryder's "Detroit Medley" and, as bootleg recordings have affirmed, a celebratory take on the Temptations' 1966 soul classic "Ain't Too Proud to Beg." The latter was a duet with Miami Steve.

No Bruce

The night after the tour opening, the E Street Band put on an extremely rare gig without the Boss at the Ya Ya Lounge in New Orleans, which was owned by Lee Dorsey. Dorsey was, of course, a popular R&B artist who had big hits in the 1960s like "Ya Ya" (U.S. #7, 1961) and "Working in the Coal Mine" (U.S. #8, 1966).

This rare, Ireland-only reissue of "Born to Run" was reproduced with unique graphics alongside singles "The Promised Land," "Hungry Heart," and "The River" as a CBS 4-pack in 1983. Due to a number of editing mistakes on the labels ("Meeting Across the River" was listed as "Meeting Across the Water," Jon Landau was credited as "V. Landay," and Miami Steve was attributed as "Steve Van Landt"), the package was quickly deleted.   *Courtesy of Lost in the Flood*

The show—which was billed as an event *without* Springsteen—was the idea of Van Zandt, who agreed to play the gig at the club in exchange for Dorsey's services on the debut Southside Johnny album he was slated to produce at the end of 1975. For the gig, Miami and the band performed a series of '50s and '60s chart favorites before backing Dorsey on a handful of his own classics.

So where was Springsteen? He and his then-girlfriend Karen Darvin had already moved along to Texas, so that he could ready himself for the next gigs on the itinerary.

The Homecoming

Returning to New Jersey as the Garden State's rock-'n'-roll hero, Springsteen was booked to play two shows on October 10 at Red Bank's Monmouth Arts Center. According to reports, the theater marquee simply read "The Homecoming."

Covers for these shows included Manfred Mann's 1966 hit "Pretty Flamingo," Gary U.S. Bonds's 1961 hit "Quarter to Three"—which would be a fixture in his live set for the rest of the 1970s—and Ike and Tina Turner's 1961 single "It's Gonna Work Out Fine."

During the second of these high-energy gigs, which boasted considerably different sets, former pianist David Sancious returned to the E Street Band for a rendition of Chuck Berry's 1958 song "Carol." The song first achieved mainstream fame when it was covered by the Beatles in 1963 and the Rolling Stones in 1964.

Among those in the crowd were Springsteen's cousin Frankie, who taught him his first guitar chords, and members of the Castiles.

The Roxy

On October 16, Springsteen began a four-night, six-show run of gigs at the Roxy in Los Angeles. That first night, however, he was evidently unaware that Columbia Records had bought up the majority of the tickets for West Coast media people, industry movers and shakers, and Hollywood celebrities.

As the show progressed, the lack of crowd reaction tipped Springsteen off to the fact that this wasn't his core audience. He was playing to Jack Nicholson, Warren Beatty, Cher, Gregg Allman, Ryan O'Neal, Neil Diamond, Wolfman Jack, Jimmy Connors, Phil Spector, David Bowie, George Harrison and Carole King.

In homage to King, who cowrote many of the songs that Springsteen loved in his formative years, he dedicated a cover of her 1966 song "Goin' Back"—which was recorded by both Dusty Springfield and the Byrds—to her. The crowd was in awe.

Although being in the presence of celebrities made Springsteen uncomfortable, the first Roxy gig made him a superstar. Bob Dylan and Mick Jagger were now among his fans.

Despite the rapturous reception, he felt the night could have gone better. "For something to happen, you have to be loose," he would tell *Playboy* for its January 1976 issue. "You have to take risks, be willing to make a fool of yourself. Then it flows. Tonight wasn't bad, but we can be twice that good. You should see us when we're hot."

After the show, Jack Nicholson—a graduate of Neptune High School—is seen in the Rainbow Bar chatting for hours with Garry Tallent, also an NHS alum. During their stay in L.A., the E Street Band took an obligatory trip to Disneyland.

Dissed by Stills

Not everyone in Hollywood was backing Springsteen in October 1975. For instance, Stephen Stills—of Buffalo Springfield and Crosby, Stills, Nash and Young fame—wasn't convinced he was all that special.

"Bruce is good, but he's not that different from a lot of people," Stills said that year. "He's nowhere near as good as his hype."

Coping with Fame

Although Springsteen was becoming more and more famous each day, he was having a difficult time with stardom—and confessed that it was depressing.

"I haven't changed, but things around me have," he acknowledged to the *Los Angeles Times* the week of the Roxy shows. "I'm not sure what it all means yet. I haven't had time to sit down and decide what's new that's fun and what's new that's not."

Upon first observing a billboard for *Born to Run* atop a Sunset Boulevard building during that same trip west, Springsteen's initial, excited reaction was quickly supplanted by a feeling of uneasiness.

Yet for all the accolades and the pressures, his philosophy regarding his live gigs was unaffected. Famous or not, when he took the stage, he always had something to prove. The kids in the crowd would know it if he wasn't putting his heart and soul into his shows. As always, he did so the night of October 17, when his show at the Roxy was simulcast to millions of listeners on FM rock stations across the United States.

Meeting Dylan

With a five-day break before his next gig at the Paramount Theater in Portland, Oregon, Bruce flew back to New York to attend the surprise sixty-first birthday party of Gerde's Folk City owner Mike Porco. Porco—who booked Bob Dylan into his first Greenwich Village gigs in 1961—played a key role in the rise of the New York folk movement.

Dylan showed up with Joan Baez, various members of his upcoming Rolling Thunder Revue, and a film crew. Springsteen and Dylan were introduced, and they joined forces for a rendition of "Happy Birthday" for Porco. It has also been suggested that Dylan offered Springsteen an opportunity to join him on the road as part of the Rolling Thunder Revue.

Springsteen wound up turning down Dylan's offer because he had his own touring obligations. Besides, taking Dylan up on his offer would mean that Springsteen wouldn't be able to bring his own band along.

Time and *Newsweek*

On October 27, 1975, *Time* and *Newsweek* ran their infamous cover stories on Bruce Springsteen. Coordinated by Mike Appel, Springsteen looked at the covers with amazement and disbelief. At just twenty-six, he was, in his own words, just a simple guy. As he marveled to Hilburn in 1975, "I'm not the president."

The dueling covers began when Bob Altschuler, the vice president of publicity at CBS, called Appel to inform him that *Newsweek* wanted to do an article on Springsteen. But because *Time* had already written about Springsteen in a recent earlier issue, Appel told Altschuler that he was only interested if they put him on the cover. Appel thought that would be the end of it until Altschuler called back a week later to notify him that he had, in fact, gotten word from *Newsweek*. Barring a significant news event, Springsteen would be featured on the cover.

Appel was in disbelief when he called Springsteen to tell him. Although he was caught completely off guard, he hesitantly agreed. While writer Maureen Orth got to work on her story about Springsteen—whom she would dub "the great white hope of rock and roll"—Appel and Altschuler had begun conspiring to get their client on the cover of *Time*.

"Just tell them *Newsweek* gave him the cover and we want to talk to them as well," Appel told Altschuler. "We don't have anything to lose right now, so all we can get told is to go screw ourselves," Appel remembered in *Down Thunder Road*. He then called Springsteen to share the news that a *Time* cover was also in the works. Springsteen again resisted until Appel convinced him that if they could pull this off, they would know he had "made it."

Appel had convinced the editors at *Time* to put Springsteen on the cover by berating them. At the time they were considering putting New York City's Mayor Beame on the cover until Appel abruptly but effectively told them by phone, "You'll eventually have to put [Bruce] on your cover. Right now you have a chance to be visionaries. Six months from now you're functionaries."

En route to Los Angeles ahead of the Roxy shows, *Time* writer Jay Cocks—who was a friend of Jon Landau's—accompanied Springsteen and the E Street Band and conducted all of his interviews on the five-hour 747 flight. The end result was a glowing feature that offered a different perspective from Orth's piece, "Making of a Rock Star."

The Hype

As *Newsweek* explained, Bruce Springsteen was already experiencing "superstar culture shock" when Orth first met with him. Denying that he was any kind of phenomenon, he told her that "the hype just gets in the way."

When both cover stories hit newsstands that same October day, which was a feat that neither Elvis Presley, the Beatles, or the Rolling Stones had accomplished, Springsteen felt as if he was losing control of his career. Instead of celebrating, he was taking it hard.

In a subsequent interview with Ray Coleman, he balked at all of the mainstream PR, saying that the publicity "made me look like I'd come up from nowhere."

Some critics began to ponder whether his ascent was genuine or if it was the net result of record company promotional tactics. In the *New York Times*, music critic Henry Edwards wrote, "Springsteen's lyrics are an effusive jumble. His melodies either second-hand or undistinguished and his performance tedious. Given such flaws there has to be another important ingredient to the success of Bruce Springsteen: namely, vigorous promotion."

Even if it wasn't entirely untrue, such suggestions really bothered Springsteen. He was also upset over Columbia's heavy promotion of Landau's quote, and ultimately believed that publicizing him as "the future of rock" was a very big mistake.

"I felt the thing I wanted most in my life—my music—being swept away, and I didn't know if I could do anything about it," he told Coleman. For a while, in the final quarter of 1975, Springsteen was a miserable superstar.

No More Interviews

Miami Steve sought to downplay his friend's frustrations to a *Playboy* scribe with a sense of humor; it appeared as if the hype was leaving a negative impression not just on the Boss but also on the members of his E Street Band. "With these two stories, everybody's gonna be asking us what it's like to be a phenomenon. I don't even know how to spell the word. Is that with a P or an F? There are journalists hanging around [Asbury Park] interviewing our friends. Record scouts hunting for the Asbury Park sound. We gotta live there, too, you know."

Meanwhile, Springsteen put Appel on notice. He wasn't doing any more interviews. And with the exception of a couple that he had scheduled to promote his European debut performances, he stuck to his guns for the rest of the year.

Tearing It Up

Upon the E Street Band's arrival in London in mid-November 1975 for a handful of European shows to promote *Born to Run*, Springsteen was very much on edge about the state of his career. He unexpectedly lost his temper upon arrival at the Hammersmith Odeon in London when he saw posters in and around the venue that proclaimed, "At Last London Is Ready for Bruce Springsteen." He tore as many of them down as he could in a fit of rage.

Springsteen was so upset that he very nearly canceled the November 18 show. He ordered buttons that read "I have seen the future of rock and roll at the Hammersmith Odeon" be destroyed.

"It was nothin' to do with the place," he said of his reaction to the posters in 1985's *Springsteen*. "It was me. It was the inside world. It's a hard thing to explain, but I learned a lot about my strengths and weaknesses in those days, especially on that particular night."

This show—which was originally planned for a live radio broadcast but canceled at the last minute when Mike Appel feared Springsteen's tirade might result in an inferior performance—was in fact filmed. The complete show was included on DVD in the 2005 30th anniversary box set of *Born to Run*.

Springsteen also played gigs at Konserthus in Stockholm, Sweden, on November 21, RAI Amsterdam on November 23, and another show at the Hammersmith Odeon on November 24 before returning to the United States for a month of East Coast sell-out dates.

You Better Not Pout

On December 2, 1975, Bruce and the E Street Band played the first of two shows at Boston Music Hall. These gigs marked the live debut of "Santa Claus Is Coming to Town," a song that would be recorded later in the month and rush-released to rock radio as a promotional recording. Days later, on December 5, Springsteen, Clemons, and Van Zandt cut a pair of Christmas messages for Bethesda, Maryland, rock station WHFS, en route to a three-night stand at Georgetown University.

Shows at Bucknell and Seton Hall led up to the famed performance of "Santa Claus," which was tracked live at C. W. Post College on Long Island on December 17. By the time Springsteen and the group got to Kleinhans Music Hall in Buffalo, they had shifted to a new Christmas nugget, performing "Here Comes Santa Claus" instead. Although it was well received, Springsteen reverted back to the former during shows Canadian shows just days before the holiday.

Recorded live at C. W. Post College in December 1975, Springsteen's version of "Santa Claus Is Coming to Town" was immediately serviced to rock radio for the holiday and became an instant favorite. The song was given this promotional pressing in 1981 when it was commercially released on a CBS charity album in 1981 and as an official Springsteen B-side as the flip of "My Hometown" in 1985.

Courtesy of 991.com

Guest DJs

In Philadelphia after Christmas to play a four-night, sold-out stand at the Tower Theatre, Springsteen, Van Zandt, Tallent, and Federici dropped in on old friend Ed Sciaky during his air shift at WMMR-FM. Taking over the airwaves, the E Street Band broke with the increasingly predictable album rock format to spin records by the Drifters, Sam and Dave, Van Morrison's Them, Buddy Holly, Sam Cooke, and Otis Redding.

Although it never materializes, Springsteen's show on December 30—the third of the four-night run in Upper Darby—was recorded for a potential live album.

Havin' a Party

With 1975 behind them, Springsteen, Van Zandt, and Bittan returned home to the Jersey Shore from Philly to take in the New Year's Day evening concert by Southside Johnny and the Asbury Jukes at the Stone Pony.

Springsteen and Bittan joined in on several numbers, while Van Zandt played a more significant role with his former band. After all, he was slated to produce Southside's upcoming debut LP for Epic Records.

One Hell of a Year

By the end of December 1975, *Born to Run* had sold 1.2 million copies, and Bruce Springsteen was a household name. In an interview with *Business Week* in early 1976, Bruce Lundvall—who had just replaced Segelstein as the head of Columbia—gave his thoughts on how it happened.

"You don't go right to the public to sell a new performer," Lundvall said. "You sell him to your own company first, then to the trade, and then to the record buyers."

Meanwhile, Springsteen—who had technically earned around $190,000 in 1975—plunked down a piece of his earnings on his infamous black 1960 Corvette. But at the time, his life had little room for a lot of possessions.

"I throw out almost everything I ever own," he told *Melody Maker* in late '75. "I don't believe in collecting anything. The less you have to lose, the better you are, because the more chances you'll take. The more you've got, the worse off you get."

14

Runaway American Dream

By late March 1976—just as combined sales for the *Born to Run* album and its respective singles had generated $1.25 million in royalties for Laurel Canyon—things were becoming increasingly strained between Springsteen and Appel.

Despite the *Time* and *Newsweek* covers, Bruce Springsteen was hardly a wealthy star—he had just three grand in the bank. Rightfully, he couldn't help but wonder why he hadn't gotten his cut of the loot.

To make matters worse, Appel had gone to Columbia in November 1975 to ask for a $500,000 advance—which was sanctioned by the label and made payable to Laurel Canyon. When he learned about this payout, Springsteen became incensed that Appel had kept the money—of which he believed the bulk belonged to him.

Shrewdly, Appel tried to use Springsteen's share of the advance as a means to manipulate his only client to re-sign with him, promising more favorable terms than his original deal. But his plan backfired by midsummer 1976 when Springsteen—now fully resentful of the Laurel Canyon head—sought counsel and fired him.

Landau's Coup

Although Jon Landau didn't become Springsteen's official manager until 1978, Mike Appel's initial suspicions about the one-time *Rolling Stone* editor turned out to be true. As Springsteen's closest confidant, Landau was staging a coup that began during the *Born to Run* sessions and took noticeable form with the *Newsweek* cover story. It was no secret that Landau—who was friends with reporter Maureen Orth—was consulted heavily for the article.

The five-page cover article mistakenly named Landau as Springsteen's manager. Whether he cited himself in that role to Orth, she made the assumption on her own, or it was a bona-fide editing error, the story left an unforgiving Appel royally pissed. As lines became drawn, Appel did everything in his power to keep Landau from producing Springsteen's fourth studio album.

Springsteen's Contract

According to Appel, he always intended to renegotiate with Springsteen when he became a star. But his desire to have Springsteen sign on with him again under new terms prompted the performer—who had become more and more distrusting of Appel—to take a close look at the original deal. He didn't like what he read.

En route to San Mateo for a family visit that winter, Springsteen touched down in Los Angeles, where Landau was producing sessions for Jackson Browne's *The Pretender*. Landau met him at the airport, and the two went to a restaurant to look over the paperwork. Landau told him that the deal—especially the fifty-fifty money split—was downright awful.

During the conversation, Springsteen explained to Landau how Appel was holding onto his share of the $500,000 advance as leverage to force him to sign with Laurel Canyon again. If he didn't accept the proposed contract, Appel insisted he would hold the artist to the letter of the original paperwork.

That struck Landau as a bullying tactic and a conflict of interest. When Springsteen discovered his royalty rate on his first two records—three points on retail—was the same as Landau's agreement to merely produce Browne's latest, he flipped out. He wanted an attorney.

Lawyered Up

On Landau's recommendation, Springsteen had attorney Mike Mayer look over his contracts. The first thing Mayer struggled with was Appel's involvement in so many areas of Springsteen's career. Mayer wondered how, as his manager and his producer, Appel could have the best financial interest of his client in mind.

Landau also recommended Springsteen team with Mike Tannen, a music business adviser and lawyer who counted Paul Simon as a client and had, at times, managed artists. Tannen stepped up and agreed to help Springsteen tighten up his business affairs.

Saying No to Appel

Springsteen began turning down a lot of the proposals that Appel threw at him throughout 1976. In January, for instance, when Springsteen was low on dough, Appel came to him and pitched a radio special that would help raise $250,000. Springsteen said no.

Later, Craig Electronics approached Appel with an opportunity for the Boss to star in his own, one-hour, prime-time concert special on NBC Television. Springsteen could be as experimental as he wanted, and the appearance would earn him a cool million bucks. He said no. The special ultimately went to Bob Dylan, who had initially been approached but held out for more money.

In the spring, Appel had managed to book Springsteen as the only U.S. artist at the closing concert of the 1976 Summer Olympic Games in Montreal. He passed on the opportunity for singular, global exposure.

Another idea Appel hatched, for a summer tent tour, was quashed by Springsteen. The plan was to travel around North America with a 6,000-capacity tent, free of unions, that Springsteen's crew would pitch on college campuses. With the tent being waterproof, run on generators, and with air conditioning, Appel's plan seemed strong at first. But after speaking about it with Appel, Springsteen realized the heat, the mud, and a ton of other potential disasters made it a stupid idea.

Finally, Philadelphia concert promoter Larry Magid approached Appel with an idea that would earn Springsteen a million bucks tax free. All he'd need to do was headline a one-day, Fourth of July "New Jersey Bands" concert at JFK Stadium. But Springsteen was still a decade away from playing stadium concerts, and after he witnessed giant prog-rockers Yes play the same venue without video monitors, he declined the offer. He couldn't see the stage from the back of the stadium and knew, whatever the payout, he just couldn't put his hard-working fans through such an inferior concert experience.

When asked about turning down these opportunities later in the year, Springsteen—according to *Down Thunder Road*—said, "I can make twenty bucks for dropping my pants on Broadway, too, but I don't do it."

A Formal Accounting

In March, Mayer sent a formal request to Appel that demanded an accounting of all monies due Springsteen. Two weeks later, Appel sent the breakdown of outstanding bills and owed salaries.

According to Laurel Canyon in a letter sent to Mayer two weeks later, Springsteen was owed $76,000 less two weeks salaries for his road crew, or $6,150.00, and outstanding bills of $38,450. He had merely $31,400 coming to him.

In a letter dated March 23, Mayer—acting on behalf of Springsteen—demanded full payment of $45,000, which also included his $14,000 retainer fee.

Dad Advice

That same month it was looking as if there might be an agreement between Springsteen and Appel after all. Bruce had suggested they tear up the old contracts and work off of a handshake agreement.

Springsteen was willing to forgive Appel for taking advantage of him when he was a naïve kid if he could agree to new terms. In addition to some financial corrections, Springsteen wanted all of his publishing back, which Appel was apparently considering.

A few days later, however, Appel had changed his tune. Suddenly he was against the handshake agreement, which angered Springsteen. Why wouldn't Appel take him at his word?

In meetings with Mayer, Appel balked about the drastic reduction in his percentages and the notion of having Landau continue to produce Bruce's records. He also only wanted to give Springsteen back half of his publishing, retroactive to *Greetings.*

Appel was acting on the advice of his father—who told him to stick to his guns. In doing so, he walked away from his last chance to make up with Springsteen. It would later prove to be the biggest mistake of Mike's management career.

Locking Out Appel

The last week of March, Springsteen sent Appel a letter advising him that he had formally obtained legal representation. He let Appel know that he had informed his record company of his claim for outstanding unpaid royalties in the amount of $153,000. Springsteen's lawyers had requested that said CBS royalties be held in a provisional account until Laurel Canyon had paid the $45,000 he was due.

More importantly, Springsteen advised Appel that he was hitting the road that month for three months of tour dates. He offered Laurel Canyon a 15 percent commission to be paid upon receipt of the $45,000. He advised Appel that this agreement—which Appel quickly signed—did not imply that any other disputes had been resolved.

Although he signed the interim agreement, Appel never received his commissions for the tour, which were held by Springsteen's accountant. Springsteen would later attest that Mike got what he deserved. "It is like this, man," Springsteen would later explain. "Somebody stabs you in the fucking eye and you stab them in the fucking eye."

Meanwhile, he had inked with Premier Talent—the Frank Barsalona–led company that once booked tours for the Beatles—and landed a $100,000 advance to keep his organization afloat.

If that wasn't enough, the $153,000 royalty payment from CBS went directly to Springsteen's accountant. Appel had become completely closed off from his client.

Saying No to Marsh

Above all else, Springsteen felt he deserved to own his songs. When he found out that he needed to get Appel's permission so that music writer Dave Marsh could publish the lyrics from "Born to Run" in his planned book of the same name, he called Appel to make the request.

Appel, who had been left out of all things related to Springsteen business by May 1976, told Springsteen to forget it, unless he wanted to consider reteaming under a new deal. Due to the legal troubles that would ensue, Marsh held up publishing the book until 1979.

After this experience, Springsteen became determined to get controlling interest in his publishing back no matter how long it might take. It was his art. Nobody else deserved to tell him where and when he could reproduce it.

Yetnikoff Sides with His Star

In addition to legal and financial guidance, Springsteen also met with Walter Yetnikoff, the head of CBS, without Appel's knowledge in the early summer of '76. Yetnikoff made clear that his allegiance was with Springsteen. The label head knew that the contract was a poor one and that he would step in and mediate if necessary.

Yetnikoff also told Springsteen that an artist who sells a million records ought to get at least a half million dollars at minimum and that the company was willing to renegotiate. More than anything, Columbia wanted a new studio album and urged Springsteen to get to work. Via Jimmy Iovine, Bruce arranged for studio time, anticipating Landau would be done working with Jackson Browne—whose own sessions were marred by his wife's suicide—and be back in New York by August.

Appel Sticks Out His Chest

On July 2, 1976, Appel contacted CBS Records' executive Bruce Lundvall to inform him that he was aware that Jon Landau had been selected to produce the next Springsteen record with the label's blessing. In his letter, which was also sent to Yetnikoff and Bruce, he advised the company that Landau had no authority to assume that role.

Appel cited the agreements between Laurel Canyon, Ltd. and CBS, signed June 9, 1972, and his contract with Springsteen. He explained that he wanted to work with the company in accordance with its agreements.

Appel was making it clear that he had contractual control of Springsteen's next record and wanted Landau to have no part of the next project. In Springsteen's copy of the letter, Appel enclosed a personalized note advising him to live up to his contractual obligations.

The Beverly Wilshire

After being out of contact with Springsteen and his new handlers for nearly three months, Mike Appel and his wife ran into Springsteen and the E Street Band during a trip to Los Angeles in late July. Appel walked onto the back patio at the Beverly Wilshire Hotel and was stunned to find the members of the E Street Band and members of the Asbury Jukes lounging poolside during a trip to CBS Records' Annual Sales Convention.

Although Springsteen had already planned to go ahead with a lawsuit against his manager, he gave no hint of it as they exchanged pleasantries like they were old friends. If the rest of the band—most obviously Miami Steve—acted awkwardly surprised, Springsteen was his same old usual self. He sat down to chat cordially with Appel and his wife for a spell. A few days later, on July 27, Springsteen took the first formal step to get Appel out of his life when he filed suit against him.

Bruce's Lawsuit

Springsteen named Mike Appel, Laurel Canyon Management Inc., Laurel Canyon Ltd., and Laurel Canyon Music Inc. in his lawsuit. He alleged "Fraud, Undue Influence and Breach of Trust," in which he claimed—according to *Down Thunder Road*—that Appel falsely represented himself as "knowledgeable in business affairs generally, and in the entertainment business in particular; that he was a capable and experienced contract negotiator and business affairs administrator; that he was a person of good character."

The lawsuit also accused Appel of breach of contracts and failing to render an accounting of any nature until Springsteen forced his hand via Mayer. Documents filed alleged Appel "conducted business in a shockingly slipshod, wasteful and neglectful manner."

If that wasn't enough, the suit also contended Appel had misappropriated funds and withheld Springsteen's copyrighted material from author Dave Marsh against the rocker's wishes. Springsteen sought $1 million in compensatory and punitive damages.

Appel's Countersuit

A stunned Appel reviewed the suit with his attorney, Leonard Marks, that same day. Marks told the manager/producer that he should forget any notion of making amends with Springsteen. Their professional relationship was over.

Appel handed over his original contracts, agreed to Leonard's retainer, and—two days later—countersued Springsteen, CBS Inc., and Jon Landau in New York Supreme Court. His suit sought to uphold his contractual right to name Springsteen's producers for the duration of the agreement.

Appel also intended to place an injunction against the record label to prevent Landau from producing Bruce's fourth album and—by naming Landau directly—block him from producing any Springsteen records during the length of their deal.

Yetnikoff Stands by Bruce

Not long after the countersuit documents were served, Appel got a phone call from Walter Yetnikoff. Yetnikoff told him that, regardless of what his legal claim suggested, CBS was moving forward with plans to track a Springsteen album with Landau.

In a certified letter sent to Appel in advance of Springsteen's suit, CBS—via its attorneys—made it clear that it wanted to stay neutral. The difficulties between Appel and his client, the letter insisted, had nothing to do with CBS Records.

During their brief phone conversation, Appel told Yetnikoff that he had no intentions of allowing it. He meant it.

On August 4, CBS sent another certified letter to Appel letting him know that as a result of his legal action against Springsteen, Landau, and the label, it was obvious he would no longer be able to furnish a new recording by Springsteen as required.

Appel Is Fired

On August 4, Springsteen—via his attorneys—officially discharged Appel. In a certified letter sent to Laurel Canyon's offices, Appel was informed that Springsteen had rescinded all agreements with him related to personal management, recording, and music publishing based on his fraud and breach of trust. Appel's improper accounting of Springsteen's income and expenses were named in the letter. The document also described certain elements of Appel's conduct as "tortuous in nature."

Fein

Five days later, Marks filed a motion on behalf of Laurel Canyon in New York State Supreme Court, seeking a preliminary injunction to prevent Springsteen and CBS from recording new music unless the plaintiff [Appel] either produced or designated the producer for the project. Marks cited the March 1972 agreements between Bruce and Appel and the agreement between Laurel Canyon and CBS from June 9, 1972.

Judge Arnold L. Fein ultimately honored the injunction, which prevented Springsteen from breaching the agreement. Springsteen would need Appel to approve of any recording he was going to make.

After the injunction was granted, in early September, CBS began backpedaling. A letter sent to Appel, the company's executive vice president, Walter Dean, wrote, "In light of what promises to be a protracted dispute between you and Bruce Springsteen, we withdraw our exercise of the option [to record the fourth album with Landau]."

That same month, Springsteen's lawyers appealed the decision, but they lost in the Appellate Courts. It was a unanimous five-to-none decision in favor of Fein's injunction.

Adele Tries to Patch Things Up

Into the fall of 1976 and winter of 1977, CBS encouraged the parties to come to a settlement. The label feared that a prolonged dispute would diminish Springsteen's presence among the fickle record-buying public.

Perhaps the sweetest and most innocent gesture in the movement to try and get Appel and Springsteen to reach an amicable agreement came from Adele. Mrs. Springsteen sent Appel a letter and a book called *Legal and Business Problems of the Record Industry Workshop*. Speaking in *Down Thunder Road*, Appel marveled, "It's just what a good mother would do to get her 'boys' back together again!" Of course, after all the depositions and mud-throwing, it was way too late for that.

The Settlement

Unhappy with the outcome under Mayer's direction, Springsteen aligned with a new attorney in November by the name of Peter Parcher. Under Parcher's guidance, the legal battle between Bruce and Appel dragged out until a settlement was reached on June 1, 1977. According to Leonard Marks, once Appel finally realized that he could never reestablish his relationship with Springsteen, he waved the white flag.

Although the courts had been in Appel's favor, the public sided with Springsteen, effectively ruining his career in artist management. Appel took his settlement, which equated to a pair of payouts in late 1977 and early 1978 in the amount of $350,000 each.

BILL GRAHAM PRESENTS

AN EVENING WITH
BRUCE SPRINGSTEEN
AND THE E STREET BAND~
SATURDAY, OCTOBER 2, 1976, 8:00 PM. PARAMOUNT THEATRE, Oakland. Tickets: $5.50, $6.50, $7.50. Available at BASS and the Paramount Box Office (465-6400).

There is a 60c computer charge on all advance BASS sales. Tickets available at the following BASS outlets: Bill Graham's 1333 Columbus, San Francisco and Bill Graham's Hayward, 22451 Foothill Blvd., Hayward; all Pacific Stereo Stores in No. Calif. & Reno; Liberty House, S.F.; Bullocks in Palo Alto and Cupertino; ASUC; San Jose Box Office; Odyssey, Santa Cruz & Livermore; Banana Records, Fremont; Eastmont Mall, Oakland For BASS information and reservations dial T·E·L·E·T·I·X.

A poster for the E Street Band's October 1976 gig in Oakland, California, this show was part of Springsteen's "Lawsuit" tour. Although it was designed to keep the organization afloat while he sorted out his legal predicament with Mike Appel, it didn't stop Springsteen from fleshing out his sound with the added expense of his own brass section, the Miami Horns.
Courtesy of Robert Rodriguez

Aside from the $700,000, he also retained royalties on the first three records and 25 percent of the publishing on those albums. In 1983, in desperate need of cash, Appel sold his rights back to Bruce for $425,000. The following year he sold the production rights to Springsteen for an undisclosed sum. By this time, he and Springsteen were on speaking terms again.

The Depositions

In depositions that took place in August and November 1976, a lot of interesting information was disclosed. Here are some of the key revelations:

1. Springsteen admitted that he never looked at his contracts. "That's my problem," he disclosed in a deposition on August 16, 1976. "I never looked at Mike Appel, and I found out that I don't own a fucking thing that I wrote."

2. Bruce felt he had been swindled, telling Appel's attorney Leonard Marks, "I wrote 'Born to Run,' every line of that fucking song is me and no line of that fucking song is his. I don't own it. I can't print it on a piece of paper if I wanted to. I have been cheated."

3. Bruce was loyal and grateful to the E Street Band's members for the sacrifices they made early on and assured Appel's lawyers they were not prima donnas. In one meeting he recounted how his band once slept in Jimmy Cretecos's mother's attic. On another occasion they slept in houses that stunk from cat feces.

4. Springsteen revealed what he earned between 1973 and 1975. He started off with $35 per week, which jumped to $50, and to $75 and $100. By 1975, he and the band made $200 weekly, which had jumped to $350 weekly by 1976.

5. In 1974, Springsteen acquired a $5,000 piano—which was considered extravagant for the time. He balked that although Appel arranged for him to have it, he did not buy it for him. In the words of the Boss, who used the instrument to write much of the material on *Born to Run,* "I paid for it with my own money."

6. According to Springsteen, Appel promised him two additional points on *Born to Run* for producing the record, but never listed it on the accounting he received from Laurel Canyon in March 1976.

7. In October 1975, Springsteen had been asked by Dr. Pepper's advertising agency, Young and Rubicam, to consider a future television collaboration.

8. When asked why he turned down the tent tour that Appel had proposed, Springsteen snapped at Marks, "You want to do law in a tent? I will not play my guitar in a tent."

The Springsteen Clause

In the wake of the legal wrangling between CBS and Mike Appel, record companies began to alter their traditional agreements to specify that—should there be a disagreement between the independent producer or production company and the recording act—the label has the right to deal directly with the talent. The independent producer would still be entitled to royalties, but he or she would have no power to stop the artist from recording new music.

Springsteen on Appel

A year after the resolution, Springsteen—who was often mum on the subject—did open up about the suit to Hilburn during his 1978 tour. "What it all came down to was principle. He worked hard for a long time—we all worked hard—and he sacrificed and, okay, he deserved something for it. But what I wanted was the thing itself: my songs . . . ."

15

I Got the Radio on, and I'm Just Killing Time

1976–1977

Despite his legal wrangles with Mike Appel, which kept him out of the studio for all of 1976 and much of 1977, this was an active period for the Boss. He headlined three successful U.S. tour legs and collaborated live with a number of out side artists, including Gary U.S. Bonds and Patti Smith.

He also provided some covert help to friends who were working in the studio, including Southside Johnny and the Asbury Jukes and Ronnie Spector. Those loyalties aside, Springsteen began to think about his next studio album and knew that just as he had changed since the unveiling of *Born to Run*, his music, too, would undergo a shift.

Boss Acres

In early 1976, Springsteen established a new residence in Holmdel. Located across the Parkway from the Garden State Arts Center and adjacent to the Bell Labs facility known as "Telegraph Hill," the big white farm house was the focal point of the property. Before long, the members of his band and crew would call it "Boss Acres," while Springsteen would ultimately prefer to name it "Thrill Hill."

It was fifteen miles from Asbury Park, the city he helped make famous a few years earlier. Toney Holmdel was certainly a world away from that shoddy Shore town, but close enough if he needed a beer, a little nightlife, or felt compelled to take part in an unplanned jam session.

Although the farm, which was a rental, was sparsely furnished at first and had seen better days, the peeling, white 1930s house had more comforts than Springsteen had ever known. Replete with a pool, a top-notch stereo, a barn, and a horse stable, the house inspired Springsteen to become an equestrian soon after he moved in.

With his motorcycle, a new pickup truck, and his vintage 1960 Corvette out in front, "Boss Acres" was home. It would become the place where Springsteen would shape some of his most enduring songs.

Standing Up for Southside

The U.S. Bicentennial Year got underway with Springsteen helping Van Zandt—who was producing and playing guitar on Southside Johnny and the Asbury Jukes' Epic debut. When the record, titled *I Don't Want to Go Home*, was released that May, it boasted Springsteen credits on "You Mean So Much to Me" and "The Fever"—the two tunes he wrote for the record.

Elsewhere, Clarence Clemons added the bass vocal on the latter under the nom de rock "Selmon T. Sachs." As the project's producer/guitarist, Van Zandt wrote the memorable title cut and another number, "Sweeter Than Honey," overseeing the sessions at the Record Plant that winter.

Springsteen also penned the liner notes for Southside's debut. Remembering their years bonding together at the Upstage, he wrote, "It's time to speak the names of the lost soldiers, 'cause the music on this album—Johnny's music—is something that grew out of those friendships and the long summer nights when there was no particular place to go and nothing to do . . . except play."

When the time came to help get the word out about the Jukes' first long player, Springsteen did all he could, playing with the group at the Stone Pony on many occasions. When Southside Johnny took the stage over Memorial Day weekend 1976 at the Stone Pony—where his group had previously been the house band—the E Street Band was there to show support.

The concert, which was hosted by Philadelphia's FM powerhouse WMMR and simulcast live on May 30 to regional East Coast radio stations, drew participation from Clemons, Weinberg, Steve Van Zandt, former Ronette Ronnie Spector, and Springsteen, who helped close the event with "Havin' a Party."

Hangin' with King

On March 7, Springsteen was tapped to sing with one of his childhood heroes when Carole King—who wrote or cowrote a number of 1960s classics including the Shirelles' 1961 chart-topper "Will You Love Me Tomorrow" and the Monkees' 1967 classic "Pleasant Valley Sunday," among countless others—headlined the Beacon Theatre.

Springsteen performed a duet of King's own "Loco-Motion" during her encore. King, of course, is best known for her landmark 1971 album *Tapestry*, which has sold more than twenty-five million copies.

Chicken Scratch

Four days after the E Street Band's invite-only dress rehearsal at the Stone Pony, Springsteen launched the second leg of the *Born to Run* tour. The trek—which was conducted without Mike Appel's involvement—went fairly smoothly.

Because of its at times illogical tour routing and attention to tertiary concert markets, the six-week run of dates became known as the Chicken Scratch tour by

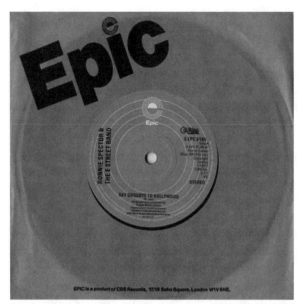

Produced by Steve Van Zandt, this cover of Billy Joel's 1976 song "Say Goodbye to Hollywood" was billed to Ronnie Spector and the E Street Band. Although the Boss plays guitar on the track, he wasn't officially credited because of his then-ongoing suit with Mike Appel.   *Courtesy of Lost in the Flood*

the band and crew. Launching in Columbia, South Carolina, on March 25, the trek closed in mid-May in New Orleans.

In addition to staples from *Born to Run* and favorites from his back catalog, Springsteen continued to enjoy performing rock-'n'-roll classics like "Raise Your Hand," Gary U.S. Bonds's "Quarter to Three," Mitch Ryder's "Detroit Medley," The Isley Brothers/Beatles classic "Twist and Shout," Manfred Mann's "Pretty Flamingo," and his favorite teenage anthem, the Animals' "It's My Life."

As part of his onstage shtick, and a visual comment on his lengthy gigs, Bruce was often carted offstage on a stretcher during the finale. In keeping with his work ethic, he would always return for another encore.

At times, venues sold out quickly—as was the case with gigs at Virginia Tech and a hastily planned show at Ovens Auditorium in Charlotte that was announced just five days before its date. But other performances, especially in Deep South cities, were a bust. In Tennessee locales like Johnson City, Knoxville, and Chattanooga, Springsteen only sold around a thousand tickets each in venues that held three and a half times that.

He may have been a magazine cover star, but his sales didn't always show it. A surprise 5,000-seat sellout at Birmingham's Boutwell Auditorium aside, shows in Little Rock and Shreveport were the biggest flops of the tour, with 600 and 300 respective seats sold.

Forgetting Max

With such a sparsely attended gig, it's no wonder that Springsteen wanted to leave Chattanooga behind. In a hurry to split, the E Street Band's tour bus made it an hour out of the city, en route to its next show in Nashville, when the group realized Max Weinberg was missing. He caught up with them that night.

Choate Charity

At the request of John Hammond, Springsteen agreed to play a private school benefit in Wallingford, Connecticut, two weeks into the tour. If the confines of the snooty boarding school known as Choate Rosemary Hall left Springsteen feeling out of his element, he was comforted by the fact that some of his core fans—including Philadelphia DJ Ed Sciaky—made the three-hour journey north to support him.

Behind the first few rows of loyalists rocking out to "Thunder Road" and "Rosalita" were faculty, students, and family who were there to support the pricey prep school.

Rockin' Opryland

If the Byrds were the first rock group to play the Grand Ole Opry, the fact that they took the Ryman Theater stage in 1968 while in the city recording their country-rock classic *Sweetheart of the Rodeo* practically negates that fact. Arguably, the E Street Band was the first bona-fide rock-'n'-roll outfit to gig at the Opry and clearly the first to perform at the facility's then-new home inside Opryland USA Theme Park.

Although the show wasn't a sellout, the 4,500-seat auditorium was two-thirds full, affirming that there was a substantial Springsteen following in the Music City in the spring of '76.

Calling Elvis

Following his April 29 performance at the Ellis Auditorium in Memphis, Springsteen, Van Zandt, and CBS publicist Glen Brunman took a cab for a late dinner. After midnight, the cab driver recommended a place near Graceland. But when the cabbie mentioned the estate of Springsteen's boyhood idol Elvis Presley, he forgot all about food.

"I saw a light on," Springsteen told Philadelphia DJ Ed Sciaky two years later. "And I say, 'I gotta find out if he's home, Steve.' So I jumped over the wall, a stone wall. And the cabdriver is going, 'Man, there's dogs in there. You're gonna get it. You're gonna be in trouble.'"

Although Springsteen never got the opportunity to meet the King, he did make it to the front door, where he knocked and knocked. But his hopes of jamming with the "Hound Dog" bard in his estate's notorious Jungle Room were dashed when Presley's security escorted him out. When Springsteen tried to explain that he too was famous, the guard told him that he was sorry but Elvis was in Lake Tahoe.

Rockin' the Cadets

Two weeks after the Chicken Scratch tour wrapped, Springsteen accepted a pair of lucrative military gigs. The first took place at the U.S. Military Academy at West Point in New York State. At a performance before an audience of cadets on May 27, some civilians were granted tickets, but they were relegated to the back of Eisenhower Hall, behind the Academy attendees, who were pretty motionless in their dress whites.

The next night, the E Street Band took the stage at the U.S. Naval Academy in Annapolis, Maryland. Fittingly, the show marked the inclusion of a rousing encore as Springsteen led the group through Frankie Ford's 1959 hit "Sea Cruise."

Nice Tone

Springsteen traveled to his old haunt the Main Point in Bryn Mawr, Pennsylvania, on June 21 to check out his former bandmates David Sancious and Ernest "Boom" Carter. Playing in their new outfit, Tone, Springsteen joined the group for one number and hung out with the one-time E Streeters backstage.

Time for a Shave

The Bryn Mawr show also marked the last time Springsteen would ever perform with his beard. Sometime after he returned to Holmdel, he reinvented himself by shedding the facial hair that had been his scruffy trademark since the dawn of the 1970s.

Friends, including journalist Dave Marsh, didn't immediately recognize Springsteen. In keeping with his makeover, his raggedy jeans, and guinea tee were gone. He looked downright handsome.

Bicentennial Man

Two weeks after Springsteen showed up to support the Asbury Jukes as they rocked *Crawdaddy* magazine's tenth anniversary party in Manhattan, Springsteen and the E Street Band celebrated the United States' 200th anniversary by participating in Southside Johnny's Independence Day gig at the Stone Pony.

After a memorable gig by Lyon, Shore area fans who hung around the Asbury Park venue got the surprise of their lives when Bruce and the E Street Band took the stage after midnight and played a number of staples—including "Tenth Avenue Freeze Out" and other *Born to Run* favorites—for stunned attendees.

Two weeks later, Springsteen—who by now knew the importance of making an impression on those who sold and promoted records by new artists—accompanied Miami Steve and the Asbury Jukes during a trip to the CBS Records

Annual Sales Convention in Los Angeles. Southside Johnny opened the convention, which was branded "The Family of Music—1976" with a forty-minute set that featured guest guitar by Springsteen on "The Fever" and "I Don't Want to Go Home." The superstar assisted Lyon in being extremely well received, performing a vocal duet on the latter.

The Miami Horns

Springsteen needed to tour to keep his organization afloat as his lawsuit with Appel carried on. Sure he had a $100,000 advance from Premier Talent, but most of that went toward his legal bills.

Going back on the road didn't have to be the same old-same old, however. As his image overhaul asserted, Springsteen wasn't above trying new things, including wearing a suit onstage. A creative shift in the music's presentation was most notable and came after tapping Southside Johnny's horn section—which included saxophonists Carlo Novi and Ed Manion plus trumpeters Tony Palligrosi and Rick Gazda—for a six-show run at the Monmouth Arts Center in August '76.

These dates—which also included stops at the Palace in Waterbury, Connecticut, and Massachusetts' Springfield Civic Center—marked the debut of several new songs, including "Rendezvous," "Something in the Night," and "The Promise." A cover of the Dovells' 1963 U.S. #3 hit "You Can't Sit Down" was also introduced into the live set as an encore with staying power.

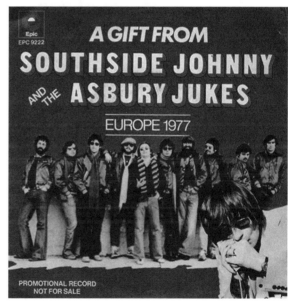

The "Lawsuit" Tour

After the success of the brass section during the preliminary Lawsuit tour dates, Steve Van Zandt helped Springsteen assemble his own Miami Horns in time for West Coast roadwork late the following month. Joining the E Street Band for the entire tour, the second Miami Horns lineup boasted

This rare four-song 7-inch EP, released as a promo 45 designed to promote Southside Johnny and the Asbury Jukes' 1977 tour, culled tracks from its first two records. It included songs written by Springsteen ("The Fever") and Steve Van Zandt ("I Don't Want to Go Home" and "This Time It's for Real"). The last tune, "Love on the Wrong Side of Town," was a collaborative effort between Van Zandt and Springsteen.

Courtesy of 991.com

A Coke but no smile, this picture of Springsteen leaning against his motorcycle in 1977 was rarely used—although it was included in a news item about his lawsuit that ran in *Rolling Stone* that year. This photo, taken outside of Ralph's Bar and Gas Station on Route 34 in Holmdel, was one of the first public images of a clean-shaven Springsteen. It was autographed for the proprietors, Ralph and Sharon Arentsen.   *Courtesy of Kenneth Hoerle*

Philadelphia-based players Ed De Palma (sax), John Binkley (trumpet), Steve Paraczky (trumpet), and Dennis Orlock (trombone).

Getting underway in Phoenix at the Veterans Memorial Coliseum on September 26, this show was remarkable as it represented Springsteen's first headlining arena gig. Well-attended California shows in Santa Monica, Oakland, Santa Clara, and Santa Barbara followed.

Dion

Shortly after Springsteen's headlining gig at the Santa Monica Civic Center on September 30, he accompanied Miami Steve to the Roxy in Los Angeles to catch a late-night performance by 1960s icon Dion. Introducing them as "honorary Belmonts," the man behind hits like "Runaround Sue" and "I Wonder Why" asked the two to provide backing vocals on his encore of "A Teenager in Love."

Van Zandt had known Dion DiMucci since late 1972, when he joined him on guitar for a New Year's Eve oldies gig in Miami (which is how his nickname originated). Springsteen first met Dion during his visit to L.A. the previous

October, when he had been invited to a Phil Spector–produced recording session featuring the singer.

Quarter to Three

On October 22, 1976, during a week off from the road, Springsteen drove the thirty miles from Holmdel to Seaside Heights to catch a show by one of his all-time favorites, Gary U.S. Bonds. Entering the venue as a paying customer, Bonds had no idea who Springsteen was when Fat City's proprietor introduced them.

According to an unattributed early 1980s interview cited by *Brucebase*, Bonds remembered the night this way: "The club owner came over to me during the show and mentioned that Bruce Springsteen was in the audience and wanted to come up and play. Bruce who? I didn't recognize the name! But the guys in my band did, so I said ok. When I introduced him the place went crazy."

On a borrowed guitar, Springsteen assisted Bonds on "New Orleans," "Dear Lady Twist," "Twist Twist Sonora," "School Is In," and his own concert staple "Quarter to Three." Afterwards, the two hit it off, and Springsteen invited Bonds to join him the following week during his series of shows in New York."

Double Sellout at the Spectrum

Despite the fact that Springsteen had always resisted playing arenas, his concert booker Barry Bell managed to convince him that big halls could be played effectively. Springsteen was, above all else, concerned about his fans' experience.

In order to meet the demand for tickets in Phoenix, he relented. Next, during a pair of dates at the Philadelphia Spectrum, he presented the show as a giant theater gig. Screening off the back of the stage with a large curtain, he hired local specialists, the Clare Brothers, to oversee the sound. The afternoon of the show, the E Street Band performed its full, three-hour set during sound check.

At the shows, on October 25 and 27, Springsteen rendered covers of the Phil Spector–penned 1963 Darlene Love classic "A Fine, Fine Boy" (done as "A Fine, Fine Girl"), and the 1967 Eddie Floyd soul nugget "Raise Your Hand."

Six-Night Stand

After the cavernous Spectrum gigs, Springsteen's run of six sold-out shows at the Palladium Theatre felt downright intimate. But the late October/early November concerts at the 2,800-seat Manhattan opera house still allowed Bruce to accommodate seventeen thousand New York area fans.

As promised, Bonds joined Springsteen for a rousing "Quarter to Three" during the second night, while new songs "Something in the Night" and "The Promise" remained set constants. On October 30 and November 3, Patti Smith joined the band during "Rosalita," which included a snippet of the Beach Boys' 1963 smash "Be True to Your School."

Then, on November 4, the final night of the tour, Springsteen asked Ronnie Spector to join him for three of her Ronettes classics, "Baby I Love You," "Walking in the Rain," and "Be My Baby." He also delivered a forceful take on the Animals' "It's My Life," which was cowritten by Brill Building veteran Carl D'Errico (who was in the house as a VIP guest). Late in the set, Springsteen played another Animals classic, "We Gotta Get out of This Place."

For his efforts, Bruce was invited to the D'Errico residence in New York three nights later for a home-cooked meal. Together, he and D'Errico jammed out acoustically on "It's My Life" among other songs.

Second Leg

Springsteen began 1977 by helping Van Zandt with Southside Johnny material, copenning a trio of songs ("Little Girl So Fine," "Love on the Wrong Side of Town," and "When You Dance") for the Jukes' sophomore album *This Time It's for Real.*

He also joined the E Street Band on guitar to record a one-off single with Ronnie Spector that Van Zandt had produced. The song, a cover of Billy Joel's "Say Goodbye to Hollywood" that featured Springsteen on guitar, was officially released that April, although he couldn't be credited because his legal fracas with Mike Appel had yet to be resolved.

When the Boss resumed the Lawsuit tour in Albany, New York, on February 7, the Miami Horns were still in tow. During the thirty-three-show run, which wrapped in late March, Springsteen continued to road-test new songs like "Action in the Streets," "Don't Look Back," and the ever-evolving "The Promise," which was now being delivered with just piano accompaniment.

Early in the tour, he first incorporated a monologue in the middle of one of his songs, using "Backstreets" to implement a practice that he would long repeat. By the time of the E Street Band's show at Toronto's Maple Leaf Gardens on February 13, the group's four-hour gigs began to be divided by a brief intermission, which allowed the band to hydrate and hit the lavatory.

Speaking of Spector, she—along with the vocal duo of Flo and Eddie—accompanied the E Street Band during a show at Cleveland's Richfield Coliseum on February 17 for several Ronettes favorites, plus a rendition of the recently tracked "Hollywood."

Another memorable cover—this time of Jackie Wilson's "Higher and Higher"—made Springsteen's four-night stand at the Music Hall in Boston some of the best of the trek. The loyal Boston audiences were frenzied and in awe of the Boss.

The Asbury Park All Star Revue

Springsteen's commitment to his friends, especially Southside Johnny, was evidenced by his routine guest appearances in the 1970s. On April 17, he hit the Stone Pony to join Lyon and the Jukes on celebratory versions of "The Fever," "I Don't Wanna Go Home," "You Mean So Much to Me Baby," and "Havin' a Party."

Four weeks later, after Johnny fell ill shortly before a trio of sold-out gigs at the Monmouth Arts Center in Red Bank, guitarist Van Zandt stepped in and saved the shows for fans and the Jukes. Members of the E Street Band collaborated with members of Southside's group, Ronnie Spector helped out, and Van Zandt sang lead on a number of tunes that typically featured Lyon.

Shore music fans also got the E Street Band in all their glory, pumping out lively takes of "Thunder Road," "Rendezvous," "Backstreets," and "Born to Run" during these May 1977 impromptu dates.

DICESARE ENGLER Productions Inc. Presents

BRUCE SPRINGSTEEN
in concert at
St. Vincent College
MARCH 11th 1977 8PM

Tickets available at St. Vincent College Bookstore and National Record Mart

A souvenir of the E Street Band's March 1977 performance in Latrobe, Pennsylvania, this show was hosted by St. Vincent College, a small Catholic liberal arts college and Benedictine monastery. Pittsburgh-based DiCesare-Engler Productions promoted the gig. *Courtesy of Brucebase*

Elvis in Philly

Springsteen may have been elated to learn that he was finally free of Mike Appel when a settlement was reached on May 27, the Friday before Memorial Day weekend. But he couldn't help but feel deeply saddened after the concert he and Steve Van Zandt witnessed in Philadelphia the following night.

Springsteen's earliest musical idol was in bad shape during his gig at the Spectrum in Philadelphia. Perhaps fearing this or possibly still feeling embarrassed for crashing Graceland thirteen months earlier, he elected not to play his celebrity card at the venue despite his connections.

Instead, he and Miami caught the show from the audience, but the King had clearly lost his magic—he was bloated and zonked on prescription drugs. The

May 28 show wound up being one of the last for Presley, who died on August 16, 1977, at just forty-two years old.

In the five years since Springsteen had witnessed him at Madison Square Garden in June 1972, Elvis had succumbed to drug abuse. His delivery of Frank Sinatra's "My Way" was unintelligible; on a rapid-paced "Jailhouse Rock" he was out of breath. In an interview the following year, Springsteen would recall how he and Van Zandt drove back to the Jersey Shore in silence, clearly stunned at how far his hero had fallen.

Addicted to Performing

During his downtime from the road and the studio, Springsteen found himself becoming antsy. Sitting around Thrill Hill writing the songs that would comprise his next album, the serious nature of the material—which was mirroring the struggle in the lives of his friends and family members—he found himself looking for something fun to do.

He missed the stage—anyone who had seen his recent run of gigs knew he lived for performing. At times it seemed as if he was addicted to it.

Sure, he was helping raise the profile of his friends in the Jukes. But they were helping him fill a void when his tour bus wasn't rolling. With a need to be where the action was, Springsteen would regularly jump in one of his cars and take off for shore venues, especially the Stone Pony. Throughout '77—when he wasn't thinking about the shape his next album would take—he might show up to jam with local bands.

Playing formative rock-'n'-roll numbers like "Jailhouse Rock" and "Sea Cruise" with Bob Campanell's band the Shakes on a borrowed guitar, as he did in May, or hopping up to jam with Billy Hector's band the Shots—who had taken over for the Jukes as the Pony's house band—on "Funky Broadway" was sometimes just as exhilarating as fronting the E Street Band in a basketball arena.

16

We Drove Eight Hundred Miles Without Seeing a Cop

Bruce Stories

The Mystery Lady

Part of the magic of a Springsteen show comes from the stories he's told. A classic, which he'd repeat during his 1975 dates as he'd introduce "Pretty Flamingo," had to do with a mystery lady. He would tell the tale of how he'd sit on the steps of his house on South Street in Freehold every day around 4:45 p.m. hoping to catch an eye of the beautiful, young businesswoman as she strolled through the heart of Freehold.

Onstage at the Roxy, Springsteen recounted how he and his pal Van Zandt would think of ways they might impress her. They'd tell her they were in a band. They'd sit on the steps with their guitars and hope she'd notice how cool they were. It never worked.

"She was the kind of girl who made you feel dumb about stuff," he told the crowd. "We didn't know her name. Every day, we tried to make each other find out her name. We tried to get the crazy kid on the block to go up and ask her name; he couldn't do it."

Years later, she was still on his mind. He wondered, as he introduced his cover of the 1966 Manfred Mann hit, if he ran into her, if she might be impressed by the fact that he had albums in Tower Records or a billboard on Sunset Boulevard.

Dr. John

During a May 1978 show, Springsteen gave a shout-out to the dentist who fixed his front tooth after it fell out while he was sleeping.

"I gotta stop eating all them hamburgers," Bruce joked to the crowd while thanking Dr. John Winterhouse. "It was gonna be me and Leon Spinks."

Spinks, of course, was the dentally challenged heavyweight champion who had beaten Muhammad Ali in a fifteen-round decision on February 15 of that year.

Santa in Cleveland

Sometimes Springsteen's onstage tales were pure fiction, as was his hilarious introduction of "Santa Claus Is Coming to Town" during the New Year's Day *Darkness* tour closer in Cleveland. Such is the case of his story about Christmas Eve 1965.

He explained that he had been listening to the Phil Spector Christmas album when he was thrown out of his house, so he went down to the beach, where it was snowing. The Student Prince had a sign on its door that read, "Home for Christmas."

"So I went down under the jetty to get out of the snow," he said, with a chuckle, "And who was sitting there but Miami Steve with his guitar . . . And we're going, 'This Christmas stuff is just a bunch of bullshit, that's lies . . . that's for kids . . . that's a joke . . .

"Santa Claus, he's dead, he fell out of his sleigh over Newark," he continued, "And then we heard this noise that woke us up and we looked way down the boardwalk . . . " and he began his version of the classic Spector holiday number.

Meeting Kovic

In the summer of 1978, Springsteen ran into Ron Kovic—author of the book *Born on the Fourth of July*—while he was living in Hollywood at the Sunset Marquis Hotel. One afternoon Kovic observed Springsteen swimming in the pool and rolled over in his wheelchair and introduced himself.

"You're that guy?" Springsteen asked, giving him a surprised look. "I just read your book. I couldn't put it down." A couple days later, Kovic went to open the door of his hotel room and discovered Springsteen's back catalog and a note that read, "If my music can touch you and move you as much as your book moved me, that will mean a lot to me. Bruce Springsteen."

Springsteen also invited Kovic up to see him at Winterland in San Francisco. The Boss told the audience how much *Born on the Fourth of July* had meant to him and spoke fondly of Kovic to the crowd, before dedicating "Darkness on the Edge of Town" to him, as Kovic sat on the edge of the stage with tears in his eyes.

Anyone with a Brain Transplant?

Springsteen's use of humor onstage was well known, but his banter during the middle of "Detroit Medley" during his *No Nukes* gig at Madison Square Garden on September 21, 1979, was classic.

"I've been asked by the management of the hall to make an emergency announcement. It's an emergency, medical announcement," he warned the audience. "If there's anybody in the house that has a weak heart or a weak stomach or has recently had a heart or brain transplant, please leave the hall during the next few minutes of the show as it might be dangerous to your health."

Springsteen went on to tell the joke to the crowd that he and the E Street Band were selling an insurance policy.

Before the Boss resumed the high-energy song, he explained, "It don't hurt too much, you might get away with a short trip to the emergency room when we do this. And we might even survive with just a light case of shock when we do this."

Stardust Memories

During his tour in support of *The River*, Springsteen may have been a major star, but he wasn't above interacting with fans. During a Denver tour stop, the Boss borrowed a car and went out by himself to the movies one night.

While Springsteen was in line for popcorn, a fan recognized him and asked if he'd like to sit with him and his sister. Afterward, the kid felt enough of a connection to ask Springsteen if he'd like to come home with him to hang out.

He went along with them into the suburbs. When they walked through the front door, the kid's parents were on the couch with the television on, reading the newspaper. At first, they didn't believe it was actually Springsteen in their living room until their boy brought out an album with his face on it.

The stunned mother suddenly started screaming, but after she settled down, she cooked him a nice meal, sliced him some watermelon, and he had the company of some real people for a few hours.

"That's something that can happen to me that can't happen to most people. And when it does happen, it's fantastic," he told *Musician* days later. "I went back to that hotel and felt really good because I thought, 'Wow, what a thing to be able to do. What an experience to be able to have, to be able to step into some stranger's life.'"

The Glove or the Guitar

As he introduced "Glory Days" to the Meadowlands Arena crowd on August 5, 1984, Springsteen spoke of his love of the New York Yankees as a kid. "Before I wanted to play the guitar, I wanted to be a baseball player," he explained.

In his grade-school years, he made this his main focus, and, when he was seven, he began playing in the Freehold Colonial League, the precursor to Little League. As a freshman in high school, he played in the Babe Ruth League, but by the time he was fifteen, he realized he couldn't hit, throw, or catch.

"I wasn't gonna let those details stop me," he joked. For a while, he was able to juggle his love of baseball—which was during the week—with his pursuit of rock 'n' roll on Friday and Saturday nights, until a rained-out game was rescheduled for an early weekend morning.

Springsteen, who had gotten to bed late, pretended to be sick, but his team only had eight players and really needed him. They goaded him into playing and he suited up, but when he missed an easy catch in the outfield, he hung up his glove for good.

Bruce Meets Bubbles

In late September 1989, Springsteen took a long motorcycle trip—en route to the Grand Canyon—and wound up stopping in at Matt's Saloon, a biker bar in Prescott, Arizona. A local outfit, the Mile High Band, was onstage and stunned to discover that the Boss, who had rode in from Los Angeles, was in their favorite watering hole.

Bruce ordered a beer and took the stage with the house band for versions of "Sweet Little Sixteen," "Don't Be Cruel," "Route 66," and his own "I'm on Fire," but passed on an offer to play "Pink Cadillac" during his hour onstage when he couldn't remember the words.

By the time he was done playing, attendance at the bar just off Route 89 rose from around one dozen to one hundred. Springsteen—accompanied by three motorcycle companions and a bodyguard in a van—left behind a swarm of autograph seekers.

During his visit, he also learned of barmaid Brenda "Bubbles" Pechanec's tall medical bills. A week afterward, the cancer survivor received a check from Springsteen for $100,000 to help with her expenses.

His Hometown

At a 1990 concert in Los Angeles for the Christic Institute, Springsteen explained how he used to get in his car and go back to his old neighborhoods. "I'd always drive past the old houses I used to live in, sometimes late at night," he told the crowd. "It got so I would do it really regularly, two, three or four times a week. I went to see this psychiatrist."

The doctor helped him understand what he was doing. "He says, 'Well, what you're doing is, there's something bad happened there, something went wrong and you keep going back to see if you can fix it, somehow make it right,'" Springsteen explained.

"I said, 'Yeah, that is what I'm doing,'" he continued. "And he said, 'Well, you can't.'"

17

Tonight I'll Be on That Hill 'Cause I Can't Stop

Darkness on the Edge of Town

In the two years since *Born to Run* made him a star, Bruce Springsteen had a lot of time to consider how he wanted to present himself in the future. In the wake of his success, as he was exposed to new people and new ideas, he was changing.

Following the optimism he had established on his third record, Springsteen felt obligated to test that hopefulness. He also felt it was his duty to make sure he believed in the lyrics he'd be singing to his fans night after night.

In early 1976, he started to demo titles like "Dawn Patrol," "You're Gonna Cry," and "Drifter's Barrio." And that was just the beginning. By the time he was clear of his lawsuit with Mike Appel and ready to press the record button, he had seventy songs.

Changes

Just as his songwriting had evolved—becoming more serious—other facets of Springsteen's life were different. He was no longer a scruffy, jeans-wearing McDonald's devouring simpleton. He had become more sophisticated.

He had split with his longtime girlfriend Karen Darvin and moved on to a new relationship with photographer Lynn Goldsmith. His musical tastes shifted but remained as broad as ever. He absorbed the *Saturday Night Fever* soundtrack, the Sinatra catalog and country music.

Springsteen had started to wear suits onstage, but most fans would come to identify him as the flannel-shirt-sporting, working-class pinup who adorned the cover of his next record. He continued to take cues related to his image from Dylan.

"We'd go through pictures of Dylan and talk about Bob's hair, Bob's shirt, Bob's shoes," Lynn explained to Sandford. "He'd buy old clothes at Trash and

Vaudeville in the Village, then make them appear even more used by running over them with the car. He never wanted me to [sell] a picture of him smiling."

Atlantic Studios

In June 1977, Springsteen and the E Street Band finally got to work on his fourth album, which was tentatively titled *American Madness*, at Atlantic Studios in New York. He and his advisor Jon Landau were the project's official producers, with Van Zandt working in a supporting production role and Jimmy Iovine again serving as Springsteen's engineer.

The first night, the band put down demos of twenty songs they had perfected during recent roadwork and in subsequent rehearsals. Titles they attempted included "Rendezvous," "The Promise," "Frankie," "Don't Look Back" and "Something in the Night." Only the latter wound up making the album's final cut when it surfaced under a different name a year later.

Bruce and Steve

As products of the same 1960s Jersey Shore band scene, Springsteen and Van Zandt had shared experiences and similar ambitions from a young age. Van Zandt—who was the yang to Springsteen's yin—was content to take a supporting role in the groups he played in—whether the Asbury Jukes or the E Street Band—as Springsteen put himself out in front. From the earliest days of their friendship and as they evolved, they complemented each other and made each other stronger musically and otherwise.

In the spring of 1977, two years after Van Zandt joined the band, Springsteen wanted to acknowledge the sizable impact his guitarist had made to the group. And having seen firsthand how well he managed to produce Southside's first two albums, he knew Van Zandt would be an enormous help in the production of his fourth record.

"I think Steve has more influence over Bruce than anyone else," Columbia Records executive Peter Philbin told Hilburn in 1985. As for Van Zandt's effect on *Darkness on the Edge of Town* and the E Street Band efforts that followed, Philbin acknowledged the emotional connection between Miami and the Boss.

"Steve innately knows how Bruce feels," Philbin explained. "He has a better sense than anyone, and that's important because Bruce doesn't talk about how he feels a lot. You either know it or you don't, and Steve is the best at knowing."

Perhaps no better proof exists than the footage from 2010's documentary *The Promise*, in which Springsteen and Van Zandt can be seen working together in the studio in early 1978. Fleshing out a new song, "Sherry Darling"—which was a contender for *Darkness* before it wound up on 1980's *The River*—the two are clearly having the time of their lives singing aloud as one bangs on the piano and the other pats out a rhythm with drumsticks.

Hangin' with Keith

During Springsteen's time at Atlantic Studios that summer, his evening sessions abutted the Rolling Stones' efforts mixing *Love You Live*. After they were introduced, Miami Steve and Keith Richards became fast friends.

Van Zandt was pleased to learn that Richards was a fan of his production work with the Asbury Jukes. He couldn't help but be dazzled. The Rolling Stones were, of course, one of his favorite bands of all time.

"Fire"

In spite of his disappointment with Elvis Presley's Spectrum show in June 1977, Springsteen wrote a song with Elvis in mind. But there was no indication that the King ever got to hear it. The month he submitted "Fire" for consideration, Presley died.

Springsteen instead handed the song to rockabilly revivalist Robert Gordon, who tracked the song the following year with guitarist Link Wray. Then, in 1979, the Pointer Sisters topped the chart with their rendition of the tune, which had since become a recurring number in the E Street Band's live set.

Returning to the Record Plant

As work progressed on what would eventually become known as *Darkness on the Edge of Town*, Springsteen decided he wasn't happy with Atlantic Studios, which was supposedly state of the art. From a comfort standpoint, however, it lacked many of the amenities that the E Street Band had gotten used to during the *Born to Run* sessions.

For instance, the Record Plant had an exercise area, a nice kitchen, and a couple of sleeping rooms that came in handy during Springsteen's marathon recording sessions.

In addition to those comforts, the main impetus for moving was Springsteen's extreme displeasure with the

This unique Japanese sleeve for "Badlands," which captures Springsteen performing in a suit during his 1977 Lawsuit tour, is noticeably different from most of the other releases surrounding *Darkness on the Edge of Town*, which tended to mirror the stark photography of the album's jacket. *Courtesy of 991.com.*

acoustics at Atlantic. The stiff drum sound he was getting from Max Weinberg's kit was a constant source of frustration. After many different approaches, none that worked well, he had had enough. He told Landau they needed to get back to their old facility.

Unfortunately, this shift didn't happen immediately. The Record Plant had already been booked, which meant Springsteen would have to keep working at Atlantic for the rest of the summer. He would return to the Record Plant that autumn.

Stick!

According to Max Weinberg, the advent of the Beatles' final album, *Abbey Road*, changed the way drums were recorded in rock 'n' roll forever. Many high-end studios such as Atlantic incorporated small, padded drum rooms that removed the resonance. In doing so they stripped away what Weinberg described as "a big Thrashing drum sound," the result Springsteen wanted.

Springsteen and Van Zandt came up with a term for that nonresonant sound. They called it "Stick." Whenever Weinberg's playing resulted in that boxy sonic product, they would torment him—as evidenced in the 2010 documentary *The Promise*—by yelling "Stick!"

"If you listen to the Darkness album," Weinberg told the *Star-Ledger* in 2010, "one of the first songs we recorded was 'Prove It All Night.' You'll hear that kind of mid-'70s dead drum sound. But then if you listen to the song, 'Darkness on the Edge of Town,' [which] was the last song we recorded . . . there was the sound!"

By March 1978, when Springsteen returned to Studio B at the Record Plant, it was being rebuilt and management was hesitant to let him use it. Stripped down to a concrete floor, there was no padding—only studs on the walls. But he insisted on working in such an environment, and when Weinberg hit the drum, the classic Springsteen drum sound—heard on his future records—was achieved.

The Boss's Rules

Being in the E Street Band was a good deal for its members—they were paid very well, and they had health coverage. But like any workplace, there were rules. And although Bruce was okay with booze and brews after the gigs when the work was done, the Boss had little tolerance for drugs and implemented a one-strike policy.

As the songwriter and bandleader, Springsteen also oversaw the musical arrangements. He would, at times, welcome input from members of the group, but he would regularly veto contributions that didn't fit his vision.

In the studio, Springsteen pushed his members. They would work from around 8 p.m. to midnight every day. Retakes were just part of doing business with a perfectionist like Springsteen. When the album was done, the 42nd attempt at "Candy's Room," the 49th stab at "Prove It All Night," and the 46th rendition of "Racing in the Street" were chosen.

Springsteen acknowledged his creative compulsions in 1978, talking to the *Chicago Tribune*. "Anyone who works for me—the first thing you better know is I'm gonna drive you crazy," he explained. "I don't compromise in certain areas."

The Boss's Goals

After the hype of his breakthrough album, Springsteen took some time to reflect on who he wanted to be. He came to the conclusion that he wanted to be a musician first—a rocker as opposed to a rock-'n'-roll star. He'd been a part of the record company's machine before and knew there was a difference.

One wrong decision could forever taint what he had built. He felt a responsibility to his fans to continue to deliver quality records and an ace live show. "You have got to keep constant vigilance," he explained in *Springsteen*. "You got to keep your strength up because if you lose it, then you're another jerk who had his picture on the cover."

With the aim of writing about life in a small working-class town like Freehold Borough, he fused his love of powerful, emotional rock-'n'-roll singles like the Animals' "It's My Life" and "We Gotta Get out of This Place" with the uneasiness of adulthood living paycheck to paycheck. Songs like "Prove It All Night" and "Factory" were the outcome.

At times, Springsteen almost felt guilty about his success. What made him any more deserving than those around him? Feeling a sense of responsibility to the blue-collar men and women he grew up with, he drew on their lives as much as his own. In doing so, he crafted some of the most poignant songs he'd ever write.

Only the Lonely

When he was off the road, Springsteen would sequester himself in his dark, cavernous house. Here he allowed the loneliness to propel his songs in a stark, somber direction. The mood of the material was different from anything he had attempted before.

He thought about growing up with his father. In the twenty years he lived with him, he never once witnessed Doug have a friend at their house. He felt sad for his father, but began to understand what made him tick.

For days on end, Springsteen would keep to himself. It was something he was not only comfortable with—his privacy had become increasingly important since he became famous—but knew was necessary to render the music and lyrics for the project he would name *Darkness on the Edge of Town*.

If he needed to break free or find outside inspiration, Springsteen would go for a ride. On his motorcycle or in his hot rod, the dusty beach roads weren't far off. And as he learned during the making of his previous record, they often helped inspire him.

Upon its completion, Springsteen acknowledged that the romance of *Born to Run* had been supplanted by isolation. "It's sort of like I said, 'Well, listen, I'm twenty-eight years old and the people in the album are around my age.' I perceive 'em to be that old," he told Walter Dawson of the *Memphis Commercial Appeal* in 1978. "And there's less of a sense of a free ride than there is on *Born to Run.* There's more of a sense of, 'You wanna ride? You're gonna pay.' And you'd better keep riding."

"And maybe you'll make it through," he added that year in a conversation with *Crawdaddy*, "but you ain't gonna make it through 'til you been beat, you been hurt, until you been messed up. There's hope, but it's just the hope of, like, survival."

John Ford

Cinema began to prominently inform Bruce's writing during the sessions for *Darkness,* most notably on "Badlands," which was named for the 1973 film of the same name. Although he hadn't seen the movie at the time he wrote the tune, the movie poster in a theater lobby gave him artistic stimulation.

The movies of director John Ford also influenced the songs. Bruce observed how each film had a similar confrontational scene, but that Ford shot each one differently to keep his films from becoming redundant.

"There was a lot of continuity in his work. I liked that," Springsteen said to Hilburn of Ford's work, which included *The Man Who Shot Liberty Valance* and the film adaptation of John Steinbeck's *The Grapes of Wrath.* "You [could then] go back to the previous movie and have a clearer understanding of where he was coming from. What he was saying in this film was changing the shape of what he said in another one."

Springsteen also found himself studying the films of Robert Mitchum and Arthur Ripley. He was also drawn to the realistic struggles of '40s and '50s film noir like Jacques Tourneur's *Out of the Past.*

It took 49 takes to get the sound of "Prove It All Night" to Springsteen's liking, which may explain why this 1978 45, pressed in Holland, is a virtual reproduction of the Frank Stefanko-shot *Darkness on the Edge of Town* cover, save for some different fonts.   *Courtesy of Lost in the Flood*

Hankerin' for Hank

During the recording period, Springsteen found himself drawn to country music, specifically Hank Williams, but later Johnny Cash and others. He appreciated that the lyrical themes in country were adult oriented.

In a 1995 interview with Will Percy, Springsteen spoke of how the genre shaped his work from this era. "[It] had a lot of effect on my writing because I think country is a very class-conscious music," he said. "I was always trying to shoot for the moon. I had some lofty ideas about using my own music to give people something to think about the world, and what's right and wrong. I'd been affected that way by records, and I wanted my own music and writing to extend themselves in that way."

Plotkin

With most of the record tracked by January 1978, Landau tapped Chuck Plotkin—who had been the head of A&R at Elektra/Asylum—to come to New York to mix the project. Springsteen was looking for a less elaborate sound to fit the material he had written for his fourth album, and after befriending Plotkin during their shared efforts on Jackson Browne's 1976 album *The Pretender*, Landau knew he was the man for the job.

Plotkin helped render what Bruce would describe in *Songs* as "a tighter, more modern mix." His personality—a balance of no-nonsense and cutting humor—forced Bruce to make quicker decisions than he was used to, in order to bring the record to completion.

Obsessing over the Songs

Although he had amassed dozens of new songs, the ones that Springsteen had earmarked for the record—including "Badlands," "Prove It All Night," and "The Promised Land"—were labored over the longest. Verses came slowly as Bruce strove to create a lyrical theme and an overall tone for the project. Building off of *Born to Run*'s spiritual hopefulness, he inflected a certain cynicism that came with adulthood and its real problems.

"I wanted my new characters to feel weathered, older, but not beaten," he explained in *Songs*. Weeks would pass until certain lyrics on numbers like "Adam Raised a Cain" and "Racing in the Street" felt right. They came together gradually, line by line. As songs developed that better fit the theme of the project, others fell out of favor. "Don't Look Back," for instance, was set for the album until Springsteen perfected "Darkness on the Edge of Town" extremely late in the session in March '78, bumping it off the record.

Track by Track

Crafted over eleven months, *Darkness on the Edge of Town* was Springsteen's first real attempt at making an artistic statement. The slow-brewed, artful musical statement asserted that he would much rather record an album that was true to his feelings.

It was also an indication that Bruce was still suspicious of success. Recoiling from the pop landscape, two of the record's most immediate songs—the afore-mentioned "Fire" and "Because the Night," which became Patti Smith's biggest-ever hit—were given away.

To Springsteen, what the album stood for as a whole was far more important than the singles it would spawn. Decades later, it stands tall as arguably the most uniform of his landmark albums.

"Badlands"

Springsteen had yet to see the 1973 Terrence Malick film that gave this song its title. Starring Martin Sheen and Sissy Spacek, "Badlands" portrays a man in his late twenties who is down on his luck and frustrated. Despite his pessimism, he is optimistic enough to still believe in love, hope, and faith. When all is said and done, he rises above it all.

Released as a UK single on July 21, 1978—as this promo-tional copy's paper label reveals—the musical allure of "Badlands" owed much of its contagiousness to the Animals' "Don't Let Me Be Misunderstood." Over three decades later, Springsteen would admit to the intentional similarities of both songs.   *Courtesy of Lost in the Flood*

A powerful song steered by Max Weinberg's forceful drums, a blistering twin guitar attack, and the Boss's electrifying, heartfelt vocals, it was the album's second single. Surprisingly, it failed to break the Top 40 upon its release on August 14, 1978 (it stalled at #42). It has since become one of the signature anthems in Springsteen's canon.

The song's social observations are on point—poor men do want to be rich, and the wealthy do aspire for power—but the lyrics were a tough go. "'Badlands', that's a great title, but it would be easy to blow it," he told *Rolling Stone* in 2010. "But I kept writing and I kept writing and I kept writing and writing until I had a song that I felt deserved that title."

Of its similarity to the Animals' hit "Don't Let Me Be Misunderstood" Springsteen admitted in 2011, "That's the one I was rippin' off! I flipped it from minor to major and it's basically the same riff."

"That's how it's done kids!" he continued, joking with bandmate Steve Van Zandt on his *Underground Garage* radio program, as the host broke out in a fit of laughter.

"Adam Raised a Cain"

Springsteen's intent in this song was to use biblical images to explain the complexities of his relationship with his father. As with most of the songs on *Darkness*, it was emotionally autobiographical, if not completely true. He would later reveal that this song—along with several others on the record—was a way for him to communicate with his dad at the time. On the surface he and Doug connected well enough, but his lyrics went much deeper. He was exploring the complications of their bond.

If "Adam Raised a Cain" sounds a little harsh in its presentation, that was Springsteen's plan. He told Chuck Plotkin that he wanted it to contrast against the melodic songs it was sequenced alongside. To get the mix he was after, he told Plotkin to imagine a movie where two lovers are having a picnic. Then abruptly the film cuts to a dead body. The song would be that body.

"Something in the Night"

As one of the first demos attempted for the record, Springsteen knew this song was a keeper from the outset. In a sense, it picks up where *Born to Run* left off, depicting Springsteen riding down Kingsley in Asbury Park with the stereo blasting. Hoping to numb himself from the strife in his life, he sings of plans to get a drink.

Singing about innocence lost with a piercing piano accompaniment, it's hard not to think that "Something in the Night" is—at least in part—a reaction to the shock Bruce felt when he learned Mike Appel owned his songs. As he seethes that "Nothing is forgotten or forgiven" it's believable, emotional, artful and unforgettable.

"Candy's Room"

When asked by *Rolling Stone* in 2010 if Candy was a prostitute, Springsteen responded, "Does it really matter? I'll never tell."

Whether she's a hooker, a stripper or just a maneater, it makes no difference to the song's character, "Candy's Boy"—which was the title of the song where these lyrics originate. He's in love with her and although Bruce never makes it clear if she returns the sentiment, it seems doubtful. As the narrator, he pledges that she wants to be with him, but this notion comes across as delusional.

Sonically, "Candy's Room" begins with a soft, piano-accompanied introduction, gives way to accelerated-heartbeat drums, and peaks with an explosive, intoxicating guitar solo. The arrangement is ideally matched to the lyrics and takes the listener through the gamut of emotions in this brief but commanding classic.

"Racing in the Street"

Considered his best-ever song by the authors of *The New Rolling Stone Album Guide* and American folk-rock icon Bob Dylan alike, Springsteen carefully placed this track—which makes a nod to Martha and the Vandellas' "Dancing in the Street"—as the closing number on side one of *Darkness*.

"I wanted my street racers to carry the years between the car songs of the '60s and 1978 America," he wrote in *Songs*, explaining how he crafted the material to represent his own hopes and fears. With this record, Springsteen was committed to making his characters sound genuine. Because their stories were based on real people, he knew they had to be believable.

Steeped in the local Asbury Park car culture of the 1970s, where muscle cars circled the Circuit, he made sure his grease monkey lingo was authentic. He name checked Fuelie heads and Hurst shifters and made sure the small block 396 he sang of did in fact work in a '69 Chevy.

Still, the heart of the dirgy ballad is a relationship gone wrong. At first, Springsteen's character's passion for racing offered a thrilling escape from his blue-collar job, as he and his partner Sonny covered the Northeast on nights and weekends, gambling against other hot rodders. But when his wife—the woman whose heart he won years earlier after a street race—begins to lose interest in the lifestyle and their relationship in general, the song ends on a dour note.

Do they split? Does he kill her? Do they reconcile? Springsteen never gets specific; he only reveals that they drive to the ocean to cleanse themselves of their sins. From a musical standpoint, there is mostly melancholy and just a faint hint of sanguinity in the tones of the track, which counts a memorable Roy Bittan piano intro, the ticking drum rim taps of Mighty Max, and the sad, lilting organ of Danny Federici. Of course, Springsteen's sincere yet solemn delivery is what makes it the prevailing, ultimate Springsteen composition.

"The Promised Land"

Unlike the bulk of the songs on the album, which took dozens of takes to perfect, the record's third single was finalized after just the fifth attempt. But that's not to say Bruce didn't agonize over it. Although the chorus came quickly, the verses took a long time to complete.

Springsteen also struggled over the final mix of the song to the point that it held up the release of the record by two weeks when the second side of the disc had to be remastered.

He returned to New York City, where he listened to the entire record, but something about its presentation seemed wrong. "'Promised Land' came up on the second side, it just wasn't the right mix," he told *Mojo* writer Mark Hagen in January 1999, before revealing that he flew immediately back to California to repair the project. "My life at the time was extremely focused, probably to the detriment of the records," he continued. "But very often these things were created amid a mess and you don't know what you're doing until you're done."

As for the harmonica-laden, durable rocker, Springsteen nicked its title from a 1965 song by Chuck Berry. The song's message—which suggests that damaging thoughts and dreams distract us, hurt us, and hold us back—is ultimately uplifting. That sentiment, coupled with the track's alluring execution, easily place it among the best Springsteen has to offer.

"Factory"

Inspired by his father's tenure at a nearby plastics plant, where he wound up losing part of his hearing because workers weren't offered earplugs in those days, Springsteen reflects back on memories of his daddy coming out of the plant when the afternoon whistle blew. Coming back out of the gates to meet his young family, he looked just a little less alive than he did the day before.

Unlike the songs on *Darkness* that took weeks and months to piece together, "Factory" was crafted in approximately twenty minutes. It was a pensive nod of appreciation for the sacrifices both his dad and his mom made to keep the family afloat, and it was evidence that he could relate to the common man.

At one point, Springsteen laughed remembering how his father told him that the only tunes by him that his dad ever liked were the ones his boy had scribed in his honor.

"Streets of Fire"

Springsteen may refer to this song's character as a self-professed loser wandering out on the tracks, but within the confines of the song, he's a winner pouring his heart out. It careens along as the piano and the drums pound out his frustration, and although he sings of being tricked and lied to, Springsteen does so as he roars along, riffing on some of the most moving guitar work he's ever tracked.

As for the intensity of this song—which at the very least touches on his falling out with Laurel Canyon—the Boss would tell Ed Sciaky in August 1978 that it was carved from real-life events.

"You're always writing about you," he told the DJ. "You're talking to yourself—that's essentially what you're doing when you write—and to other people at the same time. There's a little more of it—I don't know what you call it, the first person or second person—and a little more directness [on this album] . . . I guess in a way this album was a little more real for me than some of the other ones."

"Prove It All Night"

With the first single off of the record, Springsteen was conveying to his fans that success at anything—whether music, relationships, or financial independence—required sacrifice. In order to live up to the promise of the title, commitment was required on some level.

As a love song, "Prove It All Night" was the next logical step after "Thunder Road," which itself took its cue from "Rosalita." But unlike those uplifting, optimistic numbers, this devotional ode was a lot more serious.

His grand re-entry onto the music landscape after a two-and-a-half-year absence from the charts, Bruce's statement—released in mid-May '78—wielded an infectious chorus, memorable guitar lines, and Clarence Clemons's potent saxophone.

These were all elements of his 1975 breakthrough smash, but despite enthusiastic airplay on FM rock outlets, "Prove It All Night" only reached #33. But Springsteen was okay with the chart performance of his new 45. After all, he had always considered himself an album artist.

Although he had competition from the disco movement, Meat Loaf, the soundtrack to John Travolta's oldies movie *Grease*, the Rolling Stones' blockbuster *Some Girls*, and Bob Seger's *Stranger in Town* that summer, the single paved the way for very strong album sales. The musical proclamation Springsteen had chosen to help usher in his new record was an effective choice. *Darkness* peaked at #5.

"Darkness on the Edge of Town"

Revisiting the narrator of "Racing in the Street," the album's title song finds our subject alone. Although he is still in the company of his loyal partner Sonny, he is broke and his wife is gone—she presumably left him for another man who could provide a more normal and upscale life.

Near the end of his rope, Springsteen's character has lost the things that once mattered to him. He can either go off the deep end or reevaluate and start over.

By the title track's last verse, the character is faced with growing up. He'd dedicated but uncertain, as evidenced by the pledge, "Tonight, I'll be on that hill." Or as Springsteen acknowledged in *Songs,* "by the end of *Darkness,* I'd found my adult voice."

Praise

When music critics got their ears around *Darkness* two weeks before its June 2, 1978 release, it was widely, although not unanimously, praised. Leading the charge was Landau's old pal and future Springsteen biographer Dave Marsh, who wrote a feature review in the July 27 issue of *Rolling Stone.* "Like Elvis Presley and Buddy Holly, Springsteen has the ability, and the zeal, to do it all," Marsh insisted, before adding, "It feels like the threshold of a new period in which we'll again have "'lives on the line where dreams are found and lost.'"

Elsewhere, *Time* said, "Darkness passes the romantic delirium of Born to Run, cuts deeper, lingers longer," while *Crawdaddy* scribed, "Pain never used to show on him . . . but now he is owning up to it, doing for desperation what he did for release. The effect is unsettling, then staggering."

On the other side of the coin, *New Times* called it a "debacle," while the *Village Voice*'s Robert Christgau wasn't sure where he stood. He branded it "flawed and inconsistent" and then awarded it a B+.

Outtakes

With so much material to choose from, Springsteen had a diverse array of song styles to work with. He would later recognize that had he wanted, with numbers like "Rendezvous," "Fire," "I Wanna Be with You," and "Because the Night" he could have crafted an album of bona-fide pop songs. Although he would actually do that in 2010, when he released *The Promise,* a lost double album of unreleased

Springsteen was actively involved in the early years of Southside Johnny and the Asbury Jukes career, writing and cowriting key material up to 1978's *Hearts of Stone*—seen here in its Japanese pressing. Jukes cofounder and E Street Band guitarist Steve Van Zandt couldn't help but take it a step further, producing Southside's first three studio records and writing the bulk of the group's songs.

Courtesy of 991.com

tunes from this period, in 1978 he threw out all but the ten most important songs.

"Goin' Back" was an upbeat Bo Diddley–influenced number, while "English Sons" was a foot-stomping rocker. "The Ballad" was just that—a slow, reflective song. Classic Phil Spector records spawned "Get That Feeling," while Springsteen envisioned a string section for "Drive All Night," which was considerably longer than the version he later crafted on 1980's *The River*. Another track, "Sherry Darling," was cut only to see release on his next studio offering, while "Hearts of Stone" and "Talk to Me" were both handed down to Southside Johnny for his third record.

Other titles left by the wayside included "The Iceman," "Let's Go Tonight," "Outside Lookin' In," "The Loser," "Say Sons," "Taxi Cab," "Spanish Eyes," and "The Way." Anything that broke with the tension Springsteen was after was a goner.

And even with those deemed most imperative, there were many variations. At one point "Factory" boasted a violin part, while "Candy's Room," recorded in late '77, was a hybrid of two outtakes—"The Fast Song" and "Candy's Boy." Meanwhile, the title track—which was first recorded at Atlantic Studios in the summer of 1977—was experimented with and revisited. In one later incarnation, it actually brandished a rockabilly guitar line.

Ten Facts About *Darkness on the Edge of Town*

1. The album almost came out in the fall of 1977 under the title *Badlands*. Cover art was even readied, but Springsteen pulled back the record's release when he felt it wasn't ready.
2. Several other titles were also considered, including *Racing in the Streets*, the aforementioned *American Madness*, and *History Is Made at Night*.
3. In addition to making reference to Martha and the Vandellas' 1964 smash "Dancing in the Street," "Racing in the Street" also makes lyrical nods to drag-racing numbers like the Beach Boys' "Don't Worry Baby" and Jan and Dean's "Dead Man's Curve." Musically it acknowledges the Crystals' Phil Spector classic "Then He Kissed Me" and Van Morrison's "Tupelo Honey."
4. "Adam Raised a Cain" was licensed for use in the movie *Baby It's You*, which was directed by John Sayles, the man behind the camera on Springsteen's videos for "Born in the U.S.A." and "I'm on Fire."
5. "Streets of Fire," "Factory," and the title song were all cut live in the studio.
6. Springsteen once said that the characters on the record reminded him of the worn faces in the Garden State's blue-collar bars. "They're not looking to punch anybody out," he was quoted in the book *Point Blank*. "They want to be punched."
7. The album's cover photographer, Frank Stefanko, was still working by day in a meat market when he shot Springsteen for the project.

8. Advance pressings of the record weren't supposed to be played by radio until Columbia Records gave the go-ahead, but certain stations in meccas like Los Angeles, San Francisco, St. Louis, Detroit, New York, and Cleveland just couldn't wait, airing the album on May 18, two weeks ahead of release. One company, the Century Broadcasting group, which owned many of the violating stations, was sent cease-and-desist notices on May 19.

9. Springsteen was against a vast marketing campaign after the overdone hype of his previous record. He only wanted the album advertised in cities where he was slated to appear on tour. Finally, Columbia advertising head Dick Wingate reached a compromise, allowing Springsteen to design the ads, which the artist appreciated, in order to get the word out nationally about *Darkness*.

10. Talking about his favorite records of 1978, Pete Townshend said of *Darkness*, "When Bruce Springsteen sings on his new album, that's not about 'fun.' That's fucking triumph, man."

18

You've Got to Live It Every Day

Springsteen's 1978 Tour

It's Official

In July 1978, Springsteen's producer Jon Landau was officially his manager. Of course, he had gradually, albeit unofficially, occupied the role since Springsteen gave Mike Appel his walking papers in mid-'76.

After this protracted trial period, Springsteen was completely confident that the arrangement was the right fit for him. Landau's approach was far different from his predecessor's. Instead of offering edicts, he helped Springsteen weigh out his options in a way that wasn't condescending. Landau guided him, always with his client's best interests in mind, but the Boss ultimately called the shots.

Under Landau's guidance, he began to see the benefits of playing world-famous venues like Madison Square Garden. More and more fans were clamoring to see him perform—how could he refuse them?

Then there was the merchandise Springsteen had always refused to sell. Landau made him realize the kids wanted mementos like T-shirts and tour programs. By not offering them for sale, he would be letting them down.

Good Rockin' Tonight

On May 23, 1978, five days after tour rehearsals at the Paramount Theater in Asbury Park, Springsteen launched the *Darkness* tour at Shea's Theatre in Buffalo. The first of 109 shows that ran until New Year's Day 1979, the trek—which balanced arenas like the Philadelphia Spectrum and Long Island's Nassau Coliseum with large theaters—had many high points and very few lows.

Songs like "The Promise" and "Independence Day" may have been left off the new record, but they still found their way into his live set, as did a new tune, "Point Blank," that would ultimately appear on his next album. His shows were also graced with rockabilly covers from his youth that he had been rediscovering on the road. Eddie Cochran's "Summertime Blues," Jerry Lee Lewis's "High School Confidential," Elvis Presley's "Heartbreak Hotel" and "Good Rockin'

Tonight," Billy Lee Riley's "Is That All to the Ball Mr. Hall," and Buddy Holly's "Not Fade Away" were just some of the numbers he played.

Meanwhile, Bruce also played a diverse array of cover songs from outside of the rockabilly genre throughout the tour. They included renditions of the Bobby Fuller Four's "I Fought the Law," the Beatles/Isley Brothers classic "Twist and Shout," Hank Williams' "I Heard That Lonesome Whistle Blow," the Kingsmen's "Louie, Louie," Bob Dylan's "Chimes of Freedom," and Jimmy Cliff's "The Harder They Come."

Bruce's Backstage Tenet

By the start of the tour, Springsteen initiated a strict rule regarding backstage access before E Street Band gigs. No visitors were allowed.

Parties were fine after the show, but Springsteen wanted the group and the crew focused on the show as the start time approached. The Boss's edict—like his thorough sound checks—was just another way of ensuring that his live show was the best it could be.

Springsteen Makes a Music Video

Three years before MTV's emergence, Springsteen lensed his first music video— a live performance of "Rosalita" that was shot at the Memorial Coliseum in Phoenix on July 8. In this explosive clip of Springsteen putting his all into the song with the E Street Band accompanying him, they all appeared to be having the time of their lives.

When the video music channel went live on August 1, 1981, this was the only Springsteen clip at its disposal. In November 1982, that changed when a video of "Atlantic City" was premiered.

Zevon

Springsteen made a surprise guest appearance at singer/songwriter Warren Zevon's Portland, Oregon, gig on June 23, hopping onstage during the encore to play guitar and harmonica on the song "I'll Sleep When I'm Dead." But Springsteen's appearance at the Paramount Theater stop on Zevon's *Excitable Boy* tour wasn't the first time the two had shared the limelight.

The Boss had turned out for a promotional, late-night gig at the Manhattan club Trax earlier that year. During that St. Patrick's Day gig, Springsteen and stars like James Taylor, Linda Ronstadt, the Allman Brothers Band's Dickey

Springsteen launched his extensive tour in support of *Darkness on the Edge of Town* at Shea's Theatre in Buffalo, New York, on Tuesday, May 23, 1978. Ten days later, on June 2, the record was officially released.   *Courtesy of Brucebase*

Betts, and others backed Zevon on a rousing rendition of his hit "Werewolves of London."

Indy Strippers

On June 6, just two weeks into the tour, the E Street Band was already up to shenanigans when it invited a crew of strippers onstage during its gig the Convention Center in Indianapolis. Employees of the infamous gentlemen's club the Red Garter proudly strutted their stuff for ticketholders during Springsteen's encore.

Busy with Busey

The night after his sold-out show at the Forum in Inglewood, California, Springsteen was hanging with actor Gary Busey—who was the star of that year's acclaimed film *The Buddy Holly Story*. Together they went down to the Sundance Club in Los Angeles to check out a gig by the Old Dog Band, which included Busey's brother David on drums, with both men taking the stage for a song.

A month later, Busey was in Philadelphia for Springsteen's return sell-out engagement at the Spectrum. On night one, Gary helped the Boss on Holly's classic, "Carol." On night two, he assisted with another Buddy Holly number, "Rave On," plus a rapturous version of Gary U.S. Bonds's "Quarter to Three."

Returning to the Roxy

When the word slipped out on L.A. radio station KMET just after the Forum show had concluded that Springsteen was returning to the Roxy—the small,

Ticket stubs from the first and third nights of Springsteen's August 1978 headlining shows at Madison Square Garden. On the third and final night of the run, he brought his mom, Adele, onstage during an encore rendition of Gary "U.S." Bonds's "Quarter to Three."

Courtesy of Brucebase

infamous venue he played in 1975—diehard fans hurried down to the club's box office and camped out for tickets. Yet for the many that weren't lucky enough to be in attendance on July 7, when the band took the stage for a heart-stopping show, Springsteen's handlers had arranged for the gig to be simulcast in L.A. to the station's listening audience.

Aside from being several hours long, it marked the live introduction of "Point Blank" and "Independence Day"—both songs that would turn up on Springsteen's next studio album. The latter was delivered with only piano accompaniment.

We're a Happy Family

Springsteen was always delighted to have his family in the audience. During one of the L.A. shows, he addressed them during his live set.

"I think my mother and father and sister are here tonight," he told the Roxy crowd with a chuckle during the FM broadcast. "For six years, they've been following me around, trying to make me come back home . . . Every time I come in the house, they say, 'It's not too late, you could still go back to college.'

"My father, he used to give me a hard time all the time, he never used to let up," the Boss continued, smiling as the crowd listened intently. "It was always, 'Turn it down, turn it down, turn it down.' So tonight, I've got three million watts. I'm playing a hundred times louder than my stereo ever was—and he comes to see me!"

The Springsteen clan continued to support him just a month after Doug, Adele, and Pamela flew down from San Mateo for Bruce's L.A. shows. His mom and sister turned out for his first-ever concerts at Madison Square Garden. The three-night run at MSG spanned the nights of August 21–23 and saw him make a number of onstage acknowledgments to his family.

The first night, Springsteen dedicated a version of Chuck Berry's 1958 song "Sweet Little Sixteen" to his youngest sister Pamela. After the show, he spent time with sisters Pam and Ginny backstage. He also welcomed his old friends Gordon "Tex" Vinyard—who managed the Castiles—and his wife Marion to the event, which marked his first time headlining the ultimate New York venue.

After the show, he would tell WABC-TV's Joel Siegel that it was the most important night of his life. "I called my mom and said 'Ma. Listen. I have reservations for you, come and see me tomorrow night. And she said, 'I can't. I'll miss work.'" Springsteen explained, laughing.

"I want you to come and see me," he told her. "Just take the day off. So she came. And the crowd was great. The kids were great. It was good," he added quietly, hiding his emotion and looking away from the television camera.

The second night at the Garden, Bruce brought Pam out onstage during "Quarter to Three." During the last night of his engagement, his mom—who evidently took a couple of days off from her job to make the trip back east—came onstage and ordered her boy to play one more encore. "You can't say no if mom requests 'Quarter to Three,'" he informed the crowd as Adele humorously shook her finger at her son as the crowd roared.

Beaver Brown

Looking for a place to unwind after the E Street Band's August 25 show at Veterans Memorial Coliseum in New Haven, Springsteen and the band went over to the notorious rock club Toad's Place. It was here that Bruce first encountered Beaver Brown, the John Cafferty–fronted rock band that was heavily influenced by the Boss.

If it's true that imitation is the sincerest form of flattery, then Springsteen was clearly cajoled as he and Clarence Clemons joined Beaver Brown—the Rhode Island–based band who played Springsteen covers in its set—for a cover of "Rosalita." Springsteen and Cafferty also huddled together to figure out what else they could play, before delivering the Dovells' "You Can't Sit Down," the Swingin' Medallions' 1966 hit "Double Shot of My Baby's Love," and Wilson Pickett's "In the Midnight Hour."

We're Not Done Yet

During the *Darkness* tour, the Boss stunned fans a couple of times by returning to the stage after the house lights had come up. In one such instance, at the Providence Civic Center, Rhode Island Springsteen fans who hung around after "Quarter to Three" got an extra special treat.

Ten minutes after leaving the stage following the presumed encore, the E Street Band came back on to turn out an extended version of "Tenth Avenue Freeze Out."

Springsteen pulled a similar stunt after the band's December 15 concert at Winterland in San Francisco. Just as fans thought that gig—which was broadcast to the Bay Area via KSAN—was well over, Springsteen came back out to treat the five thousand attendees to one last tune. Informing the audience that they were off the radio but going to do one last tune, he introduced "Twist and Shout" by explaining that it was the first song he ever learned to play on guitar.

Don't Forget the Lyrics

Having gone several years without playing "Lost in the Flood," Springsteen decided to dust off the *Greetings* number during the trek, pulling it out for the first of just a few rare performances. With only piano accompaniment, he treated the audience at Pittsburgh's Stanley Theater to the tune on August 28.

Before he began the song, he confessed to his fans that he wasn't sure he remembered all of the words. In order to avoid any mistakes he opens his personal, handwritten lyrics notebook to get the job done. After the *Darkness* tour, the song would be out of Bruce's concert repertoire until 2000.

Cleveland Rocks

Following their Cleveland concert obligations at the nearby Coliseum, Springsteen and Miami Steve traveled over to the Agora to join Southside Johnny for his late-night headlining gig. Van Zandt, who performed with the Jukes whenever possible, played lead guitar for the entire show, while Springsteen jumped onstage late in the second set.

Asbury Jukes fans got a special treat as the Boss offered Johnny an assist on "The Fever," "I Don't Wanna Go Home," and "Havin' a Party." According to reports, this show didn't wrap up until 4 a.m. the next morning.

Meeting Seger

With a night off until his own show in Saginaw, Springsteen and his entourage took his tour bus to Michigan's Pine Knob Music Theater in Clarkston on September 2 to check out a performance by Bob Seger and the Silver Bullet Band. Springsteen—a fan of Seger's records and aware that his breakthrough hit "Night Moves" had been inspired by "Jungleland"—was curious to see what the Silver Bullet Band's live show entailed.

Seger was on tour that summer promoting his own hit album, *Stranger in Town*, which boasted the classics "Hollywood Nights," "Still the Same," "Old Time Rock and Roll," and "We've Got Tonight." After the show, Springsteen and Seger spent some time getting to know each other. They hit it off quickly, talking about the music business and even singing together on some oldies.

As a result of their meeting, Springsteen was inspired to perform the Chuck Willis nugget "Hang Up My Rock 'n' Roll Shoes" during his own gig the following night.

Capitol Thrill

After a run of Midwest gigs in the first week of September that concluded at Notre Dame University, Springsteen returned to play the New York City area. Three concerts were lined up at the Palladium, and three more were set for the Capitol Theatre in Passaic, New Jersey.

All six shows were sold out, with the New Jersey shows being more significant, if only because one of the concerts was broadcast live on New York's WNEW-FM. According to *Brucebase*, that gig—held on September 19, 1978—is one of the best all-time Springsteen concert recordings. With superb renditions of the non-album tracks "Because the Night" and "Fire," plus stellar performances of "Racing in the Street" and "Thunder Road," the sound quality was also top-notch.

The lone sound check for this gig marked early attempts of "The Ties That Bind," a new song called "Go Away (Come Close)," and versions of Led Zeppelin's "Whole Lotta Love," the Hollies' "I'm Alive," and Johnny Cash's "I Walk the Line," among others.

The third night, September 21, also marked the celebration of Springsteen's twenty-ninth birthday. Although it was commemorated two days early, concert promoter John Scher and Bruce's own band and crew made the milestone memorable when an attractive woman popped out of a giant cake onstage.

Santa in September

Three months ahead of Christmas, Springsteen took to the stage at Boston Gardens for a marathon four-hour gig that represented an early holiday gift. It wasn't the rendition of Elvis Presley's "Good Rockin' Tonight" that opened the show or the rare occurrence of "New York City Serenade," but the delivery of "Santa Claus Is Coming to Town" that surprised everyone in the crowd.

Springsteen informed the audience that he didn't think he'd make it back to Boston in time for the holidays. Therefore he was serving up his version of the Christmas staple well in advance of Mr. Claus's arrival. He also played the song in Atlanta just days later.

Springsteen Gets the Knack

During the E Street Band's month long break in touring that October, Springsteen went west. On a holiday in Los Angeles, he hung at the Sunset Marquis and befriended members of the up-and-coming rock outfit the Knack.

On October 17, he joined the group at the Troubadour for renditions of Buddy Holly's "Not Fade Away" and Bo Diddley's "Mona." A year ahead of their massive hit "My Sharona," Springsteen and the band's drummer Bruce Gary jammed in his hotel room on the latter's original tune "Rendezvous."

Back at Boss Acres

Just days away from the final two months of touring commitments behind *Darkness on the Edge of Town*, Springsteen and the E Street Band reconvened at his home in Holmdel to rehearse in his barn. He called it Telegraph Hill Studio, despite the fact it was little more than a place to jam.

The group attempted several new songs with titles like "Tonight," the Buddy Holly–inspired "Wild Kisses (I'm Gonna Treat You Right)," "Janey Needs a Shooter"—a song he would give to Warren Zevon—and "The Ties That Bind," which, of course, would surface on his next studio release.

Princeton Vibes

When roadwork resumed on November 1, it was in Springsteen's backyard. The E Street Band hit the stage to the delight of fans, who danced and jumped with such excitement that the floor in Princeton University's Jadwin Gym was

vibrating up and down. The show resulted in structural damage to the building and marked the last major rock show ever held in this facility.

Bruce Goes Bang

Following Springsteen's gig at Cobo Hall in Detroit on December 30, the E Street Band descended on Cleveland's Richfield Coliseum for a pair of anticipated New Year's shows. Unfortunately, one of the two concerts was marred by the poor judgment of a presumably intoxicated fan.

Late into the New Year's Eve gig, as midnight came, the band rang in 1979 with "Auld Lang Syne." But not long after, an audience member near the front of the stage tossed a lit firecracker in Springsteen's direction during "Good Rockin' Tonight." When it exploded dangerously close to him, Springsteen lost his marbles for a minute and rep-

This 1978 *Creem* magazine cover finds Springsteen posing with his Esquire guitar. He picked up his beloved guitar for just $185 in May 1972 at Phil Patillo's Guitar Shop in Belmar, New Jersey.   *Author's Collection*

rimanded the unidentified fan from the stage. After regaining his composure, Springsteen carried on with the show, but it rightfully pissed him off.

The following night, January 1, 1979, when the band took the stage, Springsteen was in improved spirits for the show that boasted a staggering thirty-two-song setlist. It helped that it was the final night of the trek, but rarities like a cover of the Rolling Stones' classic "The Last Time," and the overall loose and playful tone of the gig, made it a memorable one.

19

We're Runnin' Now, but Darlin' Will We Stand in Time?

The River

A week and a half after the *Darkness* tour had concluded, the E Street Band—sans Miami Steve—gathered together at the Lock, Stock and Barrel, a club in Fair Haven, New Jersey, for Clarence Clemons's thirty-seventh birthday party. Springsteen sang lead on covers of "Mustang Sally," "Kansas City," "I Saw Her Standing There," and "Rock and Roll Music" during the celebration, which also marked the second-to-last time the group would perform together in front of an audience until the following September.

In March, following a planned two-month break that allowed Springsteen time to plot his next record, the E Street Band reconvened for sessions at a new Manhattan facility called the Power Station. Intermittently, he had played out locally when friends like Robert Gordon—who had scored a minor hit with "Fire"—and Rhode Island rockers Beaver Brown played the Fast Lane in Asbury Park.

During a break from studio work that June, the E Street Band went to Los Angeles to attend the wedding of its lighting technician Mark Brickman. In a reception held at the Whisky in Los Angeles, Springsteen and the group shared the stage with Boz Scaggs and Rickie Lee Jones for a series of originals like "Thunder Road" and an assortment of obligatory covers.

Hey Ho, Hungry Heart

In the spring of 1979, the Ramones touched down at the Fast Lane during a North American tour in support of their fourth studio album, *Road to Ruin*. Springsteen was a fan of their records, especially their latest single, "I Wanna Be Sedated," and went to catch the band's March 29 show in Asbury Park to show his support.

Afterward, he hung out backstage with frontman Joey Ramone, and the two got along well, even singing a few tunes together. Then the Queens-born punk singer suggested that Springsteen write his band a song.

He obliged, pumping out "Hungry Heart." But when Jon Landau heard the contagious tune, he recommended that Springsteen keep it for his upcoming record. When it became his biggest hit to date the following year, he was glad he did.

Home Demos

Aside from the unreleased material that Springsteen had road-tested in 1978, he wrote a number of songs at home. Some titles included "Everybody's Looking for Somebody," "I Don't Know," "Looking Out for Number One," "I Want to Start a New Life," and "You Gotta Fight."

One song, "Chevrolet Deluxe," was a gloomy number similar to what became "The River," while "White Town" had a reggae touch. He would extract lyrics from the latter for his song "Jackson Cage."

Rough sketches of songs like "You Can Look (But You Better Not Touch)" and "Held Up Without a Gun"—which became the B-side of "Hungry Heart"— were also worked on at home in Holmdel in 1979.

The Ties That Bind

When Springsteen and the E Street Band joined forces at the Power Station in late March to begin work on his fifth studio album, Van Zandt was asked to serve as an official producer—alongside Springsteen and Jon Landau—on the project.

The Power Station was located inside a renovated Manhattan cathedral, which allowed the group to achieve a big sound. The musicians hit the ground running, beginning with "Roulette," an urgent, politically charged song written in response to that year's catastrophic Three Mile Island nuclear accident. Sessions for the record proved to both fun and productive.

Over the next few months, Springsteen tracked a ten-song album he would title *The Ties That Bind*. Although "Roulette" would find itself relegated to outtake status, he had finished and

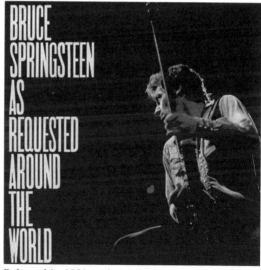

Released in 1981 at the end of *The River* world tour, *Bruce Springsteen as Requested Around the World* was a promotional album that joined the five sturdiest tracks from his latest album ("Sherry Darling," "The River," "Cadillac Ranch," "Hungry Heart," and "Out in the Street") with four fan favorites ("Born to Run," "Badlands," "Prove It All Night," and "Rosalita (Come Out Tonight"). *Courtesy of Lost in the Flood*

sequenced the record. He planned to open it with the title track and include the songs "Cindy," "Hungry Heart," "Stolen Car," "Be True," "The River," "You Can Look (But You Better Not Touch)," "The Price You Pay," "I Wanna Marry You," and "Loose Ends."

In September, the album was mastered and submitted to Columbia Records. Photographer Frank Stefanko was again commissioned to shoot Springsteen for the album jacket, and word soon reached retailers via the label that the Boss would have a new record in the shops for the Christmas season.

But Springsteen continued to write and record, and changed his mind about releasing the long-player. He withdrew the album, much to the disappointment of his fans, his label, and the music business as a whole.

"I felt that it just wasn't good enough," he said of the lost record in *Songs*. "The songs lacked the kind of unity and conceptual intensity I liked my music to have."

Springsteen and the E Street Band continued working on the project for another year. When his follow-up to *Darkness on the Edge of Town* was finally released in October 1980, seven of the ten aforementioned songs would be on it.

Meanwhile, hardcore fans willing to pay enough wound up with bootleg copies of the project anyway, when reel-to-reels of the master found their way into the wrong hands. As for bootlegging in general, such releases had become a significant concern for the Springsteen camp by 1979.

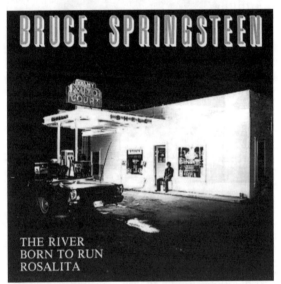

THE RIVER
BORN TO RUN
ROSALITA

Utilizing artwork that would surface again thirty years later as part of 2010's *The Promise* packaging, this 12-inch pressing of "The River"—backed by "Born to Run" and "Rosalita"—from May 1981 included the Boss's UK tour dates from the time on the reverse sleeve.
Courtesy of 991.com

Bootleg Blues

While Springsteen once took a relaxed attitude to fans taping his shows—going so far as to tell bootleggers recording his 1978 FM simulcast from the Roxy to roll their tapes—rehearsal and demo recordings of new, unreleased music had begun to seep out. It presented what he, Landau, and Columbia Records all considered a very serious problem.

Concerts were meant for the public, which was why he could look the other way, but new material was a work in progress and in many cases was never meant to be heard by the public. Bootlegs that were originally made by fans for other fans had become big

business. When he saw astro-
nomical prices on unauthorized records that sounded
really bad, he felt as if he
and his fans were both being
ripped off.

Landau put his foot down
in May 1979, telling *Rolling
Stone*, "Bruce spends a year of
his life conceiving and exe-
cuting an album so that it will
perfectly reflect the musical
statement he wants to make.
Then these people come
along and confiscate material
that was never intended for
release on an album, sell it
and make a profit on it without ever paying anyone that's
involved. It's just out-and-out
theft."

Springsteen's camp went
to court in Los Angeles and
New Jersey, filing suit against
bootleggers for copyright

Springsteen's second U.S. single from *The River*, "Fade
Away," was a haunting, organ-laden ballad that kept it from
duplicating the success of the infectious U.S. #5 hit "Hungry
Heart." Most sales were to his core fans, who wanted the 45
for the non-LP tune "Be True," a leftover from the album's
sessions.   *Courtesy of 991.com*

infringement, unfair competition, and unauthorized use of name and likeness.
Although these suits weren't completely carried out, they scared the bootleggers
enough to pull them off the market. More importantly, they prevented scores
more from being illegally released.

"The people who were doing it had warehouses full of records, and they were
just sittin' back getting fat," Springsteen told Dave DiMartino the following year.
"Rushing and putting out anything and getting 30 fuckin' dollars for it. And I
just got really mad about it."

No Nukes

Springsteen signed on for a series of "No Nukes" concerts in September 1979
that were held under the banner of MUSE—Musicians United for Safe Energy.
He did so at the encouragement of his good friend and the event's coproducer,
Jackson Browne.

The aim of these four shows at Madison Square Garden—which also featured
the Doobie Brothers, Tom Petty and the Heartbreakers, Crosby, Stills and
Nash, Bonnie Raitt, and others—was to raise awareness about the dangers of
radioactive-fueled energy and help finance a pro-solar and antinuclear initiative.

Springsteen and the E Street Band played the benefit on September 21 and 22, performing abridged sets that balanced fan favorites like "Prove It All Night," "Rosalita," and "Jungleland" with yet-to-be-released songs like "Sherry Darling" and "The River"—the latter of which premiered at these gigs. Springsteen also performed a duet with Browne, delivering a memorable version of "Stay," the 1960 Maurice Williams and the Zodiacs doo-wop classic.

As for the audience reaction, a reporter from the *Boston Phoenix* called Springsteen's first appearance "the most frenzied I've ever heard." Of course, the crowd grew impatient in the lead up to the Boss's headlining appearance. Tom Petty would later admit that he thought he was being booed as the audience clamored for "Bruuuce." Meanwhile, Graham Nash told a scribe from *Rolling Stone*, "I learned never to open for Bruce Springsteen."

An official release of "Stay" and Springsteen's renowned concert staple "Devil with the Blue Dress Medley" followed in late '79, when a three-record, various artists set, *No Nukes*, hit store shelves. Like the concerts, proceeds from the album went to the antinuclear cause.

Back to Work

The overwhelming response Springsteen got from the MUSE audiences made him want to give them an album that was a cut above the norm. Springsteen didn't want to just take up space on store shelves; he wanted his name on the best records in his fans' collections.

As 1980 approached, the E Street Band went back into the studio. An abundance of tunes were tracked, but Springsteen's instinctive approach meant that there would be more and more misfires as he tried out many, many songs. He was determined to let the group play live and see what developed, but he

also kept his built-in bullshit detector on at all times in order to keep the bar high. The net result, as he would explain in *Songs*, was "more pop songs in a looser conceptual framework."

This Brazil pressing of Springsteen's 1980 smash "Hungry Heart" is significant because it was mastered at 33 1/3 RPM and it marks the only appearance of "Stolen Car" as its B-side. All other markets featured the non-LP track "Held Up Without a Gun" on the flip of "Hungry Heart." *Courtesy of Lost in the Flood*

Atlantic City Expressway

On January 9, 1980, long before Jon Bon Jovi (then Jon Bongiovi) was a rock-'n'-roll superstar, he was just a kid from Sayreville, New Jersey trying to make a name for himself. One cold night, as his band—the Atlantic City Expressway—played the Fast Lane, he was joined onstage by one of his heroes. Together they sang renditions of two Springsteen tunes in the A.C.E.'s repertoire—"Prove It All Night" and "The Promised Land."

The cover image of a collectible three-LP vinyl box set released in 1980. Produced for export, it counted UK copies of Springsteen's first three records.   *Courtesy of 991.com*

Contrasts

Bruce had hoped to mirror his live shows—where slow, serious numbers would be offset by exhilarating rave-ups—on his next record. After the seriousness of *Darkness*, he wanted paradoxes. This time out, the emotional range of his album needed to also allow for the fun, energetic, party-like atmosphere of his concerts.

When *The River* was said and done at the end of the summer of '80, the song sequencing balanced the frolicsome against the somber. It was Springsteen's intent to reflect the inconsistencies of life through his music, where joyous experiences might follow morose ones—and vice-versa.

When fans flocked to record stores upon the two-LP set's release on October 17 and brought *The River* home, they got to experience a dichotomy similar to Springsteen's live gigs, right in the comfort of their own living rooms.

The River

Springsteen's fifth album covered difficult subject matter, including the challenges faced by adults with families and responsibilities. The title track, for instance, was inspired by the struggles his brother-in-law faced trying to make ends meet for Bruce's sister Ginny and their children as a construction worker during the recession of the late 1970s.

The Boss would later reveal that "The River" helped fuel the writing of his 1982 album *Nebraska,* while another album track, "Stolen Car," would inspire some of the songs on 1987's *Tunnel of Love.*

In many of the songs, he was acknowledging that, for a lot of people, many of the little things were worthwhile, if not heroic. "Little things that happen in a kitchen or something, or between a husband and a wife or between them and their kids; It's a grand experience but it's not always big," he told the *Los Angeles Times* in 1980. "There's plenty of room for those kinds of victories and I think the records have that."

Track by Track

With *The River,* Springsteen was reacting to the records he had already made. If

A rare Japanese handbill from 1980 designed to promote Springsteen's involvement in the *No Nukes* album, which culled tracks from his September 1979 performances at Madison Square Garden. The live album—which helped raise awareness of the dangers of nuclear power—also included tracks by the Doobie Brothers, Jackson Browne, Bruce Springsteen, James Taylor, Crosby Stills and Nash, and Tom Petty, among others.   *Courtesy of 991.com*

Darkness had a modern production value, his next offering—which was beginning to look like a double album—needed to reflect the spontaneity of his concerts. With the help of Steve Van Zandt, who was a student of 1960s garage rock, the project took on a less refined sound than its predecessor, incorporating exuberance without sacrificing the professionalism Springsteen and the band had become known for.

"The Ties That Bind"

Written on the road in 1978, Springsteen first debuted this song live that fall. Originally slated to be the title cut of his scrapped '79 album, he still felt the song was strong enough to open his weighty 1980 double album. Supposedly influenced by the Searchers' "Needles and Pins" and Creedence Clearwater Revival's "Who'll Stop the Rain," it was tracked in The Power Station's wood-paneled studio with microphones over Max Weinberg's drums to capture an ideal snare sound.

Although the song never earned the attention it deserved on the radio—likely because it was never released as a single even though it deserved that honor—its chiming guitar lines and Springsteen's stellar lyrics about heartbreak still made it a favorite of fans. Since the E Street Band's 1999 reunion, the pensive but upbeat song has been a regular part of Springsteen's live set.

"Sherry Darling"

Easily the funniest moment on *The River* and one of the most fun, this frat-party sing-along about a pain-in-the-ass mother-in-law was conceived during the *Darkness* sessions but held over.

A showcase for Clemons's saxophone and Springsteen's amusing remarks about Sherry's mama yappin' in the backseat, the memorable number is, at its core, a love song. When it was released in certain territories as a single in 1981, it showed a more playful side of the Boss than had been heard in years.

"Jackson Cage"

Juxtaposed against its lighthearted predecessor, "Jackson Cage" was just the opposite. An ode of understanding extended to a downhearted woman who feels isolated, dejected, and emotionally abused, it may be one of the starkest, rawest songs in Springsteen's songbook and arguably the most jarring on *The River*.

"Two Hearts"

Doing an about-face from the song that it follows, Springsteen's "Two Hearts" turns out to be another one of his finest garage rock numbers. Evoking elements of the great 1960s guitar-driven singles he and Van Zandt were weaned on, it's an upbeat shot of optimism aimed at the lovelorn.

Bruce assures his listeners that they, like he, will love again. And just as loneliness sucks and heartbreak hurts, it's the reason we all need to keep searching. As the Boss

Pressed for the Spanish market in 1981, this unique art for "The River" single boasts a photo of Springsteen with the E Street Band. The picture was taken from the lyric sheet of its parent album.   *Courtesy of 991.com*

explains with a little help from a harmonizing Steve, "Two hearts are better than one."

"Independence Day"

Written in 1977 and originally considered for *Darkness*, this song is based on Springsteen's turbulent relationship with his father. He loves his father, but the fact that they are so much alike constantly has them at each other's throats, until he leaves, acknowledging in his lyrics that the house isn't big enough for the both of them.

Springsteen's heart-wrenching vocal on "Independence Day" ranks it among the best he's ever tracked. The sad accompaniment—whether Roy Bittan's soft piano, Clarence Clemons's somber saxophone part, or the delicate acoustic guitar strums—provides the ideal backing for what has to be one of Springsteen's most sincere recordings.

"Hungry Heart"

Released as a single on October 21, 1980, "Hungry Heart" became Springsteen's biggest hit to date, peaking at #5 in the U.S. in December. An infectious song about a roaming man's infidelities, the tune—which was written in under a half an hour—supposedly extracted its title from a line in the poem "Ulysses" by Alfred, Lord Tennyson.

Recorded with Springsteen's vocals sped up slightly and counting harmony vocals from the Turtles' own Mark Volman and Howard Kaylan (aka Flo and Eddie), the massively popular track wound up being named single of the year in the 1980 *Rolling Stone* Reader's Poll.

Although the single flopped in the U.K. where it stalled at #44, former Beatle John Lennon was a fan of the song. On the day of his murder, December 8, 1980, Lennon called "Hungry Heart" "a great record" when he was asked about it, and compared it to his own comeback single, "(Just Like) Starting Over."

"Out in the Street"

Tracked in the spring of '80, "Out in the Street" was one of the last songs recorded for *The River*, and its optimism was nearly its death knell. Bolstered by the intertwining vocals of Van Zandt, Bittan, and, of course, Springsteen, its chorus is infectious, making it one of the shining stars of the album.

Yet the Boss very nearly pulled the tune—which tells the tale of a construction worker who lives for Friday nights and the good times that come with the weekend—from the record. "It's about people being together and sharing a certain feeling," he said in *Springsteen*. "It's about people being together and sharing a certain feeling. I know [the feeling] is real, but it's hard to see sometimes."

"You go out in the street, and there's a chance you get hit over the head or mugged," he explained. "The song's not realistic in a way, but there's something very real at the heart of it."

"Crush on You"

An explosive, heart-pumping rocker with a rockabilly spirit, the song tells about a man walking down the road when a gorgeous woman—clearly out of his league—pulls up at the light in a 280Z or some other pricey "Hong Kong special" of the era. Springsteen ponders whether the object of his desires is a waitress, a bank teller, or a Rockefeller heiress.

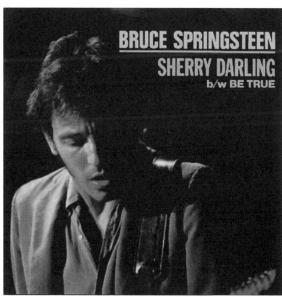

Released as a 7-inch single in European markets in 1981, "Sherry Darling" was arguably the most upbeat number on *The River* and a great forum for the saxophone work of Clarence Clemons. *Courtesy of 991.com*

Describing her as "C'est Magnifique," his imagination runs wild as the band stomps and shakes behind him. Although it may not be the finest number on *The River*, in terms of rock-'n'-roll merriment, it's aces nonetheless.

"You Can Look (But You Better Not Touch)"

As vibrant and fun as the song it follows, this number recalls the spirit of Eddie Cochran and Jerry Lee Lewis, as Springsteen puts a hillbilly affectation on his vocal delivery.

Matched with a twangy guitar lead, the sing-along chronicles the frustration of a young man who has to suppress his animalistic tendencies as a lady writhes in front of him on the television. Later, when he gets alone with a gal he nicknames "Dirty Annie" at the drive-in, he gets interrupted by a tap on the glass just as he is about to have his way with her.

"I Wanna Marry You"

A lilting devotional ballad aimed at a single mother of two, whom Springsteen's character watches from afar but hopes to marry, this song is either lyrically hopeful or downright sad. As he thinks of what he'll say to her, his pitch will be to tell her that, although he probably won't be able to make her dreams come true, he might be able to help them along.

Yet for all of his pleading, one never knows if he ever actually approaches her to explain how he feels. Whether real or imagined, the song's presentation—with the church organ playing of Danny Federici building the framework—is downright magical.

Based on its backing vocal arrangement—which recalls classic doo-wop and white soul—it becomes one of the more unique numbers on *The River*. Still, Springsteen's guttural crooning is what carries the song and makes it convincing.

"The River"

Launched with an unforgettable harmonica part that will come to signify some of Springsteen's future work, this song—penned about his sister Ginny's life—was partially inspired by lyrics from the 1950 Hank Williams song "Long Gone Lonesome Blues."

The song first came to him in his New York hotel room while he was working at the Power Station, when he started singing another Williams tune, "My Bucket's Got a Hole in It." He drove home to Holmdel that night and wrote the song that same night. Using a narrative voice, his character—presumably his brother-in-law—sat on a barstool telling his story to a stranger on the next stool.

"I based the song on the crash of the construction industry in late '70s New Jersey and the hard times that fell on my sister and her family," Springsteen wrote in *Songs*. When Ginny first heard the song unveiled at the No Nukes shows, she visited her big brother backstage, gave him an embrace, and knew—without him saying it—that he had written it about her.

The sleeve for the original 1981 UK 45 RPM release of "The River." The song, which was inspired lyrically by the Hank Williams song "Long Gone Lonesome Blues," was backed with "Independence Day." The latter was written in 1977 and was initially considered for *Darkness on the Edge of Town* but was held over for *The River*.   *Courtesy of 991.com*

"Point Blank"

This bleak, six-minute ballad was the last song recorded for the project. With a theatrical piano line, it traces the downward spiral of a drug-afflicted girl that the narrator once imagined he had a future with.

The promising young woman he used to canoodle in the Asbury Park rock clubs is now a heroin addict waiting on her welfare check. Springsteen took the title of this powerful story song from the 1967 Lee Marvin movie of the same name.

"Cadillac Ranch"

A high-energy number and live favorite—as evidenced by its presence on the 1986 box set *Live 1975–85*—"Cadillac Ranch" is one of Springsteen's car songs. The song—which name checks 1950s NASCAR champion Junior Johnson and actors James Dean and Burt Reynolds—is an acknowledgment of the love a working man has for his vintage Caddy, replete with Eldorado fins and whitewalls.

For the track, Springsteen returns to singing in the same Southern drawl heard in "You Can Look (But You Better Not Touch)" as he utters about his desire to visit the popular Texas tourist stop. It was named for the ten classic Cadillacs that are buried hood-first at an angle in the wheat field at Ant Farm near Amarillo.

A photo of the ranch is featured in the artwork for *The River*. Later, Springsteen was photographed for 1984's *Born in the U.S.A.* tour program at the artistic display, running alongside the graffiti-covered cars.

"I'm a Rocker"

A contagious, beat-driven number, this playful, rollicking track is hard to dismiss. It's little wonder it was a staple of his live set on many tours. In this song written about a damsel in distress, Springsteen's macho superhero character promises to save the day.

Dismissing James Bond and Secret Agent Man, not to mention Kojak and Columbo, he professes he is the right man to lift her spirits. Based on the groove of this soaring winner, he's a sure bet to help anyone mend a broken heart.

"Fade Away"

An organ-touched, pained ballad, this song was a favorite of Steve Van Zandt's, but its slow arrangement meant that it was short-lived in Springsteen's live shows. Although it was the second single from *The River*, its despairing narrative kept it from becoming more than a modest hit.

After incorporating it into their live set in the 1980s, Southside Johnny and the Asbury Jukes covered the tune on the 1997 live record *Spittin' Fire*. In Van Zandt's mind, however, it still had staying power nearly thirty years after it was tracked; he referred to it in a 2008 *Rolling Stone* Q and A as "one of those funny, lost little gems."

"Stolen Car"

This somber track focuses on a failing marriage, whose subject goes as far as to steal cars in order to feel alive. Part of him hopes to get arrested so that he can slip away from his wife, but he never gets pulled over, and his unhappy life with her trudges forth. The notion that jail seems more alluring than the marital prison he's already living in affirms his hopelessness.

Backed by just a piano, a synthesizer, and some soft tympani, Springsteen would go on to cite "Stolen Car" as another song that marked a change in his approach to songwriting as he approached *Nebraska*.

"Ramrod"

Another number penned for *Darkness on the Edge of Town* but held over for *The River*, this sexually charged song has been a recurring part of the E Street Band's shows for decades. Its joyous, high-energy presentation—augmented by a fabulous Clarence Clemons sax solo and Danny Federici's chirping organ—earned the acknowledgment of author Stephen King, who named it one of his Top 10 favorite rock songs of all time.

As for Springsteen himself, he once admitted that the Duane Eddy–like tune was one of the saddest things he'd written—obviously not because of the music, but because the character was so anachronistic.

"The Price You Pay"

A fusion of the solemnity heard on *The River*'s ballads and the hooks heard on both "Hungry Heart" and "The Promised Land," this is one of the secret weapons of an album chock-full of great songs. Melodic and reflective, "The Price You Pay" is an underrated, mid-tempo number. Its magic wasn't lost on Emmylou Harris, who covered it in 1981 on her album *Evangeline*.

"Drive All Night"

At eight and a half minutes, this love ballad is one that few fans cite, but there's a magic power in its slow rendering, thanks in part to Clemons's unhurried sax part. Some have argued that the song suffers from a lack of self-editing, and truth be told, Springsteen could have made "Drive All Night" far more effective by fading it out at the five-minute mark. As it stands, the track gets a little dull at the end, making it the album's lone dud.

"Wreck on the Highway"

Springsteen's delivery of this song, inspired by the Roy Acuff tune of the same name, has tinges of country music, but the acoustic guitar and organ assist him in telling a haunting story of a man who comes upon a terrible auto accident on a two-lane road.

Amid the spitting rain, the blood and glass on the roadway—not to mention an injured driver—the narrator gets out of his car to see if he can help, and as he does so, he ponders his own mortality. In the final verse, home safe in the arms of his loved one, he continues to be haunted by the images of what he witnessed.

Springsteen would reveal that the song came very quickly, almost automatically. He was surprised later, based on how much he liked it, that he put such little effort into it.

Outtakes

With twenty-five completed songs, Springsteen had four sides of material for the record and a handful of B-sides when sessions wrapped in August 1980. Non-LP material like the aforementioned "Held Up Without a Gun" and "Be True"—the flipside of "Fade Away"—were the only numbers from the work at the Record Plant to see release until 1998's *Tracks* box set.

Countless variations on the songs that made the record were tracked, including "Stolen Car"—which originally began under the title "Son You May Kiss the Bride."

Many others, including the four that were held over when he decided against releasing *The Ties That Bind*, eventually surfaced on *Tracks* or never emerged.

"Cindy," "From Small Things (Big Things One Day Come)," "I Wanna Be Where the Bands Are," "Loose Ends," "Mary Lou," "Restless Nights," "Rickie (Wants a Man of Her Own)," "Roulette," "Slow Fade," and "Take 'Em as They Come" are among these outtakes.

Ten Facts About *The River*

1. All told, *The River* cost $500,000 to make.
2. In April 1979, work was halted on the album when Springsteen crashed a three-wheeled motorbike into a tree, requiring three weeks of recuperation.
3. The Clash were forced to move their sessions for their own double album, *London Calling*, from the Power Station to Electric Ladyland when Springsteen's fall 1979 sessions ran over.
4. In anticipation of the record in the summer of 1980, many FM stations began playing Springsteen's version of "The River" that appeared in the *No Nukes* film. Jon Landau and Columbia Records issued cease-and-desist letters to stop them from airing that rendition.
5. "Held Up Without a Gun" was included on the original track list for the album. When Springsteen changed his mind and pulled it that September, early pressings of the album cover had to be reprinted.
6. Since its release in 1980, *The River* has sold more than five million copies in the U.S. alone, where it has been certified quintuple platinum by the Recording Industry Association of America.

7. *Rolling Stone* listed the record as #250 in its 2003 ranking of the 500 Greatest Albums of All Time.

8. On November 8, 2009, the E Street Band performed *The River* in its entirety at Madison Square Garden.

9. The title track was released as a single in several Western European territories in May 1981. It reached #35 on the U.K. singles chart. It was not released in the U.S.

10. "Sherry Darling" and "Cadillac Ranch" were also issued as singles outside of the U.S. in 1981.

Critical Reaction

Critics were largely positive, with *Musician* calling *The River* "Springsteen's best album," while the *Village Voice* praised the project by writing, "the condensed song craft makes this double album a model of condensation—upbeat enough for the radio here, delicate enough for a reverie there, he elaborates a myth about the fate of the guys he grew up with that hits a lot of people where they live."

Of course, not everyone felt the same. *Trouser Press* panned it, writing, "*The River*'s attempt to make a statement is buried in an avalanche of repetition and evident lack of inspiration."

Commercial Reception

The River was Springsteen's first chart-topping album. The fact that it was a double disc made that all the more impressive, as the cost of the record was—at $11.98—a little less than twice what a normal album cost at the time. It sold 1.6 million copies in the first two months of release.

The album's second single was an odd choice. As a slow, organ-tinged ballad, "Fade Away" made a great album cut but an inferior single. The fact that it stalled at #20 confirmed this notion. Barnburners like "Two Hearts" and "Cadillac

The cover of an extremely rare 1981 4-track 12-inch promotional EP titled *Killer Tracks from The River*. Pressed in Japan, this release—which only features Steve Van Zandt, Clarence Clemons, and Springsteen on the sleeve—was limited to approximately 100 copies and included "The River," "I Wanna Marry You," "Hungry Heart," and "Point Blank."   *Courtesy of 991.com*

A 1979 newspaper ad promoting specialty programming on Cleveland rock station WMMS, including a Sunday night broadcast of "Rare Springsteen" material.   *Author's Collection*

Ranch" or the melodic rockers "Out in the Street" or "The Ties That Bind" would have all been better choices. As it was, the album's shelf life only lasted as long as Springsteen's ongoing tour, which was a wrap by mid-1981.

Just after his album reached #1 in November 1980, Springsteen was asked by *Musician* what, if any, goals remained, to which he responded, "Doing it is the goal. It's not to play some big place, or for a record to be Number One. Doing it is the end—not the means. That's the point. So the point is: What's next? Some more of this. But bigness—that is no end. That as an end, is meaningless, essentially. It's good, 'cause you can reach a lot of people, and that's the idea. And after tonight, you go out and you reach more people, and then the night after that, you do that again."

20

Ten Years Burning Down This Road

Springsteen Tours 1980–1989

The River Tour

In late September 1980, the E Street Band came together in Lititz, Pennsylvania, to prepare for *The River* tour opener, which got underway on October 3 at the University of Michigan in Ann Arbor. Special guest Bob Seger joined the band for its finale rendition of "Thunder Road," which Springsteen played—quite unusually—for the second time that night. The Ann Arbor show was also notable because somehow he forgot the lyrics to his trademark single "Born to Run."

Thankfully, his devoted audience knew all the words to the set-opening number and gladly helped him remember them. His connection with his audience was something that had grown stronger year after year. It was more than mere fan adulation; when he met his loyalists out on the road, they had a connection that didn't need to be spoken.

As a means of rewarding his fans, Springsteen and his handlers came up with a "ticket drop"—a way of getting last minute VIP tickets that have gone unclaimed by the media and special guests into the hands of hardcore fans. On the day of the shows, astute Springsteen disciples could stop by the venue box office and oftentimes score awesome seats.

Throughout October, the Boss covered Midwest cities like Chicago, St. Paul, Milwaukee, and St. Louis, traveling westward performing in theaters and arenas. Gauging the success of his shows not by the audience reaction or the following day's newspaper review but by his own assessment, Bruce had trouble sleeping on those rare nights that things went wrong. Performing was still the thing that made him feel the best—the most alive.

Three weeks into his roadwork but a night ahead of a Seattle Coliseum gig on October 24, Springsteen took a walk from his Olympic Hotel room to the nearby Old Timer's Café where the Montana-bred Lost Highway Band was playing. During a break in the band's set, Springsteen asked a band member—who didn't instantly recognize him—if he could sit in. "Only if you can stay in tune," they told him, as Springsteen strapped on a borrowed guitar and led the group

These unused silkscreen After Show passes from Springsteen's 1980 tour would have been given to grant backstage access at E Street Band concerts in Houston, Texas; Largo, Maryland; and Baton Rouge, Louisiana.   *Courtesy of 991.com*

through three 1960s rock classics, "Route 66," "Gloria," and "In the Midnight Hour."

On Halloween night, the E Street Band launched the set with a cover of Jumpin' Gene Simmons's 1964 novelty hit "Haunted House" at the L.A. Sports Arena as Springsteen was carried onstage in a coffin and chased by ghoulish roadies during his guitar solo. The next night, Jackson Browne came out to duet on "Sweet Little Sixteen," a number Springsteen first joined Browne on during his headlining gig at the L.A. Forum two and a half months before.

Throughout the tour, Springsteen was keeping the members of the E Street Band on their toes, regularly deviating from the setlist. Following his two-night stand at the Summit in Houston on November 15, Springsteen explained himself to the *Houston Post* in an interview that ran a week later. "I had to stop the guys in the band and say, 'Listen, just forget the list, don't look at it anymore, don't start anything until you hear me call it.' I was calling a lot of 'em—"Growin' Up," "Crush on You," "Fade Away," "Stolen Car"—different things from night to night. That's the way it goes . . ."

On a different night, Springsteen tested the band by calling out "Midnight Hour," a Wilson Pickett classic that they hadn't rehearsed. "We all just about fainted," Steve Van Zandt told *Musician* in January '81. "Funky [bassist Garry Tallent] didn't even believe we were doing it until about the second chorus." Just the same, everything sounded tight.

With a five-day break, the band resumed the tour with its first show in Chicago, with the live debut of Elvis Presley's "Mystery Train" as the finale. Routed back to the East Coast the week of Thanksgiving, a pair of D.C. area shows at the Capital Centre in Largo, Maryland, on November 23 and 24 were followed by two homecoming area gigs at Madison Square Garden on the 27th and 28th. The first night, Springsteen dedicated "Darkness on the Edge of Town" to his former drummer Vini Lopez, while "Growin' Up" was served up

This ticket stub, dated November 23, 1980, came from the first of Springsteen's two Washington, D.C.–area gigs at the Capital Centre.   *Author's Collection*

with an acknowledgment to John Hammond, who signed him after hearing the song.

Arena shows in Pittsburgh, Rochester, Buffalo, and Philadelphia continued into December. Speaking to the Spectrum crowd the night after John Lennon was suddenly killed, Springsteen admitted, "It's hard to come out and play tonight when so much's been lost. The first record that I ever learned was a record called 'Twist and Shout' and if it wasn't for John Lennon, we'd all be in some place very different tonight. It's an unreasonable world and you have to live with a lot of things that are just unlivable and it's a hard thing to come out and play but there's just nothing else you can do."

A week before Christmas, Springsteen was back in the Big Apple for two additional Madison Square Garden shows. Three days after the holiday, he performed a three-night stand at Nassau Coliseum in Uniondale, New York, including a New Year's Eve concert that—at four hours and thirty-eight minutes—may be the longest Springsteen show ever performed. During the New Year's Countdown, Springsteen sprayed champagne into the crowd, soaking much of the front row. He had good reason to celebrate; 1980 was a tremendously successful year. (Note: The version of "Merry Christmas Baby" that was released on the 1987 benefit CD *A Very Special Christmas* was recorded on this night.)

Springsteen and the band went back on the road in late January 1981 playing shows in Toronto, Montreal, and Ottawa before again canvassing the U.S. heartland. A variety of cover versions began to emerge, including Bobby Fuller's "I Fought the Law," Woody Guthrie's "This Land Is Your Land," and Wilbert Harrison's "Kansas City"—which was played specifically for the audience at that city's Kemper Arena.

As the tour made its way into the Deep South, Johnny Cash's "Folsom Prison Blues" was incorporated into his regular encore "Detroit Medley," while "Twist and Shout" was also a routine show closer. Seven weeks after it began, the second leg of *The River* tour concluded at Indianapolis's Market Square Arena on March 5. For all of Springsteen's hard work, he had dropped twenty pounds, going from 150 to 130 pounds, slimming down to a twenty-six inch waist.

European *River*

A week after his run of North American dates were complete, Springsteen called Jon Landau to let him know that he was seriously ill. He was sick with a serious bout of the flu that left him with laryngitis and a fever. If he wasn't near death, he felt crummy enough that his upcoming European tour dates would need to be bumped back a few weeks until he regained his strength.

Finally, on April 7, he made his first European concert appearances since 1975, launching a two-month run of shows at the Congress Centrum in Hamburg, Germany. In addition to staples from Bruce's own songbook, fans across Eastern Europe—from France and Spain to Belgium, Holland, Denmark, and Sweden—were treated to an arsenal of new covers, like John Fogerty's "Rockin' All Over the World," Creedence Clearwater Revival's "Who'll Stop the Rain"

A set of After Show-only passes from Springsteen's July 5, 1981, gig at the all-new Brendan Byrne Arena in New Jersey's Meadowlands. He and the E Street Band played a then-unprecedented six-night stand at the arena, selling a whopping 125,000 tickets. *Courtesy of 991.com*

and "Run Through the Jungle," Elvis Presley's "Follow That Dream" and "I Can't Help Falling in Love," and Arthur Conley's "Sweet Soul Music."

The E Street Band's show in Manchester, England, saw Bruce premiere Chuck Berry's "Johnny Bye-Bye," which he, of course, would later alter to incorporate lyrics about Presley's passing and release as the B-side to "I'm on Fire." Days later, during a six-night stint at London's Wembley Arena, Springsteen reworked Jimmy Cliff's "Trapped" into the captivating and emotional number later heard on the 1985 *U.S.A. for Africa* benefit album.

Springsteen closed his first lengthy European trek at Birmingham's International Arena with a pair of dates on June 7 and 8. On the first night, he couldn't help but feel elated when he was joined onstage by one of his idols, the Who's guitarist Pete Townshend. The rock legend responsible for albums like 1969's *Tommy* and 1971's *Who's Next* played with the E Street Band on "Born to Run" and the "Detroit Medley."

Back in America

Following a one-off solo performance on June 14 at the Hollywood Bowl as part of his continued antinuclear efforts and an onstage meet-up with Gary U.S. Bonds—for a rendition of his comeback hit "This Little Girl"—in San Francisco the night after, Springsteen flew home to New Jersey to attend Max Weinberg's wedding in East Orange.

During the June 20 festivities, the E Street Band's members played a lengthy set that included "You Can Look (But You Better Not Touch)," "Hungry Heart," and a rendition of Tom Waits's "Jersey Girl," which Springsteen dedicated to the just-married Rebecca Weinberg.

When the Weinbergs returned from their honeymoon, Max rejoined the E Street Band for an unprecedented six-night opening stand at the 21,000-seat Brendan Byrne Arena in the Meadowlands. Springsteen launched the shows—which ran from July 2 to July 9 and saw all 125,000 tickets sell out in one day—by sprinting out ahead of the band onto the stage. The first night, as he publicly unveiled the aforementioned Waits song, he told the Garden State audience, "This is something that we learned for you . . . and it's for all the Jersey Girls."

Subsequent stands at the Philadelphia Spectrum (five nights), Illinois' Rosemont Horizon (two nights in July, three more in September), and the L.A. Sports Arena (five nights) proved that Springsteen and the E Street Band had hit their commercial stride.

The first night of his Los Angeles engagement, on August 20, was an important one for Springsteen, because he donated proceeds to the Vietnam Veterans of America Foundation, a nonprofit that he cared deeply about. The show opened in an unusual fashion for fans as the organization's president, Robert Muller, spoke to the crowd. Surrounded by war veterans in wheelchairs, Muller touched on the joy that rock 'n' roll brought to the members of his foundation before Springsteen took the stage for a poignant take on CCR's "Who'll Stop the Rain."

The band and crew rewarded themselves for their hard work in 1980 and 1981 with a late September trip to Honolulu. The trip doubled as an opportunity for Clarence Clemons to marry Christina Sandgren, as the group's members, management, and significant others—including Springsteen's then-girlfriend, actress Joyce Hyser—looked on. As with Weinberg's wedding, the party turned into a lengthy jam session. It was also the last time the members of the band would play together for an audience until 1984.

Looking back on what the group had achieved not only with its yearlong tour but in general, Steve Van Zandt told *Backstreets* magazine, "What we accomplished could have been accomplished in any little town in America. I think it's really great that Bruce and I did it for New Jersey. It gave hope to all the Des Moines of the world."

A stub from Springsteen's May 20, 1981, concert at Bingley Hall, on the County Showground in Stafford, England.
Courtesy of Brucebase

The *Born in the U.S.A.* Tour

After Steve Van Zandt's exit, Springsteen knew he'd have some big shoes to fill. In the third week of February 1984, with no decisions yet made about a replacement, he invited his old friend Nils Lofgren to his three-story brick mansion in Rumson for the weekend. For Lofgren, who had just been released by his record company, it was a welcome distraction to spend time with the Boss jamming, talking, and going to bars.

The pair happened to be watching MTV together when the network announced that Little Steven had officially left the E Street Band. When Springsteen explained to Lofgren that he wasn't yet sure of Steve's replacement, Lofgren asked for an audition. Springsteen was a little surprised but ultimately took him at his word, and in June 1984, he got the job.

A warm-up gig with the full band was held on June 8 at the Stone Pony, weeks in advance of the official tour launch. Two nights later, Bruce and Nils were back at the Asbury Park club joining Cats on a Smooth Surface for a series of covers of songs by

A ticket stub from Springsteen's September 14, 1985, gig at the Cotton Bowl in Dallas. During the Boss's encore, a fan with a prosthetic leg held the artificial limb high in the air. He rewarded the fan with his very own song— an unruly cover of Creedence Clearwater Revival's "Travelin' Band." *Author's Collection.*

Them, John Lee Hooker, the Animals, the Rolling Stones, and John Fogerty. A week later, the group held rehearsals at the Clair Brothers' facility in Lititz, Pennsylvania, where sound and lighting coordination was perfected. Later, the band crashed a live show by Lancaster-area band the Sharks, taking the stage well after midnight on June 21 for an unannounced six-song set.

Three days later, during rehearsals on June 24 in Red Bank, at the site of Clemons's defunct club Big Man's West, Lofgren—who had been hired not only to play guitars but provide backing vocals—was continuing to suffer from recurring laryngitis that stemmed from a bout with mononucleosis. In a bit of a panic, Patti Scialfa, a locally bred singer who had recently befriended Springsteen and previously sang on an unused session for *Born in the U.S.A.*, was invited to audition. At the end of the following day, after continued rehearsals, she was officially hired as a member of the E Street Band.

Four days later, Scialfa was with Springsteen at the St. Paul Civic Arena for the start of the tour. At first, it was a little nerve-racking. "Ten minutes to showtime, they still didn't know where they were going to put me," she told *Q* magazine in 1993. "I ended up by Max [Weinberg]. I had a big notebook with my words like cramming for school down at my feet."

The concert was the first in a fifteen-month, 156-show trek that was long on new material—Springsteen played eight songs from *BITUSA*, a handful from *Nebraska*, and the public unveiling of his cover of the Rolling Stones' politically charged 1968 classic "Street Fighting Man." An acoustic rendition of "No Surrender," the unexpected return of "Growin' Up" at some shows, plus rare covers of the A's "A Woman's Got the Power"—for his mother—and Dobie Gray's "Drift Away" during his ten-night, mid-August stand at the Brendan Byrne Arena in the Meadowlands are also noteworthy parts of the first leg of the tour.

Springsteen's 1985 Summer tour program was sold as a souvenir to attendees of his British and Irish concerts. Notable among them were his sold-out finales at Wembley Stadium, which marked the brief return of E Street guitarist Steve Van Zandt as a guest player during encores.   *Courtesy of 991.com*

Backstage at the Joe Louis Arena in Detroit, Springsteen revealed that he was losing three to five pounds a night. With his onstage three- to four-hour fitness regimen, coupled with weight training that had his biceps bulging and a six-mile daily jogging routine under the advisement of a personal trainer, it was no wonder he was sculpted. His only indulgence was his nightly backstage rubdown.

As the trek continued, he attempted Sam the Sham and the Pharaohs' "Wooly Bully," ZZ Top's "I'm Bad, I'm Nationwide," the Rivieras/Ramones favorite "California Sun," Freddy Cannon's "Tallahassee Lassie," and revisited Jimmy Cliff's "Trapped," which the E Street Band first attempted in 1981. During a night off in Pittsburgh that September, Springsteen dropped in to play with Joe Grushecky's Iron City Houserockers.

On a short break in the tour days later, he joined Southside Johnny at the Morris Community Theatre in Morristown, New Jersey, for a pair of Wilson Pickett numbers ("In the Midnight Hour" and "Mustang Sally") and "Twist and Shout." In mid-December, after a wildly successful five-month caravan, the band's '84 roadwork wrapped in Atlanta with a pair of shows at the Omni that each featured the return of Van Zandt—as a guest—playing on six encores, including the obligatory holiday favorite "Santa Claus Is Coming to Town."

"It's the greatest feeling on earth," Springsteen said, explaining the allure of touring to *People* that fall. "It's like a circus. You just kind of roll in, walk into somebody's town and, bang! It's heart to heart."

On January 4, the E Street Band resumed touring, starting up in Hampton, Virginia, and wrapped up the first extensive North American leg late in the month in Syracuse, New York. A pair of tour surprises in Greensboro, North Carolina, began on the 17th at the Rhinoceros Club when Springsteen hopped onstage with Boston band the Del Fuegos for versions of the McCoys' 1965 chart-topper "Hang on Sloopy" and Ben E. King's iconic 1961 #4 smash "Stand by Me." The following night, at the Greensboro Coliseum, both Gary U.S. Bonds and one-time Steel Mill member Robbin Thompson joined the Boss for "Twist and Shout."

Bruce in Brisbane

During an eight-week break from touring, Springsteen participated in the all-star charity single "We Are the World" and picked up an American Music Award and a Grammy Award for Best Single of the Year and Best Rock Vocal, Male Category, respectively for "Dancing in the Dark." He also shared the stage with Madonna and Prince on the latter's "Baby I'm a Star" at a February 23 concert at the Los Angeles Forum before heading Down Under to begin his first-ever tours of Australia and Japan.

Springsteen's first Australian performance took place at the Sydney Entertainment Centre on March 21. The first of a five-night, nonconsecutive run marked covers of Elvis Presley's "Can't Help Falling in Love" and Creedence Clearwater Revival's "Travelin' Band." The next night, during an already booked Neil Young show in the same venue, Springsteen joined in during an encore of "Down by the River." A week later, during a downpour at the 50,000-seat QE II Sports Centre in Brisbane, the E Street Band rolled out "Who'll Stop The Rain."

A four-night stand at Tokyo's Yoyogi Olympic Pool, plus a gig in Kyoto and a pair of dates in Osaka, closed out this successful, monthlong trek.

Born in Europe

On June 1, after a month off in which Springsteen married Julianne Phillips at the Oswego Lake Country Club in Oregon on May 14, followed by a honeymoon in Italy spent at the Lake Como villa owned by designer Gianni Versace, Bruce launched a massive European Stadium tour. The opening date, at Ireland's Slane Castle, was the biggest crowd Bruce had ever played, with possibly one hundred thousand people in attendance, including Eric Clapton and the Who's Pete Townshend, both of whom joined him onstage. The show

This UK 12-inch single—which featured material from Springsteen's 1986 box set *Live/1975-1985*—was released in 1987. It counted a concert rendering of "Born to Run" and the A-side, with performances of "Seeds" and "Johnny 99," on the back.   *Courtesy of 991.com*

EURO-TOUR 1985

JUNE 1: DUBLIN: Castle Slain	JUNE 16: FRANKFURT
JUNE 4: NEWCASTLE: St. James' Park	JUNE 18: MUNCHEN: Olympic Stadium
JUNE 5: NEWCASTLE: St. James' Park	JUNE 21: MILANO
JUNE 8: GOTEBORG: Ullevi	JUNE 23: MONTPELIER
JUNE 9: GOTEBORG: Ullevi	JUNE 25: ST. ETIENNE
JUNE 12: ROTTERDAM: Feyenoord	JUNE 29: PARIS
JUNE 13: ROTTERDAM: Feyenoord	JUNE 30: PARIS
JUNE 15: FRANKFURT	JULY 3: LONDON: Wembley Stadium
	JULY 4: LONDON: Wembley Stadium
	JULY 6: LONDON: Wembley Stadium
	JULY 7: LEEDS: Roundhay Park

This poster commemorated the E Street Band's June and July 1985 tour dates through Europe. A summer break followed that fourth leg of Springsteen's trek in support of *Born in the U.S.A.*, before the group returned to the road to rock U.S. stadiums that fall.   *Author's Collection.*

was equally unique as it marked the only time the E Street Band played the Beach Boys' "When I Grow Up to Be a Man."

At Springsteen's Gothenburg show, during his "Twist and Shout" encore, Swedish fans jumped so hard that the structural supports of Ullevi Stadium, which was built on a layer of clay, nearly caused the venue to collapse. Construction crews purportedly worked diligently to extend the concrete pillars to bedrock in time for the next evening's show.

Gigs in the Netherlands, West Germany, France, and Italy gave way to a trio of concerts at London's Wembley Stadium in early July that marked the debut of a new song called "Seeds." Also of note, on the second and third nights, Little Steven returned as a guest player for encores. Although Springsteen was supposedly asked to perform at Live Aid at Wembley on July 13, he declined, claiming he needed a break. As a concession—following the E Street Band's final U.K. gig at Roundhay Park in Leeds—Springsteen did lend his massive stage to the cause.

Last Leg

In preparation for the final, stadium leg of the *Born in the U.S.A.* tour, Springsteen and the band reconvened at 129 Monmouth Street in Red Bank, once the home of Big Man's West, for two days of rehearsals on July 30. On August 5, the band went back to work with sold-out shows at RFK Stadium in Washington, D.C., plus sports stadiums in Cleveland, Chicago, and Philadelphia.

At Three Rivers Stadium in Pittsburgh, just days into the trek, the E Street Band launched the show with "Born in the U.S.A." Midway through the song,

Springsteen was puzzled when he recognized he was down two members. Somehow Roy Bittan and Lofgren missed their cue to take the stage—they were in a nearby room playing ping-pong as the gig got underway. Following this incident, the Boss began taking a head count at the start of every performance to avoid a recurrence.

In mid-August, Springsteen returned to the Garden State for the first four of six nights (two shows were added and played at the end of the month) at Giants Stadium in East Rutherford. In between this impressive run, a concert planned for Sullivan Stadium in Foxboro Massachusetts had to be withdrawn—much to the disappointment of the many Boston-area Bruce fans—when the concert permit application was received too late.

Perhaps the most unusual gig of the entire tour took place at the Cotton Bowl in Dallas when a fan with an artificial leg took it off and threw it up onstage during "Stand on It," the night's planned finale. "This man just took off his leg," Springsteen chuckled into the microphone. "Hold it on up, man . . . Wait a second . . . this man took that last song too literally . . . but he gets a song." The owner of the prosthetic leg was rewarded with a fiery rendition of Creedence Clearwater Revival's "Travelin' Band."

Nine days later, on September 22, the E Street Band's planned show at Denver's Mile High Stadium had to be postponed because of a predicted snowstorm that failed to materialize. The next night, with freezing temperatures, the show went on, with fans dressed in heavy coats and blankets, as if they were attending a Broncos football game. Similar weather followed the next night, as Springsteen made up the canceled concert.

Four gigs at the Los Angeles Memorial Coliseum closed out the *Born in the U.S.A.* tour, with Springsteen debuting his rendition of Edwin Starr's classic "War." Bruce—unfamiliar with the lyrics in an era before teleprompters were common in the concert industry—actually taped the lyrics to his arm. Two nights later, the version that appeared on his 1986 concert box, *Live/1975-85*, was recorded alongside the newly written "Seeds" and six other songs. During the 1985 tour finale, on October 2, Springsteen brought his wife, Julianne, onstage to dance with him during "Dancing in the Dark." On the last two encores, for John Fogerty's "Rockin' All over the World," and "Glory Days," manager Jon Landau took the stage to play guitar.

The last gesture was an affirmation of just how far the two had come together. It was also an indication that it was in Springsteen's best interest to continue to follow the career guidance of Landau. Under his direction, Springsteen had become the biggest rock star in the world.

Rockin' the Clubs

Springsteen didn't go back on the road formally until 1988, but 1987 was an active performing year. On April 12, for instance, he and several members of the E Street Band joined Cats on a Smooth Surface at the Stone Pony for rollicking live staples like "Darlington" County," "Cadillac Ranch," and "Light of Day"—which had recently been released as a single by Joan Jett for a movie of the same name. Jon Bon Jovi joined Springsteen on the encore, "Kansas City."

After recording in California late that spring, the Boss came back east to rock the Jersey Shore, taking the stage for club gigs with local reggae band Jah Love at the Green Parrot in Neptune and Key Largo in Belmar, where he cooked up Bob Marley–inspired takes of "Born in the U.S.A." and "My Hometown." Springsteen also jammed at the Pony with headliners Marshall Crenshaw, Little Steven, and the Band's own Levon Helm that August. Meanwhile, a pair of Cats shows at the historic Asbury Park venue again offered fans the rare opportunity to catch surprise, intimate E Street Band performances.

On September 14, Springsteen served as best man at Danny Federici's second wedding to Kathlynn Helmeid at Asbury United Methodist Church. From there, the wedding party flew to Janesville, Wisconsin, for a reception two days later where the E Street Band played.

Nine days later, Springsteen was in Philadelphia for U2's massive, attendance-shattering concert at JFK Stadium. During the show, which also featured Little Steven as opening act, the Irish band's frontman Bono asked eighty-five thousand fans if they wanted to play his guitar. In unison, they all responded yes. He then asked, "Does Bruce Springsteen want to play my guitar?" Suddenly, the Boss walked out onstage as the crowd erupted to join in on a cover of Ben E. King's "Stand by Me."

Sans Lofgren and Clemons, the E Street Band unexpectedly took the stage at McLoone's Rumrunner in Sea Bright on Halloween to test out some *Tunnel of Love* songs like "Brilliant Disguise" and "Tougher Than the Rest." This performance came a week after the memorial service for John Hammond, who died on July 10. Out of respect for the man who signed him to Columbia Records, Springsteen played Bob Dylan's "Forever Young" at the October 22, St. Peter's Church event.

Springsteen continued to be seen out, playing with Bobby Bandiera and Cats at the Stone Pony that fall, while showing up at a benefit for the Rumson Country Day School on November 6, where he appeared with the Fabulous Grease Band. He closed out '87 with December performances in New York, where he participated in a Carnegie Hall tribute to Harry Chapin and a Madison Square Garden benefit for homeless children alongside Dion, Paul Simon, Ruben Blades, Lou Reed, James Taylor, and Billy Joel.

Tunnel of Love Express

The 1988 *Tunnel of Love Express* tour brought about a number of changes for Springsteen fans. The staging of the E Street Band was considerably different from previous tours. A reflection of his desire to downsize, he went back to arenas for the North American dates. Meanwhile, during private tour rehearsals at the

Fort Monmouth Expo Center in New Jersey in late January, his veteran band members were in different spots. Weinberg was downstage, and Scialfa—once on the fringes—was now out in front with Springsteen.

When the tour opened on February 25 in Worcester, Massachusetts, Scialfa shared the mic with Bruce on a number of songs. Reflecting their fiery new romance, they flirted heavily during their onstage interactions. As with the *Tunnel of Love* packaging, the Boss dressed differently, too. Wearing black jeans and a black dress shirt, Springsteen, now thirty-eight, was a changed man.

While it was billed as an E Street Band tour, it didn't always feel like it. Like the album he was plugging, a good part of Springsteen's set took on a midtempo vibe. He went so far as to

Springsteen's *Tunnel of Love Express* tour—from which these backstage passes originated—was notable because it marked the increased presence of Patti Scialfa in the E Street Band's live shows. Behind the scenes, his marriage to Julianne Phillips was crumbling as his romance with Patti was heating up. *Courtesy of 991.com*

alter his trademark anthem, "Born to Run," turning it into an acoustic blues number, although the magic of past tours was evident in places, as with "You Can Look," "Rosalita," and the ever-present "Detroit Medley."

The Horns of Love—which now featured saxophonists Mario Cruz and Eddie Manion, trombonist Rickie "La Bamba" Rosenberg, plus trumpeters Mark Pender and Mike Spengler—were also in tow at the Centrum and remained for the tour, which wrapped on May 23 after a five-night engagement at Madison Square Garden.

While there wasn't as much variation in the tour's live sets, sound checks in Atlanta and Largo, Maryland, were where a lot of the excitement was. In advance of these shows, Springsteen attempted covers of Van Morrison's "Tupelo Honey," "Crazy Love" and "Into the Mystic"; Bob Dylan's "Just Like a Woman" and "One of Us Must Know (Sooner or Later)"; Elvis Presley's "Don't Be Cruel," "All Shook Up," and "Heartbreak Hotel"; plus songs by the Everly Brothers, Chuck Berry.

Later in the tour, during a Tacoma sound check, Springsteen and the band worked through Buddy Holly's "That'll Be the Day" and Roy Orbison's "Crying," which Springsteen would debut weeks later during his May 16 gig at

Madison Square Garden. Just days before, at the April 23 show at the Los Angeles Sports Arena, he had the crowd sing "Happy Birthday" to Orbison, who was in attendance.

While the surprise, late-night club-hopping that once was so prevalent had fallen by the wayside by 1988, Springsteen and Lofgren did drop into the Maple Leaf Bar in New Orleans on May 11 to check out a few tunes by the New Orleans Blues Department. They joined the band for a handful of songs, including John Lee Hooker's classic "Boom Boom."

European Tunnel

Immediately after the North American tour concluded, Bruce returned home to Beverly Hills. Three nights later, and with a two-and-a-half-week break before the European tour opener, Springsteen joined John Mellencamp onstage at Irvine Meadows in California for a cover version of Bob Dylan's classic "Like a Rolling Stone."

Days after opening the seven-week stadium trek at Stadio Comunale in Turin on June 11, Springsteen made headlines. Rock's man of the people was observed playing "I'm on Fire," "The River," and "Dancing in the Dark" with a group of Rome street musicians on a borrowed guitar in front of a small crowd. Later in the tour, on July 23 in Copenhagen, Springsteen was again seen busking—this time with Danish street musician John Magnusson.

A massive show at Wembley Stadium on June 25 was made more notable when Edwin Starr joined the E Street Band on his legendary "War," while the second of two Rotterdam stadium gigs marked the first-ever performance of Bob Dylan's "Chimes of Freedom." Days later, during a lengthy gig at Stockholm Stadion in Sweden, Springsteen tracked the live version of "Chimes" that was the title cut of his subsequent EP.

Amnesty Tour

When the *Tunnel* tour through Europe was over (it wrapped on August 3 in Barcelona), Springsteen went home to the Jersey Shore. The E Street Band took a four-week break from the road, before resuming roadwork on September 2, as part of the multiple-artist, global Amnesty International *Human Rights Now!* tour. But by August 21, he was getting itchy and went down to the Stone Pony to play with his pals in Cats on a Smooth Surface. Three nights later, he joined his friend and forthcoming tourmate Sting for a version of "The River" at Madison Square Garden. He had so much fun, he went back again the next night, August 25, and did the same song, before helping out on the Police classic "Message in a Bottle."

A full band rehearsal for Springsteen and the E Street Band took place at Wembley Stadium in London on September 1, following sets by Sting, Peter Gabriel, Tracy Chapman, and Youssou N'Dour. For the tour, Springsteen cut his typical three-plus hour set down to seventy-five minutes. Staples like "Born in the U.S.A.," "The Promised Land," and "Thunder Road" gave way to the evening's all-star closing songs, "Chimes of Freedom" and Bob Marley's "Get Up, Stand Up."

European meccas like London, Paris, Budapest, Turin, and Barcelona were quickly covered before the trek started globe-hopping to stadiums in expected (Montreal, Toronto, Philadelphia, Los Angeles, Tokyo) and unexpected locales (San Jose, Costa Rica, New Delhi, Athens, Harare, Zimbabwe, Abidjan on the Ivory Coast, Sao Paolo, Brazil) over the course of the seven-week conscience-raising tour.

Iconic American folksinger Joan Baez joined Springsteen in Oakland on September 23 for a rousing take on Dylan's "Blowin' in the Wind" before Roy Orbison took the stage to sing "Happy Birthday" to Springsteen, who was celebrating his thirty-ninth year.

If such nights were memorable, perhaps his most impassioned performance came during the first of two concerts in Argentina. The first, held at Estadio Mundialista in Mendoza, was broadcast on Chilean television. During the gig—which was about half Argentinean and half Chilean—Springsteen praised the crowd of thirty thousand for its fight for democracy amid the regime of Augusto Pinochet. He heralded his audience while acknowledging that it was an example of courage and determination for people around the world.

When 1988 roadwork was over, the members of the E Street Band were happy for the payday. But performances on the trek, which would wind up being its last with Springsteen until 1999, were bittersweet. In Sandford's book, Tallent said, "maybe the band should have ended after *U.S.A.*," adding, "The *Tunnel* tour wasn't the real thing. The magic was gone."

Bruce, the Special Guest

As winter 1988–89 approached, Springsteen kept a low profile, turning up for a Tarrytown, New York, gig to join folksinger John Prine in mid-November. On November 26, while in the Bay Area to visit his parents for Thanksgiving, Bruce joined Southside Johnny and the Asbury Jukes during their set at the Stone in San Francisco. Back in Jersey, a week before Christmas, he sang "Santa Claus Is Coming to Town" with local musicians.

In January 1989, Springsteen inducted Bob Dylan into the Rock and Roll Hall of Fame and dedicated "Crying" to the memory of Roy Orbison, who died a few weeks before. With no official performances for the rest of the year, Springsteen kept busy during a spring spent in L.A., taking the stage twice at Mickey Rourke's Hollywood club, Rubber, playing with local acts like the Mighty Hornets for covers of Mitch Ryder's "C. C. Rider" and Ben E. King's "Stand by Me."

The summer of '89 began with Springsteen back east, taking the stage with Max Weinberg's side outfit, Killer Joe, at the Stone Pony and singing Elvis's own "Loving You" for Roy Bittan at his June wedding to Denise Rubin at the

Carlyle Hotel in New York in early June. Guest stints at the Pony and other Jersey Shore venues like Martell's in Point Pleasant and the Rumrunner in Sea Bright with everyone from Nils Lofgren, Jimmy Cliff, Southside Johnny guitarist and longtime friend Bobby Bandiera, Cats on a Smooth Surface, the X-men, the Fabulous Grease Band, and La Bamba and the Hubcaps.

Other Springsteen cameos of note included a June 14 performance of "Down by the River" with Neil Young at Jones Beach on Long Island and a June 30 appearance with Jackson Browne at Bally's Casino in Atlantic City. A July 2 visit to the Café Bar in Long Branch saw Springsteen play six songs with his longtime friend Gary U.S. Bonds.

On August 11, he took the stage at the Garden State Arts Center in Holmdel with Ringo Starr's All Starr Band—which included E Street members Nils Lofgren and Clarence Clemons. Springsteen helped out on Beatles numbers "Get Back" and "With a Little Help from My Friends," plus Starr's own 1973 smash "Photograph" and Little Richard's "Long Tall Sally," which the Fab Four covered early in their career.

World Tour '88

Another souvenir from the Boss's *Tunnel of Love World Tour '88*, this twenty-page UK tour program replicates the cover photo from Springsteen's '87 album. *Courtesy of 991.com*

A fortieth birthday celebration at the Rumrunner came a night after the Boss played with Jimmy Cliff at the Stone Pony, joining in on "Trapped." The party included the entire E Street Band plus Little Steven getting together to jam on "Around and Around," "Sweet Little Sixteen," "Stand By Me," "Glory Days," "Havin' a Party," and "Twist and Shout."

The year 1990 was a remarkably quiet one in the public sense for Springsteen. He performed at a pricey, private Rainforest Foundation benefit with Paul Simon, Sting, Don Henley, Bruce Hornsby, Herbie Hancock, and others at the Beverly Hills home of movie producer and businessman Ted Child. Tickets for this February dinner/concert were $5,000 each. Attended mostly by Hollywood's elite, it raised $1 million for the Amazon ecosystem.

A few weeks later, Springsteen and Bob Dylan were invited to join Tom Petty and the Heartbreakers at the Forum for a pair of songs. On October 29, Springsteen and Petty jammed again, this time at Petty's San Fernando Valley home. The frontmen—backed by producer and Electric Light Orchestra brainchild Jeff Lynne and various Heartbreakers—ripped through a run of oldies like "Little Red Rooster," "Mr. Tambourine Man," and "Wipeout," just for the fun of it.

Then, on November 16 and 17, Springsteen took the stage at the Shrine Auditorium for the first of two acoustic headlining concerts to benefit the Christic Institute. These gigs featured special guests Jackson Browne and Bonnie Raitt collaborating on the encores, "Highway 61 Revisited" and "Across the Borderline." The shows also marked the public debut of songs like "Red Headed Woman," "When the Lights Go Out," "Real World," and his future hit "57 Channels (And Nothin' On)," which was still a year and a half away from release.

21

Maybe Everything That Dies Someday Comes Back

Nebraska

By mid-1981, the five year lease on Springsteen's Holmdel farm had run out. He established new residences in Rumson—which was close to the water—and Colts Neck, where he maintained a sprawling farm. Between his time in these two residences, he seriously started to think about his next studio album.

After a whirlwind year and a half, Springsteen didn't go out much. He read Flannery O'Connor, watched films, and wrote songs. The key for him at this phase in his creativity was to ensure that the details and the emotion were ideally balanced.

Intent on tracking demos of his new songs at home as a means to be less wasteful with studio time, Springsteen sat down in a bedroom chair at his Colts Neck home on January 3, 1982, and started playing into a Teac Tascam Series 144 four-track recorder that his guitar technician Mike Batlan had set up for him. With just the machine, which was bought for $1,050; a few microphones; his voice; a harmonica; a tambourine; a mandolin; an organ; and his acoustic guitars, the Boss tracked fifteen new songs—most in just a few takes—mixed them through an old Gibson guitar unit into a ghetto blaster, and brought them to the E Street Band.

But when the group came together in April and May for sessions at the Hit Factory in New York, the sessions weren't working out the way Springsteen had hoped. A few songs were keepers (some of them ultimately made it to his 1984 album *Born in the U.S.A.*) but key numbers like "Atlantic City" and "Mansion on the Hill" lost something when the E Street Band electrified them.

"It became obvious fairly soon that what Bruce wanted on the record was what he already had on the demo," Max Weinberg would tell *Rolling Stone* in April 2011. The band's electric treatments of the songs removed the haunting, barren vibe that his original cassette had captured.

By June 1982, on the encouragement of Van Zandt—who felt the intimacy and the great cinematic mood of the original cassette was just extraordinary—Springsteen and Jon Landau were seriously considering releasing the songs from the demo as is, save for some difficult technical alterations by Chuck Plotkin.

"It's amazing that it got there," Springsteen told *Rolling Stone* in December 1984, "'cause I was carryin' that cassette around with me in my pocket without a case for a couple of weeks, just draggin' it around. Finally, we realized, 'Uh-oh, that's the album.'" Springsteen would reveal that it was a struggle to transfer the audio vinyl, due to high levels of distortion coming through during the mastering process. It was eventually remedied, but there was real talk of making it a cassette-only offering.

This August 1984 E Street Band ticket stub is a souvenir from the second of Springsteen's ten nights of sold out Meadowlands Arena shows.
Author's Collection

Track by Track

With the project ready for release, Landau and Springsteen brought the record to Columbia. Walter Yetnikoff was at a loss for words. This was nothing like "Hungry Heart." The label wondered how it might find exposure on album rock radio, which had become downright slick by the summer of 1982 thanks to the popularity of bands like Journey, Asia, and Van Halen.

"Nebraska"

The album's title song is sung from the perspective of nineteenth-year-old Charles Starkweather and is based on the true story of his eight-day killing spree in 1958, in which he and his fourteen-year-old girlfriend Caril Ann Fugate executed eleven people. Setting a bleak tone for the album, Springsteen sings about Starkweather's crimes, his trial, his conviction, and his looming execution.

Inspired to write 1978's "Badlands" after seeing the movie poster for the Terrence Malick film of the same name, he eventually watched the movie in 1980 and penned this song, which was later covered by Chrissie Hynde of the Pretenders and singer/songwriter Steve Earle.

In advance of writing "Nebraska," Springsteen interviewed Ninette Beaver, who wrote the 1974 book *Caril*, via telephone about Fugate. He very nearly titled the song "Starkweather."

"Atlantic City"

Springsteen penned this number at a time when the impoverished Oceanfront city was hoping to recover economically with the advent of legalized gambling. But by the early 1980s, the newly built casinos only served to emphasize the stark differences between the glimmering Las Vegas-inspired tourist destinations and the crime- and drug-afflicted parts of the city.

The UK sleeve for "Atlantic City," Springsteen's limited 45, was released in November 1982. Backed with "Mansion on the Hill," Springsteen's song—partially inspired by a Philadelphia mob killing—was the first of his singles to be made into an official music video treatment. The clip, which received modest rotation in the early days of MTV, consisted of black-and-white footage of the run-down shore town. He did not appear in the video.
Courtesy of 991.com

In order to make good on the bills that, as Springsteen describes, "no honest man can pay," the song's character gets involved with the mob as a hit man. The opening lines of the tune—culled from newspaper headlines at the time—refer to the front-porch nail bombing of Philadelphia mob man Phil "The Chicken Man" Testa, who was killed in March 1981 following the execution of his boss, Angelo Bruno.

The song has since been covered by the BoDeans, the Band, Counting Crows, Hank Williams III, Pete Yorn, Eddie Vedder, the Gaslight Anthem's Brian Fallon, and the Hold Steady, among many others.

"Mansion on the Hill"

Springsteen once revealed that this song, written from a child's perspective, was based on memories of a place his dad used to bring him and his sister Ginny when they were little. Parking along a road adjacent to the highway, they'd look inside the steel gates at how the wealthy lived and dream.

Sharing its title with a 1948 song written by Hank Williams, it was later covered by American country hero Johnny Cash on the 2000 Sub Pop tribute album *Badlands: A Tribute to Bruce Springsteen's Nebraska*.

"Johnny 99"

Taking its premise from a newspaper headline—in which the Ford Motor Company closed its Mahwah, New Jersey, plant in 1980 after thirty-five years—Springsteen wove the tale of a New Jersey auto worker who went off the rails one night out of economic despair.

The man, named Ralph, gets drunk on gin and wine and kills a night clerk. For his crime, he is sentenced to ninety-nine years in prison but instead asks to be executed. Because of his punishment, those surrounding his case come to nickname him "Johnny 99."

Although stripped down in its presentation, the musical vibe of the song is steeped, somewhat ironically, in upbeat rockabilly. As with the character in "Atlantic City," Springsteen's Johnny also has "debts no honest man can pay."

As with the song that precedes it on *Nebraska*, Johnny Cash liked it so much that he also recorded it for an album he titled *Johnny 99*. John Hiatt and Los Lobos have also recorded the song.

"Highway Patrolman"

Penned from the standpoint of Joe Roberts, a lawman who regularly finds himself getting his troublemaking brother, Frankie, out of one mess after another, this classic story song finds Springsteen at his most inventive lyrically. Musically, he fingerpicks his guitar part, sings, and plays a soft harmonica.

The heart of the tale begins upon Frankie's return from Vietnam in 1968, when he gets into an altercation at a bar, attacking and killing a boy. When Joe receives the radio call, witnesses describe his brother as the assailant. He takes off into the rural Michigan night in pursuit of Frankie. Close on his brother's trail, Joe watches as Frankie crosses over into Canada, allowing him to get away with murder.

Johnny Cash also recorded this song for his 1983 album *Johnny 99*.

"State Trooper"

Influenced by the 1977 song "Frankie Teardrop," by New York avant-punk outfit Suicide, Springsteen hatched the idea for the song while returning home one night from the city via the New Jersey Turnpike.

Based on a homicidal character who is afraid of what he might do if he were to be pulled over, the song is as grave as the imagery it depicts. Coming out of the Holland Tunnel and blowing past the glowing Kill Van Kull in Bayonne and Bayway Refinery in Elizabeth, one can just envision how Springsteen came up with the references in "State Trooper."

In 1996, Steve Earle covered this song on his LP *Live*. Ten years earlier, the Cowboy Junkies recorded a version on their debut LP *Whites Off Earth Now!!*

"Used Cars"

This autobiographical song depicts Springsteen growing up working class in Freehold. It may have been the most self-revelatory number he had written to date when it was released in 1982.

Describing the scene as his father test-drove a used car along Michigan Avenue in Freehold in the early 1960s, Springsteen's crystal-clear depiction of his sister sitting up front with him eating an ice cream cone while his mother rode in the back twirling her wedding ring is unforgettable.

Yet as the family celebrates its big day, honking its horn as the neighbors come to see the family's new used car, Bruce is already dreaming of bigger things. When his number comes in, he pledges, he will never ride in a used car again.

Ironically, when the Boss did actually hit it big, he favored and ultimately collected used cars from the 1950s and 1960s, despite the fact that he could own and drive any car he wanted.

"Open All Night"

As the lone track on *Nebraska* to boast electric guitar, this Chuck Berry–influenced rocker depicts a man driving alone through the New Jersey night to meet his girlfriend, who waits tables at Bob's Big Boy several hours away.

One of Springsteen's infamous "car songs"—this time it's a late '60s Mustang Cobra Jet he sings of—inflects some much-needed humor into the album. When he finally reaches his gal Wanda, for instance, the two eat fried chicken together but, without napkins, wipe their hands on a Texaco road map.

"My Father's House"

Based on the relationship between Springsteen and his dad, the song—like "Factory," "Independence Day," and "Adam Raised a Cain" before it—finds the Boss growing up and looking to finally put behind all of the animosity that had existed between them through the years. He sings of the night he returned to the house where he was raised, only to find the woman who lived there now shooing him away through her chained front door.

"My Father's House" also appears to find Springsteen, then thirty-two, pondering his faith through the song's utilization of biblical references, such as the line "our sins lie unatoned" and the title itself. In 1986, Emmylou Harris covered the song on her album *Thirteen*.

"Reason to Believe"

A sarcastic look at faith, Springsteen begins this song by singing of an old man poking a dead dog he had struck on Highway 31 with a stick, hoping it might spring back to life.

Elsewhere, a woman works hard for the love of her life until he up and leaves her, and she prays that he'll come back. As the album's closing number, the contemptuous "Reason to Believe" was delivered with the same bare-bones presentation as the other tracks on *Nebraska*.

Describing it to Jon Landau in a note reprinted in *Songs*, he explains it was "culled from my own experience driving down Highway 33 on my way to Millstone [New Jersey]." Introducing the song in Oakland in 1984, Springsteen said, "Here's a song about blind faith. That is always a dangerous thing, whether it's your girlfriend or if it's in your government."

Critical and Commercial Receptions

When it dropped on October 4, 1982, Springsteen's sixth record went largely unnoticed by the industry. *Nebraska,* ostensibly a folk album, was deemed a vanity project. The LP charted in the U.S. Top Five when loyalists ran out and grabbed copies.

However, the stripped-down offering was such a departure in production and delivery from his previous records that he stunned certain fans and temporarily alienated some others. As with the Columbia Records staff, the barrenly arranged *Nebraska* was not the follow-up to *The River* they were anticipating. Little by little, over the next few decades, Springsteen fans would slowly succumb to its desolate presentation and its thought-provoking charms.

But at first, only the music critics recognized the merits of *Nebraska. Time* called it "an acoustic bypass through the American heartland, sounds a little like a Library of Congress field recording made out behind some shutdown auto plant."

Meanwhile, *Rolling Stone* insisted "this is the bravest of Springsteen's six records; it's also his most startling, direct and chilling." Lastly, the *New York Times* dubbed it his "most personal record, and his most disturbing," adding, "It's been a long time since a mainstream rock star made an album that asks such tough questions and refuses to settle for easy answers—let alone an album suggesting that perhaps there are no answers."

Springsteen's Bleak Music Video

Springsteen had no plans to tour behind the record—he was busy throwing his all into making the bona-fide rock album everyone was clamoring for. Instead, he took advantage of the fledgling music video channel MTV.

But Bruce's first foray into music video was a dreary, black-and-white clip for "Atlantic City." It featured footage of the urban blight of its namesake and no film of Springsteen whatsoever.

When it debuted on MTV, it was with little fanfare. It scored medium rotation for a few weeks, but without the hooks and bombast of his past songs, it was soon shelved.

Outtakes

When Springsteen pared his fifteen contenders down to ten, he left stark renderings of future album tracks like "Born in the U.S.A." and "Downbound Train" off the record. An unplugged version of "Pink Cadillac"—which became one of his most notorious B-sides—plus titles like "Child Bride" (later revised into "Working on the Highway") and "Losin' Kind" were also scratched from the song list.

Twenty Years After

Two decades after he released *Nebraska*, Springsteen reflected on the creative detour he took after the massive success of *The River*. Speaking to *Entertainment Weekly* in 2003, he said, "We were doing good, makin' a lotta dough, but when you're in the spotlight, it makes you hyperaware of what you're doing, and that can make you more self-conscious than you need be.

"I wrestled through all those things, and I found my own way of alleviating those pressures, partly by making an experimental record like *Nebraska*—that helped me feel very balanced. . . . I just had to get my feet back into what felt like real life. I always come back to the same thing: It's about work."

22

I'm Ready to Grow Young Again

Born in the U.S.A.

S ave for a cross-country journey he took in his vintage dark blue Camaro with a friend, Matty DiLea, Bruce Springsteen spent much of 1982 and 1983 working on new songs at his homes in New Jersey and Southern California. In his newly acquired Hollywood Hills residence, he had a makeshift studio with an eight-track recorder set up in his garage, again with the help of Mike Batlan.

When he was back east, Springsteen could often be found hanging out in the clubs on the Jersey Shore. If one thing was clear after the wood-and-wire approach of *Nebraska*, the Boss had the urge to rock again, whether it was with Cats on a Smooth Surface at the Stone Pony, the Iron City House Rockers at Clarence Clemons's own Red Bank club Big Man's West, the Stray Cats at the Fast Lane, Dave Edmunds up at the Peppermint Lounge in New York City, or John Eddie at the Brighton Bar.

As Springsteen would admit in one of his new songs, "No Surrender," which he penned in late '83, he could feel his heart begin to pound when he performed John Lee Hooker's "Boom Boom" and the McCoys "Hang on Sloopy" with local bands. He may have been easing into his mid-thirties, but he still had ambitions that involved drums and guitars. As always, nothing else made him feel as happy as living the dream.

Miami and Southside Get Hitched

Just as Springsteen was getting serious about rock 'n' roll again, two of his closest friends, Miami Steve Van Zandt and Southside Johnny Lyon had gotten serious about life. Both tied the knot in 1982.

On August 10, Lyon and his bride Jill Glasner were married in Asbury Park in a celebration that saw members of the Asbury Jukes and the E Street Band share the stage.

Then, on New Year's Eve, 1982, Van Zandt and his fiancée Maureen Santoro were married. After being serenaded by Percy Sledge—who sang his enduring classic "When a Man Loves a Woman"—the Chambers Brothers performed at the reception, which also found best man Springsteen and Van Zandt rocking out.

Feeling Blue

At times throughout 1983, Springsteen was feeling down in the dumps. According to a friend speaking on anonymity in Christopher Sandford's *Point Blank*, at one point he admitted he "went through a shitty time. I thought of blowing out my brains."

Springsteen was lonely. Sure he could have companionship, but he longed for a relationship. He confessed to Marsh that his depression was a problem in the months leading up to his seventh album. "I thought, 'This can't be happening to me. I'm *the guy with the guitar.*'"

Despite his fame and his money, happiness was eluding him. With therapy, and a shift to a healthier lifestyle—which included six-mile runs, pumping iron, and eating better—he snapped out of it.

Good Luck, Goodbye

Springsteen's outlook wasn't helped by the announcement that his right-hand man, Steve Van Zandt, was leaving the band to go out on his own. By 1983, E Street's guitarist made it clear to the Boss that he could be counted on to help produce and record most of what would become *Born in the U.S.A.*, but he would then be leaving the band to pursue his solo career full time.

Little Steven and the Disciples of Soul had already earned some notoriety. In the winter of 1983, Van Zandt had a modest hit with his debut album, *Men Without Women*, and its Motown-inspired single, "Forever." Meanwhile, a new, politically charged album, *Voice of America*—to be led by another single "Out of the Darkness"—was already in the works for 1984.

All of this solo activity, including North American and European headlining roadwork with the Disciples of Soul, left Steve out of most of the later sessions for Springsteen's new record. He also excused himself from a massive upcoming E Street Band tour to support it.

Ironically for Springsteen, the heartfelt song he penned about Van Zandt's departure from the band also helped to pull him out of his depressed state in late 1983. Written about their bond coming up, "Bobby Jean" seems like a love song to a woman at first, but its deeper emotional meaning was an earnest reflection of their nearly twenty-year friendship.

The Hit Factory

In May 1982, following the completion of *Nebraska*, Springsteen and the E Street Band recorded a three-week session at The Power Station recording studio in Manhattan. During this time frame an array of unreleased tracks were worked on in addition to the songs "Born in the U.S.A.," "Darlington County," "Working on the Highway," "I'm Goin' Down," "Glory Days," and "Downbound Train," all of which made it onto the record.

The band had previously cut the upbeat "Cover Me" and the haunting "I'm on Fire" in early 1982 during sessions in which they also unsuccessfully attempted to record the songs that wound up on *Nebraska* in their original demo form.

A year later, in studio sessions between April and June 1983 at the Hit Factory, the E Street Band continued to plug away at a full-on electric rock record, cutting "My Hometown" amid a host of outtakes.

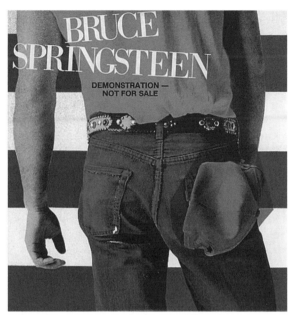

Murder Incorporated

By the summer of 1983, Springsteen believed that his next album was finished. Collecting the best of the songs he had stockpiled over the past eighteen months, the proposed

Released as a promotional EP in the fall of 1984, this pressing of "Born in the U.S.A." was serviced to radio and was backed with "Shut Out the Light," "Pink Cadillac," "Jersey Girl (Live)," and "Santa Claus Is Coming to Town."

Courtesy of Lost in the Flood

song sequence, titled *Murder Incorporated,* was compiled on cassettes that he circulated to the band, its management, and certain individuals at Columbia Records.

But, as with *The Ties That Bind* in 1979, Springsteen changed his mind and continued working on the project for the next six months. In late 1983, he perfected "No Surrender" and "Bobby Jean."

Track by Track

For the new record, Bruce had recruited Bob Clearmountain to work alongside Plotkin and Toby Scott, mixing the record. With a reputation of turning rough tracks into shiny, affable gems, as was the case with the Rolling Stones' 1981 classic *Tattoo You,* Clearmountain delivered the ultimate end product, *Born in the U.S.A.*

"Dancing in the Dark"

In January 1984, just as Springsteen was thinking about moving along to the mixing and mastering phases of his record, Jon Landau pushed him to come up with a blockbuster lead single. Although he was miffed at his manager's

The long awaited single

DANCING IN THE DARK

B/W "Pink Cadillac" (Unavailable elsewhere)

This ad for the extended version of "Dancing in the Dark" ran in the now-defunct UK music weekly *Sounds* in June 1984. It also announced the B-side, "Pink Cadillac," which quickly became one of Springsteen's best known non-LP tracks. *Author's Collection*

recommendation, having delivered eighty songs in two years, he went away and came back with the sure-fire smash Landau wanted.

"Dancing in the Dark" satisfied Landau but—when rendered with its pronounced synthesizer line and bold electronic drumbeat—worried Springsteen quite a bit. It was the Boss's most deliberate pop song yet.

On May 4, exactly one month ahead of his first rock album in three and a half years, Bruce Springsteen finally released the single. But unlike any previous Springsteen 45s, "Dancing" embraced technology to present a fresh, modern sound that helped launch its parent album into the stratosphere.

If the track's upbeat, hook-injected delivery suggested otherwise, the song's character was depressed at first about getting older and his dumpy home. Then, with the encouragement of a lady friend, he talks himself into leaving his anger and frustration to the side for a while, and they head out on the town in pursuit of some fun.

"Born in the U.S.A."

If its sound was soldierly, aggressive and direct, the lyrics behind what would become one of Springsteen's best-known but most misunderstood songs came from the perspective of an underappreciated Vietnam veteran. Having returned home to America in the early 1970s, the character in the title track of his seventh album relayed the dissatisfaction, sadness, and rage felt by those personally scarred from the only war that the United States had ever lost.

Unfortunately, the frustrations expressed in the song's verses were often overshadowed by the perceived patriotism heard in the chorus. Yes, it was very much about American pride, but it was also about American shame.

A powerful musical arrangement that meshed the Boss's cathartic vocals, a chiming, collaborative guitar/synthesizer hook, and Max Weinberg's thundering snare drum rolls, "Born in the U.S.A." was recorded during full band sessions in May 1982. Springsteen chose the third take, which Weinberg told *Backstreets* in 1984 was "the greatest experience I've ever had recording."

With the initial buzz around the album, "Born in the U.S.A." was an immediate favorite on FM rock stations upon its release. It was given a shot in the arm commercially on October 30, 1984, when it was released as the third single from Springsteen's album of the same name. It was boosted again by a memorable music video directed by John Sayles that became a staple of MTV around the turn of '85 and pushed its single to #9 in the *Billboard* Hot 100.

The first person outside of his immediate camp that Springsteen ever played the finished take of "Born in the U.S.A." for was Bobby Muller, the president of the Vietnam Veterans of America organization at the time. During the playback, Muller gave Springsteen—who was aiming to depict a blue-collar man who felt detached from his family, his neighbors, and his government—an approving smile.

The song was inspired, at least in part, by Ron Kovic's 1976 Vietnam book *Born on the Fourth of July*, about a disenchanted, wheelchair-bound veteran. Springsteen picked up a copy of the paperback in a Phoenix drug store in 1978, shortly before he and Kovic had a chance meeting in a Los Angeles hotel. Springsteen told Kovic that he had just finished his book, and the two spoke at length about disenfranchised 'Nam veterans.

"Cover Me"

Springsteen planned to give this song, originally written and recorded as a demo, to Donna Summer until Jon Landau heard it and—as with "Hungry Heart" three years before it—refused to let it go. Springsteen instead wound up giving another song, "Protection," to the disco giant.

The demo take of "Cover Me" was deemed so good by Landau that it wound up on the record. With its danceable beat and glimmering guitar lines, Springsteen's manager/producer knew immediately that the song had serious hit potential.

Landau was right. When it was released as the record's second single on July 31, it was instantly popular. It went on to peak at #7 in the U.S. charts.

"Darlington County"

Arguably Springsteen's most hilarious song, it tells the tale of two rich (albeit dumb), trouble-seeking buddies from New York City who drive down to South Carolina. A live favorite, "Darlington County" is a playful and memorable piece of top-down, heartland rock 'n' roll.

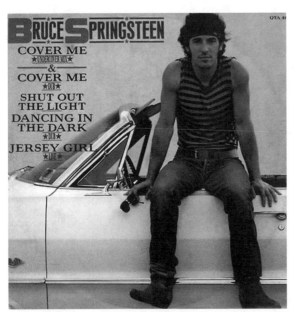

Arthur Baker's reworked "Undercover Mix" of "Cover Me" was released as a commercial 12-inch single in 1984. Bonus tracks included a dub mix of the same track and a dub treatment of "Dancing in the Dark," plus the non-LP offerings "Shut Out the Light" and "Jersey Girl (Live)."

Courtesy of 991.com

"Working on the Highway"

At first considered for *Nebraska*, this primitive rock-'n'-roll song was reworked in the spring of 1982 at the Power Station studios. A recurring song in Bruce's live shows, this shuffling *BITUSA* album track is as contagious as they come.

Lyrically, it picks up where Bobby Fuller's "I Fought the Law" left off. The title tells it all, as it offers two different viewpoints—one of a county employee, the other a worker on a prison road gang.

"Downbound Train"

A somber, mid-tempo song about a man who loses his job and his wife, "Downbound Train" was one of the few keepers from Springsteen's 1982 sessions with the E Street Band where they attempted to electrify the *Nebraska* material.

Ironically, one of the Boss's biggest champions, writer Dave Marsh—who has made a nice living through his Springsteen biographies—criticized the song in his book *Glory Days*, calling it "incredibly sloppy" and "the weakest song he has released since the second album."

"I'm on Fire"

One night in February 1982, during the aforementioned electric *Nebraska* sessions, Springsteen conjured up a rhythm that reminded him of one by Johnny Cash and the Tennessee Three. Worked on live in the studio with keyboardist Bittan and drummer Weinberg, the song is one of Springsteen's most sexually charged numbers yet, replete with a soft rockabilly beat and atmospheric synthesizers.

Released as the fourth single from *Born in the U.S.A.* in early 1985, it peaked at #6 in the U.S. and reached #5 in the U.K.

"My Hometown"

Based on a childhood memory of Springsteen's in which he drove down Main Street in Freehold in the family Buick sitting on his dad's lap, this heartfelt song also explored the ramifications to the community when the local rug mill closed and a racially charged incident took place in the borough during his teen years.

As the seventh single from Springsteen's seventh album, it reached #6 on the *Billboard* charts soon after its November 21, 1985, release.

"No Surrender"

This anthem very nearly missed making the final track listing of *Born in the U.S.A.*, but the Boss was ultimately convinced by Steve Van Zandt at the last minute to keep it. Springsteen wasn't comfortable with the song's message—clearly nobody could hold out and succeed all the time. Life had its concessions and defeats.

"He argued that the portrait of friendship and the song's expression of the inspirational power of rock music was an important part of the picture" Springsteen wrote in *Songs*. To this day, it was a good call. "No Surrender" is a favorite among fans.

"Bobby Jean"

Springsteen never makes it immediately clear if this is a love song about a woman or an ode to a close personal friend, but through the years it has been ascertained that this classic was in fact written about his relationship with Steve Van Zandt.

With its direct, moving lyrics like, "Now you hung with me, when all the others turned away . . . turned up their nose," Springsteen marvels how they always liked the same bands and had the same fashion sense. With its chiming piano line and Clarence Clemons's superb sax solo, and Springsteen's from-the-gut

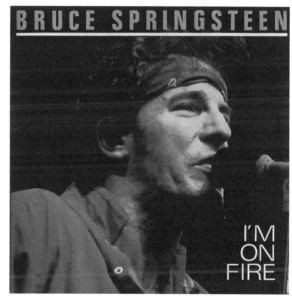

Released as a promotional single in 1985, this sleeve for "I'm on Fire," featuring a photo of Springsteen singing onstage, was unique to the Spanish market.

Courtesy of Lost in the Flood

Bruce Springsteen My Hometown

B side: Santa Claus Is Comin' To Town

Springsteen may have been a multimillionaire by this point in his career, but he still identified with the common people he was raised beside. "My Hometown" may have been based on his childhood memories in Freehold, but working-class men and women around the world identified with it. *Author's Collection*

vocals, the song is as brilliant emotionally as it is structurally.

To hear it is to know it— "Bobby Jean" is among his best songs ever.

"I'm Goin' Down"

The infectiously rockin' sixth single from *Born in the U.S.A.* was nearly bumped from the record at one point as Springsteen and Landau went back and forth over whether to include it or "Pink Cadillac." Topically, it is a commentary on the differences between men and women.

Released as a formal single in the fall of 1985, more than three years after it was recorded, it reached #9 in the U.S. pop survey, despite the fact that there was no accompanying music video.

"Glory Days"

One of the most recognized Springsteen songs—it is a staple of baseball games throughout North America—this was the fifth proper single from the album. Musically, it's easily the most celebratory number on *Born in the U.S.A.*—from the organ fills to the intoxicating mandolin solo—which explains why it hit the U.S. Top 5 in mid-1985.

Its relatable lyrics talk about getting drunk, pining for the youthful days when life was about playing high school baseball and turning boy's heads, before kids and divorce and responsibility took over.

Interestingly enough, one verse—which makes reference to the narrator's father working at the Metuchen Ford plant assembly line until he was let go—was officially published with the lyrics but excluded from the actual recording.

Critical Reaction

When reviews of *Born in the U.S.A* began to surface in late May and early June, in tandem with its release, the response was overwhelmingly positive. *Rolling Stone*'s

Debby Miller gave it five stars, its highest honor, heralding its "rowdy, indomitable spirit" and adding, "[Bruce] may shove his broody characters out the door and send them cruising down the turnpike, but he gives them music they can pound on the dashboard to."

The *Los Angeles Times'* Robert Hilburn wrote, "the conflict between the rousing arrangements and the frequently downbeat themes offers an interesting psychological tension" while the *New York Times'* Stephen Holden called the album "Mr. Springsteen's most comprehensive vision of American life to date."

Naming Springsteen "the most idolized keeper of the flame of American rock and roll, imaginatively coming to grips with the new rhythms and

With Springsteen sporting the same headband and leather jacket seen in his "Born in the U.S.A." video, the sleeve of the "Glory Days" maxi single was instantly identifiable. The previously unreleased track "Stand on It" lured in fans who already owned its parent album.   *Courtesy of 991.com*

textures of 80's popular music," Holden was not alone in his assessment of the record. By year's end, the consensus of critics ranked it at the top of the *Village Voice* Pazz and Jop poll.

Commercial Response

Released on June 4, 1984, *Born in the U.S.A.* debuted at # 9 in the U.S. and began its ascent to #1 on the *Billboard* 200, where it remained from July 7 until it was knocked down to #2 by Prince's album *Purple Rain*. The Purple One remained at the top spot for the next twenty-four weeks, with Springsteen at #2 until he pulled ahead of Prince again on January 19, 1985. It ultimately sold more than twenty million copies, making *Born in the U.S.A.* one of the best-selling albums of all time.

Born in the U.S.A. produced seven Top 10 singles over nineteen months beginning in June 1984, tying the number of excerpts Michael Jackson had with his 1982 smash *Thriller*. The album remained in the U.S. Top 10 for eighty-four weeks.

With the success of the record, Springsteen was a rich man. He would never need to worry about money again, and was able to help his family and friends.

Although Springsteen's first motivation was always the music, as a man who grew up poor, he welcomed wealth. "It's an inanimate thing, a tool, a convenience," he told *Rolling Stone* in '84. "If you've got to have a problem, it's a good problem to have."

The Videos

Aside from the tried and true mediums of radio and old-fashioned publicity, the ascent of MTV was perfectly timed with Springsteen's 1984–85 promotional campaign. Four of *Born in the U.S.A.*'s seven singles had accompanying music videos, and the importance of the channel wasn't lost on the Boss, who knew that its ability to reach millions of music fans was essential to his continued popularity.

"Dancing in the Dark"

This video featured actress Courteney Cox, later of *Friends* fame, dancing

onstage with Springsteen. Shot at the St. Paul Civic Center in Minnesota at the outset of the *Born in the U.S.A.* tour, the clip was directed by suspense and horror movie director Brian De Palma, who cast Cox.

"It was scary," Cox remembered, speaking to NBC's *Dateline* in 2004. "I just imitated what [Bruce] did. Whatever he did, I followed." Springsteen obviously liked her moves as he couldn't stop smiling at her throughout the iconic video, for which she was paid $350. It debuted on MTV on July 10, 1984.

Released on May 4, 1984, a month in advance of its parent album *Born in the U.S.A.*, "Dancing in the Dark" was a bona-fide smash single, with its modern synthesizer treatment and pulsing beat. Unfortunately the song was kept from topping the U.S. singles chart by Duran Duran's "The Reflex" and Prince's "When Doves Cry." Although it stalled at #2, the single became synonymous with the summer of '84. Its video helped launch the career of actress Courteney Cox.

Courtesy of 991.com

"Born in the U.S.A."

The second promotional film from the album, for the disc's title cut, premiered in December 1984. Directed by filmmaker John Sayles, the clip meshed performance footage of Springsteen in concert with affecting images of mid-'80s America, including Vietnam veterans, their Amerasian children, oil refineries, cemeteries, and waving flags.

"I'm on Fire"

Also shot by Sayles, the video for "I'm on Fire" finds Springsteen in the role of a mechanic who dreams about the beautiful, wealthy customer whose vintage Ford Thunderbird he services. She clearly has a thing for him, too, and always asks that he take care of her car.

As the clip progresses, Bruce finishes his work on the car and drops it off at her mansion in the hills. After pondering ringing her doorbell, he sticks the keys in her mailbox and ventures off into the night.

Marking Springsteen's first attempt at acting, it debuted in April 1985, and later, in September, it was named the Best Male Video at the MTV Video Music Awards.

"Glory Days"

The last video for the record was also made with Sayles, and began airing in June 1985. Opening with Springsteen in the character of a working-class dad playing baseball with his son, the clip soon cuts away to the E Street Band performing the song in a townie bar/pool hall.

Steve Van Zandt, who had been out of the band for two years at the time of the filming, is seen playing guitar alongside Springsteen and providing backing vocals in the spirited video. It also marks the first on-camera footage of newer members Nils Lofgren and Patti Scialfa.

As the song ends, Sayles cuts back to Springsteen with the boy, as they wait for Julianne Phillips—Springsteen's then-new wife—to pick them up at the ball field. The exterior footage was shot at Miller Stadium in West New York, New Jersey, while the performance footage was lensed at the legendary Hoboken rock club Maxwell's.

Inspired by Johnny Cash, Springsteen's haunting, memorable ballad—upheld by synthesizer—"I'm on Fire" was an unexpected worldwide hit. This EP release, from early 1985, added the non-LP tracks "Johnny Bye Bye," "Shut Out the Light," and an enduring take on Tom Waits's "Jersey Girl (Live)." *Courtesy of 991.com*

Remixes

As part of a trend that began in the early 1980s with new wave rock acts, studio hands and noted DJs began remixing records for club play. By 1984, Springsteen got in on the act, hiring Arthur Baker, who had previously worked with Afrika Bambaataa and New Order.

Baker—who was responsible for the dance mix of Cyndi Lauper's 1983 breakthrough "Girls Just Wanna Have Fun"—first reworked "Dancing in the Dark," turning it into a dance music favorite and making it the best-selling 12" single of 1984. Despite pushback that summer from some of his core rock-'n'-roll audience, who disliked the "Blaster Mix" treatment of the song, Springsteen had already commissioned Baker to revise "Cover Me," unveiling the "Undercover Mix."

This rendition, released in October, incorporated a new bass line, new backing vocals, incorporated dub components, and also charted at #11 on *Billboard*'s dance survey. The final Baker/Springsteen collaboration, for the 12" "Freedom Mix" of "Born in the U.S.A.," saw release in January 1985.

It was drastically different from the original and emphasized the shame of the song by eliminating a lot of the bombast of the source track. Baker cut up Springsteen's vocals and altered it to the point where it wasn't the same song. As a result, it failed to place on the Hot Dance/Club Play chart.

This Portuguese pressing of "Santa Claus Is Coming to Town" was rare because it was the only market that saw the song released as an A-side. Unlike in other territories, "My Hometown" was placed on the B-side.

Courtesy of Lost in the Flood

B-sides and Outtakes

Among the songs left off the record, a number wound up as B-sides, including "Pink Cadillac," "Shut Out the Light," "Janey, Don't You Lose Heart," "Stand on It," and "Johnny Bye Bye"—a song cocredited to Chuck Berry that developed out of the *Darkness* leftover "Let's Go Tonight"—all saw staggered release between May 1984 and September 1985.

"This Hard Land" and "Murder Inc." were scrapped in 1983 but revisited as new tracks on 1985's *Greatest Hits* album, while "A Good Man Is Hard to Find (Pittsburgh)," "Wages of Sin," "Cynthia," "My

Love Will Not Let You Down," "TV Movie," "Lion's Den," "Brothers Under the Bridges" "Car Wash," "Rockaway the Days," "Man at the Top," and "Frankie"—a song that dated back to 1976—were all included on the 1998 box set *Tracks*. "County Fair" and "None but the Brave" were included on the bonus disc of 2002's *The Essential Bruce Springsteen*

With the twangy, rockabilly sound "Pink Cadillac" getting nearly as much attention as "Dancing in the Dark" in mid-1984, a picture disc celebrating the famed B-side—but featuring both tunes—was released.   *Courtesy of 991.com*

"Follow That Dream," originally recorded by Elvis Presley in 1962, "Sugarland," "The Klansman," "Seven Tears," "Fugitive's Dream," "One Love," "Betty Jean," "Unsatisfied Heart," "Richfield Whistle," "Little Girl Like You," "Delivery Man," "Don't Back Down," "Out of Work," "Love's on the Line," "Club Soul City," "Angelyne," "All I Need," "Hold On (To What You Got)," "Savin' Up," "On the Prowl" "Now and Forever," "Summer on Signal Hill," "Beneath the Floodline," "Light of Day"—which surfaced in its live form on *MTV Unplugged*—and "Protection," a song given to Donna Summer, were all attempted. Some of these recordings are in circulation among fans, and all are presumably still in Springsteen's vaults.

23

What I Got I Have Earned

Live/1975–85

The year 1986 was Bruce Springsteen's quietest since he became a public figure. But it wasn't as if he recoiled from the spotlight. Early in the year he gathered available members of the E Street Band to perform a pair of gigs at the Stone Pony.

Despite an estimated worth of $50 million as of October '85, he was staying true to his philosophy that he wanted to be a rock musician as opposed to a rock star.

A January benefit for laid off 3M workers was Springsteen's first opportunity to gather the E Street Band—sans Bittan, who was unavailable—at the Stone Pony. Then in March, the band played a surprise nine-song set just for the fun of it, opening with the non-LP live favorite "Stand on It" before playing songs from his '78, '80, and '84 studio albums. This Stone Pony show marked Springsteen's last with the E Street Band until April 1987.

He split his time between New Jersey and California, spending much of the year writing, adjusting to life off the road as a married man, and readying his sprawling five-LP, three-CD box set *Live/1975-85*. He had ideas of how he might poke a hole in the superstar bubble that accompanied *Born in the U.S.A.* With his next album he would look to scale things back to a level of fame that he could be comfortable with.

"Seeds" Planted

In November 1985, just weeks after the 1985 tour was wrapped, Jon Landau sent the Boss a tape of four live recordings—including "Born in the U.S.A.," the recent "Seeds," "The River," and the Edwin Starr original, "War" as part of a proposal for a concert album. When Springsteen went back and listened to a 1975 performance of "Thunder Road" recorded at the Roxy in L.A., he finally began to seriously consider an official concert record and went as far as pondering it as a double album.

As with any project that bore his name, Springsteen obsessed over the live album, which quickly ballooned to five LPs and three CDs. He would listen to dozens of takes of each song in an effort to find the best possible version. From there, he would add overdubs with the help of Chuck Plotkin. Finally, after eight months laboring over the music, he handed it over to Bob Clearmountain to mix. But the packaging still occupied his time. According to one report, the Boss sorted through ten thousand photos in an effort to compile the art for the planned sixty-two-page accompanying booklet.

Bring on the Box

For more than a decade, Springsteen had resisted the pressure to put out a live album. Although such projects had been considered in 1976 and again in '78, he was still hesitant to ready such a release as late as 1984. When asked about the possibility of a concert project in 1984 by the BBC's *Old Grey Whistle Test*, Springsteen said, "A live record, a lot of times you're doing things that you've done already. I think it'd probably be a little boring to work on."

But when a press release was issued on September 11, 1986, announcing that an epic Springsteen box set was slated for a November 10 release, advance orders were colossal. With requests for 1.5 million copies, the forty-track *Live/1975–85* became the largest cash-volume preorder in the history of the music business.

Two weeks before its release, rock radio was cleared to play excerpts from the box, which had been serviced to FM outlets in the form of eight-song promotional samplers. With anticipation incredibly high, thanks to Springsteen-loyal radio outlets like WMMR in Philadelphia, WNEW in New York, and WMMS in Cleveland, fans lined up outside of record stores the night before to guarantee they would get their copies.

Not surprisingly, *Live/1975–85* debuted at #1 in the U.S., selling three million copies in its first month. Columbia invested $3 million promoting the project, pulling in $30 million in sales. Springsteen's cut wasn't too shabby—he grossed a cool $7 million.

Unfortunately, by the end of the first quarter of

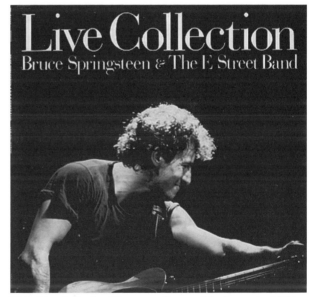

This *Live Collection* EP—manufactured in Japan in 1987—included concert renditions of "For You," "Rosalita," "Fire," and "Incident on 57th Street". A companion EP, *Live Collection II*, was also released with live takes of "Johnny 99," "Working on the Highway," "I'm on Fire," "Bobby Jean," and "Born to Run."
Courtesy of 991.com

1987, the pricey box set stopped selling. It ultimately sold a little over four million copies, which made it anything but a failure.

Essential Tracks

Amassed from thirty live shows Springsteen had in the Thrill Hill vaults, the material represented on *Live/1975–85* was extracted from sixteen shows, including gigs held at the Roxy in Los Angeles (in 1975 and '78), San Francisco's Winterland (1978), Arizona State University (1980), Nassau Coliseum (1980), New Jersey's Meadowlands Arena (in 1981 and 1984), Giants Stadium (1985), and the L.A. Coliseum (1985).

Launched with his piano-only rendition of "Thunder Road," from his first run of landmark shows at the Roxy in 1975, the album's key allure—at least in Springsteen's mind—was to present songs as he had originally intended them to sound. "The audience allows you to attack something with a lot more intensity," he told Marsh in *Glory Days* of the box set versions of "Badlands" and "Darkness on the Edge of Town."

Released in late 1986 in tandem with his *Live/1975-85* box, Springsteen's live cover of Edwin Starr's "War" was backed with the seasonal concert number "Merry Christmas Baby."

Courtesy of 991.com

"War"

The record's first single was originally considered as the B-side of "My Hometown" a year earlier until the idea for a live album took shape. Released in November 1986, it fared well commercially, turning the E Street Band's version of Edwin Starr's 1970 antiwar anthem into a #8 Hot 100 hit.

Springsteen began to play the song on Jon Landau's recommendation, although it took some time for the band to deliver a version he could live with. Performed in response to Ronald Reagan's foreign policy at the time, it emerged late in the *Born in the U.S.A.* tour and was recorded live at the Los Angeles Coliseum on September 30, 1985.

"Raise Your Hand"

Springsteen's official version of the Eddie Floyd classic, this tune was cowritten by Floyd and Booker T. and the MGs guitarist Steve Cropper. The song was a staple of the E Street Band's live set during the *Darkness* tour.

"Because the Night"

Springsteen, of course, gave this song to Patti Smith for her 1978 album *Easter* after producer/engineer Jimmy Iovine convinced him to do so during a ride to Coney Island in an orange Mercedes. In 1993, thanks to a popular cover recorded by 10,000 Maniacs, the song became known to a new generation of music fans.

Issued as part of a UK double-45 box set in 1987 with the live "Born to Run" single, this rare 7-inch—known as CBS BRUCE B2—paired live versions of "Spirit in the Night" and "Because the Night." *Courtesy of Lost in the Flood*

As for this live rendition—which was recorded on December 28, 1980, at Nassau Coliseum—it was the only Springsteen-sanctioned version of the tune until 2010, when he released his own 1978 studio performance on the lost album *The Promise*.

"Seeds"

In what may be one of the most affecting songs Springsteen has ever penned, he tells the plight of a man who desperately seeks work and is living homeless in his car. Although it debuted during his 1985 concerts, the version heard on *Live/1975–85* is the lone take on this track officially available.

"Jersey Girl"

Previously released as the flipside to "Cover Me" in 1984, this live take on Tom Waits's notorious *Heartattack and Vine* has since become a memorable if not obligatory part of many of his New Jersey shows. Performed live during his 1981 run of shows that opened the Brendan Byrne Arena, "Jersey Girl" is the last of the album's forty songs.

"Fire"

Live/1975–85 was already falling off the charts when a single for "Fire" was released in February 1987. Springsteen's first official release of the song he wrote first for Elvis Presley—which was made famous by the Pointer Sisters—wasn't able to revive it. Stalling at #46, it was his first single since "Badlands" to miss the U.S. Top 40.

All the Kids Are Dancin'

Springsteen's Other Concert Albums

In Concert MTV Plugged

In support of his 1992 dual releases *Human Touch* and *Lucky Town*, Springsteen was tapped to record an episode of *MTV Unplugged*. But fans expecting an intimate, acoustic performance from the Boss got quite the contrary when—after a solo rendition of the previously unheard ode to his wife, "Red Headed Woman"—he and his touring band plugged in and delivered an electrifying set of music.

Following the September 22 taping and subsequent airings, a CD version was released in Europe only on April 12, 1993, in conjunction with Springsteen's ongoing European tour. Plans for a limited, ninety-day release in that market eventually gave way to a proper North American release on August 26, 1997.

As for his alteration of the MTV franchise, the program's producer, Alex Coletti, told *Q* in 1993, "When you have the chance to work with Bruce, he can do what he wants. It was a fantastic show and it still had a lot of 'Unplugged's' feel. It was very small, very intimate—and that's all part of what makes 'Unplugged' special. But it was very loud."

As for material, Springsteen's set included subdued takes on classics like "Growin' Up" and "Thunder Road," yet only the latter made the CD—which was long on recent songs like "Better Days," "Living Proof," "Human Touch," and "My Beautiful Reward." The aforementioned "Red Headed Woman" and the first official release of "Light of Day"—which Joan Jett first tracked in 1986—were the disc's only new songs.

With the strictly limited European release, *Q* called it "a pretty good Springsteen live album," adding "there's enough under the Boss's travel-battered bonnet to take him a good few miles further yet down the rock 'n' roll highway."

Four years later, *Entertainment Weekly* called it "an excellent sampling of the 1992 Bruce." Asserting that the Boss's storytelling "is priceless," the review said "his best moments are when he's alone with his guitar or backed by Roy Bittan's piano."

Bruce Springsteen and the E Street Band: Live in New York City

Released on March 27, 2001, this double live album was a companion to the DVD release of his first-ever major televised concert. Chronicling the E Street Band's massively popular 1999–2000 Reunion tour, it was recorded during the final two gigs of the trek at Madison Square Garden. The HBO special of the same name received six Emmy nominations and earned two resulting Awards.

As for the double CD, it contained two new songs—"Land of Hope and Dreams" and the controversial ballad, "American Skin (41 Shots)." Springsteen wrote the latter about the New York Police Department killing of Amadou Diallo. The former was written by Springsteen to restate the purpose and ideas behind the Reunion tour.

The album—which included fan favorites like "Jungleland" and "Badlands" peaked at #5 on the *Billboard* 200.

Hammersmith Odeon London '75

Recorded in London on November 18, 1975, this double album (and concert video) was a document of the E Street Band's first European excursion. Released on February 28, 2006—following its appearance as both a single release and part of the *Born to Run 30th Anniversary Edition* box set the previous November—the performance was initially dismissed by Springsteen.

This white-label promotional copy of the E Street Band's Reunion Tour was sent to the media in advance of the proper double-CD release of *Live in New York City*. The concert album provided a stopgap Springsteen release to fans as he worked on the songs that would comprise his acclaimed 2002 effort *The Rising*.   *Author's Collection*

In advance of the show, which was his first U.K. gig ever, the rocker was rattled by the guerrilla marketing Columbia had done. So although there was documentation of this period in his career, he was hesitant to review it. "I'd paid no attention to it. I never looked at it . . . for 30 years," he wrote in the liner notes. But after *The Rising* tour, and in anticipation of the *Born to Run* commemorative releases, he looked at the film and listened to the performance and was impressed.

Despite its historical content, which included snippets of Van Morrison's "Moondance" in the midst of "Kitty's Back," an early

Doors slam, birds won't sing, and, before long, the song's subject is alone in a bar pondering an extramarital affair. Although it doesn't reflect the country genre sonically, "One Step Up" had all the elements of a Nashville smash. Kenny Chesney realized this in 2002 when he covered the song on his chart-topping album *No Shoes, No Shirt, No Problems*.

Ironically, the song's haunting backing vocal was delivered by Patti Scialfa, the woman Springsteen left Phillips for. They would, of course, eventually marry and raise a family together.

"Tougher Than the Rest"

Although it was never released as a single in the United States, this track f4ared well in Europe upon its June 1988 release. It follows an a capella opening number, "Ain't Got You," and its slow, rhythmic presentation sets the sonic tone of *Tunnel of Love*.

Originally conceived as an upbeat, rockabilly-influenced number, the final version of the song finds Springsteen's character assessing his shortcomings in his pursuit of love. Admitting he's rough around the edges, his song-subject spots a woman across the room and hopes she will dance with him and possibly take a chance with him.

The song's allure made it a Top 20 hit in the U.K. among other European countries. It fared well in Austria and the Netherlands and peaked at #3 in Switzerland's singles chart.

"Spare Parts"

Also released as a single outside of North America on September 12, 1988, "Spare Parts"—with its fiery guitar part and pounding rhythm—is easily the hardest-rocking song on *Tunnel*. Counting Federici, Weinberg, Tallent, and guest harmonica player Wood, the song was a modest performer, reaching the Top 40 in the U.K.

Lyrically, it weaves the tale of Janey, an unwed mother who is ditched by her baby daddy, Bobby. After struggling to support the baby on her own, she ponders killing her infant son, but ultimately finds hope and, instead, baptizes him.

Videos

Five music videos were produced for the album, with four of the promotional clips directed by U2 veteran Meiert Avis. The first, for "Brilliant Disguise," finds Springsteen singing the song directly into the camera as he sits on the edge of chair on a Sandy Hook soundstage. Unlike most videos that had aired on MTV up to this point, the clip was unique because it was captured in a single shot, with Bruce singing a live vocal over the song's musical track. There were no edits, which was ironic because it was nominated in the Best Editing category as well

This 1988 four-track UK EP for "Tougher Than the Rest" offered Springsteen fans the opportunity to get their hands on the non-LP rarities "Roulette" and "Be True." Both songs were recorded in 1979 for an album Springsteen ultimately shelved and reworked into his double LP *The River.*   *Courtesy of 991.com*

as the Video of the Year class at the 1988 MTV Video Music Awards.

The next clip, for "Tunnel of Love," finds Springsteen in full adult mode, wearing a dark suit jacket and leaning against a wall singing. Avis adds a nice black-and-white image to this video, which was shot at Palace Amusements in Asbury Park. Here Bruce dresses more like a grown-up than ever before. His fashion fits the adult theme of the song.

More straightforward was Springsteen's official clip for "One Step Up," which found the Boss strumming a black acoustic guitar and lip-synching the tune into a microphone. Stark winter scenery of him driving alone in a vintage car, stopping for a passing train, evokes the serious tone of the tune. In addition to performance footage shot at the Expo Theater in Fort Monmouth during *Tunnel of Love Express* tour rehearsals, other footage—including the Boss dressed as an old man—was shot inside the Wonder Bar in Asbury Park.

"Tougher Than the Rest" caused some controversy upon its debut in late 1987. Featuring live concert footage from his then-ongoing Tunnel of Love Express trek, Avis augmented the video with brief scenes of straight and gay couples at Springsteen concerts.

The final video for the record, for "Spare Parts," was helmed by director Carol Dodds and shot live in the U.K. during the *Tunnel of Love Express* tour. It featured footage of industrial England and a fiery performance of the song by the E Street Band.

Commercial and Critical Reception

Considering its shift in approach, *Tunnel of Love* did extremely well commercially, topping the Billboard album charts in the weeks after its release. On the strength of its U.S. singles, it went on to sell five million copies, which was just the sort of modest success that Springsteen and manager Jon Landau had hoped for.

Reviews were strong, with *Newsweek* calling it "the best album Springsteen has made." Meanwhile the *Chicago Reader* wrote, "Tunnel of Love is a finely crafted album, careful, cautious, lyrically brilliant in places."

Tunnel of Love has a loose story line: boy meets girl, marries girl, loses girl, misses girl," wrote Stephen Holden in the *New York Times*. "[It] isn't an intellectual breakthrough . . . with *Tunnel of Love*, he's no longer sure of anything. But he's facing his fears head-on."

Finally, *Rolling Stone*'s Steve Pond explained, "*Tunnel of Love* is precisely the right move for an artist whose enormous success gloriously affirmed the potential of arena rock and roll but exacted a toll on the singer. *Born in the U.S.A.* sold 12 million copies mostly because it was the best kind of thoughtful, tough, mainstream rock and roll record—but also because it was misinterpreted and oversimplified by listeners looking for slogans rather than ideas."

Tunnel of Leftovers

In addition to the *Tunnel of Love* tracks—which also included "Ain't Got You," "Cautious Man," "Valentine's Day," "All That Heaven Will Allow," "Two Faces," "Walk Like a Man," and "When You're Alone"—Springsteen had a number of leftover songs when he wrapped work on the record.

"Lucky Man" was the B-side of "Brilliant Disguise," while "Two for the Road" wound up on the flip of the title track. Both of these, plus three more—"The Honeymooners," "The Wish," and "When You Need Me"—were also included on the 1998 four-disc rarities offering *Tracks*.

Recordings of "Beneath the Floodline," "Walking Through Midnight"—a song cowritten with Southside Johnny—and the studio rendition of "Seeds," which was heard in its live form on *1975–85*, are still in the Boss's vault. Another tune, "Part Man, Part Monkey," was revisited again during sessions for *Human Touch* in 1990.

Tunnel of Love Express Tour CD

Released in February 1988, this five-song promotional disc was designed to increase airplay of the track "One Step Up" and raise awareness of Springsteen's imminent U.S. tour. Boasting another album extract, "All That Heaven Will Allow," plus the rarities "Roulette," "Be True," and the infamous B-side

This thirty-track, double promotional CD, titled *Bruce Springsteen 70's to 80's: The Future of Rock 'N Roll*, was issued in Japan in 1988. Boasting fourteen classics from his first decade as a recording artist and sixteen from his 1980s output, the collection is one of the most sought after by Springsteen's enthusiasts. *Courtesy of 991.com*

"Pink Cadillac," the *Express Tour* EP lists the first thirty dates of the trek on the back jacket.

Chimes of Freedom

In August 1988, while Bruce Springsteen and the E Street Band had been on tour as a part of the multiple-artist Human Rights Now! Tour, he released a live EP to benefit Amnesty International. Consisting of live material tracked during the Boss's 1988 live shows, the EP's title track was, of course, his rendition of the Bob Dylan classic "Chimes of Freedom."

Recorded in Stockholm's Olympiastadion on July 3, '88, Springsteen's rendition of the thought-provoking Dylan folk classic earned it and the rest of the EP some attention at U.S. rock radio, although it quickly fizzled out due to poor timing and minimal promotion.

As for the remaining material, two of the tunes—"Born to Run" and "Tougher Than the Rest"—were captured during Springsteen's April 27, 1988, live show at the Los Angeles Memorial Sports Arena. The E Street Band's concert version of "Be True," which was originally the B-side to "Fade Away," was tracked on March 28 at the Joe Louis Arena in Detroit.

26

Cuddle Up

Springsteen's Girlfriends and Wives

Karen Darvin

T his Texas-bred, blonde model was Springsteen's girlfriend around the time of his 1975 ascent to fame, and she regularly accompanied him on tour. According to *Point Blank* author Christopher Sandford, he would sometimes take the stage with a pair of her panties in his pocket. Darvin went on to start a relationship with rocker Todd Rundgren in 1979, who she married and had two sons with.

Lynn Goldsmith

After splitting with Darvin by 1977, Springsteen had a brief relationship with a woman named Joy Hannah and then, also briefly, he dated a seventeen-year-old high schooler before he met Goldsmith, a rock photographer who went on to publish a book of her 1978 pics of him called *Springsteen: Access All Areas*. He and Goldsmith wound up breaking up in 1978 when she found a letter and some pictures from another girl, actress Joyce Hyser.

Joyce Hyser

Hyser—a brown-haired, brown-eyed New Jersey–bred actress who appeared in the 1985 teen film *Just One of the Guys*—began a relationship with Springsteen in 1978. By early the next year, she had lived with him at his New Jersey home for part of 1979.

Hyser accompanied Springsteen on the road in support of *The River*, and—at thirty-one—he felt ready to settle down. However, when he reportedly proposed to her in the early 1980s, she declined.

Just the same, when asked about it in a 2010 interview with the blog, *Back to the '80s*, Hyser said, "Bruce and I were together for almost five years. I grew up with him. We are friends to this day."

Julianne Phillips

Springsteen first met aspiring actress Julianne Phillips, twenty-four, backstage in Los Angeles in late October 1984 when his tour booker, Barry Bell, introduced them. Phillips, an Elite model from Oregon who had appeared in a .38 Special music video, was over a decade younger than Bruce.

Within a week of meeting, they were arm in arm. And the relationship made sense for Springsteen, who was anxious to settle down. He fawned over her whenever she appeared backstage—much to the chagrin of his new backing singer Patti Scialfa, who wanted to be more than friends with the Boss.

By Thanksgiving 1984, Phillips was already sharing Springsteen's residences with him. They spent Christmas in Rumson. Her first public outing with him was at the 1985 Grammy Awards. They vacationed in Maui.

Beneath the surface, they were fairly different people. She grew up well-off, while he was a self-made man. She had an ear for Lionel Richie and didn't care much for Elvis. But Springsteen felt she was the one, and he asked her to marry him on May 3, 1985.

They didn't waste much time, setting a wedding date of May 15. But when he saw the way the paparazzi descended on Phillips's hometown of Lake Oswego, Oregon, when the news broke that he was in town, he pushed their legal nuptials forward to after midnight on Monday, May 13, when they were married in Phillips's family's church.

In an effort to throw the media off their trail, the couple held their wedding reception a day later at a local country club. Steve Van Zandt and Clarence Clemons were Springsteen's best men. They honeymooned at a villa on Lake Como, Italy, that was owned by fashion designer Gianni Versace.

Springsteen spent much of 1986 and 1987 getting acclimated to married life, but when he went back to roadwork behind his *Tunnel of Love* album, Patti Scialfa was often front and center on many of the new numbers. Springsteen and Scialfa had a sexual connection. When Phillips saw the 1988 stage show, she left and flew home to Oregon.

By May, their marriage was over. Springsteen and Scialfa explored their passion and got caught by paparazzi. Pictures of them canoodling made the tabloids. Phillips filed for divorce in August 1988.

The Boss and Phillips were officially divorced in March 1989. She signed a nondisclosure agreement and received a $20 million settlement.

Patti Scialfa

Springsteen first introduced himself to singer Patti Scialfa in early 1983, when he went to watch and presumably jam with Jersey Shore rocker Bobby Bandiera at the Stone Pony. The attractive redhead in jeans and cowboy boots was backstage when he struck up a conversation with her. "We've met," he told her. "Have we?" she said, acting coy, as if she didn't remember.

Scialfa and the Boss went out for a hamburger one night and had a casual relationship. In the process of making *Born in the U.S.A.*, he asked her to sing backing vocals on one song. It didn't make the album.

For a decade, he had mulled bringing a female presence into the E Street Band. Scialfa auditioned as a backing vocalist and got the gig just days before they went on his 1984–1985 World tour.

Springsteen had a playful relationship with Scialfa. He teased her and called her by her birth name, Vivienne. She began to develop deep feelings for him, but by this time—the summer of '85— he was already married to Phillips.

Fast-forward to the *Tunnel of Love* tour, Scialfa played a prominent role in the shows, bumping and grinding with Springsteen. By the summer of '88, they were officially together, as he began to work out a divorce settlement.

Extracted from Patti Scialfa's 1993 Columbia Records debut, *Rumble Doll*, this UK single release of "As Long as I (Can Be with You)" also included "Line of Faith" and "Spanish Dancer." The album was coproduced by Springsteen. *Courtesy of 991.com*

Despite his tendencies to keep himself guarded, Scialfa had spent enough time with Springsteen in the six years since they met to really know him. He felt comfortable with her, which helped him get past his fears of getting married again. "Patti had a very sure eye for all my bullshit," he told *Rolling Stone* in 1992. "She recognized it . . . it was [her] patience and understanding that got me through."

By Christmas 1989, Scialfa was pregnant and gave birth to their first son, Evan James on June 25, 1990. The couple were married the following year, on June 8, 1991, in their Beverly Hills home. Among the ninety guests were E Street Band members Van Zandt, Federici, and Bittan, plus Jackson Browne, John Fogerty, and Bonnie Raitt.

Scialfa was already two months pregnant with their second child when they tied the knot. Their second child and first daughter, Jessica Rae, came into the world on December 30, 1991. The family continued to grow when a second son, Samuel Ryan, was born on January 5, 1994.

27

Waitin' for That Shout from the Crowd

A Dozen Indispensable New Jersey Springsteen Shows

The 1970s

In Springsteen's first decade as a headliner, his Garden State gigs were usually a cut above his standard performances. These shows—which drew diehard locals, friends, and family—were celebratory events that attracted packed crowds at a time when E Street gigs weren't a guaranteed sellout.

Trenton War Memorial, Trenton, November 29, 1974

This special gig marked the live debut of new drummer Max Weinberg and pianist Roy Bittan. The first of two shows at the 1,800-seat venue also included violinist Suki Lahav and marked a cover of Elvis Presley's "Wear My Ring Around Your Neck."

A rare, far-reaching reworking of Dylan's "I Want You" and an early, string-augmented presentation of "Jungleland" make this one of the dream 'Steen gigs.

The Carlton Theatre, Red Bank, October 11, 1975

In the throes of his promotional efforts for *Born to Run*, Springsteen returned to the Jersey Shore area on October 11 to play two shows in one night at the Carlton Theater—which would soon be known as the Monmouth Arts Center and finally, the Count Basie Theatre. The Marquee at the club simply read "Homecoming," because everyone in the area knew very well who was headlining.

Finally out of the bars, Springsteen was now a theater-grade act on the fringes of superstardom. Everyone from Cousin Frankie—who taught him the guitar—to friends from The Upstage era, plus area kids just getting into him, gave him the warmest of welcomes.

The second show, which included former E Street Band member David Sancious sitting in on "Carol," affirmed this. The night ended with four encores that left the crowd breathless.

Monmouth Arts Center, Red Bank, August 1, 1976

The same week his legal battle with Mike Appel caught fire, Springsteen launched the first of six incendiary gigs in Red Bank in order to drum up some cash to keep his organization afloat. But these are no mere run-of-the-mill E Street shows—he activates the first incarnation of the Miami Horns, using players from the Asbury Jukes.

The show also marks the public debut of the fan favorite "Rendezvous," which remained unreleased until 1998's *Tracks*. Springsteen also tried out the *Darkness* album track "Something in the Night."

Capitol Theater, Passaic, September 19, 1978

Bootlegged for more than thirty years thanks to a high-quality three-and-a-half-hour FM broadcast on WNEW-FM, this powerful, magical show saw the debut of "Point Blank" and "Independence Day"—songs that would make *The River*.

Springsteen dedicated "4th of July, Asbury Park (Sandy)" to "everybody in Sea Bright, Long Branch, Point Pleasant, Belmar, Bradley Beach," adding, "Somehow I lived in every one of those places."

The 1980s

By the 1980s, New Jersey Springsteen gigs always had a certain distinction. Whether launching the state's first world-class arena or tearing the roof off of the Stone Pony, shows in Springsteen's backyard were the ultimate E Street experience.

Brendan Byrne Arena, East Rutherford, July 2, 1981

It may not be "The House That Bruce Built," but it might as well be. Springsteen has played the Meadowlands Arena dozens of times since he opened the venue—then known as Brendan Byrne Arena—on July 2, 1981. A six-night sellout stand in any arena was unheard of at the time, even for the biggest acts of the time like the Rolling Stones, but that was the kind of draw he had become in his own backyard.

Springsteen made the shows special, with the first gig in front of twenty-thousand fans iconic for the unveiling of his soon-to-be-classic take on Tom Waits's "Jersey Girl."

When he took the stage on July 2 with a rousing version of "Born to Run," Springsteen was met with a deafening roar. Clearly the crowd approved of him as much as he approved of them.

"That was the best show ever," Springsteen told *Rolling Stone* after the tour launch. "We couldn't hear each other onstage. I felt like the Beatles."

The Stone Pony, Asbury Park, June 8, 1984

Four weeks ahead of the *Born in the U.S.A.* tour, Springsteen and the E Street Band—including new guitarist Nils Lofgren—took the stage in Asbury Park following a show by John Eddie. Marking the public debuts of the new album's title track, plus "My Hometown," "Darlington County," and "Glory Days," Springsteen's twelve-song set got underway around midnight and was a surprise to many of the several hundred at the Stone Pony.

Brendan Byrne Arena, East Rutherford, August 20, 1984

The last gig in an unprecedented ten-night stand at the arena saw the E Street Band tear through thirty-three songs. Special for the return of one-time guitarist Steve Van Zandt—who helped Springsteen out on the Dobie Gray 1973 soul staple "Drift Away" and *The River* favorite "Two Hearts"—this night also marked the brief return of the Miami Horns. Springsteen recruited the horn section for the evening to bolster "Tenth Avenue Freeze-Out."

McLoone's Rumrunner, Sea Bright, October 31, 1987

This has to be the best Halloween ever for Springsteen fans lucky enough to have been in the house as Bruce and the E Street Band (sans Lofgren and Clemons) took the stage under the billing "The Terrorists." In the spirit of the night and to help preserve their anonymity, the group wore hangman masks during "Stand on It"—the first of a dozen tunes. The set marked the live debut of *Tunnel of Love* material and an encore of CCR's "Bad Moon Rising."

Convention Hall, Asbury Park, March 18, 1999

Two weeks ahead of the E Street Band's Reunion tour launch in Barcelona, Springsteen opened this 3,000-seat venue on the Asbury boardwalk for a pair of benefit gigs. Billed as hour-long public rehearsals, tickets were sold for $20; however, fans on the first of two consecutive nights were treated to nearly three hours of tunes. The excitement of the first night was heightened by the concert premiere of "My Love Will Not Let You Down" and the new number "Land of Hope and Dreams." Police were relaxed for these shows, allowing dozens of fans without tickets to hang out on the beach outside of the hall to listen to the music.

From 1999 Onward

The spectacle of Springsteen's home-state gigs with his reconstituted band had grown by leaps and bounds after a decade of dormancy. Tickets to certain shows became incredibly hard to come by. Meanwhile, his record-setting arena and stadium appearances were made more special by the fact that he meant so much to so many in his native New Jersey.

Continental Airlines Arena, East Rutherford, New Jersey, July 15, 1999

In May 1999, Bruce Springsteen and his reunited E Street Band sold a staggering three hundred thousand tickets in a record thirteen hours for fifteen nights of gigs at the Continental Airlines Arena in East Rutherford. The July shows were lucrative for scalpers, including some who were able to get more than $1,000 a pair for prime seats in Internet auctions.

Despite this fact, Springsteen was trying to look out for his fans when he implemented his own initiative against scalpers for the shows by limiting one pair of tickets per customer for the entire engagement. Those able to score seats in the first seventeen rows would need to show two forms of ID—including the credit card used to buy the seats—at the venue box office the night of the show to pick up their tickets, where they would then be escorted directly to their respective sections.

It had been fourteen years since Springsteen and the E Street Band played at the complex during their *Born in the U.S.A.* tour for a six-night stand at Giants Stadium. And the Meadowlands facilities had been Springsteen's unofficial home since he launched what was then-known as the Brendan Byrne Arena with the aforementioned six sold-out shows in July 1981.

With the E Street Band absent for more than a decade, loyal Garden State fans highly anticipated the shows, and upon Springsteen's arrival, loyalists took in tailgate festivities that began at 2 p.m.—long before the Boss's 7:30 set time. Promoters set up a faux boardwalk amusement promenade that recalled the postcard image of Asbury Park in Springsteen's youth. On the side of the arena, facing Route 3, promoters draped a fifty-by-thirty-foot banner that proudly proclaimed, "Bruce Springsteen and the E Street Band. Sold Out 15 Shows."

Elsewhere, there were food concessions of the ilk found in Seaside Heights, plus Bruce karaoke, a Springsteen look-alike contest, games of chance, and a beach volleyball court complete with sand imported from the Jersey Shore town of Lakewood. One hundred kegs of beer were rolled in for concessionaires to pour in a parking lot beer garden.

"We knew that people were going to be here early, tailgating, so we figured that we should do something fun for the fans," Teri Festa Webb, director of marketing for the Meadowlands complex, told the *Star-Ledger*. "There's nothing more Bruce than the Jersey Shore and we figured we'd bring the Shore up north. It's going to look like the boardwalk and smell like the boardwalk. You know, with that cheesesteak aroma."

As for the opening night, it was an exhilarating show, with the one-two punch of "My Love Will Not Let You Down"—from the recent *Tracks* box—and "The Promised Land" kicking things off. The twenty-six-song set was long on surprises including the autobiographical number "In Freehold," a pair of *Tom Joad* numbers, and his soundtrack hit "Streets of Philadelphia." Not surprisingly, the late-show appearances of "Born to Run," "Bobby Jean," and "Thunder Road" reaped the most applause.

Count Basie Theatre, Red Bank, May 7, 2008

Performed as a benefit for the venue that Springsteen had rocked off and on for more than three decades, this show reportedly raised $3 million to help with restoration costs for the eighty-year-old theater. In what was originally slated as a solo gig, the E Street Band's members and the Mighty Max Horns found themselves cramped onstage for their first theater show since 1980.

These shows consisted of back-to-back performances of *Darkness on the Edge of Town* and *Born to Run*. As Springsteen told the crowd, "we're gonna start with Darkness, so we don't send you home suicidal." As the band got underway with "Badlands," there was a problem. After the false start, he told the audience, "we fucked it up already! I knew there was a reason why we didn't do this. Maybe we shouldn't do it!"

But it went on to become one of the most intense and magical nights in the history of the E Street Band. Following the final notes of "Jungleland," Springsteen led his musicians through the playful *Darkness* outtake "So Young and In Love," plus a rare "Kitty's Back," an explosive "Rosalita (Come Out Tonight)," and a jovial take on Eddie Floyd's "Raise Your Hand."

Giants Stadium, East Rutherford, New Jersey, October 9, 2009

Known as the last of three "Wrecking Ball" gigs at Giants Stadium, these were the last-ever shows at the legendary football stadium before it was torn down to be replaced by a new, state-of-the-art facility. During his May 2009 run at the Izod Center next door, Springsteen announced that the band would be back to East Rutherford to "say goodbye to old Giants Stadium . . . Before they bring the wrecking ball, the wrecking crew is coming back!"

During these concerts, he unveiled a sentimental song written specifically about the occasion, called "Wrecking Ball." The October 9 gig marked the final time the E Street Band would grace the stage at Giants Stadium, which it first played twenty-four years earlier, on September 1, 1985. Bookending his shows similarly, the Boss closed out the run of shows with a powerful, albeit fitting performance of his entire *Born in the U.S.A.* album.

Honorable Mentions

These shows weren't actually in the Garden State, but considering how many suburban New Jersey kids flocked to College Park for their undergrad degrees, and how much of the state's rock community had been served by WNEW-FM in the 1970s, these gigs very nearly qualify among the best in Springsteen's backyard.

University of Maryland Field House, College Park, April 28, 1973

In the classic sense, this is hardly the penultimate E Street Band show, as Springsteen served as the opener for headliner Chuck Berry and undercard act Jerry Lee Lewis. But because he and the boys *backed* Berry, it must be noted.

Berry came through the backstage door five minutes ahead of his gig. When Springsteen asked what tunes they were playing, Berry—according to Springsteen's account in the 1987 documentary *Hail! Hail! Rock and Roll!*—snapped back, "We're going to do some Chuck Berry songs."

Ironically, onstage, Berry—who was riding high thanks to his comeback hit "My Ding-A-Ling"—told the E Street Band to "Play for that money, boys." But they were playing with the rock 'n' roll pioneer for free. There was no additional fee for backing him. Berry, meanwhile, snatched his cash and left immediately after the show.

The Bottom Line, New York, New York, August 15, 1975

If it's impossible to single out exactly which of the ten shows over five nights (August 13–17) ranks the best, the fact that the first set on August 15 was broadcast and recorded by fans for posterity makes it the best known and most cherished of these gigs. Few would argue with the *New York Times* assessment that Springsteen's historic engagement at the Greenwich Village venue "rank[s] among the great rock experiences of those lucky enough to get in."

Many of the attendees were writers, record company people, and radio programmers who were glomming off of Columbia Records' massive ticket buy. The buzz was big among music industry fixtures in Manhattan, most of whom were hot to see Springsteen—especially on the heels of Jon Landau's "I have seen rock and roll's future" announcement in the *Real Paper* a year earlier.

Those fans in the Tri-State area who didn't get a ticket to these watershed gigs at the now-defunct venue near New York University got an ample dose of Springsteen anyway as he previewed his forthcoming *Born to Run* material.

During the simulcast on 102.7 WNEW-FM in New York, Bruce played nearly all of his new album, including the title cut, "She's the One," "Thunder Road," and "Tenth Avenue Freeze-Out," plus covers of Gary U.S. Bonds's "Quarter to Three," Jackie DeShannon's "When You Walk in the Room," and the Crystals' "Then (S)he Kissed Me."

28

In the Dumps with the Mumps as the Adolescent Pumps His Way into His Hat

Debacles, Dangers, Controversies, and Embarrassments

Garden Party

Most rock acts would be elated to play Madison Square Garden, even as the opening act for headliners Chicago. But after playing with the wildly popular jazz-rock collective on its spring 1973 arena tour, Springsteen was a total mess over the assignment.

The forty-five minute slot just wasn't enough time for him to work his magic on a loyal crowd, let alone a sea of ten thousand strange faces. Although Mike Appel convinced him the run of arena gigs would be good for his career, the outcome was far different.

"I went insane during that tour," Springsteen told *Crawdaddy* in 1974. "It was the worst state of mind I've been in, I think, and just because of the playing conditions for our band." Clearly, he just wasn't ready to play such massive venues.

Springsteen was still two years away from his *Born to Run* persona, and by comparison his gigs were still relatively subdued. By the time he made it to the Garden for a pair of shows on June 14 and 15, he had gotten experienced in being on the receiving end of boos.

Exiting the stage on the second night, Bruce was upset and let Appel know it. Unfortunately, his fusion of rage and tears was witnessed backstage by Columbia executives.

"In those days, Bruce never liked to do the big halls," drummer Vini Lopez told the *Star-Ledger* in 2000. "He didn't even like doing theaters. We did coffeehouses. It wasn't only for the sound, but just for being close to the people."

Appel's Crazy NFL Proposition

Springsteen's 1970s manager Mike Appel was as pushy as he was inexperienced. According to Dave Marsh in *Born to Run*, in advance of the release of Springsteen's debut album, Appel was crazy enough to call NBC Television, the network carrying the 1973 Super Bowl, to suggest that in lieu of "The Star Spangled Banner," they should instead use a new antiwar song penned by Springsteen during the broadcast.

When a producer for the event declined to use the Springsteen original "Balboa vs. the Beast Slayer," Appel gave the NBC staffer a rash of shit and insisted that he would call him some day to remind him of his mistake. Before hanging up on him, Appel—who had mortgaged his home to keep Springsteen's career on track—also threatened to have the producer fired.

Even though Appel's version of events is different—he claims to have suggested that Springsteen sing "Balboa" before "The Star-Spangled Banner"—few can deny that his persistence did pay off on other occasions. His brazenness helped get Springsteen in to see John Hammond a year before, and in 1975, his doggedness famously landed the Boss on the cover of *Time* and *Newsweek*.

Dissing AM Radio

Although AM Radio was still vastly popular in 1974, Springsteen—who grew up on Top 40—insulted a lot of programmers in a 1974 interview with Paul Williams. He explained that he first stopped listening to the hit format "because it got really trashy."

Springsteen called it "a wasteland" and took aim at now-classics like Andy Kim's "Rock Me Gently," plus Paper Lace's "The Night Chicago Died" and Bo Donaldson and the Heywoods' "Billy, Don't Be a Hero."

Springsteen clearly wasn't a fan of the songwriters behind said hits. Speaking about Peter Callander and Mitch Murray of Paper Lace, he said, "Oh God. If somebody shot those guys, there's not a jury in the land that would find them guilty."

It's the Bomb!

During one of the first gigs on Springsteen's *Born to Run* tour, on October 2, 1975, in Milwaukee, the E Street Band received word of a bomb threat, just seven songs into the gig. The Uptown Theater was cleared, and police went through the facility, replete with bomb-sniffing dogs, to ensure the safety of the place and its attendees.

Springsteen and the boys decamped to a local watering hole during the ninety-minute evacuation. When the audience was granted reentry and the band went back onstage, they were noticeably buzzed. With bootlegs like *Milwaukee*

Bomb Scare Show as proof, Springsteen sounded a little wasted as he asked the crowd if they were "loose" during a cover of Chuck Berry's "Little Queenie."

Panic in Detroit

On October 4, 1975, the night of the E Street Band's show at Detroit's Michigan Palace, something went wrong with Springsteen. For the first known time in his history as a performer, he refused to go on.

According to reports, he was frozen, curled up in the fetal position in the dressing room. Ultimately, Steve Van Zandt talked some sense into his friend, who had lost his mind for the moment. Meanwhile, once onstage, Springsteen didn't give his fans as much as a hint that something had upset him as he and Steve carried out a duet of the Temptations "Ain't Too Proud to Beg."

Not long after, Springsteen opened up to Robert Hilburn about the adjustments to fame. "At that moment, I could see how people get into drink or drugs," he explained. "Because the one thing you want at a time like that is to be distracted—in a big way."

Poster Shredding

Springsteen's four-date European trek got off to a bad start when he arrived in London in November 1975 and saw posters promoting his two U.K. dates that seriously irked him. In the wake of the media circus in the U.S., he was burnt out on the hype about him, but the British were just getting started.

Stickers printed up by CBS U.K. using the "I saw rock and roll's future and its name is Bruce Springsteen" and posters proclaiming "Finally. The World is Ready for Bruce Springsteen!" were everywhere within a four-block radius of the Hammersmith Odeon. Springsteen was royally pissed. So much so that he personally canvassed the area ripping down the posters he could remove and tearing them in shreds.

"I've never seen him so subdued," Miami Steve told *Rolling Stone* after the November 18 gig.

Six days later he played the Odeon again. This time he brought his A-game, performing a three-hour concert that featured nine encores.

Racists in London

On the final night of Springsteen's brief tour, after his redeeming Odeon show, the band returned to their hotel rooms. However, Clarence Clemons—who was in the company of some black acquaintances—was told by prejudiced management staff that his visitors could not be allowed up to his quarters.

Instead of getting mad at the xenophobic personnel at the front desk, Clemons changed into his wildest stage outfit and got even. Returning to the lobby, the Big Man managed to intimidate and embarrass several Caucasian businessmen as they returned to their rooms with their ladies of the night, questioning them on whether they were registered guests.

Springsteen Slams Columbia Records

By the time of *Born to Run*'s ascent, Springsteen was taking aim at his record company for the Dylan comparisons that accompanied his first two records. He deemed it a mistake and said to *NME* reporter Andrew Tyler in November 1975, "How can they expect people to swallow something like that?"

"It blows my mind how [Columbia] can underestimate people so much," Bruce seethed. "I was trying to tell these guys at the record company, 'wait a second, you guys. Are you trying to kill me?' It was like a suicide attempt on their part. It was like somebody didn't want to make no money."

Springsteen was also irked by the placement of quotes from Landau's famous article in press kits and advertising to plug his third album. While he was deeply moved by Landau's words, he was bothered by the way the company took the praise out of context and used it to hype his record. "It pisses me off," he told Tyler. "When I read it, I want to strangle the guy who put that thing in there."

Artistic Improvements

During his summer 1978 tour stop in Los Angeles, Springsteen became so uncomfortable with the billboard advertisement for his new album, *Darkness on the Edge of Town*, that he decided to access the rooftop of the six-story Sunset Strip building where the sign was located to deface it.

On July 4, before his show at the Forum, Springsteen, Van Zandt, Clemons, Tallent, and members of their crew climbed onto the roof of the Sunset Strip building where the billboard promoting *Darkness on the Edge of Town* sat. With twenty cans of spray paint, Springsteen and his gang made some alterations.

Plans to put a mustache on the giant picture of his face were thwarted when Springsteen couldn't reach his nose. Instead, they tagged the phrases "E Street" and "Prove It All Night" on the sign. Describing the prank to the Forum crowd, he told the audience that they "made some artistic improvements."

The Firecracker Show

During Springsteen's New Year's Eve gig in Cleveland in December 1978, a fan near the front of the stage hurled a firecracker in his direction at the Richfield Coliseum that caused quite a scare. Exploding just beneath Bruce's right eye, the matter seemed to upset Van Zandt more than anyone.

"If anyone saw the cat that threw that firecracker, man," Steve balked, "[he] almost took [Bruce's] fucking eye out."

After making sure he was okay, Springsteen was only a little more diplomatic. "I've seen people hurt at shows with firecrackers before," he told the crowd. "I don't want nobody throwing that shit in here."

"I'm gonna have a good new year anyway," he told the audience as he led the band into "Good Rockin' Tonight." Although he was upset over the incident, he was a complete professional, pushing out eight additional numbers before wrapping up the night.

Break a Leg

One Saturday in mid-April 1979, Springsteen's tour booker Barry Bell brought a friend, comedian Robin Williams, to the rocker's New Jersey farm. But as Williams—who had previously met Springsteen—and Bell drove up Bruce's driveway, they caught him off guard as he was riding on a motorized three-wheeler with his then-girlfriend, actress Joyce Heiser.

Distracted, Springsteen crashed the motorbike into a tree, injuring the muscle in his leg. Despite the pain, he held off on going to the emergency room until the leg became so swollen that he could no longer resist.

While he managed to avoid a fracture, specialists diagnosed severe muscle damage and insisted on three weeks of rest so that the injury could properly heal.

Don't Shoot Me

In September 1979, Springsteen signed on to play the MUSE benefit shows at Madison Square Garden. But when he learned that photojournalist Lynn Goldsmith, his former girlfriend, would be the concert's official photographer, he made a request to organizers that she not shoot his sets.

But at one point during the show that marked his thirtieth birthday, Springsteen jumped down into the front rows of the Garden to grab Goldsmith after he caught her taking pictures of him, violating their agreement. He brought her back up onstage with him, pulling her by the arm, telling the audience, "This is my ex-girlfriend," before picking her up like a caveman and carrying her backstage, where she was removed from the show.

Days later, a report in the *New York Post* claimed that Goldsmith was planning to sue Springsteen for $3 million "for public humiliation and for being manhandled." No suit was ever filed.

Born to Forget

When Springsteen took the stage in Ann Arbor, Michigan, on October 3, 1980, to launch his first tour since 1978, few would imagine that he'd forget his signature anthem. But as the E Street Band started up the show's first number, "Born to Run," he did just that.

"I knew it was gonna happen," Springsteen said to Marsh in 1980, speaking of his inability to recall the lyrics to his enduring hit. "I'd just listened to the song about ten times backstage, tryin' to remember 'em. But my mind just went blank. All of a sudden, though, I heard the words in the back of my head, and I realized, holy smokes, the kids are singing them to me. It was a real nice gift."

Caught in the Act

In the midst of the Phoenix stop of *The River* tour, Springsteen went a little crazy during "Rosalita" and jumped from the side of the stage. His destination was the top of the speakers some nine feet below him, but he missed.

Tragedy was averted when roadie Bob Werner broke Springsteen's fall, keeping him from landing on the concrete floor. Werner wasn't as lucky—he incurred a sprained wrist.

As the song rolled on longer than it should have, no one in the E Street Band or the crowd could see what transpired. Then the neck of Springsteen's guitar stuck up out of the air. He followed with a boyish grin, climbing back onstage and resuming the tune, much to the delight of his fans.

Not NOW

In the spring of 1982, Springsteen found himself under scrutiny by the New York branch of the National Organization for Women. The ladies of NOW were displeased with Bruce's repeated use of the term "little girl" in his lyrics and began a campaign that pled with the Boss to stop using such language in his tunes.

In addition to a publicity campaign, the organization spread its sentiments about Springsteen via telephone and letter writing efforts. An unnamed representative for Springsteen insisted that the use of "little girl" was a rock-'n'-roll term, NOW balked and insisted Bruce was writing and singing sexist music.

If so, the record-buying public didn't seem to mind. Springsteen continued to use the phrase in 1985's "I'm on Fire," one of his biggest-ever hits.

What an Ass!

When Springsteen's backside met the American flag for the cover of *Born in the U.S.A.*, it prompted a strange reaction during the summer of '84. Some people actually thought the Boss was urinating on the flag. Meanwhile, scores of women couldn't stop staring at his Levi's–clad buttocks. Either way, the publicity was priceless.

Saying No to $12 Million

In 1986, the Chrysler Corporation sought to use Springsteen and his smash "Born in the U.S.A." in an advertising campaign for its line of minivans. But Bruce turned down Chrysler Chairman Lee Iacocca's $12 million offer.

If Springsteen couldn't be bought, the patriotic message in the song was commercially viable enough that a song called "The Pride Is Back"—sung by Kenny Rogers—became a massively successful campaign, boosting sales of the vehicles.

The Boss, of course, has yet to endorse a product to this day.

Don't Show

A planned concert for New Jersey's East Freehold Park was proposed for May 29, 1986, as an outdoor benefit show to promote the Jersey Artists for Mankind single. Although no members of the E Street Band, nor Springsteen himself, were confirmed for the show, an application for a concert permit by organizers six weeks prior started rumors among music fans.

With a park capacity of just twelve thousand, the Freehold town officials' fear that the event could draw one hundred thousand music fans prompted the event cancellation when the permit was yanked on April 22. Although he never officially agreed to rock his hometown, the Boss was seriously considering making an appearance. Unfortunately, the show never took place.

Road Dogs

In 1987, two former Springsteen roadies, Mike Batlan and Doug Sutphin, filed suit against the Boss seeking $6 million in punitive damages and back overtime pay.

"We're suing him for massive violations of labor laws which resulted in our being cheated out of hundreds of thousands of dollars," Batlan—Springsteen's former guitar tech who helped produce *Nebraska*—said in a letter to *Q* magazine at the time. "Can a man be a hero to the working class while simultaneously spending millions of dollars in a legal battle to keep the workers of his own Industry exempt from the protections of labor law?"

When Batlan and Sutphin exited in 1985, Springsteen gave them $250,000 in severance—quite a generous parting gift at the time. he eventually settled out of court for $200,000 in September 1991, just six days before the trial in the case was to begin. A year later, he commented on the suit, calling it "disappointing. I worked with these two people for a long time, and I thought I'd really done the right thing. And when they left, it was handshakes and hugs all around," Springsteen explained. "And then about a year later, bang! The Boss contended that Batlan and Sutphin had been treated extremely well. The men were either disgruntled, looking for a nice payday from their famous former employer, or both.

Before the Fame Is Lame

In 1998, Springsteen went to court in London to prevent the record company Masquerade Music from releasing a record of his old demos and outtakes. "You need to protect your work, your music and the identity that you've worked hard to present," Springsteen told *Uncut* in 2002 of his efforts to prevent the release of *Before the Fame*, a project consisting of old demos and outtakes.

"I'm not losing sleep at night over it, but I'm protective of it where I can be," he explained. Springsteen's legal team was ultimately able to have the unsanctioned album project withdrawn.

41 Shots

Bruce Springsteen caused a tremendous controversy in June 1999 when he premiered the song "American Skin (41 Shots)" at Philips Arena in Atlanta during the E Street Band's Reunion tour. A social commentary set to music, Springsteen chronicled the incident of February 4, 2009, when four Bronx plainclothes police officers fired forty-one gunshots, killing Amadou Diallo, a twenty-three-year-old Guinean immigrant who was mistaken for a rape suspect.

When it heard about the song soon after, the New York Police Department reacted unfavorably, with City Police Commissioner Howard Safir telling the *New York Daily News*, "I personally don't care for Bruce Springsteen's music or his song," in an article asking cops to avoid attending and/or working security at Springsteen's upcoming ten-night stand at Madison Square Garden.

"He goes on the boycott list," Bob Lucente, president of the New York State Fraternal Order of Police, said of Bruce, calling him a "fucking dirtbag" in the presence of reporters. Diallo's parents had the opposite opinion after meeting with Springsteen after the first MSG gig on June 12.

Diallo's mother Kadiatou first heard the song in its entirety during a Springsteen show at the Garden. "He invited us to meet him backstage," she told *AARP the Magazine* in 2009. "He hugged me in a very warm, affectionate way."

After introducing Mrs. Diallo to Patti and the rest of the E Street Band, Springsteen showed Mrs. Diallo to the VIP section. She was deeply touched. "I was stunned," she added, "because I thought, 'He's going to come and be like this big celebrity singer.'" Later, Springsteen donated money to four New York City colleges for scholarships in Amadou's honor.

Whistlin' Dixie

In early 2003, Natalie Maines—frontwoman for the Dixie Chicks—spoke out in a London concert about her disagreement with U.S. president George W. Bush about the ongoing invasion of Iraq. The media picked up on the story, which wound up causing quite a controversy and prompted many country music fans—who are typically conservative—and programmers to revolt against one of the genre's most popular acts.

"The Dixie Chicks have taken a big hit lately for exercising their basic right to express themselves," Springsteen said in an official press release. "To me, they're terrific American artists expressing American values by using their American right to free speech. For them to be banished wholesale from radio stations. And even entire radio networks, for speaking out is un-American."

Springsteen explained that the ongoing pressure at the time by government and big business to conform flew in the face of freedom. "I do want to add my voice to those who think that the Dixie Chicks are getting a raw deal, and an un-American one to boot. Send them my support," he concluded.

Canceling Halloween

In October 2008, the Springsteen's made news by announcing that there would be no Halloween festivities at their Rumson home. In past years, he and his wife, Patti Scialfa, had erected a detailed holiday display at the gates of their estate, but concerns over safety and the overwhelming popularity of the annual event meant that he put the kibosh on trick-or-treating.

"So as not to inconvenience you this Halloween, due to 'catastrophic success' (read: too many visitors for the neighborhood to handle) and concern for the safety of kids and parents, we won't be having our usual Halloween display this year in Rumson," read a post on Springsteen's official website. "We wish everyone a safe and Happy Halloween! Thanks, Bruce and Patti."

In previous years, the Springsteens had masked characters dole out candy to trick-or-treaters as they allowed visitors to walk up onto their well-decorated main driveway. Many even speculated that Springsteen or Scialfa were behind the masks.

Ugly Rumors

When accusations surfaced in August 2006 that Springsteen had an affair, he took to his official website to refute the reports. "Due to the unfounded and ugly rumors that have appeared in the papers over the last few days, I felt they shouldn't pass without comment. Patti and I have been together for 18 years—the best 18 years of my life. We have built a beautiful family we love and want to protect and our commitment to one another remains as strong as the day we were married."

In April 2009, while Springsteen was on tour in Houston, reports suggesting that he had another affair seeped out when he was named as the other man in a Monmouth County divorce complaint filed by Red Bank resident Arthur Kelly. The papers contended that Ann C. Kelly of Long Branch "has committed adultery with one Bruce Springsteen, who resides in Rumson, N.J. and Colts Neck, N.J., at various times and places too numerous to mention."

Springsteen responded to these allegations via Shore Fire Media, his public relations representatives, by directing the media to his 2006 response. He had no further comment.

Greatest Mistake

In January 2009, Springsteen was regretting a deal he made with Wal-Mart to sell an exclusive version of his *Greatest Hits* album that recycled eleven tunes from his 1995 best-of with the "Radio Nowhere" single from 2007's *Magic*. Soon after the $10 collection went on sale at the big box retailer on January 13, fans took to the message boards at *Backstreets.com* to criticize the move, considering Wal-Mart—notorious for its antiunion stance and labor law violations—pretty much went against everything he stood for.

Springsteen's management defended the move in a *Billboard* interview. Jon Landau asserted that because Bruce's other discs were already in Wal-Mart—where he sold 15 percent of his CDs—the move was acceptable. "We're not doing any advertising for Wal-Mart," Landau said. "We haven't endorsed Wal-Mart or anybody else. We're letting Sony do its job."

But Springsteen jumped on the sword and acknowledged his new *Greatest Hits* release was a hurried decision, because his camp was in the throes of planning a lot of activities for early 2009. "We didn't vet it the way we usually do," he told Jon Pareles. "We just dropped the ball on it."

Given the company's labor history, Springsteen conceded, "It was a mistake. Our batting average is usually very good, but we missed that one. Fans will call you on that stuff, as it should be."

Springsteen's Geography Flub

On November 13, 2009, at Michigan's Palace of Auburn Hills Friday night, Springsteen addressed the crowd by the wrong state. "Hello, Ohio!" the Boss said on several occasions during the first half-hour of the lengthy gig.

Steve Van Zandt quickly whispered the geographical blunder to the singer, who was visibly rattled over the gaffe. "I'm all right," Springsteen told the crowd after the tip-off. He then laughed it off nervously, confessing, "That is every frontman's nightmare."

After the jinx, Springsteen and the band kept rolling, offering up a complete performance of the 1975 album *Born to Run*. Springsteen also performed his recently debuted new track "Wrecking Ball" and took a moment to talk up the Detroit-area charity Focus: Hope.

Following the show, Van Zandt commented on the "Hello, Ohio!" mishap, telling *Rolling Stone* that at first he thought he'd misheard the Boss. "The second time I looked at Garry and said, 'Did you hear what I just heard?' At that point I knew I had to get Bruce's attention."

What a Vidiot!

In August 2011, hilarious and embarrassing lost footage of Springsteen dancing and lip-synching to "Dancing in the Dark" emerged on YouTube. The unused video featured Bruce alone in front of the camera in a wifebeater T-shirt, suspenders, baggy pants, and a curly mane of hair.

Bruce's dancing was downright atrocious, and the clip was uncomfortable for any true Springsteen fan to watch. Thankfully, the Boss had the good sense to ditch director Jeff Stein's concept in favor of Brian De Palma's enduring treatment.

29

When It Comes to Luck, You Make Your Own

Human Touch and Lucky Town

Firing the E Street Band

September 23, 1989, marked the fortieth birthday of Bruce Springsteen. The milestone was celebrated at the Rumrunner in Sea Bright with the entire E Street Band and former member Steve Van Zandt in place.

The celebratory gig—which found Springsteen singing "Around and Around," "Sweet Little Sixteen," "Stand by Me," "What'd I Say," "Glory Days," "Havin' a Party," and "Twist and Shout"—left everyone in the Springsteen camp elated. But four weeks later, the Boss stunned his loyal crew by phoning each of the members to let them know that he was retiring the band.

"I was on tour with Ringo Starr in Japan," Clarence Clemons told Phil Sutcliffe in May 1998. "Bruce called me. He just said, 'It's over.' I thought he wanted me back home to play with him so the Ringo tour was over for me and I said, 'Sure, I'll get on the next plane.' But he said, 'No, the E Street Band is over.'

"I was shocked, hurt, angry all at once," Clemons explained. "Then after a while I thought, 'The man's gotta do what he's gotta do. Fine.' But it's still painful to think of.'"

"I soft-soaped it somehow," Springsteen told *60 Minutes* in 2007. "Or I tried, you know. And, you know, everybody had different feelings. I mean people were mad or angry and then suddenly they're okay . . . Sometimes you've got to break your own narrative."

For years it seemed like Springsteen meant to keep the group apart. However, a reunion performance in January 1995 gave the E Street Band members a glimmer of hope. But it would be ten long years before he reactivated the group in 1999 for touring purposes.

Fighting Depression

Springsteen has said that a serious bout of depression after the *Tunnel of Love Express* tour led to some drastic changes in his life. He was in a rut but didn't have the nerve to make a change. "I went through a very confusing time, a depression, really," he told *Beats* in August 1992.

"I began to reassess everything I'd gone through," he continued. "Like the success I'd had with *Born in the U.S.A.* Did I like it? Did I want to do something like that again? Was I misunderstood?"

Springsteen also thought a lot about the iconic levels his music had reached. He felt beleaguered and—as he put it—"dehumanized." Therapy helped him resolve some of his woes. He felt freer and able to step away from his past.

"I stopped chasing old ghosts. I needed to live in the present," he explained to reporter Mans Ivarsson. "In the end I was forced to drive down a road I had never traveled before. And I found love, children, and a new faith in my place in the world."

The Lure of Los Angeles

If the temptations of Los Angeles first prompted him to establish a second residence in the area a decade earlier, Bruce and Patti went Hollywood for a different reason in 1989—anonymity. Despite being one of the biggest music stars of the 1980s, the Boss was able to live a relatively quiet, normal life in California.

There were so many other celebrities in L.A. that it was rare that he would find any enthusiastic fans hanging around his neighborhood. At his homes in New Jersey, however, there were often loyal fans congregating outside of his gates.

Los Angeles was also critical in Springsteen's effort to distance himself from his past. He wanted to break free of the image that came with his name. In L.A., the present was what mattered most.

Fatherhood

On July 25, 1990, Springsteen became a father to Evan James. The following year, on June 8, 1991, he and Scialfa were married at home in Beverly Hills. Two additional children, Jessica Rae (born December 30, 1991) and Samuel Ryan (born January 5, 1994), followed.

For Springsteen, who had become accustomed to having others cater to his needs, the roles were reversed. "You can no longer spend the afternoon thinking about whether you should wear white or brown shoes," he told *Beats*. "Because kids need you there with them; they take you out of your own head and into the real world."

Fatherhood also brought him closer than ever before to his own dad. Doug started coming around a lot. The shared experience resulted in his father opening up. More than ever before, they were seeing the best in each other.

Extracurricular Activity

In Los Angeles, Springsteen kept a pretty low profile into 1991 as he started to work through some new song ideas. He stopped in on Nils Lofgren's sessions for *Silver Lining* at Ocean Way Studios in December '90, lending harmony vocals to the track "Valentine," which was released as a single in tandem with the record's March release. Springsteen also appeared in the song's music video, although the song went largely unnoticed.

He also helped out Max Weinberg during a performance at the Rumrunner in Sea Bright on January 20, singing and playing guitar on "Ready Teddy," "Tobacco Road," "Under the Boardwalk," "Jersey Girl," and "Glory Days." Bruce had flown back east to check on his New Jersey homes and make an appearance four days earlier at the Waldorf-Astoria in New York during the Rock and Roll Hall of Fame Awards, where he and Wilson Pickett played "People Get Ready," "Mustang Sally," and "In the Midnight Hour" with new inductees the Impressions, who were spearheaded by Curtis Mayfield.

That May, Springsteen collaborated on the song "Take a Look at My Heart" for the John Prine album *The Missing Years* in L.A., which ultimately earned a Grammy for Best Contemporary Folk Album. Then in July, during another trip east, Southside Johnny recruited Springsteen for his Steve Van Zandt–produced album *Better Days*, which came out in September. the Boss donated the song "All the Way Home" and lent guitar, keyboards, and supporting vocals to the track. He also sang harmony on another tune, "It's Been a Long Time."

Twice Bittan

Some of Springsteen's aforementioned depression was related to his inability to write new songs following his *Tunnel of Love* tour. When he finally broke through a yearlong writer's block at the end of 1989, he felt that the songs sounded like inferior versions of the tunes he had written for *Tunnel of Love*, or else they sounded like cast-offs from *Nebraska*. He wanted to say something new, but he was struggling.

He decided to call up Roy Bittan, the E Street Band's longtime keyboardist. Bittan shared some of his own original instrumental tunes with Bruce, who retreated to his garage studio, where the lyrics to what became the track "Roll of the Dice" poured out of him.

Bittan jump-started what would eventually be known as the *Human Touch* album, as Springsteen ran into the house from his studio one December night, woke up Scialfa at 3 a.m., and forced her to listen to the tune. "Roll of the Dice" became the impetus for *Human Touch*, a record that Springsteen would ultimately call his most soul-influenced work since *The Wild, the Innocent, and the E Street Shuffle.*

Bittan continued to work with him in his California garage, helping him with arrangements. Springsteen wrote the title track in the spring of 1990. "57 Channels" came late in the game, injecting some humor into the project.

Bittan and Springsteen operated as a two- man band for more than a year until Journey bassist and future American Idol star Randy Jackson, Toto drummer Jeff Porcaro, former Faces keyboardist Ian McLagan, trumpeter Mark Isham, former E Streeter David Sancious, Scialfa, and a number of soul singers—including Sam Moore, Bobby King, and Bobby Hatfield—helped shape the end product at A&M Studios in L.A.

When all was said and done, *Human Touch* took nearly a year and a half to make. For his efforts, Bittan earned cowriting and production credits for "Dice" and another song, "Real World." And he wasn't just the only member of the E Street Band (save for Scialfa) to survive the great purge of 1989; Bittan was the man who brought Springsteen back from the brink of disaster.

Double Shot of Bruce

Human Touch was a statement about Springsteen's growth as a man, moving past his divorce from Phillips and head-first into his life partnership with Scialfa. He was ready to embrace whatever love delivered.

With the title cut—which became the first single and was a spirited, mid-tempo rocker—Bruce sang of the need for companionship and all it entailed, whether emotion, communication, or a sexual bond.

But when he finished the record in the middle of 1991, he wasn't entirely pleased with its overall sentiment. Springsteen was a fortunate guy who was in a great marriage with two young children, but the album wasn't reflecting just how blessed he was feeling.

So he penned one more song, "Living Proof," which was inspired by Bob Dylan's "Series of Dreams," to represent how he felt about his life in the present tense. That led to a burst of creativity that resulted in the numbers he would quickly record over three weeks in the fall of 1991. It would serve as a companion album to *Human Touch* that he would call *Lucky Town*.

Soon after Springsteen announced on January 23, 1992, that the albums would be released on March 31, manager/producer Jon Landau emphasized that although the records shared certain themes, they were intended to be separate releases.

"To us they are very distinct—there's no song you could take from *Human Touch* and put it on *Lucky Town* and vice versa, which would flow and feel coherent in that context," Landau told reporter Paul Humphries.

Springsteen would later admit that he took a cue from Guns N' Roses, who had released two albums, *Use Your Illusion 1* and *Use Your Illusion 2*, simultaneously the previous autumn with great success. "I basically said, 'maybe I'll try it!'" he confessed to *Rolling Stone* in 1992.

Split Single

On March 4, nearly four weeks ahead of the new discs, a double-sided single featuring "Human Touch" backed by *Lucky Town's* "Better Days" was released. The songs were instantly popular on rock radio, and "Human Touch" peaked at #1 on the Album Rock Tracks that spring, peaking at #16 on the *Billboard* Hot 100.

Critical and Commercial Reception

In addition to its lead-off hit, Springsteen's ninth studio album boasted a popular second single, "57 Channels (and Nothin' On)," a Sonny Boy Williamson number ("Cross My Heart"), and the traditional closing number "Pony Boy," written in 1909 by Bobby Heath and Charley O'Donnell. *Human Touch* debuted at #2 in the U.S.

Meanwhile, *Lucky Town* was more upbeat, counting "Leap of Faith," "Living Proof," and "Local Hero" among its highlights. Dedicated to Scialfa and the couple's two children, Springsteen's tenth studio disc was more intimate and delicate than its companion. It peaked at #3 in the U.S.

Both were almost always reviewed together and met with mixed critical response. the *San Francisco Chronicle* wrote, "while making no new musical ground, he has created his most mature and subtle work to date." The *New York Daily News* offered praise like "The mere presence of these records is uplifting. He's given us a lot of good music at a time when we can use it."

Entertainment Weekly was less kind, calling the releases "his most confused records since his debut. It's as though his ability to craft a good record has gone the way of his working-class image." And *Rolling Stone* penned, "The aesthetic and thematic aims of *Human Touch* and *Lucky Town* would have been better realized by a single, more carefully shaped collection that eliminated their half dozen or so least essential songs."

"57" Riots

In June 1992, not long after the 1992 Los Angeles riots, "57 Channels (and Nothin' On)" was released as a single. In late April, the City of Angels erupted in violence after four L.A.P.D. officers were found not guilty in the beating of Rodney King, a black motorist. When former E Street guitarist Steve Van Zandt remixed the song for the dance floor, he injected a loop of the Courthouse chant, "No justice, no peace," turning it into a commentary on the riot that peaked at #68 on the U.S. Hot 100.

For his part, Springsteen was close to the riots, and the corner store near A&M Studios had been looted during the chaos. Burnt-out buildings were within walking distance. "It comes as no surprise that this has led to rioting," he said, acknowledging the long-standing neglect to *Beats*. "What is surprising is that [the riots] didn't occur."

30

Saw My Reflection in a Window

Springsteen's "Best Of" Compilations

Greatest Hits

The first assemblage of Bruce Springsteen singles, titled *Greatest Hits*, was released on February 27, 1995. Although it bypassed early sides and began with his breakout 1975 smash "Born to Run," the project gathered the Boss's best known singles and appended four new songs to lure in his core audience. It also included "Thunder Road," which was a classic rock radio staple but had never been issued as a proper 45.

The hits project included "Streets of Philadelphia," a single Springsteen recorded at his home studio in late 1993 for Jonathan Demme's film *Philadelphia*. Released as a single in February 1994, the non-LP number became a global smash, reaching #1 in Canada, #2 in the U.K., and #9 in the U.S. A memorable music video of the song, directed by Demme and his nephew Ted, was shot on the streets of the Pennsylvania city

The compilation was suggested to the Boss by manager Jon Landau as a means to keep the momentum that was initiated by the success of "Philadelphia" going. Springsteen—who had been working on a new studio record called *Waiting on the End of the World* that was eventually abandoned—was not averse to the idea.

"I wanted to introduce my music to younger fans, who for twelve bucks could get a pretty good overview of what I've done over the years," he told *Guitar World* that year. "For my older fans, I wanted to say, 'This still means something to me now, you still mean something to me now.'"

4 NEW SONGS WITH THE E STREET BAND INCLUDING:

"MURDER INCORPORATED"

"SECRET GARDEN"

This 1995 Columbia Records in-store display card featured the cover art for Springsteen's *Greatest Hits* on one side and this wording on the back, promoting the record's two new emphasis songs, "Murder Incorporated" and "Secret Garden." *Courtesy of 991.com*

As for the new material recorded directly for the release, Springsteen reunited the E Street Band—including Van Zandt—somewhat surprisingly in January '95. The ten-day studio session at the Hit Factory in New York found the entire band reunited in the studio for the first time since March '84 and having a great time together.

Parts of the group's regathering were caught on film for the 1996 home video documentary *Blood Brothers*. As evidenced by its footage, the collective's reconvening affirmed that any confusion or bad blood that may have existed in the years since Springsteen put the group on hiatus had been alleviated. The door was open again for future teamwork.

Essential Tracks

Aside from the indispensable classics ("Born to Run," "Thunder Road," "Badlands," "The River," "Hungry Heart," "Atlantic City," "Dancing in the Dark," "Born in the U.S.A.," "My Hometown," "Glory Days," "Brilliant Disguise," "Human Touch," "Better Days," and "Streets of Philadelphia"), *Greatest Hits* boasted one holdover from 1982 and three brand-new tracks.

"Murder Incorporated"

Recorded in 1983 during the sessions that ultimately yielded *Born in the U.S.A.*, this roaring rock number had a contagious riff and lyrics about the perils of being associated with the mob. It went on to become a staple of the E Street Band's 1999 reunion tour. Springsteen also routinely played it on his tours to support *The Ghost of Tom Joad*. It was released as a promotional 5" CD to radio in the spring of 1995 and as a commercial CD single in Austria only.

"Secret Garden"

This restrained, synth-driven love song was augmented by the sensual horn work of Clarence Clemons, or—as the Boss wrote in the liner notes of the record— "the Big Man sweeter than ever."

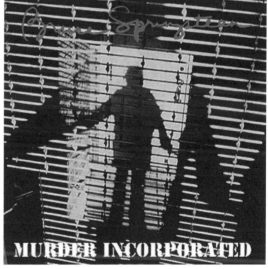

"Murder Incorporated," one of four new songs featured on 1995's *Greatest Hits* package, was issued as a promotional single in the UK The song was originally tracked in 1983 during sessions for *Born in the U.S.A.*

Courtesy of 991.com

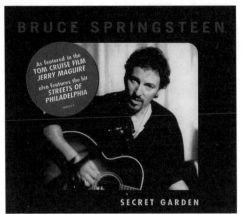

Released as a single in 1997, in tandem with its appearance in the hit movie *Jerry Maguire*, this UK CD EP pressing of "Secret Garden" also included "Streets of Philadelphia," Springsteen's other movie soundtrack smash from 1995.

Courtesy of 991.com

Upon its original release in April 1995, the single was a modest performer, peaking at #19. However, the song really picked up steam after director Cameron Crowe elected to use it in his acclaimed and vastly popular movie *Jerry Maguire*.

The "darkly erotic" tune, as Springsteen described it, became one of the most popular radio songs of 1997, thanks to a Springsteen-approved "Jerry Maguire Remix" that New York's Z100 had crafted, incorporating dialog from the movie.

"Blood Brothers"

In this ideal musical representation of the E Street Band's brief reunion, Springsteen sings of his loyalty to his legendary backing band, despite all of their time apart.

He promises, "I'll keep moving through the dark with you in my heart," and sums up his time together with Federici, Tallent, Weinberg, Van Zandt, Bittan, Lofgren, and Clemons in the liner notes by writing, "It was good to see the guys."

"This Hard Land"

"I guess this kinda sums it up with one of the ones that got away," Springsteen wrote in the *Greatest Hits* liner notes. A heartland rocker that was first attempted by the E Street Band in 1982 (this version appears on 1998's *Tracks*), the 1995 reworking is quite similar.

Outtakes and Leftovers

Notable among the songs that Springsteen recorded during the *Greatest Hits* era was "Nothing Man," a song that he first tracked in 1994 and would revisit in 2002 on *The Rising*.

Meanwhile, two others—"Without You" and "High Hopes"—found their way onto the *Blood Brothers* EP, which was issued in tandem with the VHS documentary of the same name on November 19, 1996. "High Hopes" was a cover of a song written by Tim McConnell and recorded by his band, the Havalinas, on their eponymous 1990 Elektra Records debut.

Unreleased numbers like "Back in Your Arms," and "Waiting on the End of the World"—which was first attempted with Springsteen's Other Band—were also recorded by the E Street Band in January '95. Other tunes from this era that were recorded in 1994 and are in circulation among fans include "Blind Spot," "Father's Day," and "Between Heaven and Earth."

Critical and Commercial Response

Critics are typically disapproving of "Greatest Hits" packages, and when Springsteen dropped his, he got a pretty good mauling. "We get a very uneven impression of The Boss's career," wrote *Q.* "The earliest albums are ignored; *Born in the U.S.A.*'s songs are emphasized; the recent *Lucky Town* should have sent a better delegate than 'Better Days.'"

Meanwhile, *Rolling Stone* argued, "*Greatest Hits* comes across as a collection of familiar songs, each stellar in its own right, that somehow adds up to something less than the sum of its parts. And *Entertainment Weekly* called the album's commercial intentions "disorienting, if not depressing," adding, "*Greatest Hits* leaves you wondering whether one of the most exuberant and thoughtful of American rockers believes in his own dreams anymore."

Some argued that the album was timed to draw attention to "Streets of Philadelphia," which was in contention for five Grammy Awards. They weren't wrong as Springsteen nabbed four trophies, including Song of the Year, Best Rock Song, Best Vocal Performance, Solo, and Best Song Written for a Motion Picture.

From a commercial standpoint, *Greatest Hits* had the cash registers ringing, shifting over four million copies in the U.S. and five million throughout Europe while topping the *Billboard 200*, plus the U.K., Canadian, and Australian album charts.

The Essential Bruce Springsteen

In the liner notes to Springsteen's second career overview, the Boss explained that the "new faces" at his shows during *The Rising* were the impetus for 2003's *Essential* package. A far more inclusive representation of his music than its predecessor, *Greatest Hits*, *The Essential Bruce Springsteen* included two full discs of previously

Bruce Springsteen: The Collection was a savvy repackaging of the Boss's first, second, and fourth albums in a slipcase box from 2004. Columbia, which had planned an expanded reissue of *Born to Run* for the following year, deviated from Springsteen's recorded chronology while highlighting his early output.
Author's Collection

A second volume of records packaged under the title *Bruce Springsteen: The Collection*—produced in 2005—is a little more perplexing than its predecessor. Here, *Nebraska*, *Lucky Town*, and *MTV Plugged* are curiously, if not illogically, bundled. *Author's Collection*

released music and a CD of unreleased bonus material.

The thirty-song package was an ideal introduction to the Boss, beginning with the highlights of his first two records—"Blinded by the Light," "For You," "Spirit in the Night," "4th of July, Asbury Park (Sandy)," and "Rosalita."

While it lacked "Backstreets" and "She's the One," "Racing in the Street" and "Candy's Room," "The Ties That Bind," and "Out in the Street," "Bobby Jean," and "No Surrender" and so on, it still offered newcomers to the Springsteen party a gateway to seek out the vital tunes that Executive Producer Jon Landau had disregarded.

"The idea was to present a little bit of what each album has to offer," Springsteen wrote in the notes. As a means of drawing in his dedicated followers, the bonus disc served up a dozen rarities that didn't make it onto the sprawling rarities box set *Tracks*.

Among the highlights were "Trapped"—a live Jimmy Cliff cover from the *U.S.A. for Africa* album—along with Springsteen's 1990 rendition of Elvis Presley's "Viva Las Vegas" and his own recording of "From Small Things (Big Things One Day Come)," which he had given to Dave Edmunds in the early 1980s.

"The two discs get the Springsteen story as right as is possible in 150 minutes," wrote *Pitchfork*, while *All Music* added, "It's an unexpected gift to have them officially released as a bonus disc to a hits collection, and for the hardcore it's worth buying two discs of songs you already have just to get these rarities."

Clearly some fans agreed, propelling the forty-two song, three-CD offering into the *Billboard* 200, where it peaked at #14 soon after its November 11 release.

31

The Highway Is Alive Tonight

The Ghost of Tom Joad

Solo Demos

During a break between legs on his *Human Touch/Lucky Town* tour in early 1993, Springsteen began recording a series of acoustic numbers at home in Beverly Hills. It is believed that these demos—which became the precursor to his 1995 album *The Ghost of Tom Joad*—were recorded on or around February 25, on a cassette recorder.

Many of the songs were tracked as works in progress. For instance, lines from "Angelina" and "I Dreamt My Love Was Lost" later comprised lyrics heard on the 1995 recording "Back in Your Arms," which surfaced on *Tracks*.

Springsteen would tweak another tune, "Dry Lightning," for *Joad*, but the bulk of the songs—with titles like "Blind Spot," "Don't Cross That Line," "House on Fire," and "Knife in the Back"—remained unreleased.

Joad

In March '95, after Springsteen had finished plugging the February 27, 1995, release of *Greatest Hits*—which included the temporary reunion of the E Street Band for promotional appearances—he began writing and recording a new album at his home studio, Thrill Hill West.

He wrote and recorded enough material for two albums during the seven months. One set of music was solo in the vein of *Nebraska*, and another was prepared as band material, for which he brought in E Streeters Danny Federici, Garry Tallent, and Scialfa, plus *Lucky Town* drummer Gary Mallaber, pedal steel player Marty Rivkin, and violinist and future E Street member Soozie Tyrell.

Seven of the solo tracks—including "Highway 29," "Balboa Park," and "Galveston Bay"—were picked and sequenced alongside one another at the front of the album, while the band material—which included "Across the Border" and "Straight Time"—was selected to close out the record.

From a presentation standpoint, most of the songs were driven by Springsteen's acoustic guitar. Lyrically, the tunes were observations on the ways of life in southwestern America and Mexico, with the Boss drawing heavily on John Steinbeck's *The Grapes of Wrath* and John Ford's ensuing film adaptation.

The movie had a substantial influence on the disc, as evidenced by the title. In interviews to promote the project in late 1995, he confessed that a speech by Henry Fonda in the role of Tom Joad actually made him cry.

"I think I'd read some John Steinbeck in high school, [but] there was something about the [*Grapes of Wrath*] film that sort of crystallized the story for me," the Boss told Bob Costas in a promotional interview released by Columbia. "And it always stayed with me after that, for some reason there was something in that picture that always resonated throughout almost all of my other work. It was just an image that popped out as I was sitting around on the couch messing around with the guitar."

Essential Tracks

The stories of the characters on *The Ghost of Tom Joad*, which were first heard by fans upon its release on November 21, 1995, explored the relationships between brothers and lovers who were forced to make unfortunate life choices. Springsteen's song subjects acted desperately and traveled aimlessly in the wake of political and social exclusion.

"Sinaloa Cowboys"

This number was partially inspired by a Mexican man that Springsteen encountered during a motorcycle trip into the Arizona desert with some friends. The stranger told him of his brother who died in an accident on his own motorbike, and the story stayed with him.

It was also influenced by the immigration issues that he often read about in the *Los Angeles Times* during the years he and Patti had predominantly lived in Beverly Hills. On several occasions over the years, Springsteen had traveled to the border crossings to gain his perspective on the issues he explores on "Sinaloa Cowboys."

"The Ghost of Tom Joad"

The title track to Springsteen's eleventh studio record mentions the character from Steinbeck's *The Grapes of Wrath* in both its storyline and name. But in addition to the aforementioned cues the song takes from Steinbeck and Ford, it also pays homage to Woody Guthrie's activist folk music approach, as the Boss sought to represent dusty America's unheard voices—those homeless and disenfranchised.

Featuring images of sleeping bags and tents sprawled out under bridges, transients roaming along railroad tracks and congregating around campfires as police choppers fly overhead, Springsteen's song brought the uncomfortable topic of homelessness to a wide audience.

"Youngstown"

A poignant look at the once-thriving Ohio locale where iron ruled for 170 years, "Youngstown" explores the steel industry's downfall in the area in the 1970s and the widespread struggles that ensued. Springsteen sings from the viewpoint of a Vietnam veteran and out-of-work steel mill worker who had provided for his family just as his father—a World War II veteran—had until his factory closed.

The narrative takes aim at the Youngstown Sheet and Tube Company, who were owners of Jenny (aka the Jeanette Blast Furnace). Through the song Springsteen criticizes the proprietors who made their riches off the backs of the character and his descendants, who worked at the steel plant for multiple generations until it closed in 1977.

Springsteen wrote the song after reading the 1985 Dale Maharidge book, *Journey to Nowhere: The Saga of the New Underclass*, which explored the dying steel towns of the Midwest. "Youngstown" was later praised in the *New York Times* as the best song on the album, with writer Nicholas Dawidoff saying it had "all the tension and complexity of great short fiction."

This French ad for *The Ghost of Tom Joad*—released in Europe on November 21, 1995—announced Springsteen's first album of stripped-down music since 1982's *Nebraska*.
Author's Collection

"The New Timer"

Also derived from Maharidge's book, this track looks at how working-class American men from the dying steel towns of the 1970s wound up giving up stability to become boxcar hobos. Mimicking those who lost everything during the Great Depression, these individuals—who had training for little else outside of ironwork—hopped freight trains when their worlds fell apart.

Leaving home with the hope of finding work, the Pennsylvania steelworker in the song meets up with an older man named Frank who has been riding the rails since the Depression. After they go their separate ways, "the New Timer" learns that Frank had been inexplicably murdered.

Although he dreams of someday being reunited with his family and prays for forgiveness from them for leaving, the rambling character—who at teams makes ends meet picking peaches—is shamed by his inability to provide for his family and never does reunite with them.

Critical and Commercial Reception

When the world's music bible, *Rolling Stone*, praised *The Ghost of Tom Joad* as "Springsteen's best album in ten years" and ranked it "among the bravest work that anyone has given us this decade," most critics followed suit with that assessment. The magazine heralded the Boss for "giving voice to people who are typically denied expression in our other arts and media."

But *Joad* wasn't exactly easy listening, and *Entertainment Weekly* was among its detractors. "On the surface, Springsteen's story-song approach is a smart, thoughtful move," the magazine wrote the week it was released. "But for all its nobility, *The Ghost of Tom Joad* still feels like a disappointing step back."

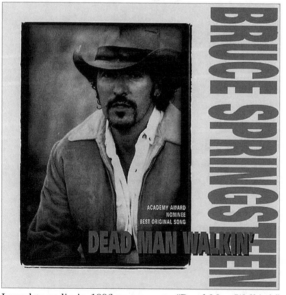

Issued to radio in 1996 to promote "Dead Man Walkin'," this single earned Springsteen an Academy Award nomination from the film of the same name.   *Courtesy of 991.com*

On first listen, *EW* pointed out that the record's unplugged approach was reminiscent of *Nebraska* but lacked "the sheer force" of "Atlantic City" and was without that effort's stray rockabilly licks. In a nutshell, the album sounded "downright depressed."

Record buyers seemed to agree, as *The Ghost of Tom Joad* failed to crack the Top 10, stalling at #11 on the Billboard 200. After eight consecutive Top 5 placements, Joad was the first studio album since *The Wild, the Innocent, and the E Street Shuffle* to fail to perform that feat.

In North America, there was no proper single, which made sense as it was arguably Springsteen's least commercial album yet. In certain European markets, however, "The Ghost of Tom Joad"—a bona-fide folk song—was issued as a single. In the U.K., however, it failed to go beyond #26.

Despite its commercial shortcomings, Springsteen was pleased with the record. So were the tastemakers in the music industry, who named it the Best Contemporary Folk Album at the 1997 Grammy Awards.

Outtakes and Extras

The most notable of the nonalbum cuts from this era, "Dead Man Walkin'" was penned in the spring of 1995 for the soundtrack of the Tim Robbins–directed movie of the same name. In some markets it was issued as a single in early 1996 and was nominated for an Academy Award, but unlike the 1994 Springsteen song "Streets of Philadelphia" (from the Tom Hanks film *Philadelphia*), it failed to grab the Oscar for Best Original Song. Springsteen was backed by Federici, Mallaber, and bassist Jim Hanson on this song, which can also be heard on the bonus disc of *The Essential Bruce Springsteen*.

Other songs from this era include "Brothers Under the Bridge," a tune that found its way onto *Tracks*. Recorded in May '95, it is unusual in that it shares a title with a completely different *Tracks* number that was recorded in 1983.

Other songs considered at the time included "Tiger Rose"—which the Boss eventually gave to rockabilly pioneer Sonny Burgess—plus "Little Things" and the curiously titled "I'm Turning into Elvis."

On a related note, Springsteen also worked with his friend Joe Grushecky in July 1995, helping cowrite "Idiots Delight," "I'm Not Sleeping," "1945," and "Cheap Motel" for the latter's December 1997 studio album *Coming Home*.

32

You Ain't Lived till You've Had Your Tires Rotated

Springsteen's '90s Tours

Lucky Town/Human Touch Tours

With his companion albums finished and submitted to Columbia, Bruce Springsteen began holding discreet auditions for his new touring band at Roy Bittan's Hollywood recording studio in March 1992. After selecting guitarist Shane Fontayne, drummer Zach Alford, and bassist Tommy Simms by mid-April, his group began rehearsals at Bittan's facility, before moving into Hollywood Center Studios Soundstage, also in Hollywood.

On May 6, the band played live for ninety minutes in front of an audience of Sony executives as a warm-up to Springsteen's first-ever *Saturday Night Live* appearance, playing "57 Channels (and Nothin' On)" and "Living Proof" three days later.

After several more rehearsals back in Hollywood that included the introduction of vocalist Bobby King, singer and multi-instrumentalist Crystal Taliefero, plus singers Gia Ciambotti, Carol Dennis, Cleopatra Kennedy, and Angel Rogers, Springsteen and his ten-piece band performed a rehearsal concert that was simulcast across North America on FM rock outlets and contained cameos by Patti Scialfa and Steve Van Zandt.

When asked why the E Street Band was put on ice, Springsteen told *Beats*, "It was time for a change; time to move on." And with the fusion of his new project and musical direction, where white rock band met black gospel choir, he was making the spiritual alterations he felt he needed to make. It was his first-ever major tour without the E Street Band.

"For the '70s and '80s, no artist could have been better served by a band than Bruce was by the E Street Band," Jon Landau told *Billboard* in June 1992. "That's just a fact. Fantastic people. Fantastic musicians. Bruce and the E Street Band could have toured forever. But at some point, he just needed to sort of shake things up, just to give himself some new challenges and new inspiration.

"After the Amnesty International tour ended, it was pretty clear he didn't want them waiting on him," Landau continued. "This was a time for everyone to make their individual moves."

Springsteen believed he owed it to himself to experiment with new musicians, and once he had the right players in place, he made a lengthy commitment. A year-long world tour kicked off on June 15 in Stockholm, and he and the band canvassed Europe, playing a monthlong run of arena shows. Unfortunately, the roadwork did little to sustain the sales numbers that he

A souvenir of Springsteen's July 1992 performance at Wembley Arena. Springsteen launched his 1992–93 tour in Stockholm, Sweden, on June 15 and wrapped it nearly a year later in Oslo, Norway.

Courtesy of Brucebase

and Landau had hoped for, but Springsteen had a good sense of humor about it, acknowledging it to the crowd of Swedes by saying, "Soon we'll overtake both Kris Kross and Def Leppard!"

At least ticket sales were still strong. When he returned to North America in late July, he launched five more months of touring with an eleven-night stand at the Meadowlands Arena.

Springsteen played to his home strongly by pulling out surprises like "Jersey Girl" and "Trapped"—both for the first time since '85—on different nights of the engagement. Other crowd-pleasers like "Darlington County," "Downbound Train," "Growin' Up," "Racing in the Street," and "Spirit in the Night" were rotated. At the July 26 gig, he brought out his mom, Adele Springsteen, for the first time in years to dance with him onstage to "Working on the Highway."

Two months later, during a series of shows at the Los Angeles Sports Arena on September 28, Danny Federici sat in with the Boss's other band for E Street classics like "Bobby Jean," "Thunder Road," "Born to Run," and "Working on the Highway."

While on the West Coast, Springsteen was forced to cancel a pair of shows at the Shoreline Amphitheater in Mountain View, California, due to illness, which he would make up two weeks later. Another gig, slated for the Rupp Arena in Lexington, Kentucky, was also postponed just six hours before show time on November 21 and rescheduled for December 17.

During his election-day gig at in Milwaukee, Springsteen dedicated "Glory Days" to President-Elect Clinton. Six days later, at Nassau Coliseum on November 9, Steve Van Zandt made a cameo with Bruce on that same number, while Long Island's own hero, Billy Joel, played piano on "Glory Days" the next night.

With December's arrival, the Boss began to play "Santa Claus Is Coming to Town" as an encore for audiences in Dallas, St. Louis, Indianapolis, Philadelphia, Boston, Pittsburgh and Lexington. At the Boston Garden gig on December 14, former J. Geils Band frontman Peter Wolf joined in on an encore of Wilson

Pickett's "In the Midnight Hour," while in Pittsburgh, local hero and Springsteen pal Joe Grushecky played on "Glory Days" and "Santa."

When Nashville transplant Garry Tallent travelled some 217 miles to the tour leg closing Lexington show on December 17 to slap the bass on "Glory Days" and "Bobby Jean," it was another instance of E Street players desperately missing their roles with Springsteen. But there was more reuniting of old Upstage pals to be done before the '92 was put to bed. Two days after Christmas, he rode down to the Stone Pony in Asbury Park to play with Southside Johnny and the Jukes on "The Fever," "It's Been a Long Time" and "Havin' a Party."

After a ninety-day break, Springsteen went back on the road in Europe for an extensive three-month tour of Europe that started on March 31. Kicking off at the SECC Arena in Glasgow, the Boss and his "Other Band" canvassed Scotland, Germany, Switzerland, Italy, France, the Netherlands, Belgium, Portugal, Spain, Denmark, Sweden, Ireland, England, and Norway.

There were a number of surprise moments during the spring 1993 trek, including the cameos of Garden State rock giants Jon Bon Jovi and Richie Sambora on "Glory Days" in Dortmund, reggae favorite Jimmy Cliff singing with Springsteen on "Time Will Tell" in Verona, and Jerry Lee Lewis taking the stage with him at Royal Dublin Society Stadium in Ireland to sing "Great Balls of Fire" and "Whole Lotta Shakin'."

As for covers, Cliff's "Many Rivers to Cross," CCR's "Who'll Stop the Rain," Elvis Presley's "Viva Las Vegas," and Curtis Mayfield's "It's All Right" were played during the tour, as was the Louvin Brothers' timeless country gospel number "Satan's Jeweled Crown." Bruce also performed "Across the Borderline" during gigs in Spain, singing part of the Little Village tune—which was penned by Ry Cooder, John Hiatt, and Jim Dickinson—in Spanish.

Impromptu performances in May found Bruce, Fontayne, Simms, and King taking over a dancing school ball at their Munich hotel to play "Lucille" and "Twist and Shout." At the end of the tour, while hanging in London's South Kensington neighborhood at the Stonehope Arms pub, Springsteen also sang "Jumpin' Jack Flash" into a karaoke machine.

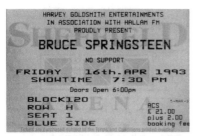

A ticket stub from Springsteen's April 16, 1993, show at the Sheffield Arena. These shows in support of *Lucky Town* and *Better Days* were performed with the "Other Band." *Courtesy of Brucebase*

At the final show, at Valle Hovin Stadion in Oslo, Bruce brought out Jon Landau to play guitar on a pair of numbers, before inviting guitar tech Rick Lapointe to sing Steppenwolf's "Born to Be Wild." Landau and the tour's head of security, Warren Kaye, also assist on the final encore, of "Twist and Shout" and "Let the Good Times Roll."

Blood Brothers

In what was not exactly a tour but live work worth mentioning, Springsteen brought the E

Street Band back into action on February 21, 1995, to perform a live club gig at Tramps in New York in support of *Greatest Hits*. The show marked the live debut of "Murder Incorporated" and included fan favorites like "Bobby Jean," "Spirit in the Night," "Two Hearts," and "Thunder Road." The intimate, invitation-only gig concluded with a rendition of the Righteous Brothers' "Little Latin Lupe Lu."

Six weeks later, the E Street Band performed again before a camera crew and a small audience of Springsteen insiders and Columbia Records staffers at Sony Studios in New York.

This ticket stub is from Springsteen's July 23, 1992, show at Meadowlands Arena. It was one of eleven sold-out shows he played at the 21,000-seat venue that summer.   *Author's Collection*

The show—which opened with his new single, "Secret Garden," and included the other three new songs on *Greatest Hits*—soon gave way to a comedy routine the Boss called "I'm Turning into Elvis." But the classics, from "Prove It All Night" and "Badlands" to "Cadillac Ranch" and "She's the One," were rapturously received.

The same day, the E Street Band appeared at The Ed Sullivan Theater in New York where they performed "Murder Incorporated" live on CBS Television's *The Late Show with David Letterman*.

Groovin' with Grushecky

Springsteen had been working with Joe Grushecky, originally the frontman for iconic Pittsburgh band the Iron City Houserockers, producing his 1995 album *American Babylon*, when he first offered to hit the road with his friend that year. After jamming live on a number of occasions that led up to a July 22 gig at the Tradewinds in Sea Bright—a night that saw Springsteen, Steve Van Zandt, and Max Weinberg playing with the Houserockers—a short East Coast tour was hatched for that October.

A four-hour private rehearsal of the Grushecky/Springsteen "October Assault" took place at the Stone Pony the night before the tour opener on October 17. Although rumors had leaked to fans that Springsteen was in tow, the shows—which also took place at Tramps in New York, the Electric Factory in Philly, Nick's Fat City in Pittsburgh, and Park West in Chicago—were formally billed to Joe Grushecky and the Houserockers.

Springsteen did take over vocal chores on some of his own songs, including "Murder Incorporated" and "Light of Day," but it became clear during the gigs that he was happiest when he was the Boss. During the second of two Pittsburgh shows on October 21, he was having difficulties with his guitar straps and jokingly let the audience know about it, as *Backstreets* would report.

"You know, I'm in the band for only a week," the Boss griped. "And they break my guitars. A beer freezes on my amps. And my fingers are bleeding."

When Grushecky cracked, "Yeah, and it's the hardest work he's done in five years," the Boss responded, "I'll let you get away with that in Pittsburgh."

In the years that followed, Springsteen and Grushecky remained tight, and when the Houserockers came to town—such as their gig at Cheers in Long Branch in December '97—the Boss joined Grushecky onstage. During a subsequent show in Pittsburgh in March 1998, Springsteen dropped in on Nick's Fat City to play a mix of covers, Grushecky originals, and his own compositions, including "Ramrod."

Taking *Joad* on the Road

On November 21, 1995, the day that *The Ghost of Tom Joad* was released, Springsteen played a solo acoustic warm-up gig at the State Theater in New Brunswick, New Jersey. Playing a ninety-minute set, the wood-and-wire approach to the Boss's music worked well in a concert hall. In addition to the title track, "Sinaloa Cowboys," and "Youngstown," the more serious-minded songs in his canon like "Adam Raised a Cain," "Darkness on the Edge of Town," and "Born in the U.S.A." were a superb fit.

The next night, at the official tour launch at the Count Basie Theater in Red Bank, Springsteen trotted out a reworked version of "Streets of Philadelphia" and a rarely unearthed "Point Blank." From there, he traveled with his guitar for a pair of concerts at the Wiltern Theater in Los Angeles, and performed "The Ghost of Tom Joad" on *The Tonight Show with Jay Leno.*

With just a few guitar cases, and a minuscule crew, the Boss had a lot more freedom. He could fly from a two-show engagement in Berkeley to a gig in Rosemont, Illinois, to a gig at the Constitution Hall in Washington, D.C., and meet these obligations with little struggle. There were no equipment trucks, let alone a tour bus, on the late '95 Theater run.

A pair of December shows at the Tower Theater in Philadelphia produced material for the following year's promotional cassette, *Bruce Springsteen: Columbia Records Radio Hour,* while a performance of "Youngstown" on *The Late Show with David Letterman* was sandwiched in between a pair of shows at the Beacon Theater in New York.

A third Beacon show, after a pair of Boston Orpheum dates, marked the rare performance of "The Wish," a song Springsteen wrote about when his mother bought him his first "real" guitar. The December 17 gig was only the third time he had ever played the tune.

He took a three-week break for the Christmas and New Year's holidays before getting back to work in Montreal on January 7. By the time he made it to Detroit, "No Surrender" was added to his set. But the big news came in Youngstown, as local and national media played up the fact that Springsteen had penned a tune about the town where the 2,600-seat Stambaugh Theatre was located.

A performance of Springsteen singing "Youngstown" on the *CBS Evening News* was matched by coverage in the *Los Angeles Times.* He was given the key to the city, as he told the crowd, "This is about the men and women who lived in this town and who built this country. It's about those who gave their sons and daughters to the wars that were fought . . . and who were later declared expendable."

When asked about the smaller venues such as the Stambaugh, Springsteen told Robert Hilburn that the quietness of the halls he had been playing was essential to mood. "The show has a lot of elements. The spoken passages are as important as the songs in a way," he explained. "It's theater and it's music. Ideally, I appear in between songs, but when the music starts, I disap-pear and the characters in the songs fill the stage with their lives and their experience."

This program was sold to attendees of Springsteen's 1995-96 *World Acoustic* tour. The Boss opened the tour close to his Jersey Shore home, playing at the Count Basie Theatre in Red Bank on November 22, 1995.   *Courtesy of 991.com*

After finishing up his January 1996 tour in Atlanta, Springsteen took his "Solo Acoustic" campaign to Europe, where he spent six weeks playing the *Joad* songs with stripped-down takes of "Bobby Jean" and "Brothers Under the Bridge." After a three-week break that afforded him the opportunity to play his Oscar-nominated song "Dead Man Walkin'" on the 68th Academy Awards, he resumed playing overseas.

A fall tour of North America again found Springsteen exploring his folksinger identity with a final leg of solo shows. The tour was launched on September 16 at the Benedum Center in Pittsburgh, and the Boss tried out a new title called "There Will Never Be Any Other for Me but You" in Providence and wrote a tune called "In Michigan," which he sang for his audience at the Miller Auditorium in Kalamazoo.

Springsteen performed a benefit show for the John Steinbeck Research Center at San Jose State University on October 26. In Tempe, Arizona, five days earlier, Nils Lofgren joined him on "No Surrender," while Danny Federici played on a pair of numbers in Santa Barbara four days later. Back east, Bruce debuted "The Hitter"—a song he would record for 2005's *Devils and Dust*—at the Landmark Theatre in Syracuse on November 13.

By Thanksgiving week, he was back on the Jersey Shore for a three-night stand at the Paramount Theatre in Asbury Park, where he played much longer sets joined by Scialfa, vocalist/instrumentalist Soozie Tyrell and Federici for all three gigs. Original E Street Band member Vini Lopez joined Bruce onstage on the second and third shows, while Upstage scene veteran Big Danny Gallagher and Steve Van Zandt joined him on the last Paramount gig. Some of the live surprises included "Wild Billy's Circus Story," "Rosalita," "Independence Day," "For You," and "It's Hard to Be a Saint in the City."

Springsteen closed out '96 road duties on December 14 in Charlotte. The gig was his 102nd show in thirteen months. And he wasn't done. On January 27, he embarked on a monthlong run through Japan and Australia.

Bruce returned to the U.S in time to attend the Grammy Awards on February 26. He performed "The Ghost of Tom Joad" on the CBS broadcast from Madison Square Garden and won the Best Contemporary Folk Album honors. Ten days later, while still on a break from touring, he joined the Wallflowers onstage at the Tradewinds in Sea Bright, rocking out with Jakob Dylan's group on "My Girl," "Brand New Cadillac," and "Not Fade Away."

A final leg of the "Solo Acoustic" tour launched in Vienna on May 6 and saw Springsteen head into new countries like Poland and the Czech Republic. The last night, at the Palais des Congres in Paris, he was joined by an old friend, singer/songwriter Elliott Murphy. Together they played Murphy's own "Diamonds by the Yard" and another number, "Blowing Down the Road (Old Dusty Road)."

33

Somebody Shake
My Brains

Tracks

In time for the 1998 holiday season, Springsteen fans were treated to a massive, sixty-six-song box set of rarities that spanned his entire career with Columbia Records. The project asserted the Boss's value as a consistently great and remarkably prolific songwriter.

Beginning with the demos he made with John Hammond in 1972 and closing with an unreleased song called "Back in Your Arms," which was tracked with the E Street Band in 1995, the project was inspired by Bob Dylan's career-spanning 1985 release *Biograph*. With the advent of *Tracks*, Springsteen would be able to expand his listeners' understanding of the music from his first twenty-five years in the recording studio.

When work stalled on an acoustic record in the fall of '97 and an electric record in early '98, Springsteen realized he might have a long gap between releases and threw his attention behind the box set idea.

Working with his recording engineer Toby Scott at his home studio, Springsteen sifted through two hundred to three hundred recordings that had been in storage at Iron Mountain and pared them down to what resulted in *Tracks*. It was eventually released on November 9, 1998.

Springsteen's only real rule for the project was that the music it housed had to be related to a record that he had already released. This ruled out any songs that would have made up any new material or any unreleased "lost" albums, such as the tunes that comprised his 2010 release of 1978's *The Promise*. Fans of *The River* and *Born in the U.S.A.* eras wound up getting an entire album's worth each of extra material.

It's important to note the absence of outtakes from *Greetings from Asbury Park, N.J.* This was an intentional move because session material from Springsteen's first record had been tied up in court proceedings that were ultimately resolved in 2001. Should a second volume of rarities surface in the future, it is likely that material from this period will be included.

A promotional poster for his sprawling 1998 rarities box set, *Tracks*, featured some of the earliest photographs taken of Springsteen as a Columbia artist. At the time, the collection's sixty-six songs spanned his career to date, beginning in 1972.
Courtesy of 991.com

The Best of the Box

If Springsteen's outtakes ranged from good to brilliant, one thing is sure. Upon hearing the tunes on *Tracks*, professional songwriters had to be in awe. From 1973's loose-feeling but flawlessly structured "Thundercrack" to '79's hook-laden rocker "Where the Bands Are" or '82's urgent "My Love Will Not Let You Down" and '87's poignant and deeply personal "The Wish," Springsteen's leftovers were unbelievably great.

The Columbia Audition

Springsteen's infamous recordings of "Mary Queen of Arkansas," "It's Hard to Be a Saint in the City," "Growin' Up," and "Does This Bus Stop at 82nd Street" were tracked at CBS Studios on May 3. 1972. These unrefined but thrilling demos overseen by Hammond are the first key recordings in Bruce's career.

"He just hits the button and gives you your serial number, and off you go," the Boss remembered in an interview with *Mojo*. "I was excited. I felt I'd written some good songs and this was my shot. I had nothing to lose and it was like the beginning of something."

Second Album Outtakes

Along with the aforementioned "Thundercrack"—which Springsteen wrote as a showstopper with three or four different pauses until "Rosalita" took its place—three other leftovers from *The Wild, the Innocent, and the E Street Shuffle* were essential. "Santa Ana" and "Seaside Bar Song" were early concert favorites that he eventually dropped because of the Dylan comparisons they elicited. Meanwhile "Zero and Blind Terry"—which originally began as "Phantoms" and "Over the Hills of St. Croix"—was also signature number in the Bruce Springsteen Band's live set.

Sifting through the songs, Springsteen realized that "Thundercrack" wasn't complete. So he called up Vini Lopez and asked if he'd be willing to come over and sing his part. "I said, 'I'd be glad to,'" Mad Dog told *Backstreets* in 1998. "So I went to his studio by his house and did the vocals. It took 40 minutes."

"He wanted the original guys to sing on it, so me and Federici went in," Lopez explained. "I knew all my parts like there wasn't any time in between, like we were just there again, like a time warp."

Born to Run and *Darkness* Leftovers

Outtakes from the *Born to Run* sessions are scarce on *Tracks*, but "So Young and In Love"—a powerful song believed to have been tracked in Blauvelt in October 1974 promptly after Weinberg and Bittan joined the E Street Band—and "Linda Let Me Be the One" represent it adequately. The latter was one from sessions at the Record Plant that Springsteen liked so much that he eventually decided he wanted to put it on his 1975 studio album. Unfortunately, he couldn't locate the master recording and wound up leaving it off.

Darkness-era leftovers are a little more abundant on Tracks. "Rendezvous" was a song recorded in 1977 but left to the side even though it had been a favorite of his live shows. Unable to find a suitable studio take, he added a live version from 1980 that characterizes the tune—which was recorded by Greg Kihn, the Knack, and Gary U.S. Bonds—well.

The melancholy "Iceman," the upbeat, horn-fueled "Give the Girl a Kiss," the original version of "Hearts of Stone"—soon given to Southside Johnny—and "Don't Look Back" also chronicle the era. As for the latter, which was dropped from *Darkness* at the last minute, it ranks as one of the best of the *Tracks* goodies.

The River Overflows

When he sacked his 1979 album *The Ties That Bind*, Springsteen put some super-rock singles on ice. Most notable was "Roulette," a blistering number about the nuclear paranoia he and many Americans felt after the Three Mile Island meltdown, but the edgy "Dollhouse," the power-pop concoctions "Living on the Edge of the World" and the superb "Where the Bands Are" rival some of the finest numbers on *The River*.

Explaining his love of power pop, which was also alive on "I Wanna Be with You," Springsteen spoke to *Mojo* of his love of the Raspberries' *Greatest Hits*. "They were great little pop records," he said. "I loved the production, and when I went into the studio, a lot of things we did were like that. Two, three, four-minute pop songs coming one right after another."

Born in the U.S.A. Extras

The original, acoustic blues incarnation of "Born in the U.S.A."—which Springsteen first tracked during his *Nebraska* recording session—was radically different from the studio version that the world came to know. In some ways it was more effective in getting its message of bittersweet patriotism across.

Elsewhere, "Wages of Sin"—recorded on May 10, 1982, at the Power Station—was what Springsteen would call "a real find" in 1998, while the rollicking numbers "Cynthia" and "TV Movie," the seven-minute "Frankie" (which had been kicking around in one form or another since 1976), and the original 1982 recording of "This Hard Land" were all winners.

"Car Wash," "Rockaway the Days," "Man at the Top," and "Brothers Under the Bridges" ('83) rounded out the unreleased material from Springsteen's most famous recording era.

Best of the Rest

Among the handful of *Tunnel of Love* outtakes heard on *Tracks*, the love song "When You Need Me" and "The Wish," which Springsteen wrote about his mother, are standouts. Telling Robert Hilburn about the latter in 1998, he said, "It's probably as autobiographical as I've ever gotten. That may be why it didn't get on the record.

"It was a combination of having recently gotten married and thinking about my mom," he continued. "I wrote a lot about my dad at particular times but she was also very central in my life."

Much of the fourth disc was comprised of songs written between 1989 and 1991 that were considered for *Human Touch*. Of the dozen tunes, "Seven Angels" balanced delicate verses with a charged refrain, "Sad Eyes" found Springsteen drawing on the pretty soul of Dionne Warwick, while "Happy" was a reflection of his life circa 1992.

"I've struggled with a lot of things over the past two, three years, and it's been real rewarding. I've been very, very happy, truly the happiest I've ever been in my whole life," Springsteen told *Rolling Stone* that year.

Reception

Although *Tracks* only reached #27 on Billboard's U.S. album survey, it reaped mounds of praise when it was released. The *Wall Street Journal* wrote, "*Tracks* adds to Mr. Springsteen's legacy as the best of America's post-Dylan singer-songwriters. Much more than a collection of miscellaneous and unconnected recordings, it shows an artist who's looked inward to find a superior means of expression."

The *Boston Globe* echoed that sentiment, writing, "what's apparent is that Springsteen left more good songs off his studio albums than most composers write in their entire recording careers."

18 Tracks

Although *Tracks* was applauded by music writers, sales of the project failed to match his first box set, 1986's *Live/1975–85*. After word leaked that a Reunion tour with the E Street Band was in place for 1999, a single disc compiled by Bruce that picked his favorites from *Tracks*, was slated for store shelves on April 12, 1999.

Titled *18 Tracks*, it included three additional but previously unreleased recordings. Yet the inclusions of "The Fever," "Trouble River," and "The Promise" failed to entice CD buyers. But it hardly hurt ticket sales. Springsteen's Reunion tour was arguably the hottest tour of '99.

34

Rockaway the Nights

Roll Call at the Rock Hall

W hen Bruce Springsteen was inducted into the Rock and Roll Hall of Fame at the Waldorf-Astoria in New York in March 1999, he paid tribute to his legendary backing group, the E Street Band. Although he was honored as a solo artist, Springsteen took the time to proudly acknowledge his notorious bandmates.

Nils Lofgren was dubbed the most overqualified second guitarist in show business. Springsteen also suggested to attendees that Lofgren—who joined the band in 1984—played ten times better than he did.

Danny Federici was touted for his natural, instinctive ability. Springsteen pledged his genuine love for Federici while saluting the organist and accordion player for bringing the vibrant feel of the Jersey Shore's boardwalks to his music through the years.

Bassist Garry Tallent was heralded as a lovely friend whose "quiet dignity" graced Springsteen's band and life, while pianist Roy Bittan was praised by the Boss for his "emotional generosity" and for giving a distinct sound to many of his finest records.

As for Mighty Max, who kept busy in the band's down years as the band leader on the Conan O'Brien show, Springsteen applauded his drummer's unique style and thanked him for delivering with power and finesse night after night.

Springsteen proclaimed his adoration of guitarist Steve Van Zandt and reminisced about their endless rock-'n'-roll alliance, describing him as a "great songwriter, producer, great guitarist." Turning to his wife Patti Scialfa, he cited her for busting up the E Street boy's club when she was asked to join, pledging his love by thanking her for "hitting all the high notes" and adding, "you're tougher than the rest."

Last but not least, he praised the Big Man, thanking saxophonist Clarence Clemons as "a source of myth and light and enormous strength for me on stage," who would always lift him up. Springsteen pledged his love for "C" and for filling his heart during virtually every E Street performance.

When U2's Bono inducted Springsteen, he cited him as "More than The Boss, he's the owner. He owns America's heart." In addition to the E Street Band, Springsteen brought his mother, Adele, up onto the dais before they played classics like "Tenth Avenue Freeze-Out" and "The Promised Land." Later,

Springsteen participated in an all-star jam session with Bono, Paul McCartney, and Billy Joel to close out the night.

It wasn't his first appearance at the annual event, which is typically held early in the year at New York's Waldorf-Astoria Hotel. In 1987, he inducted Roy Orbison. In 1988, he ushered in Bob Dylan. The Boss also welcomed his friends Jackson Browne and U2 in 2004 and 2005 respectively.

In addition to playing at the Rock Hall ceremonies, the E Street Band backed Jerry Lee Lewis at the Concert for the Rock and Roll Hall of Fame in 1995. But his support for the Rock Hall has long been evident. In a 2009 exhibit called "From Asbury Park to The Promised Land," Springsteen lent artifacts like his legendary 1957 Chevy Bel Air convertible, his 1960 black Corvette convertible, several of his guitars—including his Fender Esquire from the *Born to Run* cover—plus rare handbills, posters, and awards.

Performances of note include his participation in the 1988 induction ceremony, which found him in the company of Dylan, the Beatles, the Beach Boys, and the Rolling Stones. In 1994, Springsteen surprised many—including himself –by appearing with Guns N' Roses' Axl Rose in an unrehearsed duet of the Beatles' "Come Together" after an earthquake in Los Angeles kept Rod Stewart and Elton John from performing it in New York.

Still, his most important performance at the Rock Hall events has to be his 1989 delivery of Roy Orbison's "Crying." After inducting him two years prior, Springsteen returned to sing the song in Roy's memory. Orbison had died just weeks earlier.

35

I Close My Eyes and Feel So Many Friends Around Me

The Reunion Tour

"I don't know if it pays to project too much into the future," Springsteen told Robert Hilburn in early 1996 when asked about a full-on E Street Band reunion. "I assume at some point we will play together in some fashion again. We enjoyed getting together for the *Greatest Hits* thing. But we don't have any plans."

Two and a half years later, while plugging *Tracks*, he was a little less cryptic with the *Los Angeles Times* scribe, saying, "I've kept a pretty open mind about the whole thing," before suggesting that he wasn't yet in a position to comment on his future plans.

Springsteen's publicists at Shore Fire Media did that for him a few weeks later when they made it official. Bruce Springsteen and the E Street Band were embarking on a reunion tour—with guitarist Steve Van Zandt back in the fold. Although the December 8, 1998 press release promised details early in the New Year, all that mattered at the time was that the band was touring for the first time in eleven years.

The announcement was ideally timed considering the Boss was set to be inducted into the Rock and Roll Hall of Fame on March 16, 1999. And although Springsteen was being inducted alone, he had the members of the legendary E Street Band up onstage with him. "I wouldn't be standing up here tonight without you," he said, "and I can't stand up here now without you."

Later that night, the reunited E Street Band performed, but by that time the tour preparations were already well underway. Several weeks earlier, on February 26, Springsteen dropped in on *Late Night with Conan O'Brien*, performing "Working on the Highway" with the Max Weinberg 7. The appearance signified Weinberg's hiatus from the show to rejoin Bruce.

Contrary to previous Springsteen campaigns, the Reunion tour would start in Europe, but before the April 9 Barcelona launch, a run of private practices and a pair of public rehearsals took place in March at the Convention Hall in Asbury Park. During the audience-attended shows, from which Springsteen donated ticket proceeds to support local community centers, the band mixed favorites like "Prove It All Night," "Born to Run" and "Thunder Road" with an electric take on "Youngstown," the *Tracks* rarity "My Love Will Not Let You Down," and a new, unreleased song, "Land of Hope and Dreams."

If the idea of the Reunion tour conjured up notions of a nostalgic payday, Springsteen was aware of the risks to his reputation. Yet because he had complete confidence in the band, he also anticipated great rewards.

At the first rehearsal in early March, as they tested out songs from the box set and the new song ideas he was working on, his belief in his musicians was affirmed and then some.

Cover art for the 1999 Reunion tour program book, which was sold during the E Street Band's record-setting fifteen-date run of shows at the Continental Airlines Arena in East Rutherford.
Courtesy of 991.com

"The thrilling thing was seeing how good the band was playing," he told Hilburn in April 2000. Springsteen testified that the E Street Band was playing at its absolute best.

Europe 99

When the tour began with a pair of shows at Palau Sant Jordi in Barcelona, Springsteen made it evident to fans that the Reunion tour would be long on surprises like an E Street Band version of "Lucky Town," an unexpected performance of "Spirit in the Night" and the first rendition of "Rendezvous" since New Year's Eve 1980. In Milan, *Tracks* favorites "Where the Bands Are" and "Jungleland" were highlights.

Cameos were few on the tour, as the focus was on celebrating the band, but the show in Lyon, France, on April 28 featured the surprise vocals of guest Jon Bon Jovi on "Hungry Heart." Three weeks later, Edwin Starr joined Springsteen in Birmingham, England, for a take on "War." A trio of May shows at Earl's Court in London were bookended by a pair of real stunners: an unexpected Scialfa-Springsteen duet of "Factory" on the first night and a very rare "Meeting Across the River" on the third. The latter hadn't been played since January 1, 1979.

The E Street Band continued to mine the Boss's songbook, playing "Racing in the Street" and "Trapped" in Paris and Arnhem, the Netherlands, respectively for the first time since 1985. On the second-to-last night of the thirty-five date European leg, he dusted off "Because the Night."

A Continental Homecoming

After a two-and-a-half-week break, Springsteen and the E Street Band kicked off its 1999 U.S. touring commitment with fifteen shows at the Continental Airlines Arena in East Rutherford, New Jersey. When the gigs had gone on sale two months earlier, fans helped Bruce set a record by snatching up all three hundred thousand tickets in just thirteen hours. Springsteen—who first christened the arena in 1981 and previously played an eleven-night stand there in 1992—would hold a four-week residency at the arena, between July 15 and August 12.

"Look out, Ricky Martin, now," Springsteen told the crowd on the first night, adding "I'm filled with the spirit, baby . . . the ghost of Tom Jones," in the midst of "Tenth Avenue Freeze-Out." Springsteen also played "In Freehold" during the homecoming gig, adding a line about his recently deceased dad, envisioning "his ghost flipping the bird to everyone in Freehold." The first two songs of the gig, "My Love Will Not Let You Down" and "The Promised Land" were broadcast live, nationally on VH1.

During the run of shows, he treated his audiences to welcome performances of "Candy's Room, "The Ties That Bind," "Something in the Night," "Point Blank," and "Racing in the Street," while celebrities like Tom Hanks, Robert De Niro, Heather Graham, and Edward Norton each turned out for at least one gig.

On the last night, Springsteen introduced "Frankie," a song that first emerged in 1976, to the crowd, saying, "This is for the aficionados." Springsteen also finally played "Jersey Girl" and "Rosalita," two songs that he had held out on playing until the fifteenth night. Fans held up signs that read "Rosie," petitioning for the latter, which the Boss introduced with a chuckle by teasing, "How could I say thanks? I know there's a way."

Before he played "Rosalita" as the fifth encore, Bruce was joined by Jon Bon Jovi, his guitarist Richie Sambora and Melissa Etheridge all helping out on "Hungry Heart."

As August wound down, the E Street Band played a five-night stand at Boston's Fleet Center, where he unveiled "For You" and "New York City Serenade." The last of a three-night run at the MCI Center in Washington found Bonnie Raitt, Bruce Hornsby, Mary Chapin Carpenter, Jackson Browne, and Springsteen's cousin Frank Bruno Jr. helping out on "Hungry Heart."

A six-night Philadelphia stand included five shows at the First Union Center and one gig—held on Springsteen's fiftieth birthday—at the Spectrum. The show was very special to fans in the arena as Bruce played "Growin' Up," "Does This Bus Stop at 52nd Street," and "The Fever." It also marked the first performance of "Blinded by the Light" since April 1976. The 1999 Reunion tour dates wrapped at the Target Center in Minneapolis on November 29.

Last Leg

A three-month break from the road ended on February 28, 2000, when the Reunion tour reignited at the Bryce Jordan Center at Pennsylvania State University. Springsteen launched the show with "Lion's Den"—a *Tracks* rarity from 1982 that he played in honor of the Penn State Nittany Lions.

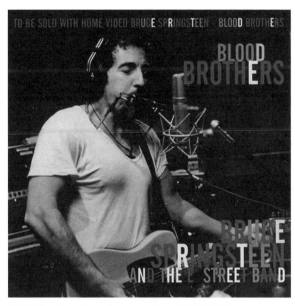

This EP, released as a bonus with the 1996 VHS documentary of the same name, included two previously unreleased tracks from the Greatest Hits era. *Author's collection*

A week later, the group toured the south, playing shows in Orlando, Tampa, Sunrise, and Dallas. During the E Street Band's gig at the Altel Arena in Little Rock, it played the symbolic "Mary Queen of Arkansas" for the first time in twenty-six years. Four days later, at the Pyramid Arena in Memphis, the Boss played Elvis Presley's "Follow That Dream," before dedicating "Land of Hope and Dreams" to Martin Luther King and Elvis.

A month later, at the Compaq Center in Houston, Steve Van Zandt left the stage in the middle of the show, apparently with a stomach problem before "Out in the Street." Showing little sympathy for his old pal, the Boss cracked, "I told you not to eat the clams."

As the tour progressed, Springsteen introduced a country version of "Dancing in the Dark" with Nils Lofgren on pedal steel and Garry Tallent on stand-up bass in Cincinnati on April 30. A week later, they put a similar country stamp on "No Surrender."

The playfulness continued in late May after a two-week break with covers of Them's "Gloria" at Arrowhead Pond in Anaheim and Elvis Presley's "Viva Las Vegas" and "Can't Help Falling in Love" in Las Vegas. While there were no covers in the set by the time the E Street Band rolled into the Delta Center in Salt Lake City on May 29, the tour premiere of "It's Hard to Be a Saint in the City" was welcome after an eighteen-year gap.

When Springsteen debuted two new songs at Philips Arena in Atlanta on June 4, the response wasn't nearly as frenzied. Opening with "Further On (Up the Road)"—a new song that would make it onto *The Rising* in 2002, he also

Springsteen and the E Street Band reunited for roadwork in 1999 after a decade apart. The tour's first leg started in Barcelona in April 9 and wrapped on June 27 in Oslo. This ticket stub is a memento from the group's concert at London's Earls Court on May 21 of that year. *Courtesy of Brucebase*

played "American Skin (41 Shots)" several songs into the set. Penned about his thoughts on the New York Police shooting of Amadou Diallo the previous February, the haunting song created a controversy (chronicled in detail in Chapter 28) that was met with disapproval from many in the NYPD.

Needless to say, when Springsteen arrived at Madison Square Garden on June 12, to close the tour with ten sold-out shows, the crowd reaction to the dirge—which he played each night—was overwhelmingly positive. "Good evening, New York, I'm so glad to be here," he said on that first night to a round of cheers. Then, jokingly, he sneered "Shut up," and the twenty thousand in the crowd roared even louder.

On the final night, Springsteen stunned nearly everyone when he played "Lost in the Flood," his rarely performed 1973 number. If that obscurity—not played since 1978—wasn't enough, he broke out a solo piano rendition of "The Promise" and another infrequent offering, "The E Street Shuffle."

Before he left the stage, he told fans, "I hope we will continue to try to do something" as the E Street Band broke into their anthem, "Blood Brothers."

36

There's Spirits Above and Behind Me

The Rising

Although the album wasn't released until 2002, Springsteen had begun testing some new songs for what would become *The Rising* with the E Street band as early as March 1999. During the Asbury Park Convention Hall rehearsals for the Reunion tour, the band soundchecked "Further On (Up the Road)" and "Waitin' on a Sunny Day."

"My big question when I put the band back together was if we were going to have real work left to do," Springsteen told *Rolling Stone* in December 2009. "I wasn't interested in going out and repeating what we'd done."

His goal was to write songs that would rival the best in his back catalog and maintain the sense of purpose that steered the band during its first two decades. With "Land of Hope and Dreams"—a number that closed out the Reunion shows—and "American Skin (41 Shots)," he felt he found that balance.

As evidenced by their appearance on 2001's *Live in New York City*, the Boss knew he had the confidence he needed to write for the E Street Band. Those songs were the catalyst for what followed. But that wasn't the only challenge.

Tryin' O'Brien

The band went into the studio with Landau and Plotkin in 2001, but things didn't sound current enough to Springsteen's ear. After talking it over with Landau, the two decided that they weren't up on the technologies that had come into play in the six years that he had been away from the studio.

After a discussion with Don Ienner, Sony Music's then-chairman suggested Brendan O'Brien, who had previously worked on records by Pearl Jam, Stone Temple Pilots, Matthew Sweet, Paul Westerberg, and Rage Against the Machine. After meeting with O'Brien, Springsteen played him demos of two new songs, "Further On (Up the Road)" and "Nothing Man."

The plan was to make an album of E Street Band songs that had the modern touches that a record ought to have in 2002. As Bruce told *Uncut* that year, "It just came down to, 'We'd like to record some good songs if we can and we'd like it to be exciting.'"

After agreeing to record at O'Brien's Atlanta studio, where Springsteen felt he'd be most comfortable, they set a date. He continued to work on new material throughout the summer of 2001.

Shore Sounds

In addition to writing in his home studio, Springsteen made it a point to return to the bars on the Jersey Shore for fun and inspiration throughout the summer of 2001, beginning with an hour-long guest appearance at the Stone Pony on May 27. The gig—which marked the twenty-fifth anniversary of Southside Johnny and the Asbury Jukes' notorious radio simulcast—found Springsteen playing on classics like "The Fever," "I Don't Want to Go Home" and "Havin' a Party."

The Boss also joined Bruce Hornsby for a performance of "Cadillac Ranch" at Red Bank's Count Basie Theatre on July 31. But the surprise of the summer occurred on August 18 in Asbury Park when he played an unannounced acoustic set at the Clearwater Music Festival. He played six songs, including the oldies "Does This Bus Stop at 82nd Street?" and "Blinded by the Light," and delivered the first known performance of "My City of Ruins."

The latter, written about the dilapidated state of Asbury Park, would surface the following year on *The Rising*. That same night, Springsteen joined Nils Lofgren for four songs at the Stone Pony and closed out an active day by singing a duet of Elvis Presley's "Suspicious Minds" with singer/songwriter John Eddie.

On September 1, he returned to the Pony to play with Clarence Clemons and the Temple of Soul on E Street Band favorites like "Pink Cadillac" and "Glory Days," plus covers of Eddie Floyd's "Raise Your Hand" and Wilson Pickett's "Mustang Sally." Up in Sea Bright two nights later, Bruce and Patti turned up at Donovan's Reef in Sea Bright, where they sat in with local outfit Brian Kirk and the Jirks for performances of "Rosalita," "Tenth Avenue Freeze-Out," and "Jersey Girl."

9/11

After Springsteen watched the Twin towers fall on the television from his Rumson home as thousands of innocent people perished that unforgettable Tuesday, he was deeply affected. Songs began to pour out of him.

In response to the terrorist attacks, he acted selflessly, traveling to Sony Studios on September 21 to perform on a national telethon called *America: A Tribute to Heroes*. Backed by Van Zandt, Clemons, Scialfa, Soozie Tyrell, and three backing vocalists, Springsteen performed an eerily fitting and moving "My City of Ruins."

A month later, he acted locally—participating alongside Scialfa, Weinberg, Joe Ely, Joan Jett, Bon Jovi, Phoebe Snow, and Sonny Burgess—as part of the

"Alliance of Neighbors" benefits at the Count Basie Theatre, which was orga-nized by Garry Tallent.

The shows, held on October 18 and 19, were played to assist the families of the 150 local victims of the September 11th tragedy, many who commuted to the World Trade Center in New York by ferry from Red Bank. For the gigs, Springsteen would again play a moving version of "My City of Ruins" with help from the Pilgrim Baptist Church Celestial Choir, plus favorites like "Bobby Jean" and "Thunder Road."

By the second or third week in September, he had written "Into the Fire" for the telethon, although he elected not to play it. From there he penned "You're Missing" and "The Fuse"—which came to him in the middle of the night as he thought about the lives that had been devastated.

"People knew people," he told *Uncut*'s Adam Sweeting. "You knew this woman and her husband, someone else's son, someone else's brother." With the elements of a story taking shape, Springsteen found himself being encouraged by strangers. One man supposedly pulled up next to him at a traffic light, rolled down his window, and told him, "We need you now."

As he drove around Monmouth County in the days and weeks after the attacks, he was stunned by the number of funerals he'd witness as he'd roll by churches in communities like Middletown, Fairview, Shrewsbury, and Little Silver. Springsteen couldn't help but be impacted. The songs came out naturally. "I'm just doing something that's useful for me," he told Sweeting. "And then hopefully in some fashion it's gonna be useful and will provide some service to my audience."

Recording *The Rising*

The bulk of the album was written between September '01 and March '02. As the songs came, he would quickly demo them. When he first reviewed "Into the Fire" and "You're Missing" with O'Brien, the producer began to provide input about song structure which was something Springsteen hadn't experienced in a long time. The Boss welcomed the feedback.

When the band recorded "Into the Fire" in Atlanta in early 2002 at Southern Tracks Studios, Springsteen knew O'Brien was the right choice. The song defi-nitely sounded like the E Street Band in the moment, which was what Bruce had wanted. Worked on from January to March with eyes on a summer release, the sessions went much quicker than any previous E Street album.

Track by Track

The Rising would prove to be Springsteen's most impressive rock album since *Born in the U.S.A.* To fans, it was an affirmation that the rebirth of the E Street Band was about much more than nostalgia.

"Lonesome Day"

Launching *The Rising* and setting the tone of the album, this memorable, mid-tempo song is written from the perspective of a grieving 9/11 widow or widower. Counting country elements, courtesy of Soozie Tyrell's violin, the song was the second single from the record, following the title track with a December 2, 2002, release. A video for the song was shot in Asbury Park with acclaimed director Mark Pellington.

"Into the Fire"

Dedicated to the 343 firefighters who perished at the World Trade Center, the song depicts images of the men and women who went up the stairs as everyone inside those buildings was running down to the street below. One of the most lyrically moving songs the Boss has ever penned, he sings of loss, "I need your kiss/but love and duty called you someplace higher."

"Waitin' on a Sunny Day"

Apparently written in (or before) 1998, this buoyant tune was soundchecked by the E Street band on June 17, 1999. For this lyrically simple love song bolstered by the Big Man's saxophone, Springsteen once revealed he took inspiration from Smokey Robinson. The contagious number was released as a single outside of North America on April 22, 2003, and has become a regular, uplifting highlight of the Boss's shows since its release.

"Nothing Man"

First written in 1994, this song depicts a hero—presumably a Gulf War veteran—who is championed in his hometown paper after his life was changed in "a misty cloud of pink vapor." It's unclear if the Boss altered any of his lyrics on this soft ballad to fit with the theme of the album, but it works in any case.

"Countin' on a Miracle"

Written in 2000, the song's message of hope against all odds was assumed by some fans to have been written in the aftermath of 9/11. Although it could be from the perspective of someone watching the Trade Center collapse on television and praying that their loved one got out alive, the reality is that the lyrics are simply about someone who is heartbroken after a breakup.

"Empty Sky"

Written in the aftermath of 9/11, it depicts the pain and acceptance that one's spouse will never return and the reminders that are everywhere, from the empty side of the bed to the void in the sky where two towers once stood so confidently. Springsteen played it every night during *The Rising* tour with a slow, haunting delivery.

"Worlds Apart"

In this message of healing in the wake of 9/11, Springsteen encourages listeners to accept people's differences. The song was written at a time when feelings of intolerance in America toward many from the Middle East were at an all-time high. In an effort to promote the acceptance of other cultures and mitigate blind hatred, Springsteen tapped Asif Ali Khan—the Pakistani-born "Prince of Qaawali"—to play on the song.

"Let's Be Friends (Skin to Skin)"

This song is unique in that it is the only one on *The Rising* that was not completely recorded in Atlanta. Springsteen tracked this at Thrill Hill East sometime between 1999 and 2001, but he did revisit it under O'Brien's guidance, adding additional instruments at Southern Tracks. Amid the somber tones of the record, this is a bright and welcome shot of E Street soul.

"Further On (Up the Road)"

After its live premiere in Atlanta in June 2000, this song—which seems to signify the regrouping of his old friends in the E Street Band—was earmarked for the record. In it, Springsteen sang "Let's take the good times as they go," delivering an optimistic message to Garry, Danny, Clarence, Roy, Max, Steve, Nils, Patti and Soozie that their work wasn't yet done.

"The Fuse"

Another number written about September 11th, "The Fuse" depicts the uneasiness felt in America as it waited for another terrorist attack. Speaking to *Uncut* about the volatile time in U.S. history, Springsteen explained, "It feels as rocky as any time since the Cuban missile crisis.

"It feels like there's a lot of forces loose in the world," he added, expressing his worries over whether we had good leadership in place at home—a not so subtle dig at the Bush/Cheney regime in power at the time.

"Mary's Place"

When Jon Landau referred to this song as "a new "Rosalita" before it had ever been unveiled, fans had weighty expectations. Thankfully, Springsteen delivered with this majestic, upbeat song that he had written about a wake.

A musical assertion that life indeed goes on, "Mary's Place" brings together all of his friends for a party—a post-funeral party. This depiction of an Irish wake is the arguable pinnacle of an amazing record.

"You're Missing"

A representation of the void felt in a home in the weeks after a 9/11 funeral, Springsteen sings of a widow in one of the most emotional songs he would ever write. He weaves the story of a wife in the kitchen tending to the needs of her children while her husband's shoes and suits sit ready for use in the closet. Newspapers pile up on the doorstep, the television's on in the den, but the house is empty because he's gone.

"The Rising"

Released on July 16, 2002, in advance of the album of the same name, Springsteen's first single with the E Street Band in seventeen years was a poignant, piercing rock song that went straight into the heart of Americans. Chronicling a fireman's ascent up the stairwell in the World Trade Center towers after the planes had struck, Bruce sings of being unable to see, trudging forward courageously, wearing "the cross of my calling" and heading toward near-certain death.

Although hardly a hit single—it stalled at #52 in the U.S.—it became one of Springsteen's most heralded songs ever. At 2003's Grammy Awards, the tune earned him the awards for Best Rock Song and Best Male Rock Vocal Performance.

"Paradise"

Played just one time on the *Rising* tour, this song attempts to get inside the mind of a suicidal terrorist who has filled his backpack with enough bombs to kill everyone in a crowded marketplace. Should he successfully carries out his mission, his reward is paradise.

"My City of Ruins"

When Springsteen played this song at a 2000 Asbury Park Christmas concert, he was hoping to inspire the local residents living amid the boarded-up homes, drug dealers, and general decay to "rise up." The song was equally motivational to Americans who first heard it in September 2011 during a national 9/11 telethon, when he introduced it as "a prayer for our fallen brothers and sisters."

Reception

Springsteen's twelfth studio album and first album with the E Street Band since 1984 performed well commercially and critically upon its July 30 release. It debuted at #1 on the *Billboard* 200 and sold 520,000 copies in its first week.

Rolling Stone gave the record its highest rating—five stars—and wrote, "With its bold thematic concentration and penetrating emotional focus, it is a singular triumph. I can't think of another album in which such an abundance of great songs might be said to seem the least of its achievements."

Meanwhile *Spin* wrote, "Obsessed with mortality and suffused with grief, The Rising is the most eloquent artistic response yet to the World Trade Center tragedy."

Finally, *Time* championed, "*The Rising* is about September 11, and it is the first significant piece of pop art to respond to the events of that day . . . The songs are sad, but the sadness is almost always matched with optimism, promises of redemption, and calls to spiritual arms. There is more rising on *The Rising* than in a month of church."

Outtakes

In addition to the live version of "American Skin (41 Shots)" that had been released in its live form on *Live in New York City*, Springsteen tracked a studio version with the E Street Band on March 2, 2001. Produced by Springsteen with Chuck Plotkin, it was issued on a promotional single in June '01.

Another song, called "Harry's Place"—which has no relation lyrically or sonically with "Mary's Place"—was also recorded during *The Rising* sessions in Atlanta with the E Street Band. Springsteen would later reveal in an interview with ABC's Ted Koppel that the rock tune about a drug kingpin was one of just two songs recorded with O'Brien that didn't make the record.

Faith on *The Rising*

If he shunned religion in some of the earliest interviews of his career, by the time of *The Rising*, Springsteen was acknowledging the importance of family and faith in his fifties. Speaking to *Today Show* host Matt Lauer in July 2002, he explained how he had a lot of aunts when he grew up with a very big extended family in Freehold.

"We had about five or six houses on one street. The church was in the middle and the convent was on one side and the rectory was on the other," he explained. "So, I've seen more weddings and funerals. . . . But there were always the aunts and uncles around me. And, I think in some fashion the older I got the more those things mattered. And, even before I was married, when my life had begun to become something very different, those were the times when I felt I needed to connect most and probably for my own purposes, really."

Springsteen also admitted to *Nightline*'s Ted Koppel that "The Rising" was, in part, about the resurrection. "I was a good Catholic boy when I was little, so those images for me are always very close, and they explain a lot about life."

"What I was trying to describe, one of the most powerful images of the 11th, that I'd read in the paper, some of the people coming down were talking about the emergency workers who were ascending," he explained. "The idea of those guys going up the stairs, up the stairs, ascending, ascending. I mean you could be ascending a smoky staircase, you could be in the afterlife, moving on."

37

You Can't Forsake the Ties That Bind

Benefit Shows, Charities, and Causes

3M

The E Street Band—sans Roy Bittan and Nils Lofgren—took the stage at the Stone Pony's "JAM '86 Hometown Benefit" on January 19, 1986 A charity gig billed as "Jersey Artists for Mankind" was the next logical step in Springsteen's crusade to try and help the 450 workers at Freehold's 3M Plant who were let go when Minnesota Mining and Manufacturing shuttered its plant.

A month prior, he and Willie Nelson had joined forces in a newspaper ad campaign, printing an open letter titled "3M: Don't Abandon Our Hometown!" in the *Asbury Park Press,* the *New York Times,* the *St. Paul Pioneer Dispatch,* and *Variety.* Springsteen urged the company to reconsider closing its video- and audiotape manufacturing facility.

During the gig, which was filmed by ABC for a *20/20* piece, the Boss played seven tunes, including the serious-minded numbers "My Hometown," "The Promised Land," "Badlands," and "Darkness on the Edge of Town."

All-Star Benefit for Homeless Children

Springsteen performed alongside Dion, Paul Simon, Ruben Blades, Lou Reed, Billy Joel, and James Taylor at this charitable event at Madison Square Garden held on December 13, 1987. Bruce delivered "Born to Run" and "Glory Days" to the crowd. He also collaborated with Dion on "Teenager in Love" and joined all performers on the finale, "Rock and Roll Music."

Alliance of Neighbors Concerts

Following the 9/11 attacks, Springsteen threw his support to the local families who lost fathers, mothers, sons, and daughters when he played three benefit gigs for the Alliance of Neighbors charity. Established to help the surviving

Monmouth County families of the September 11 terrorist attacks, the shows took place on October 18 and 19, 2001, at the Count Basie Theatre in Red Bank.

Springsteen and Bon Jovi were the main attractions of the concerts, which were held over two nights and one matinee; however, Elvis Presley's legendary backing band of Sonny Burgess, Jerry Scheff, D. J. Fontana, and Kevin Kennedy; Joan Jett; the Smithereens; John Eddie; members of the E Street Band; and others also played. Together they helped raise $700,000 for families affected by the tragedy.

Amnesty International: The Struggle Continues

Ten years after Bruce headlined the Amnesty International *Human Rights Now!* tour—which culminated in an HBO Television special—he rejoined Peter Gabriel, Tracy Chapman, and Youssou N'Dour for an Amnesty Benefit gig at the Palais Omnisports in Paris.

Springsteen collaborated with the other stars on the bill for a rendition of Bob Marley's "Get Up Stand Up" before renditions of "The Ghost of Tom Joad," "Born in the U.S.A.," "Working on the Highway," and "No Surrender."

Autism Speaks

On November 17, 2009, Springsteen opened for comedian Jerry Seinfeld at this Carnegie Hall benefit. The Boss performed "No Surrender," "If I Should Fall Behind," "Working on the Highway," and "Thunder Road" and helped raise thousands for the Autism Speaks charity.

The Bobby Bandiera All-Star Holiday Concerts

On a couple of December occasions in 2006 and 2008, Springsteen was an unannounced performer at these charity shows, hosted by longtime friend Bobby Bandiera at the Count Basie Theatre in Red Bank. Backed by Bandiera's Jersey Shore Rock and Soul Revue for each occasion, the first—from December 12, 2006—featured six numbers including a duet with Jon Bon Jovi on "Tenth Avenue Freeze-Out."

At the December 22, 2008, event, Springsteen and Bon Jovi duplicated that duet, while Southside Johnny and Gary U.S. Bonds jammed with him on the timeless Asbury Jukes number "Havin' a Party."

Bridge School

At the request of Neil Young, Bruce, Nils Lofgren, and keyboardist Danny Federici were on hand for the very first Bridge School Benefit concert. Held on October 13, 1986, to assist in educating children with severe speech and physical impairments, the event at the Shoreline Amphitheatre in Mountain

View, California, featured Springsteen, Young, and former Young sideman Nils Lofgren playing "Helpless."

Springsteen also played hits like "Born in the U.S.A.," "Glory Days," and "Hungry Heart" (with the help of Crosby Stills, Nash and Young). A standout acoustic rendition of "Fire" was captured on video and later released as the official music video in 1987.

Nine years later, Springsteen returned to Shoreline for his second Bridge School gig. A solo performance held on October 28 saw him playing numbers like "Adam Raised a Cain," "Sinaloa Cowboys," and "Point Blank." He encored with Young on two of the latter's classics—"Down by the River" and "Rockin' in the Free World."

Christic Institute

In mid-November 1990, Springsteen joined friends Bonnie Raitt and Jackson Browne for a pair of gigs at L.A.'s Shrine Auditorium to raise funds for the public interest law and political action group known as the Christic Institute. These solo acoustic shows were his first since he released the E Street Band and featured six new, previously unheard songs ("Red Headed Woman," "When the Lights Go Out," "57 Channels," "Real World," "The Wish," and "Soul Driver"). Springsteen's performances were so good that he and Jon Landau considered releasing them as an album.

The gigs helped the Christic Institute file a $24 million federal lawsuit under the RICO (Racketeering and Corrupt Influence Organizations) Act, in an effort to try to expose the CIA's participation in Iran/Contra drug smuggling activities. Unfortunately, its charges that a secret team of agents had carried out the La Penca bombing were dismissed because of lack of evidence against the individual they accused of being the bomber.

After an unsuccessful appeal, the organization was fined more that $1 million in court costs for the defendants, putting it out of business.

Come Together

When Long Branch police sergeant Patrick King was shot to death in the line of duty while ordering Chinese food on November 20, 1997, it left the entire Jersey Shore community rattled. In honor of his memory and in an effort to help his family, Jon Bon Jovi organized a benefit concert for his memorial fund, planned for early in the New Year. Springsteen—along with Scialfa, Southside Johnny, Steve Van Zandt, Bon Jovi, and his guitarist Richie Sambora—appeared at the show to celebrate King's life.

Held at the Count Basie Theater in Red Bank, the show featured Springsteen and Bon Jovi leading their legendary friends through an array of classic originals and exemplary covers. When the night was over, $112,000 was raised for King's family.

Christmas Gigs at the Convention Hall

In December 2000, Springsteen booked a pair of holiday benefit concerts at Asbury Park's Convention Hall that were different from most E Street Band gigs. The shows, which were announced five days before the December 17 and 18 gigs began, benefitted eight local charities: the Greater Asbury Park Chamber of Commerce, Epiphany House, the Center in Asbury Park and Substance Abuse Resources, the Boys and Girls Club of Monmouth County, the Women's Center of Monmouth County, the Food Bank of Monmouth and Ocean Counties, and the Parker Family Health Clinic.

For these concerts, Springsteen did his best Elvis Presley impersonation on "Blue Christmas" and took on Chuck Berry's "Run, Run, Rudolph." The E Street Band and the Max Weinberg 7 also teamed for "Merry Christmas Baby" and "Christmas Baby Please Come Home," before breaking into Boss classics like "Rosalita" and "Bobby Jean." Elsewhere, Southside Johnny and Springsteen sang a duet of "This Time It's for Real."

Tickets for the shows went on sale on December 15 and—at $50 a piece—were gone in minutes. In addition to the $360,000 grossed from the concerts, Springsteen raised an additional $65,000 by holding an Internet auction of eleven pairs of tickets, which sold for between $5,000 and $7,500 each.

In early December 2001, Springsteen returned to the Convention Hall for five shows that grossed $900,000 for charities, starting a trend that continued until 2003. In addition to the Max Weinberg 7 and members of the E Street Band, the Christmas concerts usually featured special guests like Bobby Bandiera and Southside Johnny. Others who joined in over the years included Garland Jeffreys, Bruce Hornsby, Elvis Costello, Jesse Malin, and Sam Moore.

Christmas Roadhouse

On December 19, 2004, the annual Bruce Springsteen and Friends event moved to Harry's Roadhouse in Asbury Park for a pair of concerts played on the same day. For these gigs—which started at 4:30 and 8:30 p.m. respectively—he mixed up the setlist slightly. Backed by Bobby Bandiera and his band, the Boss was accompanied by Max Weinberg and Patti Scialfa on a couple of numbers. Southside Johnny and Springsteen paired up for "The Fever" in the first show. In the second show, Willie Nile helped out on the mandatory, seasonal "Santa Claus Is Coming to Town."

Clearwater Festival

Springsteen had quietly supported Clearwater, the New Jersey environmental protection group, for a number of years. But in April 2001, after learning that the organization was holding its annual fund-raiser in Asbury Park, he turned up to play a surprise acoustic set that included his just-written "My City of Ruins."

He also served up "Bobby Jean," "This Hard Land," "Does This Bus Stop at 82nd Street?," and "Blinded by the Light." For that final number he brought fans up onstage to sing along. Springsteen also praised the folks from Clearwater and the Asbury Park City council, and announced his support of the festival and the revitalization of the city so close to his heart.

Count Basie Foundation

This full-length benefit concert for the Count Basie Theatre helped to finance renovations of the hosting venue. For the Red Bank show, held on May 7, 2008, Bruce and the E Street Band played the *Darkness on the Edge of Town* and *Born to Run* albums front to back.

A year earlier, on May 12, 2007, Brian Wilson, Beach Boys cofounder, played a full concert for the Count Basie Theatre Foundation, which saw Springsteen join in on "Barbara Ann" and "Love and Mercy." The pair of stars also autographed a Challenger surfboard that sold for $7,500 at auction before the concert.

Double Take Magazine Benefit

After first being interviewed for *Double Take* magazine in spring 1998 by Will Percy, the nephew of author Walker Percy, Springsteen stepped in to help the publication—which was founded by Harvard Professor and friend Dr. Robert Coles—when it began to suffer financial difficulties in 2003.

On February 19 and 20 of that year, Springsteen played shows at the 900-capacity Somerville Theatre in Massachusetts. Billed as an "intimate evening of music and conversation with Bruce Springsteen," these events were cherished by those in attendance as the Boss opened up about classic songs like "Does This Bus Stop at 82nd Street?" and even held a Q and A session from the stage after each tune on the first night.

Despite his participation in said events, Double Take folded in late 2004, but the memory of these famous shows lives on among Springsteen fanatics.

Doug Flutie Autism Foundation

Colts Neck, New Jersey, residents Anthony and Pam Diasco pledged $60,000 at a June 1999 Doug Flutie Autism Foundation fund-raiser hosted by Jon Bon Jovi for a private Bon Jovi concert at their home. When the show was held on their estate on December 4, Springsteen surprised the crowd by turning up with Scialfa and Southside Johnny to perform six tunes, including "Red Headed Woman," "Pretty Woman," the Rolling Stones' "It's All Over Now," and Southside's own "Havin' a Party."

Food Bank Hero

Springsteen has helped feed the needy for nearly thirty years, going beyond just writing a check and speaking up to audiences about helping local hunger organizations. He even appeared in newspaper ads for the Community Food Bank of New Jersey in 2008.

Springsteen first began donating heavily to local food banks during his *Born in the U.S.A.* tour, giving $10,000 to the Steelworkers Oldtimers Foundation during his run of L.A. Sports Arena gigs in October 1984. Similar gestures in Pittsburgh (where he donated another $10,000 to a union food bank, United Steelworkers 1397) and Denver (where he gave the same amount to the Colorado Food Clearinghouse) were just the tip of the iceberg.

His generosity helped provide food for the poor in Dallas, Nashville, Providence, Syracuse, and beyond. Before his show at the Orange Bowl in Miami in September 1985, he gave $25,000 to the Daily Bread Community Food Bank.

This trend has continued ever since, even at smaller shows. On lower-profile solo tours, such as his theater trek to support *The Ghost of Tom Joad*, Springsteen was happy to share the profits from some of his T-shirt sales. Playing at Seattle's Paramount in October 1996, for instance, he donated his $7,000 merchandise profit to a local charitable food organization.

As recently as 2009, Springsteen was helping every food bank on his tour itinerary. He had quietly become one of the most famous advocates for the issue of hunger in America. By donating two sets of four prime seats plus a meet and greet, which were auctioned at $20,000 a set for a show on Long Island, he raised $40,000 for the Regional Food Bank of Northeastern New York. But he wasn't done: he matched the donation for a total of $80,000!

The Hope Concert

Held on April 29, 2003, at the Count Basie Theatre, this show was a benefit for Jersey Shore music veteran Bobby Bandiera, whose twenty-one-year-old son Bobby Jr. suffered from an undiagnosed neurological disorder. The four-hour, sold-out show helped raise $300,000 to help cover medical care.

Springsteen was on hand to support the cause, alongside Jon Bon Jovi, Southside Johnny, Gary U.S. Bonds, and the Max Weinberg 7. "The Fever," "Thunder Road," "Kitty's Back," "Rosalita," and "The E Street Shuffle" were among the Springsteen classics played.

Hope for Haiti Now

Shortly after word broke of the devastation Haiti suffered from the earthquake, Springsteen performed Pete Seeger's classic "We Shall Overcome" on an MTV-sponsored benefit held on January 22, 2010. The song—which found Bruce accompanied by Scialfa, Charlie Giordano, Curt Ramm, Soozie Tyrell, Curtis

King, and Cindy Mizelle—was promptly made available for sale as a digital download with all profits going to the earthquake victims.

Kristen Ann Carr Fund

After the tragic death of Kristen Ann Carr—the daughter of his comanager Barbara Carr and the step-daughter of his biographer Dave Marsh—Springsteen headlined this event on June 26, 1993, in Madison Square Garden. Proceeds went to the Kristen Ann Carr Fund, which was established to fight sarcoma.

Carr, who died from cancer at just twenty-one in January 1993, had traveled with Springsteen during his 1992 European tour. Following her passing, her parents, her sister Sasha, and her fiancé Michael Solomon established the nonprofit organization that sponsored sarcoma research for teens and young adults with the disease.

Alongside Terence Trent D'Arby and Joe Ely, the Boss played material spanning his entire catalog. Unfortunately, at one point, D'Arby was booed, which sent

Appearing in a 2008 newspaper ad for the Community Food Bank of New Jersey was the next logical step for Bruce Springsteen. The Boss had been helping to feed the needy by donating money, encouraging fan donations and raising awareness on the problem for over thirty years.

Author's Collection

Springsteen into a fit of rage. According to audio from the show, Springsteen lashed out at the crowd. "Terence Trent D'Arby—need I remind some of you rude motherfuckers that everybody onstage is my guest?" he scolded.

That outburst aside, the gig raised $1.5 million, which allowed for the fund to finance a research fellowship and provide support assistance to sarcoma patients. Springsteen remembered Kristen in his 1995 Grammy speech for Song of the Year, explaining that her spirit was the backbone of the song.

Letter to the Editor

As recently as 2011, Springsteen—who has worked hard to help New Jersey's food banks for years—expressed concern about the poverty in the city and throughout the region. In a letter he wrote to the *Asbury Park Press* thanking the newspaper for giving a voice to the voiceless through its story on aid cuts to the poor, he made national news.

Springsteen praised antipoverty crusaders for providing "real information and actual facts about what is happening below the poverty line."

"These are voices that in our current climate are having a hard time being heard, not just in New Jersey, but nationally," Bruce wrote. "Your article shows that the cuts are eating away at the lower edges of the middle class, not just those already classified as in poverty, and are likely to continue to get worse over the next few years."

Light of Day

On November 3, 2000, Springsteen dropped in on the Stone Pony for the first annual Light of Day Benefit Concert (which was named in honor of his song) and helped raise more than $16,000 for the Parkinson's Disease Foundation. Although he was not on the bill, which featured the likes of Marah and Joe Grushecky, he was hotly rumored and came through with a surprise solo set that began at 1:40 a.m. and concluded at 3:15 a.m.

The following year, the event—which was founded by Joe's manager and Parkinson's sufferer Bob Benjamin—moved to the Tradewinds in Sea Bright, and although he wasn't billed, he again joined Grushecky for six encores, including "Fire," "Ramrod," and "Light of Day." Ensuing shows throughout the next decade usually occurred at the Pony, although in 2006 it was booked for the Starland Ballroom in Sayreville, and in 2010 it was held at the Paramount Theatre in Asbury Park.

Alongside Grushecky, Bruce has been the annual event's mainstay. Other artists, from Garland Jeffreys and Willie Nile to Jesse Malin, have also helped keep the yearly charity gig thriving.

Make a Wish

In December 2002, a Red Bank high school senior and National Honor Society member named Michael Antrim won a Best in Show award at the Freehold Public Library art contest for his portrait of Springsteen, which he'd named "Hometown Hero."

But, as Springsteen would learn, Antrim was plagued with Crohn's disease and was a Make-A-Wish Foundation participant. He wrote Antrim a personal letter and eventually went to his house to visit him and his mom, Kathleen.

During his stay, the Boss played a couple of tunes on guitar for them, including "The Promised Land," and even signed Michael's original portrait.

Monmouth County SPCA

When Max and Becky Weinberg held a "Kick Up Your Paws" benefit at their New Jersey residence, Springsteen showed up for the fund-raiser on the Weinbergs' farm/estate. He played with the Max Weinberg 7, rocking the 500 attendees with a mix of covers like "634-5789" and "Kansas City," plus the originals "From Small Things (Big Things One Day Come)" and "Tenth Avenue Freeze-Out."

Music for Youth

During a tribute show/benefit held at Carnegie Hall on April 5, 2007, Springsteen was honored with covers of his own songs played by the likes of the Hold Steady, Jesse Malin, Badly Drawn Boy, Steve Earle, Josh Ritter, Pete Yorn, Joseph Arthur, Juliana Hatfield, and Patti Smith. The event, titled "Celebrating the Music of Bruce Springsteen: Music for Youth Benefit," was quite a success, raising $150,000 for music education.

After sitting in the mezzanine box for much of the show, Bruce came down to take the stage, delivering "The Promised Land" and "Rosalia (Come Out Tonight)" before bringing all performers onstage to play the latter with him once again.

The Rainforest Foundation

Springsteen helped Sting and his wife, Trudy Styler, by making an appearance at their sixth annual benefit for the Rainforest at Carnegie Hall on April 12, 1995. He opened with a duet of "The River" with James Taylor and performed his recent hit "Streets of Philadelphia" before turning his appearance into a tribute to the King of Rock-'n'-Roll. After his original, humorous "I'm Turning into Elvis," he played five Presley numbers including "Viva Las Vegas," "Burning Love," and "Jailhouse Rock."

In May 2010, he again turned up for the annual Carnegie Hall event, performing "Dancing in the Dark," Bryan Adams' "Cuts Like a Knife," and an all-star version of Journey's "Don't Stop Believin'" with Elton John, Lady Gaga, Sting, Shirley Bassey, Debbie Harry, and others. Nineteen-eighties nostalgia was the night's theme.

Ranney School Benefits

Beginning in 2006, Springsteen began playing concerts to benefit the teachers and parents of the Ranney School, the Tinton Falls, New Jersey–based prep school that his son Sam attended.

Typically backed by Bobby Bandiera's band and joined by Patti Scialfa and Southside Johnny, these fun concerts—which mix classic covers with Springsteen and Southside staples—were held annually through 2010 at the legendary Stone Pony.

Rumson Country Day School

Beginning in April 2002, Springsteen performed at four annual Stone Pony concerts to benefit Rumson Country Day School. Scialfa, Southside, and Bobby Bandiera were the constants of these gigs—which were restricted to parents from the school.

At the 2003 show, Jon Bon Jovi took the stage for the second of these celebratory yearly gigs. Setlists usually balanced 1960s hits like "634-5789" and "Bad Moon Rising" with favorites from Bruce's songbook like "Darlington County" and "Tenth Avenue Freeze-Out."

S.O.S. Racism Concert

Bruce and Clarence Clemons performed on this French television broadcast of a concert held from Chateau de Vincennes in Paris on June 18, 1988. Springsteen performed two appropriate originals: "The Promised Land"—with Clemons adding a previously unheard sax part—and "My Hometown." Following an acoustic treatment of the latter, the Boss followed the same approach to fitting covers of Bob Dylan's "Blowin' in the Wind" and Creedence Clearwater Revival's "Bad Moon Rising."

St. Rose of Lima

Thirty-plus years after his last performance at his Roman Catholic grammar school as a member of the Castiles, the Boss returned to Freehold's St. Rose of Lima School on November 8, 1996. An inimitable event, the solo gig for his childhood church and school saw Springsteen dedicating "This Hard Land" to attendee Marion Vinyard, speaking about his sister on "The River," singing his famous ode "My Hometown," and unveiling a new one, "In Freehold," for the audience.

Stand Up for Heroes

At these annual November gala events, held in Manhattan to benefit the Bob Woodruff Foundation, which helps injured soldiers and their families,

Springsteen has typically played a short acoustic set and auctioned off one of his guitars, a motorcycle, or both.

He began auctioning off his bikes in 2007, when he started appearing alongside popular comedians for the charity. In 2008, he auctioned off his Harley Davidson motorcycle for $70,000. The guitar he played on numbers like "The Promised Land," "Thunder Road," and "The Rising" that year fetched $50,000.

In 2009, the all-star benefit concert found Springsteen selling off his autographed Takamine guitar. It was won by *Law and Order* actress Mariska Hargitay, who paid $50,000. In 2010, he pulled in $140,000 from another guitar, with all money going to help "Stand Up for Heroes."

"We Got the Love"

Springsteen lent his guitar playing to the Jersey Artists for Mankind benefit, joining Clarence Clemons, Nils Lofgren and other Jersey Shore music luminaries like La Bamba and Glen Burtnick on this multi-artist charity single. Coproduced by Garry Tallent at Shorefire Studios in Long Branch, an official single and video—which did not include Springsteen—were released on May 16, 1986.

World Hunger Year

Billed as "A Concert to Fight Hunger," this show—held at the Meadowlands Arena on June 24, 1993—was designed to benefit charities such as World Hunger Year, the Food and Hunger Hotline, and the Community Food Bank of New Jersey. Alongside Springsteen's "Other Band," E Street members Clarence Clemons, Patti Scialfa, and Max Weinberg; former guitarist Steve Van Zandt; Southside Johnny; Joe Ely; the Miami Horns; and Soozie Tyrell all guest on various numbers.

In addition to a full set with his new band, the aforementioned E Street members help out on "Glory Days," "Tenth Avenue Freeze-Out," "Born to Run," and "Jersey Girl" during this memorable evening.

38

I Feel a Dirty Wind Blowing

Devils and Dust

When Springsteen came off the road in October 2003, he took a well-deserved break. But by the spring of 2004, he was already back at work on his third folk album. Recorded and/or mixed between March and August of that year with the help of Brendan O'Brien, the resulting *Devils and Dust* album was actually built from songs that he had written through the years, with one tune, "All the Way Home," dating back to 1990.

In fact, the only truly new song was the title track, while much of the material had been recorded in between 1995 and 1997. O'Brien was recruited to assist the Boss with updating and enhancing the presentation of the music, which the Boss was eyeing for a 2005 release.

The thematic sequel to *The Ghost of Tom Joad* was based on songs that Springsteen had accumulated. The hushed material on *Devils and Dust* told stories of people in the American West whose lives were at risk, but unlike its 1995 counterpart, this material balanced its characters' tough experiences with some positivity.

Essential Tracks

"In every song on this record," Springsteen told the *New York Times*, "somebody's in some spiritual struggle between the worst of themselves and the best of themselves, and everybody comes out in a slightly different place." That underlying theme could be heard on the album's best songs.

"Devils and Dust"

The record's title track and lead single was first soundchecked with the E Street Band in April 2003. It told the story of an American soldier serving in the 2003 invasion of Iraq who is as uncertain as he is uncomfortable about his orders.

"What moved me the most was the idea of a young kid stationed at a checkpoint," Springsteen told NPR's Renee Montagne. "You've got a very, very short period of time where you have to decide about the car that's driving toward you, whether it's an innocent family, or whether it's your death coming at you . . . And you have to decide right, right now. There's so little room for error, and the error that you make is so very final."

Although it received little airplay and stalled at #72 after its release on March 29, 2005, it did resonate with the National Academy of Recording Arts and Sciences, who nominated it for Song of the Year, Best Rock Song, and Best Solo Rock Vocal. Springsteen took home the gong for the latter in February 2006 and performed the song on the broadcast, telling the audience "Bring 'em home!"

"All the Way Home"

This brisk number was penned in 1990 and originally given to Southside Johnny. Springsteen reclaimed the song, which he originally recorded in 1997 with the help of Chuck Plotkin and Toby Scott. Brendan O'Brien added sitar to the track in 2004.

"Reno"

The character in this song visits a hooker who reminds him of an old girlfriend, but after the deed is done, he feels emptiness and regret. An interesting look at the differences between lust and pure sexual release and the intimacy and ecstasy that can be shared between those who are truly in love, the song is among the crassest Springsteen has ever recorded as the lyric "Two hundred straight in/Two-fifty up the ass," suggests.

"Black Cowboys"

An African American teen who has grown up in The Bronx leaves behind his mom and her drug-dealing boyfriend and ventures west on this compelling number, which is essentially a short story put to music.

"Silver Palomino"

When a mother dies, her thirteen-year-old son survives her loss by connecting himself to a beautiful horse that he would watch from afar. Recorded as a solo number, O'Brien oversaw the addition of strings to the track in 2004.

"Jesus Was an Only Son"

In this hymn about Mary's love and the comfort she receives from Jesus, Springsteen embraces his Catholicism on a song about the relationship of mothers and sons. "I'm not a churchgoer," he told Jon Pareles, "but I realized, as time passed, that my music is filled with Catholic imagery. It's not a negative thing.

"I've been back to the church on many occasions," he continued, explaining that he has since befriended priests. And I've been to the convent where the nuns now give me beer, which they have in the refrigerator. I don't think they had that when I was going to school there."

"Matamoros Banks"

Picking up where *The Ghost of Tom Joad*'s "Across the Border" left off, this song reverses the occurrences that lead up to a Mexican immigrant drowning in his effort to cross the border into the U.S. It ends with thoughts of optimism as he heads out with such hopefulness for his future in the Texas border city of Brownsville.

Reception

Released on April 26, 2005, *Devils and Dust* debuted at #1 on the Billboard album survey in its first week of release, going on to sell 650,000 copies. Although the record didn't have staying power, reviews were strong.

"The heart of the CD is filled with the compassion and craft that have made Springsteen such an invaluable rock star," the *Los Angeles Times* wrote, while *Mojo* said, "an alarming intimacy is the bedrock of *Devils and Dust*."

Still, the *Village Voice's* Amy Phillips took a different stance, writing, "It's long, boring and preachy." Perhaps *New York* got it best: "[It] stands somewhere between *Nebraska* and *Joad* in terms of impact and quality, but this album doesn't merely find the middle ground between those two earlier releases: Its best songs break new ground for Springsteen."

39

Brothers and Sisters Don't You Cry, There'll Be Good Times By and By

The Seeger Sessions

The Sessions Band

As Bruce Springsteen's only album of cover material, *We Shall Overcome: The Seeger Sessions* was an homage to iconic folk musician and social activist Pete Seeger. Although it wasn't released until April 25, 2006, work on the record dated back nearly a decade, when Springsteen first recorded "We Shall Overcome" for the 1998 tribute album *Where Have All the Flowers Gone: The Songs of Pete Seeger.*

The "Sessions Band" that he would come to utilize was first hired—when they were known as Cajun/zydeco band the Gotham Playboys—to play at a "Fiesta"-themed party that Patti Scialfa had thrown for Springsteen's forty-eighth birthday. The bash, held in a field on their Colts Neck farm, featured Jeremy Chatzky, Sam Bardfeld, Larry Eagle, and Charles Giordano, musicians that he would hire to play with him to record "We Shall Overcome" along with five other Seeger tunes in his home studio on November 2, 1997.

Alongside Soozie Tyrell—a multi-instrumentalist and close friend of Patti Scialfa's—these members of the Gotham Playboys were the core of the Sessions Band that Springsteen reactivated in 2005. At the time, he was apparently considering music for a sequel to 1998's *Tracks* box, and upon reviewing the unreleased Seeger songs, he elected to move forward with a full tribute record.

The Sessions Band reconvened after a seven-and-a-half-year gap to record nine songs at Springsteen's Thrill Hill East on March 19, 2005. Springsteen's cousin, guitarist Frank Bruno, plus Patti Scialfa and the Miami Horns also joined in on these sessions.

Eight of the record's thirteen songs—including "Old Dan Tucker," "Mrs. McGrath," "O Mary Don't You Weep," "John Henry," "Jacob's Ladder,"

"Shenandoah," "Pay Me My Money Down"—the project's only single—and "Froggie Went A-Courtin" were traditional uncredited numbers that spoke volumes about American history.

As for credited numbers, "We Shall Overcome" had long been known as the most important protest song in American history, while "Jesse James" was Billy Gashade's historical ballad about the legendary outlaw.

Reception

The Boss's fourteenth studio record only slightly outperformed its predecessor, selling seven hundred thousand units in the U.S. and earning a gold RIAA certification. Meanwhile, critics were overwhelmingly positive in their assessments, with *E! Online* describing it as "quite possibly his best album since *Nebraska*." The *Austin Chronicle* called it "music-making for the sheer joy of it, and that delight overflows in a manner that's truly rare."

"Many who don't like Springsteen may love this. Many who love Springsteen may hate this," wrote *Mojo*. And finally, *Rolling Stone* added, "His most jubilant disc since Born in the U.S.A., and more fun than a tribute to Pete Seeger has any right to be."

As for Seeger, he was quite thrilled by the record and the attention. "It was a great honor," he told *Rolling Stone's* Andy Greene in 2008. "He's an extraordinary person, as well as an extraordinary singer."

We Shall Overcome: The Seeger Sessions continued to perform strongly, earning the Grammy Award for Best Traditional Folk Album in February 2007.

Years before the Seeger Sessions, Springsteen was paying homage to the folk legend on this 1998 tribute album, *Where Have All the Flowers Gone: The Songs of Pete Seeger*. Alongside Springsteen, old friends like Jackson Browne and Bonnie Raitt provided their interpretations of his everlasting songs. *Courtesy of 991.com*

40

Is There Anybody Alive Out There?

Magic

After finishing up work on the *Seeger Sessions* tour in the fall of 2006, Springsteen asked his Atlanta-based producer Brendan O'Brien to fly up to New Jersey that December to listen to a number of rock songs he had written with his next studio album in mind.

"We literally sat in his living room," O'Brien told *Rolling Stone*'s Andy Greene in 2007. "He gauges people's reactions and I have to be as honest with him as I can." O'Brien, who first worked on *The Rising*, helped Springsteen sift through the songs to see what was and what wasn't going to work.

In late February 2007, Springsteen began working on sessions for what would become *Magic* with O'Brien at Southern Tracks Studios. By early March, E Street Band members Garry Tallent, Max Weinberg, and Roy Bittan were summoned to Atlanta to participate in a five-day rehearsal and recording session, with the remaining members—Steve Van Zandt, Nils Lofgren, Danny Federici, Clarence Clemons, Patti Scialfa, and Soozie Tyrell—being brought in as necessary during the next eight weeks.

O'Brien would later explain that managing the *Magic* sessions was easier without all ten members in the room. Drawing on the members as overdubs were required just made more sense. Additionally, Max Weinberg's commitment to "Late Night with Conan O'Brien" meant that he did most of his work over one long weekend.

And when it came time to bring in the Big Man, Springsteen insisted on being in the studio. "I appointed Bruce 'Senior Vice President in charge of Clarence's saxophone,'" O'Brien told Greene. "There's a whole dynamic there that spans decades. I don't even get in the middle of it."

Lyrically, the record was driven predominantly by Springsteen's frustration with the leadership in the United States at the time. "*Magic* was obviously a response to the Bush Administration and the terrible eight years of American history that left us in the shape we are in today," he told Brian Hiatt in late 2009. "That was an angry record about how your country can disappear before your eyes, sort of very quietly in the night."

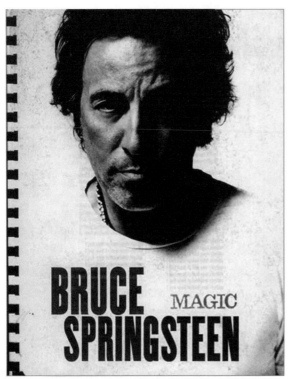

This *Magic* tour program practically replicated the sleeve artwork from The Boss's 2007 studio album.

Author's collection

Essential Tracks

With *Magic*, Springsteen was careful to keep the album tight, making sure it was concise and effective. "[It] moves like a rocket from beginning to end," Jon Landau told *Entertainment Weekly* upon its release. And because of that, the album had a certain playability that even *The Rising* lacked.

"Radio Nowhere"

The lead single from Springsteen's first rock album since *The Rising* was perhaps the most direct, guitar charging anthem he had ever done. He sounds desperate as he pleads for "a thousand guitars" and makes nods to past numbers in the lyrics.

For example, the line "dancing down a dark hole" alludes to 1984's "Dancing in the Dark," while his reference to "misty rain" is repeated from another song off *Born in the U.S.A.*— "Downbound Train."

While one-time Tommy Tutone frontman Tommy Heath was quick to allege that the Boss's lead riff and chord sequence on "Radio Nowhere" were derivative of his 1982 one hit wonder, "867-5309/Jenny" in a *Chicago Tribune* report soon after the single leaked in August 2007, there is no evidence he pursued legal action.

In any event, "Radio Nowhere" was acclaimed and well received, earning Grammy Awards in 2008 for Best Solo Rock Vocal Performance and Best Rock Song.

When asked by Foo Fighters frontman Dave Grohl which song he wished he had written at the MTV Europe Music Awards in 2007, R.E.M. singer Michael Stipe responded, "Radio Nowhere."

"Gypsy Biker"

A memorable harmonica-led number that ranks among the best on *Magic*, it deals with the sad homecoming of a U.S. soldier killed in action during the Iraq War.

"Girls in Their Summer Clothes"

Reminiscent of the lush, Phil Spector–produced pop records of the 1960s, this was the second single from *Magic* and was released on January 15, 2008, but failed to crack the U.S. Top 40. Describing the song to Dan Cairns in the Sunday *London Times*, Springsteen said, "I was interested in having a song where you get this classic image of a late summer, light on, in a small American town. And it's perfect in a way that only occurs in pop songs—when the air is just right, where the sun's sitting a certain way."

A year after its release, Springsteen pulled in a Grammy for the song during the 2009 awards in the Best Rock Song category. "I didn't even know I was up for a Grammy!," he marveled to MTV. "I opened the newspaper on Monday and saw that I had won, and thought, 'Well, that's great!'"

"Magic"

Coins disappear, cards go up sleeves and rabbits come out of hats in this ode to America circa 2006. Springsteen's title track conveys the disillusionment and apprehension he, and millions like him, felt as his country was being steered by tricksters and magicians.

"Last to Die"

The title and refrain from this song were both culled from a 1971 quote from John Kerry, who was then a representative of Vietnam Veterans Against the War. Kerry, of course, went on to become a U.S. senator from Massachusetts and the 2004 Democratic presidential hopeful who Springsteen backed on the *Vote for Change* tour.

As for Kerry's famous quote that inspired the tune? It went like this: "How do you ask a man to be the last man to die in Vietnam? How do you ask a man to be the last man to die for a mistake?"

"It's a tricky bit of business because for me the song has to have a life both outside of its political context and at the same time contain your politics," Springsteen explained to NPR's Steve Inskeep in March 2008. "Otherwise, you're stuck with a headline, or you're stuck on a soap box. And there are times for that, but for me, I want the music to have a variety of lives."

"Long Walk Home"

Initially debuted on tour with the Sessions Band in 2006, this uplifting song balances sadness and optimism. Ranked as the #38 song of 2007 by *Rolling Stone*, Springsteen explained to the *New York Times*' A. O. Scott how "a guy comes back to his town and recognizes nothing and is recognized by nothing.

"That's his experience," Bruce continued. "His world has changed. The things that he thought he knew, the people who he thought he knew, whose ideals he had something in common with, are like strangers. The world that he knew feels totally alien. I think that's what's happened in this country in the past six years."

It was also a commentary on American civil liberties at the time. "I don't need to spiel through the litany," Bruce told Inskeep. "No habeas corpus, the curtailing of civil rights—you realize how easy it is for those ideals to be subverted."

"Terry's Song"

A hidden, heartfelt track added to *Magic* two weeks after it was announced, the song was appended as a tribute to Springsteen's long-running assistant and friend Terry Magovern, who died on July 30—a month after the record had been finalized. Springsteen first played it at his friend's memorial service, which was held at the United Methodist Church of Red Bank on August 2, 2007.

Commercial Success and Critical Acclaim

At fifty-eight, Bruce Springsteen was pleased with his place in the world of music and glad to be free from labels and the absurd imaging that often accompanies pop music. "My take on the whole thing is, by the time you're my age, the race is over; these are the victory laps," he told London's *Sunday Times*. "I make any kind of music I want to make, you know? There are no rules—they're not waiting for my record at Top 40 radio next week. I'm not worried about whether I'm going to be competing with 50 Cent. All that pressure is off."

Just the same, when the Boss's fifteenth album debuted at #1 following its October 2nd release, it was one hell of a victory lap. As Springsteen's eighth #1 in the U.S., it was bumped from the top slot to #2 after one week by Kid Rock's *Rock n Roll Jesus* album, but quickly returned to #1 before sliding down to #12 in its fourth week of release.

All told, *Magic*—preceded by the lead single "Radio Nowhere"—sold more than one million copies in the United States, with a total global sales tally of just under five million units. The record was also named the #2 album of 2007 by *Rolling Stone*.

Mojo heralded it "as a State of the Union address disguised as a pop record," *Entertainment Weekly* called it "his best since *The River*," while the *Los Angeles Times* added, "it's the way Springsteen injects his American bible stories with the air of disbelief that makes *Magic* a truly mature and memorable album."

Clear Channel Controversy

Although Springsteen was a classic rock giant who helped conservative radio monopoly Clear Channel pull in millions in advertising revenue, a Fox News report released in October 2007 suggested that the company had told its classic rock radio stations throughout the U.S. to not play any music from *Magic* because it did not agree with the album's political slant. The company denied the report and countered by saying that its radio stations gave Springsteen's latest record more love than its competing stations in the format.

Magic Tour Highlights EP

Released digitally via iTunes on July 15, 2008, this four-track live EP consisted of matching videos from the E Street Band's 2008 tour and was issued to benefit the Danny Federici Melanoma Fund. The *Magic Tour Highlights* offering included "4th of July, Asbury Park (Sandy)" from March 20, 2008, in Indianapolis. It was Federici's last live performance with the E Street Band before he died.

Launched with "Always a Friend," the Alejandro Escovedo/Chuck Prophet song was tracked on April 14, 2008, in Houston and featured assistance by Escovedo. The release also featured a collaborative recording of "The Ghost of Tom Joad" with Rage Against the Machine guitarist Tom Morello.

Finally, the Byrds' Roger McGuinn joined the E Street Band in Orlando on April 23 for a performance of "Turn! Turn! Turn!," which was, of course, written by Pete Seeger.

41

Sunrise Come, I Climb the Ladder

Working on a Dream

Fourteen months after the politically steered *Magic*, Springsteen stunned fans by releasing a new album. For the first time since 1973, when he issued his first two records in one calendar year, the Boss was giving his audience a one-two punch of rock music in quick succession.

Springsteen later said that when he was completing the tracks for his 2007 album with Brendan O'Brien in Atlanta, he felt like he wasn't done writing. The producer encouraged him to keep writing, and the Boss pumped out five new songs—"This Life," "My Lucky Day," "Life Itself," "Good Eye," and "Tomorrow Never Knows"—in his Georgia hotel in just one week that became the impetus for a new album.

With *Working on a Dream*, Springsteen decided to make a rock record about transience and love. His songs of mortality and devotion embraced pop music on a grander scale than ever before, as he translated the sounds of classy, classic 1960s pop—from the Beach Boys to the Byrds. The net result was a lushly crafted collection.

Dream was tracked during breaks in the roadwork that supported *Magic* in a fashion similar to that project. Springsteen first built the foundations for the material with Bittan, Tallent, and Weinberg. The rest of the E Street Band was brought in to record their parts as the eleven songs took shape. A twelfth song, "The Wrestler," which was written for the Mickey Rourke movie of the same name, was added as a bonus track.

In an official statement announcing the record on November 17, 2008, Springsteen said, "I hope *Working on a Dream* has caught the energy of the band, fresh off the road from some of the most exciting shows we've ever done. All the songs were written quickly. We usually used one of our first few takes, and we all had a blast making this one from beginning to end.

Essential Tracks

"I realized, I do love those big sweeping melodies and the romanticism, and I haven't allowed myself much of it in the past," Springsteen told the *New York*

Times of his great pursuit of pop hooks. "When you have a little vein you haven't touched, it's full."

Perhaps Steve Van Zandt—who saw *Working on a Dream* as part of a trilogy with '02's *The Rising* and *Magic*—put it best when he assessed Bruce's talent as a pop songwriter. "In a different era he would have been in the Brill Building," Van Zandt told Jon Pareles.

"Outlaw Pete"

"That was me throwing it back to *The Wild and the Innocent*," Springsteen told Brian Hiatt of the eight-minute operetta that opened the album. Critics compared its riff to the one on a 1979 Kiss song, "I Was Made for Lovin' You."

Its lyrics wove the tale of a character who could not escape his past and must come to terms with his misdeeds to find some peace. The song's subject accepts that he will carry his sins to the grave, acknowledging, "We can't undo the things we've done."

"My Lucky Day"

This contagious, uplifting number first hooked fans of Springsteen on his new, pop-driven *Dream* when it became available for download on Amazon.com on December 1, 2008. The song's release came just one week after the title cut from its parent album was made available for free download via iTunes.

"Working on a Dream"

Released in advance of its namesake album on November 24 as a free one-day download on iTunes and Springsteen's official website, the title number at times evoked Creedence Clearwater Revival. The positive and inspiring song, which debuted live during the November 2 "Change We Need Rally" in Cleveland, Ohio, was one of the final stops in Barack Obama's successful 2008 presidential campaign.

"Queen of the Supermarket"

Delivered in a style reminiscent of early '60s soul bard Ben E. King, this ode to falling in love at the grocery store is one of the unexpected surprises found on *Working on a Dream*.

"They opened up this big, beautiful supermarket near where we lived," Springsteen revealed to *The Guardian*. "I hadn't been in one in a while and I thought, 'This place is spectacular! This place is . . . it's a fantasy land!'

"I started looking around and hmmm—the subtext in here is so heavy!," he continued. "It's like, 'Do people really want to shop in this store or do they just want to screw on the floor?'"

"Life Itself"

Released a month ahead of *Working on a Dream* as a free daily download from Amazon.com on December 28. A belated Christmas gift for Boss disciples, the dreamy, Byrds-inspired number was the third advance single—an unheard-of marketing approach at the dawn of 2009.

"Kingdom of Days"

Focusing on a couple aging together, Springsteen wrote this song to Patti Scialfa—his partner for twenty years—as a testament of his undying love. Talking about the record, he asserted his belief in a transcendence of time when in the presence of somebody he cared deeply for.

"The Last Carnival"

Considered a sequel of sorts to 1973's "Wild Billy's Circus Story," this song was written in homage to Danny Federici, who played with Springsteen for forty years and died in April 2008.

Springsteen wrote the song to come to terms with his passing, explaining to journalist Mark Hagen, "He was a part of that sound of the boardwalk the band grew up with and that's something that's going to be missing now."

The elegy featured Jason Federici playing his father's accordion as Springsteen sang, "We'll be riding the train without you tonight/The train that keeps on moving."

"The Wrestler"

This pensive number was written for the acclaimed film of the same name starring Mickey Rourke and directed by Darren Aronofsky. Springsteen penned the stripped-down number about the washed-up wrestler at the request of his actor and friend. Although it won a Golden Globe Award, it was consequently shunned by the Academy Awards, where it wasn't even nominated.

Critical and Commercial Response

The marketing push behind Springsteen's sixteenth album was sizable and began in late 2008, when a ninety- second snippet of "Working on a Dream" was aired during the November 16 Sunday Night Washington Redskins/Baltimore Ravens game on NBC Television. The aforementioned digital single release of the song, plus the releases "My Lucky Day" and "Life Itself," helped sustain public interest until the record's official street date of January 27, 2009.

Although the album leaked onto the Internet on January 12, it still sold strongly, debuting at #1 in early February. Eventually selling six hundred thousand copies in the United States and over three million globally, the record was still a success at a time when new record sales for major artists—including heritage rock act U2—were lackluster.

Reviews were mixed. *Los Angeles Times* critic Ann Powers wrote, "The best thing that can be said about *Working on a Dream* is that it's boisterously scatter-brained, exhilaratingly bad." *Chicago Tribune* writer Greg Kot was also not a fan, writing "On about half the new songs, he trots out the kind of facile imagery that would've gotten him tossed out of a Nickelback songwriting seminar."

Haters aside, *Rolling Stone*'s Hiatt penned a five-star review, while *Entertainment Weekly* gave it a solid "A." In the U.K., *NME* raved, "his 16th (16th!) studio album, sees him eschew such stylings and instead go for broke on telling tales and flashing his soul."

The *Los Angeles Times* review landed somewhere awful and awesome. It read, "Only a great artist could make an album that's at once so stirring and so slight."

42

Your Loving Grace Surrounds Me

On the Road from *The Rising* to the *Wrecking Ball*

The Rising Tour (2002–2003)

Before Bruce and the E Street Band began official road activity in support of *The Rising* in August 2002, they held ten days of rehearsals the preceding month at the Expo Theater in Fort Monmouth. From there, the band shifted into the Convention Hall in Asbury Park for four rehearsal shows.

On the morning of the third warm-up gig, held on July 30th, the E Street Band was broadcast playing new songs across North America on NBC's *Today Show*. "The Rising," "Lonesome Day," and "Into the Fire" plus "Glory Days" were all broadcast in the 8 a.m. hour. Another song, "Empty Sky," was taped for that evening's *Nightline* broadcast on ABC-TV. Two nights later, Springsteen played "The Rising" for David Letterman's CBS audience.

Barnstorming

When the tour got underway on August 7 at The Meadowlands Arena, Springsteen played a large chunk of his new album. The first leg avoided lengthy residencies as he and the band barnstormed arenas across North America and Europe, hitting forty-six cities during the first leg in order to maximize publicity and boost album sales.

Springsteen's sense of humor was alive and well when he rolled into Oregon on August 20 and cracked to the audience, "Portland . . . I got married here once. A long time ago. What was I thinking?" By the time the trek was in full swing, he began to rotate in surprises like "The Ties That Bind," "Candy's Room," "Racing in the Street" and "I'm a Rocker," "Mary Queen of Arkansas," and "Incident on 57th Street." In Chicago, Pearl Jam's Eddie Vedder sang with the Boss on "My Hometown."

On October 14, a two-week Western European trek got underway in Paris. While *The Rising* continued to anchor the show, with the title track, "Lonesome Day," "Waitin' on a Miracle" and "Mary's Place" among the new peaks. As the dates progressed, "Spirits in the Night," "Stand on It," "The Promise," and "The River" found their way into Springsteen's set. These shows closed at Wembley Arena in London with "Jackson Cage," a solo piano version of "Incident on 57th Street," "Night," and "Does This Bus Stop at 82nd Street?"

A second leg got underway days later, launching at the American Airlines Center in Dallas on November 3 with the Eagles' Don Henley joining the E Street Band on Bobby Fuller's "I Fought the Law." Yet just days into the tour, gigs in Austin, Columbus, and Indianapolis had to be postponed when Clarence Clemons required emergency surgery for a detached retina.

A week later, on November 12, the band was back in action in Cincinnati. The show marked the first concert with festival seating in the city since 1979, when eleven people were trampled to death at a concert by the Who. Four days later in Greensboro, Springsteen fell during a performance of "Waiting on a Sunny Day" and cut his arm.

At the show in Birmingham, Alabama, on November 19, singer/songwriter Emmylou Harris was asked to duet with Springsteen on "My Hometown." Four nights later in Miami, U2's Bono and the Eurythmics' Dave Stewart joined the E Street Band for a memorable rendition of "Because the Night" that was matched by a second cameo, as Dion came out to sing "If I Should Fall Behind" with Springsteen.

A weeklong Thanksgiving week break gave way to December '02 gigs in Pittsburgh, Toronto, Charlotte, Columbia, Albany and Columbus, where an obligatory "Santa Claus Is Coming to Town" made the encores. The tour leg wrapped in Indianapolis on December 17 at the Conseco Fieldhouse, but Springsteen still wasn't finished rocking. Along with the E Street Band, he performed at a private holiday party for the *Rising* tour crew and family on December 22 at the Stone Pony.

Second Leg

The second leg of the tour got started on February 28 in Duluth, Georgia, a week after Springsteen was given several Grammy trophies for his first rock album in a decade. Taking the stage, he cracked, "I'd like to thank absolutely fucking nobody."

At the Richmond Coliseum stop on March 6, the Boss's former Steel Mill bandmate Robbin Thompson and Bruce Hornsby both joined him on a cover of "Let's Go, Let's Go, Let's Go," a cover of the 1960 hit by Hank Ballard, who had recently passed. He had considered covering the Steel Mill number "Guilty," but after attempting it during sound check, he was unable to remember it.

In addition to a rare cover of the Beatles' "Tell Me Why" in Atlantic City and a surprise version of "Blinded by the Light," Springsteen performed

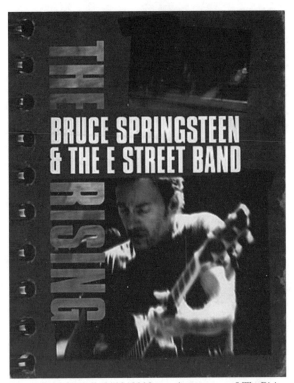

The E Street Band's 2002–2003 tour in support of *The Rising* was a massive success. Springsteen sold out an amazing ten nights at New Jersey's Giants Stadium.   *Author's Collection*

"Bobby Jean" in Providence, Rhode Island, on March 10 in memory of the one hundred people who died during Great White show at the Rhode Island nightclub, the Station, the previous month.

A relatively uneventful but triumphant trip Down Under during the last ten days of March found the E Street Band playing in Australian stadiums in Melbourne, Sydney and Brisbane, before headlining a massive gig in Auckland, New Zealand. Back on North American soil, the *Rising* Tour caravanned from Sacramento to Vancouver and across Canada, breaking after its show at Bell Centre in Montreal.

By May 6, however, the band was again in Europe, playing a pair of gigs in Rotterdam. Rotating the material kept things fresh, as they played unexpected numbers like 1978's "Something in the Night" and 1980's "Sherry Darling." The E Street Band opened its May 24 show at Stade de France playing CCR's timeless "Who'll Stop the Rain" to the rain-soaked Paris crowd. He treated crowds in London and Manchester to "Racing in the Street" and "4th of July, Asbury Park (Sandy)," respectively.

Sparks Fly at Giants Stadium

Springsteen launched the last leg of the *Rising* tour at Giants Stadium in East Rutherford with a seven-night run beginning on July 15 that resulted in an additional three August shows being added. When the rains came on July 18, he again opened with CCR, and rocked with Garland Jeffreys on "96 Tears." Three nights later, Bruce brought out Vini Lopez to play drums on "Spirit in the Night."

At Pittsburgh's PNC Park, Lofgren, Federici, and Bittan donned accordions to open the gig with "Take Me out to the Ballgame." Later that night, local star Joe Grushecky and his son Johnny joined in on "Glory Days."

"Lost in Flood" was played during the E Street Band's show at Lincoln Financial Field in Philadelphia on August 8. Two nights later at the same venue, Springsteen opened with his then-unreleased classic "From Small Things (Big Things One Day Come)" and played a fitting and full band take on "Streets of Philadelphia."

Following gigs in Chicago, San Francisco, and Los Angeles stadiums, he was back in East Rutherford. These E Street Band homecoming shows on August 28, 30 and 31, which were added after the success of the July sellouts, were outright celebrations.

On the first night, Springsteen brought out his Jersey Shore rock friend Bobby Bandiera; the second found him rocking with Marah's Serge and Dave Bielanko on "Raise Your Hand" and singing "Across the Border" with Emmylou Harris. The third and final night in Jersey, the Boss played the *Tracks* number "Cynthia" live for the first- time. "Jersey Girl" also made the set.

At Boston's Fenway Park, Peter Wolf joined the band for a closing encore of the Standells' "Dirty Water" on both nights. In Toronto, Springsteen played "My Ride's Here" in memory of the late Warren Zevon. Shows on September 13 and 14 in Washington and Chapel Hill were launched with "I Walk the Line," in tribute to the recently departed Johnny Cash.

A trio of gigs at Shea Stadium in The Bronx concluded the tour and were marked by an emotional dedication of "Into the Fire" on the second night to a firefighter who died in the line of duty. According to Springsteen, the hero had planned to attend the October 3 show for his forty-first birthday. On a lighter note, Mets pitcher Al Leiter joined in on tambourine during "Rosalita." The last night of the tour closed with Gary U.S. Bonds taking the stage for "Quarter to Three," but the final gig's best guest appearance goes to Bob Dylan, who joined Bruce for a surprise performance of "Highway 61 Revisited."

When the tour was said and done, *Billboard Boxscore* reported grosses of $222 million. According to a *Rolling Stone* report, Springsteen managed to keep a bigger share of concert gross receipts than almost anyone else in the business, due to better deals with promoters and venues. He also kept his overhead low by skipping out on epic stage designs.

Vote for Change Tour (2004)

After helping his wife Patti on a pair of songs that made it to her second solo album, *23rd Street Lullaby*, Springsteen joined her band for a pair of industry showcase performances in April 2004 at the Hit Factory, providing guitar and backing vocals on "Love (Stand Up)" and "As Long as I (Can Be with You)." He also joined her on the latter during headlining shows that September at the Paramount Theatre in Asbury Park, the Bowery Ballroom in New York, and the Roxy Theatre in Hollywood.

On October 1 in Philadelphia, Springsteen began a two week, multi-artist *Vote for Change* tour. Presented by MoveOn.org in support of the liberal political action group America Coming Together, the trek included concerts in swing states that motivated attendees to exercise their right to vote. Although the caravan—which featured Pearl Jam, R.E.M., Bright Eyes, John Fogerty, Tracy Chapman, the Dixie Chicks, and Neil Young—was formally nonpartisan, it was evident that all of the acts on the bill supported Democratic nominee John Kerry. For Springsteen's part, he held several private tour rehearsals in late September with the E Street Band at Convention Hall, including one with former Creedence Clearwater Revival frontman Fogerty.

Its political message aside, onstage Springsteen collaborations were as exhilarating as they were unusual, whether it was the Boss with R.E.M. (on "Man on the Moon") and Fogerty (on "Fortunate Son") in Philly, the E Street Band with the Dixie Chicks (on Patti Smith's "People Have the Power") in Detroit, or Springsteen with Neil Young (on Dylan's "All Along the Watchtower" and Nick Lowe's "(What's So Funny 'Bout) Peace Love and Understanding?") in St. Paul.

At the October 11 gig at the MCI Centre in Washington, D.C., stars like John Mellencamp, Bonnie Raitt, James Taylor, Pearl Jam, the Dave Matthews Band, and Jackson Browne also took the stage. On the tour's final stop at the Continental Airlines Arena two nights later, Springsteen played with Browne on his classic "Running on Empty." Browne returned the favor on "Racing in the Street." Earlier in the show, Eddie Vedder sang with Springsteen on "Darkness on the Edge of Town" and John Kerry's adopted campaign theme, "No Surrender."

As triumphant as those shows felt, earning a significant amount of media coverage and raising $10 million for America Coming Together, Springsteen was adamant about getting Bush out of office in 2004 and attended a number of Kerry's "Fresh Start for America" Rallies.

In late October he played "The Promised Land" and "No Surrender" with just his guitar at rallies in Madison, Columbus, Miami, Florida, and Cleveland. Unfortunately, for all of his dedication and hard work on behalf of John Kerry, Bush won the election.

Devils and Dust Tour (2005)

Launched on April 25, 2005, at the Fox Theatre in Detroit in support of Springsteen's latest acoustic record, the seven-month concert tour featured him performing solo, using his guitar, harmonica, a piano, and other instruments. As with the shows on his *Ghost of Tom Joad* trek, for this tour he first considered taking a band of musicians, including Nils Lofgren, but he soon decided he'd be better on his own.

"Nils and some other folks came in for rehearsals to give me a sense of if I wanted to go with something bigger," Springsteen told *Rolling Stone*. "But what tends to be dramatic is either the full band or you onstage by yourself. Playing alone creates a sort of drama and intimacy for the audience: They know it's just them and just you."

By stripping down, Springsteen had to reimagine the songs, which were recorded with a band of musicians. He rose to the challenge and set out on a North American tour of mid-sized theaters. At some venues, attendees were given a paper handout explaining that the evening's show was acoustic and "set in a theater style arrangement." Springsteen prohibited seating during the songs, and concessions were closed during the performance.

He asked for quiet at the outset of the intimate shows and warned fans to turn their phones off, at times even threatening them. At one New Jersey show late in the tour he told the crowd, "Don't fuck with me!"

The material was culled largely from his new album, *The Rising*, and *Nebraska*, but each evening featured a number of piano selections, including favorites like "Racing in the Street," "For You," "Backstreets" and "The River." Springsteen also performed rarities like "Zero and Blind Terry," "Santa Ana," and the unreleased early 1970s surprise "Song to the Orphans." While his piano playing was "perfectly imperfect" as short-lived music magazine *Harp* wrote, the loyalists who made up the bulk of his audiences for these gigs didn't seem to mind.

Fans of the E Street Band's records left the shows with mixed feelings. Clapping and singing along was discouraged as he played "I'm on Fire" on banjo. At times, the *Devils and Dust* tour felt uneven; at other moments, it was difficult listening. Springsteen's final encore at most of the performances was most perplexing. Following acoustic guitar renditions of "The Promised Land" and "Does This Bus Stop at 82nd Street," Springsteen closed down his concerts by covering Suicide's "Dream Baby Dream" on a pump organ, with a dissonant, synthesizer accompaniment coming from offstage.

A two-month European tour quickly followed, as Springsteen was able to travel light, hopping a flight from Boston to Madrid, canvassing Western Europe until late June. On his return trip to the U.S., Springsteen played an unexpected acoustic set inside Iceland's Keflavik Airport in the middle of the night.

A month of U.S. shows—typically in the East—got underway in the middle of July, which led to a six-week break. A fourth leg began on October 4 in Asbury Park at the Paramount Theatre, with the Boss donating all proceeds to the Jersey Coast chapter of the American Red Cross. Despite the inconclusive reviews, Springsteen managed to book his show into arenas in Rochester, Hartford, Uniondale, Chicago, Providence, Richmond, and Norfolk. In Boston and Philadelphia, the acoustic show demand resulted in two sellouts each at the TD Banknorth Garden and the Wachovia Spectrum.

Clearly the shows had evolved, with Springsteen reinterpreting more of his fans' favorites along the way, resulting in two solo shows at the Continental Airlines Arena and a pair of final gigs in Trenton at the Sovereign Bank Arena.

If ticket sales were sluggish in some markets, Springsteen could still pack his core fans in along the Eastern Seaboard. European sales were equally strong, with forty-six of sixty-five shows listed as sellouts. Simply put, the Boss—who had little overhead—grossed more than $33 million for six months of work.

Bruce Springsteen with the *Seeger Sessions* Band Tour (2006)

Billed as "an all-new evening of gospel, folk and blues," Springsteen's tour in support of *We Shall Overcome: The Seeger Sessions* got underway on April 20, 2006, with four consecutive rehearsal shows at Asbury Park's Convention Hall. As with the *Rising* tour, he was filmed for morning television, this time appearing on ABC's *Good Morning America* to promote the big band folk music record.

The official tour launch occurred on April 30 at the New Orleans Jazz and Heritage Festival. Much like Pete Seeger, Springsteen let the crowd—which was recovering from the previous September's devastating Hurricane Katrina—know that he was angry about the government's handling of Katrina in the days and months that followed the disaster.

Springsteen opted to launch the first leg of the tour in Europe. It got underway at the Point in Dublin in early May and wrapped in Stockholm before the month was out. The shows found him interspersing revised versions of songs like "You Can Look (But You Better Not Touch," "Adam Raised a Cain," "My City of Ruins," "Ramrod," and "Open All Night" with his interpretations of Pete Seeger's material.

Especially significant was the Sessions Band's rendering of "Bring 'Em Home," which Springsteen had tailored as a musical commentary on the Iraq War. He also delivered Blind Alfred Reed's "How Can a Poor Man Stand Such Times and Live?" with new verses that spoke to the plight of New Orleans residents in the wake of Hurricane Katrina.

The Boss continued to delve into his own material ("Atlantic City," "Into the Fire") as the tour made it back to North American soil. His itinerary began on May 27 in Mansfield, Massachusetts, and wrapped with a pair of shows at the PNC Bank Arts Center in Holmdel a month later.

Cameos of note included Joan Baez joining in on "Pay Me My Money Down" at San Francisco's Sleep Train Pavilion. At the Tweeter Center in Camden, New Jersey, Southside Johnny and Joe Grushecky sang along on the same number.

Still, the North American shows were not the sell-outs Springsteen had been used to during the past thirty years of performing. Some crowds were noticeably light. In Chicago, the outdoor venue was only half full.

The Boss went back to Europe—where there was greater interest—for the tour's third leg, playing twenty-seven shows in six weeks. Launched in Bologna, Italy in early October, the shows during this run included a new song, "American Land," plus the addition of more catalog numbers, including "The River," "Growin' Up," "Bobby Jean," "Factory," and "The Promised Land."

Springsteen also delivered a rendition of the song "Love of the Common People," which was popularized in 1983 by blue-eyed soul singer Paul Young. At Wembley Arena in London he unveiled another new song, "A Long Walk Home," about his frustration with the Bush/Cheney administration.

Magic Tour (2007–2008)

In late August 2007, news emerged from the Springsteen camp that his new E Street Band album, *Magic*, would be supported by a world tour. The Boss reassured fans he was ready to rock after his four-year foray into folk music. When asked by *Backstreets* if this was a farewell tour considering the aging of its members, Springsteen—then fifty-seven—snapped, "I envision the band carrying on for many, many, many more years. There ain't gonna be any farewell tour. I'll never do that, man—you're only gonna know that when you don't see me no more."

E Street Rock

Rehearsals began with the E Street Band on September 10 in Asbury Park, and after two weeks of closed practices, the band offered up tickets for two dry runs later in the month. The public unveiling of the *Magic* songs like "Radio Nowhere" and "Gypsy Biker" was matched by the first performance of "Thundercrack" in more than three decades. On the second night, Patti Scialfa was out in front of the group for one number—a performance of "Town Called Heartbreak"—from her recent album *Play It as It Lays*.

"We start all our tours in this building," Springsteen told the *Sunday Times* of his loyalty to the Paramount Theatre. "I guess I've been coming here since I was 16 or 17. I saw the Who here, on their first American tour, when they wrecked their instruments, and it was shocking."

"I've stood next to [Steve] since we were 16," he continued, marveling at how all of the original members were still alive and playing together each night. We had all the ups and downs that other bands have had, but we

This poster was sold at dates on Springsteen's 2008 tour with the E Street Band in support of *Magic*.   *Author's Collection*

really took care of one another. I think when I was young I felt the tug of chaos in my house, so I wanted a stable life. I like that long chain of experience."

Springsteen brought his *Magic* to Rockefeller Plaza in New York on September 28 to perform live on NBC's *Today* show, performing "The Promised Land," "Radio Nowhere," "Livin' in the Future," "My Home Town," "Long Walk Home," "Last to Die," and "Night" on the nationally broadcast morning show. That night the group played a special benefit gig/public rehearsal at the Continental Airlines Arena in East Rutherford before heading up to Hartford for the first of one hundred official shows.

The first leg meshed new classics like "Girls in Their Summer Clothes" with classics like "Born to Run" and obscurities like "Thundercrack." In Philadelphia, Springsteen played "Candy's Room" and "Cadillac Ranch," while his Chicago audience heard "Spirit in the Night" and "Thunder Road." To promote the tour and the new record, three songs ("Radio Nowhere," "Night," and "Lonesome Day") from Springsteen's October 10 East Rutherford show were released as official Internet downloads. At Scotiabank Place in Ottawa, Ontario, Win Butler and Regine Chassagne of modern rock act Arcade Fire joined in on "State Trooper" and performed their own single, "Keep the Car Running," at Springsteen's insistence.

By the time the E Street Band was in Oakland, it had played vintage numbers like "Two Hearts" and "Racing in the Street." During the L.A. Sports Arena gig on October 30, Springsteen dusted off a rare "Kitty's Back." Five days later in Cleveland, he treated fans to "It's Hard to Be a Saint in the City."

Throughout November, he continued to dig deep, playing "Growin' Up," "4th of July, Asbury Park (Sandy)," and "The E Street Shuffle." At the last date of the first U.S. leg in Boston, Peter Wolf helped out on "Tenth Avenue Freeze-Out." The concert would be the last complete performance with Danny Federici, who needed to undergo medical treatment for melanoma.

Europe '07

When the E Street Band's 2007 European tour dates got underway in Madrid, it marked the first time the band had toured without Federici. Charles Giordano— who had been in the Sessions Band—was asked to join the group as a touring member while Federici worked on beating melanoma. There was another noticeable absence as Patti Scialfa stayed behind—as she had on many of the preceding North American dates—to look after the Springsteen children, who were now teenagers who required stability and the guidance of a parent at home. To augment her often intermittent vocal role, multi-instrumentalist Soozie Tyrell was with the band on all of the *Magic* dates.

The tour was a quick success as the Boss canvassed Spain and Italy, although a gig in the Netherlands was rescheduled by a day because he had a cold. Attendees from this point forward got the December show staple "Santa Claus Is Coming to Town." By the time the leg wrapped on December 19 at The O2

Arena in London, Springsteen was ready to be home with his family. For the first time in years, he kept his holiday charity performances to a minimum.

Hartford to Barcelona

After a two-month pause, the E Street Band was back at work on February 28, kicking off its tour opener in Hartford. On this leg, audience requests via homemade signs and banners were not just honored, they were encouraged. "Rosalita," "Racing in the Street," and "Tenth Avenue Freeze-Out" were just some of the sign requests that Springsteen played.

Fans were kept guessing from show to show, as the band played exemplary numbers "Sherry Darling," "Streets of Fire," "Cadillac Ranch," "Glory Days," "Lost in the Flood," "Bobby Jean," "Detroit Medley," and "Out in the Street" in different cities.

Special guests included Bright Eyes brainchild Conor Oberst—who first befriended Springsteen on the *Vote for Change* tour—on "Thunder Road" at the Omaha tour stop on March 14. Three nights later, jazz bassist Richard Davis was brought onstage in Milwaukee to perform his original part on "Meeting Across the River."

Finally, Danny Federici returned to the band at the Conseco Fieldhouse in Indianapolis on March 20 for what sadly became his last performance with the E Street Band. Federici played on many of the songs he helped make famous, including "Asbury Park (Sandy)," "Backstreets," "Kitty's Back," "Born to Run," "Dancing in the Dark," and "American Land."

A pair of early April shows at the Honda Center in Anaheim included the guest guitar work of Rage Against the Machine's Tom Morello, playing on a newly arranged hard-rocking take on "The Ghost of Tom Joad." On April 13 at the American Airlines Center in Dallas, Jon Bon Jovi came out to sing on "Glory Days." The next night in Houston, Springsteen's Texas friends Joe Ely and Alejandro Escovedo joined the band.

That gig at Toyota Center was also significant in that it marked the first live performance of "Terry's Song," which Springsteen dedicated to his late friend Terry Magovern on what would have been his sixty-eighth birthday. Unfortunately, the mourning resumed four days later when Springsteen learned that Federici succumbed to cancer on April 17, 2008.

Federici's death prompted two shows in Florida to be rescheduled so that the band and crew could make it home to his funeral at the United Methodist Church in Red Bank on April 21. After a moving eulogy—which Springsteen made available on his official website in tribute to his fallen friend—he played three songs, "4th of July, Asbury Park (Sandy)," "Across the Border," and "If I Should Fall Behind" in his memory.

The next night he was back onstage in Tampa, with tribute film footage of Federici showing during "Blood Brothers" with Scialfa briefly on hand.

Springsteen played "Backstreets," "Growin' Up," and others in homage to Federici.

As the tour progressed, the Boss would regularly play an older song or two—such as "Spirit in the Night," "Wild Billy's Circus Story," and "It's Hard to Be a Saint in the City"—at each show.

Three weeks after wrapping the U.S. leg in Sunrise, Florida, Bruce and the E Street Band had traveled to Dublin, where the roadwork got underway at RDS Arena. On the first night, May 22, Southside Johnny Lyon came out to sing with the band on "Tenth Avenue Freeze-Out."

As the tour continued, Springsteen fueled his show with obscurities like "From Small Things (Big Things One Day Come)," "Held Up Without a Gun" (not played since 1980), and Eddie Cochran's "Summertime Blues" (not played live since '81).

He even played "Santa Claus Is Coming to Town" at a July 11 gig in Helsinki!

After a long absence, Patti Scialfa returned to the band for the final four shows of the European leg in Spain, playing shows in San Sebastian, Madrid, and Barcelona.

Springsteen Had a Homecoming

The third U.S. leg of the Boss's *Magic* tour began on July 27, 2008 in East Rutherford, New Jersey. Three Giants Stadium gigs were held over five nights, with emphasis on E Street Band classics like "Tenth Avenue Freeze Out," "Rosalita," "Blinded by the Light," and "Brilliant Disguise."

At the show on July 28, Bruce and Patti's daughter Jessica came out during "Girls in Their Summer Clothes," and she—along with some friends and Garry Tallent's daughter—was also invited onstage for the encore, "Twist and Shout." For the latter, singer Jesse Malin and Marah's Dave Bielanko also joined in. Max Weinberg's son, Jay Weinberg, got to sit in on drums during "Born to Run."

Old covers like "Little Latin Lupe Lu," "Who'll Stop the Rain," "You Can't Sit Down," "Double Shot (of My Baby's Love)," "I Fought the Law," "Then She Kissed Me," and "Boom Boom" all showed up in sets during the next six weeks. In Richmond on August 18, Springsteen stunned the crowd by playing "Crush on You" for the first time since the *River* tour.

Following the final date of the official tour routing, the E Street Band were hired as the featured act at the Harley Davidson 105th Anniversary Festival. Springsteen played his motorcycle-influenced numbers like "Gypsy Biker" and "Racing in the Street"—and brought out Danny Federici's son Jason to play accordion on "4th of July, Asbury Park (Sandy)" before breaking into the Steppenwolf classic "Born to Be Wild." The show, at the Roadhouse at the Lakefront in Milwaukee, closed with a cover of Sam the Sham and the Pharaohs' 1965 hit "Wooly Bully."

Before he left the stage, Springsteen told the audience of motorcycle enthusiasts, "We just had the greatest tour of our lives," adding, "We'll be seein' ya . . .

we're only just getting started." They also had a massive payday, grossing over $5 million from that appearance and more than $235 million in a little more than twelve months.

Working on a Dream Tour (2009)

Not only were fans of the Boss elated to have two new albums within fourteen months, but the news that Springsteen and the E Street Band were planning to head back out on the road in April 2009 after just a six-month break recalled his 1970s and 1980s work ethic.

Fifty-Nine and Feelin' Fine

Springsteen, fifty-nine, seemed tireless, delivering three-hour shows to fans from the start of the tour.

"Onstage I can't noticeably say I feel any different than I did in 1985," he told the *New York Times* in 2009. In preparation for his North American shows that spring and a European commitment that summer, Springsteen gathered the E Street Band for rehearsals at the Paramount Theatre beginning March 11. But because of Max Weinberg's existing commitment to Conan O'Brien—who was set to take over *The Tonight Show* from Jay Leno—the extensive rehearsals found Springsteen and the group working with Max's drumming son, Jay Weinberg.

Springsteen turned sixty toward the tail end of his 2009 tour in support of *Working on a Dream*. This poster was sold on that tour, which wrapped late in the year with a run of full-album shows, including complete performances of his first six rock albums.

Author's Collection

The plan would be for Max to make most shows, but in the event he couldn't leave Los Angeles—where O'Brien's show had moved—to meet the band, Jay would be prepared to sub for his father. In preparation, on some nights, the younger Weinberg would alternate with his dad on certain numbers.

The tour itself got underway on April 1 at the HP Pavilion in San Jose with set opener "Badlands" being one constant for the first leg. The sign requests continued to be popular, with Springsteen breaking out "Growin' Up," "Thunder Road," "Because the Night," "Sherry Darling," "Rosalita," and "I'm a Rocker," among others.

In addition to songs from the new album—like the title cut, "Outlaw Pete," "The Wrestler," and "Kingdom of Days"— the band also played "It's Hard to Be a Saint in the City," "The Ties That Bind," "The E Street Shuffle," and "Racing in the Street" as the tour moved eastward.

At a pair of shows in Los Angeles in mid-April, Rage Against the Machine guitarist Tom Morello was again present for electric performances of *The Ghost of Tom Joad*. During the second Sports Arena gig, Social Distortion frontman Mike Ness played with the E Street Band on his own punk classic "Bad Luck," before joining in on "The Rising."

Back east in Boston on April 21, Springsteen led the group through his first rendition of ZZ Top's "I'm Bad, I'm Nationwide" since 1984. The next night, local punk favorites the Dropkick Murphys joined Springsteen for "American Land" and "Glory Days" as that band's Tim Brennan proposed marriage to his girlfriend from the stage. During a "stump the band" segment, someone in the crowd requested the Ramones' "I Wanna Be Sedated," and the Boss obliged.

Before the North American leg wrapped with a pair of shows at the Izod Center in East Rutherford in late May, Springsteen and the E Street Band played fabulously, regardless of which Weinberg was on the drum stool. Cranking out the Troggs' "Wild Thing," the Clash's "London Calling," the McCoys' "Hang on Sloopy," the Soul Survivors' "Expressway to Your Heart," the Kinks' "You Really Got Me," the Who's "My Generation," the Rascals' "Good Lovin'," Tommy James and the Shondells' "Mony Mony," and Bob Dylan's "Like a Rolling Stone," Springsteen seemed to be enjoying himself immensely.

Unfortunately, many shows were played without Patti Scialfa—including shows close to home in Philadelphia and East Rutherford. She had fallen off her horse, and due to her injuries and her family responsibilities at home, she only appeared occasionally.

From Europe to Bonnaroo and Back

Scialfa was also absent from all of the shows on the ensuing European summer tour, which got underway with a performance at Holland's Pinkpop Festival on May 30. At this show, Springsteen was joined on "Thunder Road" by the Killers' Brandon Flowers. During the first seven shows in Sweden and Norway, Jay Weinberg played with the band.

A planned break brought Springsteen stateside for a headlining performance on June 13, 2009, at the Bonnaroo Festival in Manchester, Tennessee. Max Weinberg played the first half of the show, with Jay taking care of the second part. For the first time ever, Evan Springsteen joined his dad onstage, playing acoustic guitar on "American Land." Sign requests of "Santa Claus Is Coming to Town," "Growin' Up," and "Thunder Road" are among the highlights. The next night, the Boss was invited onstage by headlining jam band Phish, playing on three songs, much to the crowd's surprise.

Back in Europe on June 27 for the Glastonbury Festival, Springsteen joined rising New Brunswick, New Jersey-bred rock band the Gaslight Anthem, singing along with frontman Brian Fallon on their breakthrough anthem, "The '59 Sound." Fallon reciprocated the deed during the E Street Band's set, helping out on "No Surrender" during an acclaimed set on Worthy Farm in Pilton, England.

At a subsequent show at the Hard Rock Calling show in London's Hyde Park, Springsteen repeated his Gaslight cameo. In homage to the Clash and the location of the gig, the Boss opened his fiery set—later released as the DVD *London Calling: Live in Hyde Park*—with the Clash classic "London Calling."

When the band returned to its own tour dates in Bern, Munich, Frankfurt, Vienna, and Herning, Nils Lofgren would launch the shows with a historic regional song on the accordion. He did the same in Dublin, where he played "The Fields of Athenry" before the Boss rocked the RDS Arena with an explosive, thirty-song set.

The closing date on the European trek took place in Santiago, Spain, on August 2, where Springsteen busted out a completely unexpected cover of Elvis Presley's "Burning Love."

American Land

As was the practice on several recent Springsteen tour legs, the final thirty-run date run behind *Working on a Dream* got underway in Hartford on August 19. That Comcast Theatre show featured the first appearance of Manfred Mann's "Sha La La" in thirty-four years. Four nights later, Ken Casey of the Dropkick Murphys sang "American Land" with the Boss as Jay Weinberg continued to play on some or all of the songs, depending on whether Max was available.

Audience requests like "Two Hearts," "Girls in Their Summer Clothes," "Sherry Darling," and "Then She Kissed Me" continued as the tour caravanned up and down the Eastern Seaboard. In Greenville, South Carolina, on September 16, the E Street Band backed Bruce on the Rolling Stones' "(I Can't Get No) Satisfaction." Later, the Swingin' Medallions took the stage to play along with Bruce on their enduring "Double Shot (of My Baby's Love)."

Album Shows

Springsteen descended on Chicago on September 20, incorporating the entire *Born to Run* album in its proper sequence into his set. Opening with a mixed bag of songs from his back catalog, about an hour into the show the opening notes of "Thunder Road" began and the group was off. Upon the conclusion of "Jungleland," Bruce went back to mixing it up, playing the Ronettes' "Da Doo Ron Ron," and Bobby Day's novelty song "Rockin' Robin." Tweet Tweet, indeed.

Ten days later, during the E Street Band's "Wrecking Ball" run of five sold-out shows at Giants Stadium (which was set for demolition and for which he wrote and debuted a song of the same name), Springsteen again played *Born to Run*. The next show, on October 2, found him playing *Darkness on the Edge of Town* front to back.

On October 3, he played *Born in the U.S.A.* in its entirety before reverting back to *Born to Run* during his fourth gig at Giants Stadium. This October 8 show was also noteworthy as it marked Scialfa's return to the stage for the first time since Bonnaroo. The last of the "Wrecking Ball" gigs found Springsteen performing "Born in the U.S.A." once again, before closing the dates with "Jersey Girl." He also played the Rolling Stones' "The Last Time" for the first time since 1979.

Subsequent shows in Philadelphia rendered performances of *Born to Run*, *Darkness*, and *Born in the U.S.A* during a five-night stint. Special moments in the City of Brotherly Love included "Seaside Bar Song," "All Shook Up," the first performance of "The Price You Pay" since 1981, The Drifters' "Save the Last Dance for Me" and the Jackie Wilson classic "(Your Love Keeps Lifting Me) Higher and Higher"—which he hadn't played since 1977.

It was clear that the Spectrum held a special place in Bruce's heart as it was the first arena he ever really conquered back in 1976. For his final appearance there, on October 20, the E Street Band played for three hours and twenty minutes. It featured appearances by original E Streeter Vini Lopez on drums for "Spirit in the Night" and Mrs. Adele Springsteen, who danced with her son on "Dancing in The Dark."

Another *Born to Run* show occurred in St. Louis on October 25, with a start-to-finish delivery of *Born in the U.S.A.* slated for the next night in Kansas City, Missouri. Unfortunately, the show was canceled at the last minute due to the death of Springsteen's cousin Lenny Sullivan, who was the assistant tour manager.

Despite the loss, Springsteen and the E Street Band headlined the first night of the scheduled Rock and Roll Hall of Fame 25th Anniversary concerts on October 29 at Madison Square Garden. In this show, broadcast in part on HBO in the U.S., the Boss backed Sam Moore (of Sam and Dave fame), John Fogerty, Darlene Love, Tom Morello, and Billy Joel. On the second night, he was asked to play with Patti Smith on their song "Because the Night" before joining U2 on "I Still Haven't Found What I'm Looking For."

The final three weeks of touring obligations found Springsteen dedicating "Outlaw Pete" to Sullivan in Washington on November 2 before playing "Born to Run." He did so again in Charlotte the next night, before playing Van Morrison's "Brown Eyed Girl" for the first time. As the tour continued, he played *The Wild, the Innocent, and the E Street Shuffle* and *The River* at Madison Square Garden in early November. On the last night of the tour at HSBC Arena in Buffalo—which happened to be Little Steven's birthday—the Boss performed *Greetings from Asbury Park, N.J.* in its entirety, ending the *Working on a Dream* tour on an amazing high.

For 2009, Springsteen's tour grossed $93 million on just its U.S. shows and about half that again for his European efforts. When asked to look back on his decade on the road, Springsteen was pleased to have brought the legacy of his music and the E Street Band to a younger audience and happy to point out that—although he had recently turned sixty—he was still playing three hours or more on many nights..

Despite the loss of Danny Federici in 2008 and the health concerns of Clarence Clemons, who often sat onstage through most of the set, Springsteen felt strong about the future of the band.

"The E Street Band is in full power, and I certainly want to go out and continue touring," he told Brian Hiatt. "We want to take it out as far as we can go, have the guys stay happy, healthy."

The *Wrecking Ball* Tour

Although the E Street Band was largely absent from Springsteen's 2012 studio album, the tour to support that record would be a family affair. For this first album since the passing of Clarence Clemons, Bruce recruited Eddie Manion and the Big Man's nephew, Jake Clemons, to share saxophone responsibilities for the trek, which officially launched at Philips Arena in Atlanta on March 18.

Rehearsals got underway at the Expo Theater in Fort Monmouth that January and eventually shifted to the Sun Nation Bank Center in Trenton, where the group and crew tested out a new stage design. After Springsteen performed the album's first hit, "We Take Care of Our Own," on the 54th Grammy Awards broadcast on March 5, he and the band performed their first official show of the tour at the Apollo Theatre on March 9. That special event—which featured a crowd of radio contest winners, music industry{Au: Missing word(s) here? Doesn't quite make sense. GM} aired exclusively on Sirius XM's E Street Radio channel to celebrate a decade of satellite radio.

The Boss continued working with the band to perfect their stage show at the Convention Hall in Asbury Park until March 12. From there he traveled to Austin, Texas, to deliver a keynote speech at the SXSW convention on March 15. That appearance gave way to a rare, intimate two-and-a-half-hour E Street Band gig that was long on covers and featured special guests like the Animals' Eric Burdon; longtime friends Joe Ely, Jimmy Cliff, Alejandro Escovedo, and

Garland Jeffreys; Rage Against the Machine guitarist Tom Morello—who was fresh off his appearances on *Wrecking Ball* tracks "Jack of All Trades" and "This Depression"—plus members of Arcade Fire. In response to the recent, controversial Florida shooting of Trayvon Martin, Springsteen dusted off "American Skin (41 Shots)" for the Austin show.

A run of East Coast arena dates in the first month of the trek were anchored by multiple-night stands at the Izod Center in East Rutherford and New York's Madison Square Garden. Late April gigs out west in San Jose and Los Angeles gave way to a celebrated performance at New Orleans' Jazz and Heritage Festival. The Boss returned to the Garden State to play his first show ever at the Prudential Center in Newark on May 2, before heading to Europe for two and a half months of stadium gigs.

Springsteen took time out in each of these initial shows to acknowledge his fallen bandmates, Clemons and Federici, after introducing his current band members. An inspiring nightly tribute to "the Big Man," complete with images of Clemons projected atop the band on venue screens, was about celebrating the memory of Clarence and all the joy he had given fans throughout the years.

Springsteen and the E Street crew also provided fans with some surprises, including rare renditions of "The Promise" at Washington's Verizon Center and "Thundercrack" in San Jose. A volatile take on "Death to My Hometown" was an exciting new highlight of these early-tour gigs, but Springsteen saved the best for last, closing out these shows with "Tenth Avenue Freeze Out."

As this book went to press, the E Street Band announced it had booked a North American stadium leg of its *Wrecking Ball* tour. Set to launch on August 18, 2012, at Gillette Stadium in Foxboro, Massachusetts, other notable dates included performances in baseball venues like Philadelphia's Citizens Bank Park, Chicago's Wrigley Field, and Washington D.C.'s Nationals Park. A pair of concerts at MetLife Stadium—Springsteen's first in the massive East Rutherford facility that has been home to the New York Giants and New York Jets since 2010—were announced for September 21 and 22, 2012.

43

Cool Rocking Daddy

Family Life

Glad Dad

Not long after his fortieth birthday, Bruce Springsteen became a father and a family man. Celebrity aside, he spent a large part of the early to mid-1990s involved in the day-to-day activities of his children, including giving them baths, driving Evan and Jessie to school near Los Angeles, and telling them all stories. He found comfort in a quiet, normal life.

When he went on the road, Patti and the kids joined him. Although there was a nanny, Springsteen loved interacting with his children. While most celebrities thrived on attention from the media and being in the company of other actors, writers, and musicians, he would much rather take the kids to nursery school in his Ford Explorer.

During his summers back east on the farm in Colts Neck or near the water in Rumson, day trips to Sea Bright were common. In addition to homes on both U.S. coasts, the Springsteens also acquired a winter home in Wellington, Florida, an affluent equestrian community near West Palm Beach, Florida.

Family Values

As much as his own upbringing—and Patti's—helped shape his behavior and ideals as a dad, Springsteen relied on his sister Virginia and her husband Mickey early on as influences. Although they married young and suffered some financial difficulties, they persevered as a family.

Ginny, Mickey, and their two sons were icons to Springsteen in the early 1980s, at a time when he dreamt of starting his own family. It would take another decade for him to put that dream into action. "My sister's tremendously, unbelievably strong," Springsteen told *People* in 1984. "Like in the song 'My Hometown,' these are the heroic things that happen in most people's lives. Everyday things between them and their kids—just talks and husbands and wives and families . . . those talks maintain a sense of continuity and a sense of values."

Back to New Jersey

Although Bruce and Patti were happy at first raising their clan in Los Angeles, the increasingly determined paparazzi began to have a negative impact on the most routine of Springsteen family outings. By the end of the 1990s, they decided to move back to New Jersey to give their children a more normal life experience.

As much as Springsteen loved California and still maintained his house in Beverly Hills, once he and Patti had moved back east he found it increasingly hard to get away from the Jersey Shore. "The thing is, I have a big family back here," he told the *Los Angeles Times* in 1998. "That's how I grew up, with aunts, uncles, grandmothers all around me.

"It's healthy for kids to be around people who do something different," he reasoned of his and Patti's decision to raise their family far away from Hollywood. "It's just a more realistic perspective."

Striking a Balance

With the birth of his children and his marriage to Scialfa, Bruce discovered that he was able to see the difference between giving 100 percent to his job and giving 100 percent of his life to his job. As a young artist, he would use his music as a means to fill the holes in his personal life. But the importance of a family taught him he would need to balance his private existence with his public one.

"I think the fear when you are young is you will somehow be diminished by separating your energy into this and that," Springsteen told Robert Hilburn in April 2001. "In truth, it expands who you are and what you can do, your connection to the world, the way you see things, and all those feelings get funneled back into your music."

Losing Doug

When Douglas "Dutch" Springsteen died on April 26, 1998, it left a significant hole in his life. It may have taken his dad decades to accept Bruce's long hair, guitars, loud music, and unorthodox career choice, but by 1985, they were closer than ever. When the Boss came off the road that fall after a fifteen-month global tour for *Born in the U.S.A.*, he and his father took a weeklong fishing trip.

Although his father came across as Bruce's staunch nemesis in the stories he told from the stage in the 1970s and 1980s, Dutch helped to inspire some of Springsteen's most moving songs, including "Used Cars," "Mason on the Hill," "Factory," and "My Hometown."

In a statement released after his passing at seventy-three, Bruce cited his relationship with Doug as "very loving" and added, "I feel lucky to have been so close to my dad as I became a man and a father myself." Springsteen also branded his parent's fifty-year marriage as "warm and caring."

Doug's funeral Mass took place at St. Rose of Lima Church in Freehold on April 30, 1998.

Horsing Around

Since 1976, Springsteen has always maintained a wide-open piece of New Jersey farmland. It began with his home in Holmdel, where he took up an interest in horseback riding, and continued when he acquired the farm in rural Colts Neck that he and Patti still maintain.

Based in Monmouth County and a short drive to Asbury Park or Freehold or Rumson—where he maintains his other area home—or New York City, the acres of farmland owned by the Springsteens has allowed Bruce, Patti, and most recently, Jessica to pursue their love of all things equestrian.

The farm provided a sanctuary for the family that was in close proximity to everything that Bruce and Patti enjoyed from youth, whether it was the beaches, the city, or the Stone Pony. Jersey Shore–area fans have continued to respect the Springsteens' privacy.

"You can go to the boardwalk on a jammed Saturday night where there's a thousand people there and it's fine," Springsteen told *Uncut* in 2002. "People will look and say 'Hello, how you doing?' It's all just . . . it's all very do-able without much hassle, you know?"

The respect among the people from the area has allowed Springsteen to be the kind of dad he always wanted, shuttling his kids and their friends to and from activities, serving as a coach on Evan's baseball team, and supporting Jessica as she developed into a world-class equestrian rider.

In late May 2011, his nineteen-year-old daughter finished in first place with her horse, Vornado Van Den Hoendrik, in the six-bar show-jumping event at the annual Royal Windsor Horse Show. Alongside Patti, Bruce looked out of sorts in a dark pinstripe suit and polka-dot silk tie on the grounds of Windsor Castle.

Breakfast Club

On the occasions that the Springsteen family was still able to come together at their home in Colts Neck, Scialfa was happy to get up at 7 a.m. to make a big breakfast of oatmeal, pancakes, bacon, and scrambled eggs for the five of them.

The family time together gave everyone a supportive and loving starting point for whatever the day might bring. Bruce, whose parents moved away from him for a new life in California when he was just a teenager, and Patti deeply valued the time spent with their young adult offspring.

In 2011, he acknowledged that kids don't usually begin to care about their parents as people until they reach their late twenties.

"[We're] furniture until then and, as a parent, you want to be a sturdy piece of furniture if you can," he told the U.K.'s *Daily Express* in 2011. "If things don't work out, it's OK. Patti and I will always be there for them."

44

Till My TV Lay in Pieces There at My Feet

The Best of the Boss on Television

KABC

In 1978, during his stand at the Roxy in Los Angeles, Bruce Springsteen made his first television interview appearance with then KABC-TV reporter and future MTV VJ J. J. Jackson. The seven-minute segment—unheralded on a news broadcast at the time—featured live footage of "Prove It All Night" and "Rosalita" interspersed with Springsteen fielding questions.

When probed about how he managed to play for three solid hours, Springsteen laughed, "It must be desperation," before explaining that performing was the only thing he lived for, regardless of whether he was in front of an audience of ten or ten thousand.

When asked about balancing fame and integrity, he spoke of it being a state of mind. The key was to stay grounded. "If it stays real for you, it stays real for the kids you come into contact with," he told Jackson.

As for jumping into the crowd to become one with his audience, Springsteen told Jackson with a chuckle, "you usually know [it's a mistake] around the time someone socks you on the back of the head with a beer bottle."

WNET Studios

In October 1986, director Hart Perry interviewed Bruce Springsteen both alone and with John Hammond for a documentary on the latter, which ultimately surfaced on PBS stations in the U.S. on August 20, 1990. Titled *John Hammond: From Bessie Smith to Bruce Springsteen*, the film—which followed Hammond's October 1987 death—was later released commercially. The version of Bob Dylan's "Forever Young" that Springsteen sang at his revered A&R man's funeral on October 22, 1987 was heard over the closing credits.

MTV Plugged

Filmed at Warner Hollywood Studios in L.A on September 22, 1992, Springsteen's *MTV Plugged* aired on November 11 and was subsequently released on audio and video. For the program, which customarily found rock artists like Nirvana and R.E.M. playing acoustic instruments, the network allowed him to break with tradition to plug in.

The Concert for Life

On January 27, 1994, Springsteen performed his new, AIDS-inspired single, "Streets of Philadelphia" at this benefit for the tragic disease. Filmed at the Universal Amphitheatre in Los Angeles, Springsteen was backed by Roy Bittan, vocalist Bobby King, bassist Tommy Sims, and others. The footage was shown on the syndicated program *Entertainment Tonight*.

Mayfield Medley

On March 1, 1994, Springsteen attended the 36th Grammy Awards at Radio City Music Hall, appearing on the broadcast for a special tribute to soul icon Curtis Mayfield. Playing alongside heavy-hitters like Steve Cropper, B. B. King, Bonnie Raitt, Vernon Reid, Steve Winwood, Don Was, and others. Springsteen sang lead vocals on "Gypsy Woman" before taking a line of "People Get Ready."

"Thunder Road"

Springsteen returned to MTV to record a duet with Melissa Etheridge at the Brooklyn Academy of Music on February 15, 1995. The version of "Thunder Road" that aired on the channel on March 21 during Etheridge's *Unplugged* episode needed to be played twice when Etheridge forgot the words on the first try.

Letterman

On April 5, 1995, Springsteen and the E Street Band made their *Late Show with David Letterman* debut. In keeping with their *Greatest Hits* promotional efforts, the band played "Murder Incorporated" and "Secret Garden" in their entirety. Portions of "Tenth Avenue Freeze-Out" and "Money (That's What I Want)"—made famous by Barrett Strong in 1959 and also covered by the Beatles and the Flying Lizards—are also heard as the show came in and out of commercial breaks.

"One Headlight"

On the September 4, 1997, live broadcast of *MTV's Music Video Awards*, the Boss joined the Wallflowers for a performance of their then-current smash "One Headlight." Springsteen was nominated for Best Video from a Film for "Secret Garden"—which was part of the *Jerry Maguire* movie soundtrack. He lost to actor/rapper Will Smith.

Where It's At

Backed by Danny Federici and other players, Springsteen delivered strong performances of "The Ghost of Tom Joad" and "Across the Border" at New York's Sony Studios for an ABC Television special called *Where It's At: The Rolling Stone State of the Union*. Designed to commemorate the publication's thirtieth anniversary, it was recorded in January'98 and also featured a brief Springsteen interview. The program aired that May and has since been released on DVD.

A Secret History

This documentary, produced by Mark Hagen, aired on BBC 2 in the U.K. on December 5, 1998, and was designed to help promote Springsteen's new box set *Tracks*. Bruce was filmed earlier in the year performing a solo acoustic rendition of "Born in the U.S.A.," plus an on-the-spot blues number about being interviewed by Hagen. The project also included newly unearthed footage of Springsteen at Hammersmith Odeon in 1975, plus video of the E Street Band playing "Janey Don't You Lose Heart" in Los Angeles in September 1985.

The Charlie Rose Show

This hour-long interview between Springsteen and PBS news journalist Charlie Rose occurred on November 20, 1998, during the *Tracks* campaign. Arguably the best interview from the era, it trumps the one done for NBC's *Dateline* by Bob Costas that ran the following month.

Perhaps the highlight of this discussion came late in the Rose interview when Springsteen speaks of how important the E Street Band has been to his life. It's a strong hint about the Reunion tour revelation that would soon emerge.

In a fitting parting shot, he performed an acoustic "Born in the U.S.A." that was reminiscent of the original, stripped down version heard on *Tracks*.

HBO

On April 7, 2001, the Boss's first television special, titled *"Bruce Springsteen and the E Street Band: Live in New York City*, aired on HBO. Cutting the typical three hours-plus live show down to 120 minutes meant collecting only the best moments from the concert—which was filmed live at Madison Square Garden in June 2000.

Twenty-five years after he was first approached about doing his own network special for NBC, Springsteen had finally come around to the idea of being filmed for the medium. Some of the reasoning behind the program came from the fact that he regretted not filming on his *Ghost of Tom Joad* tour.

But even he Bruce and the band decided to film the shows, they weren't sure if they'd put it on television—and ultimately on DVD. *Live in New York City* ultimately got the green light because it represented the excitement, the power, and the emotion that defines a great E Street Band gig.

America: A Tribute to Heroes

Airing just ten days after the devastating September 11, 2001, terrorist attacks on New York City and Washington, D.C, Springsteen opened the two-hour all-star telethon with a then-unreleased song called "My City of Ruins." A song initially penned about Asbury Park, the decaying Jersey Shore city he helped make famous, it was a good fit for the pain and loss that the New York area, and the United States as a whole, had endured.

Broadcast live at Sony's studios in Manhattan, the show featured Springsteen surrounded by a sea of candles, plus E Street Band members Steve Van Zandt, Clarence Clemons, and Scialfa's friend Soozie Tyrell, who would eventually become a member of the E Street Band.

Reportedly viewed by sixty million people, the program—which also included performances by U2, Tom Petty, Billy Joel, Dave Matthews, Sting, Paul Simon, the Dixie Chicks, and Bon Jovi—raised roughly $150 million for the September 11th Telethon Fund.

Saturday Night Live

Springsteen's performance inside Studio 8H of the GE Building in Rockefeller Center, New York, on October 5, 2002, wasn't the Boss's first time rocking *Saturday Night Live*, but it was definitely the best. After Springsteen's first appearance with the "Other Band" in 1992, it was refreshing to see the E Street Band performing top-notch, emotive material from *The Rising* like "Lonesome Day" and "You're Missing." Host Matt Dillon and the cast in general seemed to be in awe of Springsteen and the band as the final credits of the show rolled.

The Rising on the VMAs

On August 29, 2002, the E Street Band performed "The Rising" on *MTV's Video Music Awards* live from the New York Planetarium. Introduced by James Gandolfini—Steve Van Zandt's costar on *The Sopranos*—Springsteen led the group through its comeback hit before playing a private concert for attendees.

The show balanced new songs like "Waitin' on a Sunny Day" and "Mary's Place" with classics like "Darkness on the Edge of Town" and "Thunder Road." The entire gig, which ran seventy-five minutes, occurred in the driving rain.

"London Calling"

When the 45th Grammy Awards took place on February 23, 2003, in Madison Square Garden, Springsteen and Van Zandt performed a tribute to the late Clash frontman Joe Strummer, who had died unexpectedly the previous December. Playing with Elvis Costello and the Foo Fighters' Dave Grohl, the band played the U.K. band's signature number, "London Calling."

Springsteen triumphed that night, pulling down three Grammys, two for "The Rising" (Best Male Rock Vocal and Best Rock Son") and a third for *The Rising* (Best Rock Album). Few could dispute that the Boss and his revered E Street Band were back on top.

Storytellers

Filmed at the Two River Theater in Red Bank, New Jersey, on April 4, 2005,

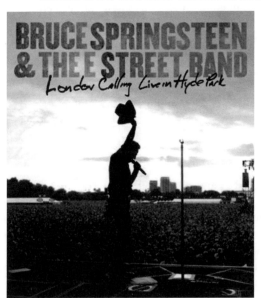

for VH1's *Storytellers* (which ran on April 23) Springsteen's performance featured songs from his various musical eras.

Beginning with the title track of his recent solo record, "Devils and Dust," Bruce quickly looked back on the different facets of his career, from 1973's "Blinded by the Light," 1987's "Brilliant Disguise," or 1975's "Thunder Road."

The actual taping of the special took three hours and included a thirty-minute Q and A session with the audience. Edited down to just under two hours, it eventually saw formal DVD release via Columbia in September 2005.

Springsteen was a big Clash fan, as evidenced by his Grammy Awards tribute to that band's fallen frontman Joe Strummer, alongside Dave Grohl, Elvis Costello, and Steve Van Zandt, in 2003. His rendering of the Clash classic "London Calling" in the 2010 DVD, *London Calling: Live from Hyde Park*, affirmed he still loved that influential punk band.   *Author's Collection*

The Super Bowl

For Springsteen fans, the E Street Band's twelve-minute, four-song half-time medley was not only the a high point of the Super Bowl XLIII, but one of the distinct highlights of a music career that has been unrivaled. Tens of millions of viewers globally tuned for the miniconcert, which came just five days after the release of 2009's *Working on a Dream*.

In an interview leading up to the show, Springsteen acknowledged two of his main motivators for choosing to play on the broadcast. First, he wanted to do it while he was still relevant and still had the chance. Second, he recognized that at his age, it was tough to get word to the public about his new releases.

So with the E Street Band, he went out onto the field at Raymond James Stadium in Tampa on February 1 and—along with a horn section and backing from the Joyce Garrett Singers on his latest single, "Working on a Dream"—he killed it. In an NBC broadcast performance that could only be rivaled by U2's 2002 Super Bowl show, he performed a medley of the aforementioned with "Tenth Avenue Freeze-Out," "Born to Run," and "Glory Days."

Springsteen "Spectacle"

Springsteen was the subject of singer/songwriter Elvis Costello's Sundance Channel performance and interview series, on a program that was split into two one-hour episodes that ran on January 21 and 27, 2010. Filmed at the Apollo Theatre in Harlem, the show was memorable as it went deeper and was more electrifying than his *Storytellers* episode.

In the company of Roy Bittan and Nils Lofgren, Springsteen played "Wild Billy's Circus Story," pieces of "The River" and "Oh, Pretty Woman" (the latter in homage to Roy Orbison), and delivered a solo rendering of the contentious "American Skin (41 Shots)."

Springsteen and Costello—along with his band the Imposters, performed Elvis's own "I Can't Stand Up (for Falling Down)," Springsteen's "Seeds," and a medley of their respective songs, "Radio Nowhere" and "Radio, Radio." Costello also delivered a stellar version of the Boss's 1980 classic "Point Blank."

"Whip My Hair"

When Springsteen, Steve Van Zandt, and Roy Bittan appeared on NBC's *Late Night with Jimmy Fallon* on November 11, 2010, the Boss and his accomplices were there to promote the release of *The Promise*. In addition to playing "Because the Night" and "Save My Love" from that project with Fallon's band, The Roots, Springsteen participated in a legendary bit of late-night television comedy.

With Fallon dressed as Neil Young and Springsteen made up as himself around the *Born to Run* era, the pair collaborated inside 30 Rockefeller Center's Studio 6B on an acoustic rendition of Willow Smith's current pop song "Whip My Hair."

I Believe in the Promised Land

Anti-Reagan Remarks

If Springsteen's political slant wasn't publicly known in the 1970s, the outcome of the 1980 presidential election was the thrust the Boss needed to make it known that he was aligned with the Democratic Party. He conveyed his disdain for Ronald Reagan in Arizona the night after the election.

Calling Reagan's victory "pretty terrifying" as he introduced "Badlands" to the audience, Springsteen would again show his disapproval of the former actor and California governor during his reelection campaign in 1984. The Boss went mental when Reagan used his name and mentioned "Born in the U.S.A" in a speech he gave about the hopes and dreams of Americans in Hammonton, New Jersey, on September 19.

Clearly, Reagan and his staffers misunderstood the cynical message of the song, which was written at a time when national pride had all but evaporated. Two days later, Springsteen wondered aloud in front of a Pittsburgh audience which of his albums was the president's favorite. "I don't think it was Nebraska," he told his fans as he introduced "Johnny 99."

"I don't think he's been listening to this one," Springsteen added of his number about an unemployed auto worker who winds up killing a convenience store clerk.

Nuclear Disarmament

On June 12, 1982, Springsteen took a public stance against nuclear weapons and stood up for peace by performing at the Rally for Nuclear Disarmament, which was held in New York's Central Park. With 750,000 in attendance, he played two songs with Jackson Browne at the concert/rally that also included James Taylor, Linda Ronstadt, and Joan Baez.

The event was broadcast live on WNEW–FM in New York and was one of the first-ever all-star Disarmament gatherings.

Support of Vietnam Veterans

In 1981, he threw his support behind the Vietnam Veterans Association by donating his earnings from a Los Angeles performance on *The River* tour. In doing so, he allowed the organization and its offshoot—the Vietnam Veterans Foundation—to become financially stable.

In a 2003 interview with the *Boston Globe*, Bobby Muller said, "Without Bruce Springsteen, there would be no Vietnam veterans movement." Muller, the head of the foundation and a disabled veteran with a purple heart, also helped inspire Springsteen's anthem "Born in the U.S.A."

Some of Springsteen's observations on the effects of the war on Americans—which were also influenced by Ron Kovic's *Born on the Fourth of July*—came firsthand. His drummer and friend in the Castiles went to 'Nam and never came home. Other friends who went to war came back scarred forever.

Springsteen has continued to support the foundation with regular donations over the past thirty years. With the attention the Boss gave to the cause, coupled with the end of the Cold War, Muller—who founded the VVA with war veteran and one-time presidential hopeful John Kerry –began to receive millions of dollars in federal money beginning in 1992.

Senator Springsteen?

An activist group known as Independence for New Jersey thought Springsteen's activism and firsthand experience with the working class might make a difference in politics. In 2002, they put his name up as a candidate for the U.S. Senate.

Although flattered, he rejected the "Springsteen for Senate" initiative, responding with a quote he lifted from General William Tecumseh Sherman, who declined an offer to run for president in 1884. "If nominated, I will not run," he told fans. "If elected, I will not serve."

Repugnant Republicans

In the early months of his presidency—long before 9/11 and the Iraq War—George W. Bush took his lumps from Springsteen, who made it known in April 2001 interviews that he would rather we did not have a Republican in office.

His liberal stance was nothing new by this point in his career, but he vowed, for the first time, to step up and take a formal stance during the 2004 election.

Iraq War

When the war in Iraq broke out in early 2003, Springsteen made a surprising statement about the conflict. "The question of whether we were misled into the war in Iraq isn't a liberal or conservative or Republican or Democratic question;

it's an American one," he told audiences on his tour to support *The Rising*, as he introduced his iconic "Born in the U.S.A."

At the same time, he accused the existing administration of taking the terrorist attacks of September 11, 2001, and using them as a blank check. Meanwhile, he pointed out, the lives of our American sons and daughters were in the balance. Citing financial woes, tax cuts that were disadvantageous to the poor, and the easing of environmental restrictions, the Boss deemed the War "a game of shadows and mirrors" in an interview with *Entertainment Weekly* that winter.

Backing Kerry

Springsteen's official endorsement of Senator John Kerry in the 2004 race for the U.S. Presidency marked the first time in his thirty-plus years in the public eye that he had backed a candidate.

He wrote a letter to the editor of the *New York Times* on August 5, 2004, announcing his support of the Democratic Party candidate, while revealing his intention of headlining the *Vote for Change* tour that followed that fall.

In his letter, he explained why he had always stayed on the fringes of partisan politics, instead opting to support causes that upheld economic justice, civil rights, human rights, and personal freedom. But in 2004, the stakes were higher than ever before.

In his opinion, the Bush administration—as he would tell *Rolling Stone* that year—"had been fundamentally dishonest and had frightened and manipulated the American people into war." He believed that, as a musician, it was his job to provide an alternative source of information to his audience.

When the tour wrapped in October, Springsteen continued to support the John Kerry/John Edwards campaign. He traveled with the senators, using his music and his influence on voters to help get them to the polls in a final push for the Oval Office in the first days of November. But Springsteen and his guitar couldn't help Kerry win the Swing States he was hoping to conquer. On Election Day, Kerry lost.

Springsteen was devastated. "Patti had to peel me off the wall," he told Jon Pareles from the *New York Times* in 2005. But Senator Kerry was deeply appreciative.

The day after Kerry's loss, Springsteen called to express his gratitude to the senator for having him involved in the campaign he believed in so much. "It was the last thing in the world I expected—a very sweet moment that meant a lot," Kerry told *AARP the Magazine*. Springsteen later caught up with Kerry after some time had passed and gave him a keepsake—the guitar he used during the rallies.

Championing Obama

After the disappointment that came with George W. Bush's reelection, Springsteen came out early and often in support of the Democratic presidential hopeful, Illinois Senator Barack Obama. He performed a series of solo performances with Obama in Philadelphia, Columbus, Ohio, and Ypsilanti, Michigan, in the first week of October 2008.

He also performed alongside Billy Joel, India Arie, and John Legend at a Hammerstein Ballroom benefit in New York on October 16. Billed as "Change Rocks," Springsteen performed two acoustic numbers before teaming with Patti Scialfa, Roy Bittan, Billy Joel and his Joel's band for the likes of "Spirit in the Night," "The Rising," and Curtis Mayfield's "People Get Ready."

Springsteen's involvement in the Obama campaign continued through to a Cleveland rally on November 2, and his overall dedication helped result in a victory in 2008. From the stage, two days prior to the vote, he delivered a speech in which he said, "I believe Senator Obama has taken the measure of that distance in his own life and work. I believe he understands in his heart the cost of that distance in blood and suffering in the lives of everyday Americans. I believe as president he would work to bring that dream back to life."

Fast-forward to the 56th Presidential Inaugural, which was billed as "We Are One: The Obama Inaugural Celebration at the Lincoln Memorial"—Bruce joined U2's Bono and the Edge, Legend, Beyonce, John Mellencamp and Stevie Wonder. At this cap to an exhilarating campaign and a shift in power, Springsteen performed "The Rising" with backing from the Joyce Garrett Singers. He also delivered "We Shall Overcome" with backing from Pete Seeger, Tao Rodriguez-Seeger, and a children's choir.

46

Lookin' for That Million-Dollar Sound

The Promise

Darkness was my 'samurai' record—stripped to the frame and ready to rumble . . . But the music that got left behind was substantial," Springsteen explained in a press release announcing *The Promise* in September 2010. Released in the U.S. on November 16 of that year—a day earlier in the U.K.—the two-CD collection made twenty-one previously unreleased songs from the *Darkness on the Edge of Town* sessions available to fans after thirty-two years in the Boss's vaults.

In the liner notes for the project, Springsteen wrote that some of the songs "perhaps could have/ should have been released after *Born to Run*." But he was affected by the bare-bones punk sounds of the time, which prompted him to make an album of tough-sounding music.

In addition to being a stand-alone release, the double-disc compilation was included in the box set *The Promise: The Darkness on the Edge of Town Story*. An amazing product, the deluxe audio/video package included an eighty-page notebook of facsimiles from Springsteen's original notebooks from the recording sessions. In addition to the alternate lyrics, song ideas, and personal notes, the Boss wrote

The sleeve for 2010's "Save My Love," a song first attempted during the sessions for *Darkness on the Edge of Town*. A lost companion album of material from that era, titled *The Promise*, was reissued in November of that year.   *Author's Collection* a new essay about his work in 1977 and 1978 on the now-classic album.

In advance of the release, Springsteen began streaming the R&B–influenced "Save My Love" on his website to help build anticipation. A harder-rocking take of "Racing in the Street" opened the set, and never-before-released recordings of "Because the Night," "Fire," and "Rendezvous" were immediate and strong.

"There isn't a weak card in this deck," Landau said in a subsequent announcement of the tracklist. "*The Promise* is simply a great listening experience." Mixed by Springsteen's longtime ally Bob Clearmountain, the project had one winning song after another, from the soul-tinged "Gotta Get That Feeling," to the delightful pop number "Someday (We'll Be Together)," to "Candy's Boy"—the precursor to "Candy's Room."

In press materials serviced to the media to help promote *The Promise*, Springsteen explained, "Rather than being a record of outtakes, it was really a separate double album that stands on its own as a piece of work."

Steve Van Zandt affirmed Springsteen's sentiment quite simply. "These cannot be considered outtakes."

Billed as "21 newly released recordings from the *Darkness* sessions," *The Promise* was equal parts celebratory and stark. This ad, featuring a timeless photo of a young Springsteen leaning on a '66 Ford, immediately resonated with all Springsteen fans.
Author's Collection

Chart Performance and Acclaim

The Promise didn't fare very well commercially, peaking at its #16 debut in the U.S. Surprisingly, it was Springsteen's lowest-charting album in his homeland since the release of his second album in 1973. It performed far better in European markets, earning Top 10 debuts in the Netherlands, Denmark, Ireland, and the United Kingdom. It was a #1 album in Germany, Norway, and Spain.

Critical acclaim was widespread. *Rolling Stone's* David Fricke awarded it five stars and called it "Extraordinary [and] fascinating," *Entertainment Weekly* gave it an A grade and praised it as "Essential." In the *Washington Post*, Allison Stewart championed it as "a revelation."

Uncut's Bud Scoppa hit the nail on the head, writing, "This music seems to have arrived from some parallel universe, enriching the history of a supreme artist at his very peak, during a vital era in rock history. What might have been, in all its overarching splendor, now is."

47

Tell Me Friend, Can You Ask for Anything More?

Significant Honors and Awards

Academy Awards

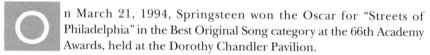

On March 21, 1994, Springsteen won the Oscar for "Streets of Philadelphia" in the Best Original Song category at the 66th Academy Awards, held at the Dorothy Chandler Pavilion.

In a 2007 interview with *60 Minutes*, he revealed how the honor changed his father's way of thinking about his career choice. "When I came home with the Oscar and I put it on the kitchen table, he just looked at it," Springsteen laughed. "And he said, 'Bruce, I'll never tell anybody what to do ever again.'"

Golden Globes

Springsteen has earned two Golden Globe Awards to date. The first came for 1994's "Streets of Philadelphia," while the second was for "The Wrestler." At the 2009 Awards, he thanked actor Mickey Rourke for reaching out to him.

"I'd like to thank Mickey," he told the audience. "Without the call I wouldn't have written the song, without his inspiration—thank you, brother, for a beautiful performance, thank you for thinking of me!"

Grammy Awards

In February 1985, Springsteen made his first appearance at the Grammy Awards with his future wife Julianne Phillips. He was invited in response to his massively successful 1984 album and its lead single, "Dancing in the Dark." The latter earned him his first Grammy for Best Male Rock Vocal Performance.

On March 2, 1988, he earned the Best Rock Vocal Performance for his album *Tunnel of Love*. Seven years later, Bruce pulled in four Grammys—including

Song of the Year, Best Male Rock Vocal, Best Rock Song, and Best Song Written Specifically for a Motion Picture for "Streets of Philadelphia."

In 1997, the Boss returned to pick up another Gramophone trophy for his album *The Ghost of Tom Joad*. It earned Best Contemporary Folk Album honors. Six years later, he was back at the awards ceremony as it acknowledged *The Rising* with three trophies: Best Rock Album, Best Rock Song (for the title track), and Best Male Rock Performance. Springsteen also shared a Best Rock Performance by a Duo or Group with Vocal Grammy with the late Warren Zevon for their *The Wind* duet, "Disorder in the House."

In 2004, he won another Best Solo Rock Vocal Performance Grammy for the song "Code of Silence," which appeared on *The Essential Bruce Springsteen* and was cowritten with Joe Grushecky. He took the same category in '05 for the song "Devils and Dust."

The year 2006 resulted in two Grammys for Bruce. He landed the Best Traditional Folk Album honors for *The Seeger Sessions: We Shall Overcome* and Best Long Form Music Video for *Wings for Wheels: The Making of Born to Run*.

Three more honors followed in 2007, including two for "Radio Nowhere" (Best Solo Rock Vocal Performance and Best Rock Song) and another Grammy for Best Rock Instrumental Performance for "Once Upon a Time in the West." The next year resulted in a gong for "Girls in Their Summer Clothes" (Best Rock Song), and then a Best Solo Rock Vocal Performance statue for '09's "Working on a Dream." In 2011, *The Promise: The Darkness on the Edge of Town Story* earned the trophy for Best Boxed or Special Limited Edition Package.

Kennedy Center Honors

Springsteen was honored alongside Robert De Niro, Mel Brooks, Dave Brubeck, and others at the 32nd Kennedy Center Honors Gala Dinner on December 5, 2009, after first being honored at a White House reception. John Mellencamp, Melissa Etheridge, Ben Harper, Sting, Eddie Vedder, and Sugarland's Jennifer Nettles sang Springsteen classics for the audience at Washington's JFK Center for the Performing Arts.

Polar Music Prize

Often considered the Nobel Prize of music, this honor was given to Springsteen on May 5, 1997, by the Royal Swedish Academy of Music. Awarded for exceptional achievements in the creation and advancement of music, it was presented by Swedish King Karl Gustav XVI. Springsteen also received a prize of $1 million kronor—the equivalent at the time of approximately $125,000.

48

Wherever This Flag Is Flown

Wrecking Ball

T hree years after *Working on a Dream*, Springsteen released his next studio effort. Titled *Wrecking Ball* after the song he first debuted in '09 during the E Street Band's final concerts at Giants Stadium, Springsteen's 2012 album found him leaving Brendan O'Brien—who had manned all of his rock efforts in the previous decade—behind to work with Ron Aniello.

Aniello was no stranger to the Springsteen camp, having coproduced Patti Scialfa's 2007 disc *Play It as It Lays*. An established producer and studio owner, the Los Angeles–based Aniello was at the helm of successful records by Guster, Barenaked Ladies, and Lifehouse. A capable multi-instrumentalist, he played alongside the Boss on much of *Wrecking Ball*.

Released on March 5, 2012, Springsteen's seventeenth studio disc was preceded on January 19 by "We Take Care of Our Own," an infectious rock song that helped build momentum for the new record. Save for the aforementioned title song, "American Land"—which was penned during the 2006 *Seeger Sessions*—and "Land of Hope and Dreams"—which first emerged on 1999's Reunion tour—the disc was comprised of all new material written by the Boss in 2011.

Speaking to Jon Stewart in the March 29 issue of *Rolling Stone*, Springsteen explained that his intention on the first half of the record was to sound "pissed off." From that point onward, he would explore more personal and spiritual perspectives. "In my music," he continued, "if it has a purpose beyond dancing and fun and vacuuming your floor to it—I always try to gauge the distance between American reality and the American dream."

From a topical standpoint, *Wrecking Ball* was a condemnation of white-collar greed and its hand in the economic downturn of the late '00s. In the wake of the American mortgage crisis, Wall Street crooks like Bernie Madoff, and the ensuing economic bailout of a number of major U.S. corporations, Springsteen felt it was necessary to write about the people and forces that brought America to a point of devastation.

Highlights

With its balance of rock bombast, Gaelic rebel music, and haunting folk, the record's title *Wrecking Ball* was an accurate description of what it entailed. Inspired, diverse in its presentation, and often downright entertaining, the album included what would likely be the final Springsteen songs to ever feature Clarence Clemons, who played on both the title track and "Land of Hope and Dreams" before he passed in June 2011.

Wrecking Ball was unique in that it found Bruce interspersing excerpts of other artists' songs into four of the numbers. "Shackled and Drawn," for instance, included a piece of Lyn Collins's 1972 number "Me and My Baby Got Our Own Thing Going." Meanwhile, the incendiary "Death to My Hometown" was laden with Alan Lomax's1959 recording of the Sacred Harp song "The Last Words of Copernicus." Elsewhere, "Rocky Ground" culled elements of the traditional gospel song "I'm a Soldier in the Army of the Lord," while "Land of Hope and Dreams" embraced a section of the Curtis Mayfield classic "People Get Ready," which Springsteen had incorporated off and on into his live show for decades.

"We Take Care of Our Own"

Springsteen's first high-profile denunciation of the U.S. government since 1984's "Born in the U.S.A.," *Wrecking Ball*'s lead single promoted a patriotic stance in the chorus, with an obvious cynicism in the verses. Matched with a memorable, rock-'n'-roll presentation, the song told of how America's "good intentions have gone dry as a bone."

The Boss also sang of those left to cope in the aftermath of Hurricane Katrina, where New Orleans residents were left helpless while "the cavalry stayed home." Impossible to discount because of its contagiousness, it was arguably the most thought-provoking Springsteen song since "The Rising."

"Death to My Hometown"

If Springsteen was influenced sonically by his friends in Celtic punk band the Dropkick Murphys, "Death to My Hometown" wasn't just a protest song, it was his most scathing indictment yet of Wall Street. Replete with a stomping beat, the track's hook came courtesy of a keen tin whistle.

"Wrecking Ball"

Initially penned in homage to Giants Stadium in the fall of 2009, when Springsteen and the E Street Band performed the venue's final concerts, the title track may have been written from the perspective of the aging stadium, but it came to symbolize much more. Revamped slightly from its original live version, the tune's refrain ("C'mon and take your best shot/Let me see what you got/Bring on your wrecking ball") was a defiant representation of the many Americans caught between foreclosure and eviction.

"Rocky Ground"

Marking the first-ever rap part in a Springsteen song—courtesy of guest vocalist Michelle Moore—"Rocky Ground" meshed the gospel approaches first attempted by the Boss on "My City of Ruins" with a hip-hop vibe reminiscent of "Streets of Philadelphia." Augmented by a Baptist choir and featuring a sample of the "I'm a soldier" line from the Church of God in Christ Congregation's "I'm a Soldier in the Army of the Lord," Springsteen uplifted the tune's solemn arrange-

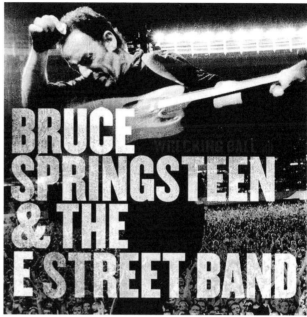

More than two years in advance of his album of the same name, the Boss released the single "Wrecking Ball," a live 45 billed to Bruce Springsteen and the E Street Band. It was recorded live at Giants Stadium during the group's last shows before the venue was torn down. It has since been replaced by a state-of-the-art facility, Met Life Stadium.   *Author's Collection*

ment with religious hopefulness, as he intoned, "There's a new day coming."

"Land of Hope and Dreams"

While performances by E Street Band members were scattered and incidental on most of *Wrecking Ball*, Steve Van Zandt, Patti Scialfa, Soozie Tyrell, and Clemons were all present in some capacity on this number. As mentioned earlier, the song revisits lines from Curtis Mayfield's optimistic soul spiritual "People Get Ready" with winning results. Unlike the concert rendering of the tune originally featured on *Live in New York City,* this version included electronic drums in lieu of Max Weinberg and was given a more concise presentation.

"We Are Alive"

Paying musical tribute to one of his longtime heroes, Johnny Cash, by lending mariachi horns to "We Are Alive," Springsteen brings to mind the latter's classic "Ring of Fire." A song for the broken people, it touches on the struggles of oppressed railroad workers, the tyranny faced by African Americans in the Deep South in the early 1960s, and the immigrants of today crossing the Mexican border into the U.S. Yet for all of the lives lost in the album's closing track, the song delivers a perspective of faith as the Boss professes, "Our spirits rise/To carry the fire and light the spark/To stand shoulder to shoulder and heart to heart."

Critical and Commercial Response

Revered music writer Robert Christgau cited the incendiary beginnings of *Wrecking Ball* in his *MSN Music* column as "heavy irony shading over into murderous rage, with refurbished arena-rock to slam it home." While *Paste* branded the disc "a big rock record," it also acknowledged that Springsteen's seventeenth was much more than that as it unfolded to reveal electronic drums, Irish folk music, hip-hop beats, blues, and gospel. Meanwhile, *Rolling Stone* scribe David Fricke called it "the most despairing, confrontation,{Au: Should be "confrontational"? GM} and musically turbulent album Bruce Springsteen has ever made" in his glowing five-star assessment.

If most mainstream press was kind—*Entertainment Weekly*'s Melissa Maerz gave it a solid "B" rating, while *NME* rated it 8 out of 10—*Chicago Tribune* writer Greg Kot knocked the record's presentation as "sterile" while insisting the Boss "lost his nerve as a coproducer, going for stadium bombast instead of the unadorned grit these stories of hard times demand."

Perhaps *Popmatters* reviewer Steve Leftridge summed the record up best by comparing it with *The Rising* and explaining that if Springsteen's 2002 disc was his "9/11 album," *Wrecking Ball* was his "Occupy [Wall Street] album."

From a sales standpoint, the record was a significant success. It debuted at #1 in the U.S., the U.K., and fourteen other countries on the strength of its singles "We Take Care of Our Own" and "Death to My Hometown." Stateside, it marked Springsteen's tenth chart-topper, tying him with his childhood hero Elvis Presley in third place. Only the Beatles (first with 19) and Jay-Z (second with 12) had achieved more #1 albums of all time.

Selected Bibliography

Countless magazines, newspapers, websites, and fanzines have covered Bruce Springsteen's lengthy career. Many were consulted in the research for *Bruce Springsteen FAQ*. For further reading, here are some suggestions:

Books

Clemons, Clarence. *Big Man: Real Life and Tall Tales*. New York: Grand Central Publishing, 2009.

Cross, Charles R. and the editors of *Backstreets*. *Backstreets: Springsteen, The Man and His Music*. New York: Harmony Books, 1989, 1992.

Duffy, John W. *Bruce Springsteen Talking*. London: Omnibus, 2004.

Editors of *Rolling Stone*. *Bruce Springsteen: The Rolling Stone Files*. New York: Hyperion/Rolling Stone Press, 1996.

Eliot, Marc. *Down Thunder Road: The Making of Bruce Springsteen*. New York: Simon & Schuster, 1992.

Graff, Gary. *The Ties That Bind: Bruce Springsteen: A to E to Z*. Detroit: Visible Ink, 2005.

Hilburn, Robert. *Springsteen*. New York, Rolling Stone Press: 1985.

Labianca, Ermanno. *Local Hero: Bruce Springsteen in the Words of His Band*. New York: Great Dane Books, 1993.

Marsh, Dave. *Born to Run: The Bruce Springsteen Story*. New York: Doubleday Dolphin, 1979, 1981.

Marsh, Dave. *Bruce Springsteen on Tour: 1968–2005*. New York: Bloomsbury USA, 2006.

Marsh, Dave. *Two Hearts: The Definitive Biography, 1972–2003*. New York: Routledge, 2003.

Sandford, Christopher. *Springsteen: Point Blank*. New York: Da Capo Press, 1999.

Santelli, Robert. *Greetings from E Street: The Story of Bruce Springsteen and the E Street Band*. New York: Chronicle, 2006.

Sawyers, June Skinner. *Racing in the Street: The Bruce Springsteen Reader*. New York: Penguin Books, 2004.

Springsteen, Bruce. *Songs*. New York: Harper Entertainment, 1998.

Music Magazines and Fanzines

AARP the Magazine

The Aquarian

BAM

Backstreets

Bass Player

Beats

Billboard

Classic Rock

Crawdaddy

Creem

Guitar World

Melody Maker

Musician

Mojo

NME

Q

Record

Relix

Rolling Stone

Sounds

Spin

Trouser Press

Thunder Road

Uncut

Zig Zag

Other Newspapers and Magazines

Asbury Park Press

Boston Globe

Chicago Tribune

Entertainment Weekly

Guardian

L.A. Weekly

Los Angeles Times

New York Times

Newsweek

Observer

People

Phoenix New Times

Playboy

Real Paper

Star-Ledger

Time

USA Today

Music Websites

www.Billboard.com
www.EIL.com
www.Exclaim.ca
www.MTV.com
www.NEM.com
www.Pitchfork.com
www.RIAA.org
www.Rockhall.com
www.RollingStone.com
www.Spin.com
www.Spinner.com

Springsteen Websites

www.Backstreets.com
www.Badlands.it
www.Brucebase.Wikispaces.net
www.BruceSpringsteen.net
www.BruceSpringsteenSpecialCollection.net
www.Brucetapes.com
www.Castiles.net
www.ClarenceClemons.com
www.DannyFund.org
www.DavidSancious.com
www.GarryTallent.com
www.GreasyLake.org
www.HopeandDreams.free.fr
www.LittleSteven.com
www.luckytown.org/
www.MaxWeinberg.com
www.montibeton.com/lostintheflood/
www.nilslofgren.com
www.NJ.com/Springsteen
www.onlybruce.de/
www.PattiScialfa.net
www.PointBlankMag.com
www.SoozieTyrell.com
www.SpringsteenLyrics.com
www.SteelMillRetro.com
www.undergroundgarage.com
www.vderlinden.nl/springsteen/

Index

THE FAQ SERIES